Megan C. Kurlychek
iversity at Albany—State University of New York

connecting theory to practice

Juvenile Justice

Kendall Hunt
publishing company

Kendall Hunt
publishing company
www.kendallhunt.com
Send all inquiries to:
4050 Westmark Drive
Dubuque, IA 52004-1840

ISBN 978-1-5249-2195-8

Published in the United States of America

To my children, Anthony and Kathryn, in honor of all they have taught me.

Brief Contents

Contents

About the Author

Megan Kurlychek is an Associate Professor of Criminal Justice at the University at Albany. Prior to entering academia she had hands on experience in policy working in the Pennsylvania State Senate and the Pennsylvania Commission on Sentencing. The most influential period of her life was from 1994 to 1999—a period now known as the "get tough" movement on juvenile crime—during which she worked as a research analyst for the National Center for Juvenile Justice researching and reporting on programs that actually worked to help, rather than hurt, wayward youth. Dr. Kurlychek brought her love for policy to her profession and to this text as she continues to draw connections between the study and practice of juvenile justice. In addition to being a Professor she also serves as Executive Director of the Hindelang Criminal Justice Center, as the Acting Director of the New York State Youth Justice Institute and as the editor for Justice Quarterly, the flagship journal of the Academy of Criminal Justice Sciences. Dr. Kurlychek continues to publish her work in key academic journals as well as presenting the results on important topics such as the sentencing of youth in adult courts and the sealing of criminal records at public policy and government conferences.

Introduction

When I first started college I thought I wanted to major in broadcast journalism—to report about everything going on in the world. What could be more interesting? However, luckily for me, most universities require a number of "general education" classes that force students to study subjects to which they may otherwise not have exposure. This is what universities call a well-rounded education. This is what I call fate. It was in just such a course—social psychology—that I found there might be something more interesting than reporting on what happens in society—understanding WHY it happens. Thus, my major was switched to Sociology—a degree to which profession I had no idea I was aspiring—but found a passion.

Within Sociology there are many subject areas to study, I quickly found my interests were in deviant behaviors—perhaps because as a college student at a large public university I was exposed to much of this by individuals who otherwise would be assumed to be law-abiding citizens. But regardless of the reason, thirty years later, I find myself as engaged and inspired by the subject area as I was when I first studied it.

One thing that has changed over this course has been my realization that just studying and understanding human behavior in society and societal reaction to human behavior is not enough. As a field, we are obligated to share these findings with practitioners and policy makers to ensure the best outcomes for society and all its members. In this text we will look closely at some of society's most vulnerable members—troubled youth. Thus, the title of this text is "Connecting Theory to Practice." Without practice our scholarly theories sit in an ivory tower and have no meaning for the millions of children growing up in America today. Without theory and scientific study, our practitioners work blindly to try and cure an ill they cannot understand. Thus, in this text my mission is to hopefully draw concrete connections between these two sometimes disjunct realms.

In doing so, I acknowledge there is too much subject matter—too many theories of delinquency—to cover in one text—at least if one hopes a student will gain something from the course! Therefore, I limit the discussion to classic and prominent theories that directly relate to the practice of juvenile justice.

The text is divided into four sections as follows:

Section 1: Defining and Measuring Delinquency

If we hope to understand a phenomenon we must first define what it is. While you might think this is simple, you know what a crime is of course, do you know what it means to be a juvenile delinquent? When was the first juvenile court started? How and why is it different than adult court? How do we gather and use statistics to understand both the problem of delinquency and the system response? These are the topics you will be addressing in Section 1 of the text.

Section 2: Understanding Delinquency

Now that we have defined delinquency, the text will take you into several key perspectives and theories that help to unravel the mystery of the etiology of juvenile delinquency in American society. These theories do not necessarily compete with each other, but all offer explanations for perhaps different parts of the problems, or different sources of deviance. Recent trends that work towards integrating theories and developing more complete pictures of child development and delinquency shape the conclusion of this section.

Section 3: Practicing Juvenile Justice

If a tree falls in the woods and no one hears it fall, does it make a sound? Perhaps you have heard this classic question—here I propose, "If a scholar develops a theory of delinquency but it has no impact on practice and solutions to the problem, is the theory useful?"

While there is of course merit to theorizing for theory itself, I remain dedicated to trying to use the empirical research of scholars to direct the development of the most beneficial programs for youth. This section of the text will take you from initial system contact with police, through the juvenile justice system's intake, diversion, adjudication and placement processes. Each stage is at once independent, yet dependent on all that comes before it, just as the youth's life outcomes after contact are dependent on the good or harm imposed by the system. Throughout this section boxes entitled "connections to theory" will be used to highlight when a specific practice draws upon and utilizes the knowledge of the theories you explored in the previous section.

Section 4: Challenges and Directions for the Future

In this final section of the text we will explore some of the most critical challenges facing the juvenile courts today such as the victimization of youth and gang violence. Each challenge, while modern, has a rich history that has led us to where we are today. With that knowledge we then conclude our learning with a brief look at where juvenile justice might head in the future and the importance of honoring the individuality and unique needs of each child and family that comes before this system for services.

While some of you are planning to major in criminology, sociology or criminal justice, others might be the "general education" student as I was once exploring a topic to which you were never hereto exposed. Whether or not juvenile justice becomes your passion, I hope that the information learned in this text will be useful to you as you navigate life in our complex society.

Section 1

Defining and Measuring Delinquency

Defining Delinquency and the Juvenile Delinquent

1

© travelview/Shutterstock.com

I can remember distinctly a day when my child's preschool held a parents day to showcase the "work" our children had been doing. Above each child's station was a sign indicating what he or she wanted to be when grown up. Answers ranged from firefighter, princess and Batman to my child's answer of "paleontologist," to which her older brother quickly responded "nerd." While we still chuckle about that day, it makes a clear point I want to make here. From early on in life we are asked what we want to be when we grow up. Inherent in this question is the idea that we are not yet complete. We are not yet who we will be—but only the beginnings of that person. Also inherent in the question is the idea that one day we will be complete—that is, grown up.

In this first chapter you will be briefly introduced to the historical ideas of childhood and adolescence as they relate to the need for a special system of justice and response to youth. Throughout this text you will find a distinct emphasis on connecting ideas to practice. This is because ultimately we respond to everyone and every situation in a manner consistent with our definitions. If we see a child as no different than an adult, then there is no need to respond differently than we would to an adult and there would be no juvenile justice system. Indeed, for much of history there was not. This chapter will introduce you to many of the ideas that lay behind the development of the juvenile justice system and then Chapter 2 will more directly address the beginnings of the system. By the end of this chapter you should be able to:

1. Document the history of the ideas of childhood and adolescence in American culture.
2. Connect these evolving ideas to the definitions of juvenile delinquency and the juvenile delinquent.
3. Define a delinquent act, a criminal act and a status offense.
4. Understand the organization and purpose of the remainder of this text.

Introduction to Delinquency

If you were to pick up a dictionary and look up the word delinquent, one of the first definitions you would find is "late." For example, someone who is delinquent on his bills is late in paying his debts. The use of the term in this book might at first seem considerably different, but it actually shares a common meaning. A juvenile who is **delinquent** is often seen as being late in developing certain things; perhaps late in developing moral notions of right and wrong or perhaps late in developing the ability to control his behavior. And, in a very real way, his behavior might incur a debt to society that he will have to pay in the currency of punishment and stigma.

Delinquent

a delinquent is a youth who commits an act that would be a crime if he was an adult

If to be delinquent is to be late—then what is a **delinquent act**? Well, in the most practical sense it is defined as an act that would be considered a crime if committed by an adult. It is an act that is against the law, but does not rise to the level of a crime because the individual committing the act is not an adult. If indeed the individual were an adult, he would be done developing—he would understand right from wrong and be able to control his actions and understand their consequences. In that case, the individual would have "**mens rae**" (a guilty mind) and would have committed a crime. But, in the case of a juvenile, it is not a crime, it is merely a delinquent act.

Delinquent Act

an act that would be considered a crime if committed by an adult

Mens Rae

a guilty mind

I have spent the last few paragraphs focused on definitions for a reason—how we define something is inherently and inseparably tied to how we respond to it. If I define a situation as dangerous, I react with fear. If I define a person as kind, I return kindness. If I define a child as not different than an adult, then I do not respond differently to the child, and his actions, than I do to the adult. But if I define the child as different, then I need a different response. This response has become our nation's **juvenile justice system**.

Juvenile Justice System

a separate system of justice designed just for processing youth

The notion of delinquency and a delinquent act have evolved over time as have definitions of childhood and adolescence. Along with these changing definitions have come changes to the way we administer justice to youth. In this first chapter of the text you will be introduced to the evolving notions of childhood and how they impact definitions of the delinquent act and the juvenile delinquent himself. In the next chapter, you will then learn how the justice system has evolved over the years in response to these changing ideas.

Today we define **childhood** as the time between infancy and adolescence—most commonly between the ages of 2 and 12. **Adolescence** then begins when a youth enters his teenage years and continues through the age of adulthood, most commonly thought of as 18. In fact, we keep inventing new periods of life such as the newly popular term "tweens," which applies to youth between childhood and adolescence—maybe 9 to 12? However, there was not always a consideration of adolescence, or even childhood, as a distinct period of life, but rather these ideas evolved over time. While the point of this text is to help you understand current theories of juvenile delinquency and juvenile justice policies, it is impossible to understand the present ideas without first acknowledging the past from which they came.

Childhood

the period of life between infancy and adolescence—most commonly between the ages of 2 and 12

Adolescence

the period of life between puberty and adulthood

Early Definitions of Childhood

The notion of childhood as a separate time of life is dated to sometime in the 1400s (Aries, 1962). According to Bernard and Kurlychek (2010), before this time, children in the care of their mothers (typically to age 5 or 6) were treated mainly as if they did not exist and children over this age were simply seen as small adults and were treated no differently than adults. This lack of a recognition of the period of life we now know as childhood is often related to high mortality rates of infants and children at that time. Even into the 1600s it is estimated that as many as two-thirds of all children born died before the age of four. It would hardly make sense to ask preschoolers what they want to be when they grow up if, indeed, they never have the opportunity to do so.

In the 1600s, infant mortality rates began to decline due to advances in our understanding of hygiene and medicine. As more children began to live into adulthood, people began to focus more on what type of adult that child would become. According to Illick (2002), the prevailing assumption about human nature in general was that we are all prone to evil. The child, unless taught otherwise, would become an evil adult. Thus, the emphasis became on viewing the child as a "potential" adult and providing teaching and discipline to ensure that his inherent evil nature would not sustain into adulthood.

It was not until the late 1800s when we find a new and broader definition of childhood that extended into a new period of life known as "adolescence" (from the Latin *adolescere* which simply means "to grow up"). Scholarly attention then began to focus on this newly identified stage of life, probably most notably with the publication of G. Stanley Halls' book, *Adolescence,* in 1904. In your lifetime you probably cannot imagine adolescence not being recognized as a distinct time of life different than childhood. After all this is when puberty hits, and all kinds of crazy changes go on in your mind and body. High school and college are major transition periods in your life as you break away from your parents, obtain independence and determine truly "what you will be when you grow up." However, much of this is actually shaped not by biology but by our social and economic systems. In agricultural and feudal societies, children simply transitioned from being, well, a child, to working on the farm, or in the family business, or being placed into an apprenticeship or even sold as an indentured servant to pay off parents' debts. Thus, there was not such a large question of what children would be when they grew up. It just happened. People did not attend high schools. Even if you ask a few generations back in your family you can probably find the first person to attend a high school. Indeed the first compulsory education law, passed in Massachusetts in 1852, only required children to attend school up to age 14 and for only three months a year.

As the economy changed, so did its need for workers. With industrialization came urbanization which amassed large numbers of youth into growing cities rather than small towns and villages. There was simply no longer a straightforward path from childhood to work and adulthood and many of these youth appeared lost. Schools and colleges became the new training grounds to mold these newly found "adolescents" into law-abiding and hard working adults, but these institutions were reserved for the children of wealthy individuals. Those who did not receive proper training and education would surely become delinquents, or as mentioned earlier—late in becoming proper adults.

Indeed the discovery of adolescence may go quite hand in hand with the discovery of delinquency. It was among this particular population of urban youth, particularly children of recent immigrants searching for a place in society and for work, that delinquency was first recorded. These children were not beyond hope as were adult criminals; after all we were all born evil. The fact that they were displaying troublesome behavior was the natural result of their human nature when not properly parented, trained and schooled. Thus, as you will see more in the next chapter—it was going to be the purpose of the juvenile justice system to "save" them.

Defining the Delinquent

In *The Cycle of Juvenile Justice*, Bernard and Kurlychek (2010) describe five distinct definitions of the delinquent that can be attached to historical periods of time. This first definition aligns closely with the discussion so far. That is the idea that the youth will ultimately become a burden on society by being a **pauper**—a poor person who does not work. These children of the poor working immigrants in America were roaming the streets, causing trouble and showing no sign of moving up in our system of capitalism. Unless properly educated and trained, they would ultimately become burdens on society instead of contributing members of the economy. Thus, in the next chapter you will not find it odd that some of the first institutions designed to house delinquents were called "training schools."

Pauper
a poor person who does not work

Shortly after this time, however, it is proposed that the rise of the social work movement that viewed children in need of care and rehabilitation would provide a related but slightly new definition of the delinquent. In this case, the definition relies on the idea that in order to become trained into productive adults, youth are dependent on their parents. This is the state in which a child enters the world, and remains until he/she can make a living for him/herself in the world. Thus, adolescents displaying delinquent behavior were seen as **dependent children** in need of such parenting from outside the home as their behavior was seen as an indicator that it was not being properly provided by the parents. This idea again will pop up in the following chapter as you see the first juvenile court being premised on the idea of "state as the parents" or "**parens patriae**."

Dependent Child
a child in need of care by the state because such care is not being provided in the home

Parens patriae
state as the parent

This definition reigned supreme for quite a long period of time, and in America, only began to change in the 1960s as society began to question much about its inherent structure. Youth were particularly active during the period of the '60s and '70s in movements such as the Civil Rights Movement and the women's rights movement that reshaped our society's thinking on many topics related to human rights in general. During this period in time, the definition of the delinquent child was changed accordingly to thus emphasize the rights of children.

Defendant

person accused in a court of law

Rather than being seen as protected by the state, the juvenile delinquent was seen as needing protection *from* the state. The state, now being seen as the oppressor of many, needed to have its power muted, and thus the rights of individuals against the state expanded. This definition of the delinquent focused more on the youth as a **defendant** and how the state might wrong, rather than correct, the child, and provided expanded civil rights to the juvenile. The resulting juvenile justice policies of this definition will again be described in the next chapter.

More recently, and as a result of high levels of adolescent violence in the late 1980s and early 1990s, the definition of a juvenile delinquent went even further away from needy children to a **hardened criminal**. Indeed, they were called a "new breed of offender" and visualized by the media as violent and deadly superpredators from which society itself needed protection. According to a warning from criminologist John DiIulio in 1995, by 2010, there would be "an estimated 270,000 more young predators on the streets than in 1990." Criminologist James Fox also joined in the rhetoric, predicting publicly that, "Unless we act today, we're going to have a blood-bath when these kids grow up" (Equal Justice Initiative, 2014). While today this is known as the "myth of the superpredator e" (***New York Times,*** 2014), as with the other definitions noted above, you will find that in later chapters that, right or wrong, it had great influence on juvenile justice policy for the nation.

From dependent child in need of care to hardened criminal in need of punishment . . . oh how our ideas of the delinquent have changed! Yet, as might have been predicted by Bernard and Kurlychek (2010), the more things change, the more they stay the same. That is, the emerging and perhaps most current definition of a juvenile delinquent is a developing adult. Now relying on evolving medical science that maps the brain development (Geidd et al., 1999; Baird & Fugelsang, 2004) and cognitive functioning of adolescents (Steinberg & Cauffman, 1996), we assert that no matter how violent the act, the child is just that and is indeed still different from an adult—that is, has not yet matured into one—and, as such, must be treated differently. Perhaps the best example of the evolution of this thinking is presented in the 2002 Supreme Court case of *Roper v. Simmons* in which the Court ruled that anyone who was under the age of 18 at the time of his/her crime could not be sentenced to death. Why? Because the death penalty is reserved for only the worst offenders "whose extreme culpability makes them . . . the most deserving of execution." According to the Supreme Court, a child under the age of 18 can simply never fall into this category because of the very nature of adolescence that "derives from the fact that the signature qualities of youth are transient; as individuals mature, the impetuousness and recklessness that may dominate in younger years can subside" (see also Steinberg & Scott, 2014). Or put more simply, because youth are still developing and are not who they will ultimately become (be it princess, Batman, paleontologist or delinquent), they simply cannot be the "worst" offenders.

Of course, each of these definitions is not accepted in its entirety by everyone at the given time point; rather these definitions wax and wane over time with the above representing what appears to have been the most popular definition at the time point where we saw significant changes to the administrative of justice to youth. While this latter topic is covered in more detail in the following chapter, in the next section, I will attach these ideas of childhood and the delinquent to the idea of delinquent acts and status offenses.

Defining the Delinquent Act

DELINQUENT ACT

As previously noted, delinquent act is typically defined as any act that would be a crime if committed by an adult. Each state and the federal justice system has its own set of codified laws that define what these acts are. These vary somewhat across states, but in general reflect the overall morals of our society. If these laws are violated by an adult, we say the adult has committed a crime. However, if these laws are violated by a youth under the age of adulthood (also noted as "under the age of criminal responsibility"), the exact same act is noted as a delinquent act. The reason it is not a crime is firmly rooted in the discussion above in which it was first promoted and more recently medically documented that children are indeed different than adults. Thus, the difference is not in the act or in its consequence, but in the age and maturity of the individual carrying out the act.

While I hinted at these differences in the quotations from the *Roper v. Simmons* case, let me clearly spell them out for you here:

1. Less mature in judgment
2. More easily influenced by outside forces
3. Not done developing (which is in part the source of differences 1 and 2)

The first is based on two factors. The first is merely lack of life experience. With age comes wisdom as we learn through mistakes. For some, those mistakes are minor; for others they are larger and may involve illegal activities. But we do not truly understand consequences of actions until we begin to experience them. Second, is the noted fact above that medical science is revealing that the prefrontal cortex of the brain does not finish developing until age 21 for girls and age 24 for males (Geidd et al., 1999). With this area of the brain responsible for reflective thought not yet fully developed, brain scans reveal that adolescents rely more on the part of the brain called the amygdala, which is the emotional center. Thus, it is easy to see how a teenager's actions could be called "senseless" or "irrational." This is also inherently tied to the notion of **mens rae** mentioned briefly before. Mens rae, which is Latin for "guilty mind," is a legal precedent for trying someone in adult court. It indicates that the individual knew what he/she was doing was wrong and still intentionally engaged in the behavior. Some believe a child is never capable of mens rae since the mind is not done developing and he/she cannot fully understand consequences of actions. Others argue that such assessments of mens rae should be individualized as some children may mature sooner than others and some crimes show more careful thought and planning (See Justice O'Conner's Dissent in *Roper v. Simmons*). This discrepancy in thinking will be discussed further in the sections discussing juvenile justice policy.

The second factor is somewhat related not only to this nature of the brain, but also to the social pressures of the teenage years in which youth are seeking to establish their identity and the role of peers becomes of high importance. Thus, a youth who might "know" right from wrong, and provide a socially appropriate answer about how to act in a given situation, may actually act entirely differently in the "heat of the moment" when surrounded by peers.

And, finally, the last point goes back to that original notion that if an adolescent is only the seeds of the adult that is yet to come, then we need to nourish those seeds. It is this last notion that perhaps most specifically calls for a different system and purpose of justice for juveniles than we have for adults. Our adult courts are designed to punish. Our juvenile courts, as you will see in more detail in the next chapter, were founded on ideas of rehabilitation and care.

This leads to another interesting point about juvenile justice in America. Because of this unique status of youth and their inability to make good decisions, our society has also determined that we need to, in a way, protect them from themselves. Thus, there are special laws that apply only to children. Violation of these laws is not referred to as a crime or delinquent act but as a **status offense**.

Status Offense

a behavior that is only illegal because of one's status as a juvenile

STATUS OFFENSE

Based on these differences between adults and children, we have as a society come up with a list of behaviors that it is "ok" for you to do if you are an adult because you theoretically understand the consequences and are capable of good decisions, but it is not "ok" for you to do if you are a kid. You can probably name some of these easily off the top of your head such as drinking alcohol, smoking cigarettes and even driving a car. Others you might not be as familiar with include "truancy," which is skipping school, and "incorrigibility," which is not listening to your parents.

FOCUS ON POLICY: Youth and Status Offenses

A status offense is a behavior that is against the law only because of one's status—in this case that status is being a minor. Typical status offenses that can lead to a child being taken into custody include:

Running away from home. A child is legally under the control of his/her parents, unless removed by the state. Thus, a child cannot simply leave the home without a parent's permission, regardless of the treatment of the child in the home.

Incorrigibility. Not only is a child not allowed to leave the home without a parent's permission, but really, a child must have their parents' permission for most behaviors. Incorrigibility is the offense of not listening to one's parents. In the United States this offense dates as far back as the Massachusetts Colony, at which time a youth of 16 years of age could be put to death for disrespecting his/her parents. Today, the punishments are thankfully much less severe, but the concept remains that the youth must obey his/her parents.

Truancy. A youth must also, at least until a given age, attend school. If a youth skips school this is called truancy and the youth can face legal consequences. Every state has compulsory attendance laws, usually to the age of 16.

In addition to these there are other acts I am sure you are aware of in which a minor cannot engage. For example, it is illegal for a minor to purchase tobacco and to purchase or use alcohol. The age for tobacco use is 18, slightly older than for dropping out of school, but less than the age at which one is allowed to drink alcohol (21 years of age). Some jurisdictions also set curfew laws for juveniles mandating that they be back in their homes by a given hour in the evening such as 10:00 pm. These are more likely to be city or local ordinances than state law, but can still lead to the arrest of a youth breaking the rule.

In the past sections you learned of various definitions of the child and the juvenile delinquent. Can you see the connections here? Which of these laws views the youth as a developing adult? As a child in need of protection? Or, perhaps, even a potentially dangerous criminal? Data also suggests that females are more likely to be arrested for status offenses, particularly running away from home, than are males who engage in the same behavior (Sickmund, 2004). Is there a reason our society might view females and males as in need of different levels of protection?

EXCLUSIONS OF YOUTH AND ACTS

While I have spent most of this chapter telling you why a child is different than an adult and called a delinquent rather than a criminal, and how and why a delinquent act is defined as different than a criminal act, I would be remissed if I did not end the chapter by telling you that every rule has its exception, and indeed this rule has many.

Just as every state in the nation has a separate system of justice for juveniles, every state also maintains laws that allow juveniles to be processed as adult criminals in certain situations. Some of these laws set statutory limits on the age and offense combinations. For example, while you may be a juvenile until age 18 in Pennsylvania, if you commit murder, you can be tried as an adult if you are over 11. That is, even an 11-year-old is supposed to know better than to kill someone. Other laws entirely remove from the definition of a "delinquent act" certain crimes such as murder, meaning that anyone committing that crime, regardless of age, can be held responsible.

BY ANDREA TORTORA
The Cincinnati Enquirer

Amid the steep hills of an eastern Kentucky coal-mining town, two young boys argued over a piece of scrap iron.

They had planned to sell the metal to a junk dealer for some pocket change. It was months before the stock market crash of 1929, yet the town of Paintsville was struggling.

The working-class residents earned their livings pulling coal out of the valleys that later would bring forth such famous country music singers as Crystal Gayle and Loretta Lynn, who grew up there.

But on May 18, 1929, Carl Newton Mahan, 6, and Cecil Van Hoose, 8, had a fight.

Cecil took the scrap of iron away from Carl, slapping him in the face. According

THIRTY PAGES PRICE FIVE CENTS

Mahan Case Finished In Kentucky, Is Belief; Boy Apparently Free

BACK IN MOTHER'S ARMS

Carl Mahan, 6 years old, Paintsville, Ky., is believed to be back in his mother's arms permanently owing to failure of J. W. Cammack, Kentucky Attorney-General, to announce that further action would be taken when he finished his study of records of the boy's case yesterday. Carl was sentenced to Kentucky State Reform School when he was convicted of having killed a playmate with his father's shotgun. The sentence was set aside by another Judge.

SLAYER

Of Playmate Safe

With Writ Between Him And Prison Sentence.

Attorney-General Ends Scrutiny Of Records

Without Announcing Plan For Further Action.

Paintsville Lad, 6, Now At Home Of Parents.

Justice Belies Charge Of Habitual Slowness

With Speed Since Fatal Quarrel Over Junk—Nation-wide Comment Drawn By Tragedy.

The Carl Mahan appeal was the big story on *The Enquirer's* front page on June 27, 1929.

to articles in *The Cincinnati Enquirer* back then, Carl ran away from Cecil, went home, and climbed up on a chair. He took down his father's 12-gauge shotgun, which was kept above the door.

Carl went back outside and shouted to Cecil, "I'm going to shoot you!" Then he squeezed the trigger.

Carl became the youngest murder defendant in Kentucky, probably in the country.

What happened next in many ways resembles what happened last Tuesday in Michigan, where another child shot and killed a playmate.

In Mount Morris Township, in eastern Michigan, a first-grade boy shot his classmate, a 6-year-old girl.

The children apparently had fought on the playground the day before. The girl, Kayla Rolland, had yelled at the boy for spitting on his desk.

The boy brought to school a gun from a relative's home. The boy, whom authorities won't identify, shot and killed Kayla. Then he put the gun in his desk and went to the principal's office.

The events of the 1929 shooting in Paintsville provide a glimpse into what may be in store for the Michigan case.

The same questions arise: Were the shooters murderers? Did they know what they were doing? Can they be held accountable for their tragic actions? If so, then how does society mete out punishment to a first-grader?

In 1929 Paintsville, the answers seemed to come fast.

Less than a week after Carl shot his friend, the skinny 6-year-old with the cowlick was on trial for murder.

The boy told the court how he came to kill his friend. Then, through the rest of the daylong trial, he lay on the defense counsel's table and sometimes slept.

After fewer than 30 minutes of deliberations, a jury convicted Carl of the lesser charge of manslaughter. The Johnson County judge sentenced him to 15 years in reform school.

The boy was released to his parents on $500 bail.

A public outcry and legal appeals followed. Some thought manslaughter wasn't enough. Others thought it was too much.

Finally, a Circuit Court judge set aside the conviction and issued a "writ of prohibition" that prevented Carl from being sent to reform school. The writ said the county judge had exceeded his authority by allowing Carl to be tried criminally before a jury. Normally, juvenile cases were decided by the county judge.

In the 71 years since the Paintsville case, states have created extensive and complex juvenile crime codes. Psychologists have created an industry out of studying child criminals. Still, child experts and psychologists disagree about whether the 6-year-old shooter is a killer or a victim. They recognize the impact that emotional and physical distress can have on a child's actions. But the concept of criminal responsibility has changed since the 1920s, said Robert Lilly, a sociology professor at Northern Kentucky University.

"The idea of holding someone else responsible for criminal behavior was not very well developed 71 years ago," Mr. Lilly said. "Children were viewed much more as adults then."

So if a child did it, the child was responsible. Parents would not be held liable for a child's actions in the America of 1929. That philosophy is in stark contrast to the social climate of 2000.

"We have a very narrow, rational, technical logic now that you can be held responsible even if you didn't intend to do it," Mr. Lilly said. "That's why people cop a plea."

In the Michigan shooting, prosecutors are calling the 6-year-old shooter a victim of circumstance and of a failed social system. The semiautomatic weapon he took to school had been left in his temporary home by friends of the boy's uncle. Police also found another stolen weapon and cocaine in the home.

Police have charged 19-year-old Jamelle James with involuntary manslaughter in Kayla Rolland's death. Police accuse Mr. James of waving the loaded pistol in front of the boy days before the shooting and leaving the loaded gun in his bedroom.

The boy will not be charged. Instead, prosecutors say, the child needs to be loved.

Culpability
how responsible one is for an act/action

Amenability to Treatment
means able to be changed through treatment

Still other laws let the determination of whether you should be tried in juvenile or adult court up to the judge or prosecutor rather than setting strict age and offense limit combinations. At the time of such a decision the judge or prosecutor should be considering the maturity of the youth, often referred to as his/her **culpability** for the offense and his/her **amenability to treatment**.

The transfer and processing of juveniles in adult courts is a topic of great public debate and will be discussed in much detail in Chapter 11. For now, just remember the earlier point that definitions are tied to policy responses. Thus, if we think a child is incapable of murder, then anyone who commits murder must in turn not be a child, and must be treated as an adult.

Key Words

Adolescence
Amenability to Treatment
Childhood
Culpability
Defendant
Delinquent
Delinquent Act
Dependent Child
Juvenile Justice System
Mens Rae
Parens patriea
Pauper
Status Offense

Chapter Summary

This chapter was filled with some definitions that you will need to remember throughout the text. First and foremost was the **delinquent act**, which is an offense that would be a crime if committed by an adult. The only reason it is not a crime is because the person committing the act is not fully formed yet and thus is not fully responsible for his/her actions and can be thought of as incapable of the required mens rae to commit a crime. Second, on the total opposite end of the spectrum, is the **status offense**. This is an act that would not be a crime if committed by an adult, but rather is *only* illegal because you are a child. Second, you have learned many definitions of a child or adolescent and how they formed into different visions of just who and what this creature is we call the **juvenile**. From a potential pauper who needs training to avoid becoming a burden on society, to a dependent child in need of care and protection, to a criminal defendant in need of protection from the system, to a hardened superpredator from whom society needs protection—all of these definitions have consequences and will be explored throughout this text. It is the first two definitions—potential pauper and dependent child—that were at the heart of the movement that led to the nation's first juvenile court and its juvenile justice system. Thus, these will be explored more in depth in the following chapter as you learn about the history of the juvenile justice system.

Discussion Questions

1. If someone asked you today what you want to be when you grow up, what would your answer be? Think back to middle school and elementary school, how would your answer have differed? What might lead you to think differently about your future today than you did as a younger child?
2. At what age do you think you are an adult? Are you one now? How do you know when you are one? Does this relate to any of the age distinctions set forth by society such as when you can vote, drive a car, drink alcohol? If not, how would you define it?
3. You were presented with several different ideas of childhood that evolved over time. Which of these were new to you? Which were familiar? You were also presented with the idea that adolescence was not always considered a distinct period of life, and now we are coming up with even more classifications such as the "tween" years. Why do you think this is so? How do you think our definition of child and adolescent might change in the next decade?
4. The chapter ended with a discussion of how sometimes children are considered adults and their actions are considered crimes rather than delinquent acts. In what situations do you think this is appropriate? At what age? For what crimes? In specific, compare the two boys, ages 6 and 8, in *The Cincinnati Enquirer* article. What might be the proper outcomes for these youth?

REFERENCES

Aries, P. (1962). *Centuries of childhood.* New York: Knopf.

Baird, A. A., & Fugelsang, J. A. (2004). The emergence of consequential thought: Evidence from neuroscience. *Philos Trans R Soc Lond B Biol Sci, 359*(1451), 1797–1804.

Bernard, T. J., & Kurlychek, M. C. (2010). *The cycle of juvenile justice* (2nd ed.). New York: Oxford Academic Press.

Editorial Board. (2014, April 13). Echos of the superpredator. *The New York York Times.*

Equal Justice Initiative. (2014, April 7). The superpredator myth, 20 years later. Retrieved from http://www.eji.org/node/893

Giedd, J. J., Blumenthal, N. J., Castelanos, F., Liu, H., Zijdenbos, A., Paus, T., . . . Rapoport, J. (1999). Brain development during childhood and adolescence: A longitudinal MRI study. *Nature Neuroscience, 2*(10), 861–863.

Hall, G. S. (1904). *Adolescence: Its psychology and its relations to physiology, anthropology, sociology, sex, crime, religion, and education (Vols. I & II).* New York: D. Appleton & Co.

Illick, J. E. (2002). *American childhoods.* Philadelphia: University of Pennsylvania Press.

Sickmund, M. (2004). *Juvenile offenders and victims national report series: Juveniles in corrections.* Washington, DC: U.S. Department of Justice.

Steinberg, L., & Cauffman, E. (1996). Maturity of judgment in adolescence: Psychosocial factors in adolescent decision making. *Law and Human Behavior, 20*(3), 249.

Responding to Juvenile Delinquency: The Creation of Juvenile Justice in America

2

In 1874 the first case of child abuse was brought before a judge in the United States. Interestingly, or perhaps, sadly, the case had to be brought to the judge's attention under laws designed to protect animals from cruelty—there were no such laws to protect children.

©New York Times, 2009.

Mary Ellen Wilson, 1874.

In this case, Mary Ellen McCormack, a 10-year-old orphan, was being abused by her adopted mother. Her birth father, Thomas Wilson, was a Union soldier who had died in battle, and her mother, unable to afford her on her widow's pension, was forced to put her up for adoption. Reports show that she was adopted by a Manhattan couple, Thomas and Mary McCormack, but her adopted father soon died and her adoptive mother turned to abusing the child.

When neighbors brought the girl's plight to the attention of authorities, a social worker, Angell Wheeler, frustrated by the lack of child-protection laws, turned to the ASPCA for help. Henry Bergh, the society's founder, took interest in the case, recruited a prominent attorney, and took the case the whole way to the Supreme Court of New York State.

Habeas Corpus

presenting the body

In this case the attorney used the writ of **habeas corpus** (remember this term—it will keep coming up) which means "presenting the body" to convince the court that Mary Ellen would be in grave danger if she were not removed from that home.

This case led Bergh, Gerry and the philanthropist John D. Wright to found the New York Society for the Prevention of Cruelty to Children in 1875, which is reportedly the first child protective agency in the world. Mary Ellen herself went on to be adopted by a new loving family, was later married, had children of her own as well as adopting an orphan girl, and died at the old age of 92.

Source: Markel, Howard. 2009. Case Shined First Light on Abuse of Children. *The New York Times*: Health. December 15, 2009.

The above example was provided to further emphasize the point that at one time, we as a society, and perhaps as a human race, did not define, care about, or respond to a stage of life called childhood or adolescence. While Mary Ellen was obviously not a juvenile delinquent, the example is given again to emphasize how our response to an event is so embedded in our definitions of it.

In this chapter you will explore the origins of the juvenile court beginning in the early 1800s and following through the turn of the 20th century. You will be exposed to the competing ideas of the time, the influence of the Progressive Movement and three key court cases that shaped forever the system of juvenile justice in America. By the end of this chapter you should be able to:

1. Identify and chronologically order the key social factors that led to the development of the juvenile court.
2. Identify the key players in the Progressive Movement and the development of the first juvenile court.
3. Discuss the key court cases in Pennsylvania and Illinois that paved the way for a juvenile justice system.
4. Describe the key ways in which the juvenile court is different from the adult court system, including philosophy, practice and terminology.

The movement to create a separate system of justice was seated in a larger social movement known as the **Progressive Era**. This era maintained a positive focus on the evolution of man and of society to an ever better state, with confidence in the role of medicine and technology to get us there. However, against this backdrop of optimism were the cold harsh realities of life in America's growing cities. As groups of **immigrants** flocked to America in search of a better life and newly freed slaves migrated to northern cities to escape segregation and overt racism, the cities became overcrowded. The newest immigrants, whether they were African-Americans fleeing the South, Irish fleeing famine in their homeland or Polish Jews fleeing prosecution, entered these cities with little resources and often without the ability to speak or read English. These populations were poor and their struggles were greatest and often most evident in their youth.

Progressive Era

maintained a positive focus on the evolution of man and of society to an ever better state, with confidence in the role of medicine and technology to get us there

Immigrants

those flocking to America in search of a better life often with little resources or the ability to read or speak English

Without a formal secondary education system as we have today and without meaningful jobs and roles for these youth in society, they often roamed the streets in groups, frequented pool halls and generally caused trouble. As their families were so often in extreme poverty, pick-pocketing and theft was also rampant. When the youth were arrested, however, there was little to do with them. Adult judges did not want to place children in adult prisons but they also did not want to ignore their acts and allow these youth to grow up to be adult criminals. What could be done?

The First Institutions for Juveniles: The House of Refuge

If it was not acceptable to put a child in an adult prison, and, furthermore, if judges believed that not doing anything with these wayward youth would only propel them into a lifetime of miseries such as crime and pauperism, then there surely had to be something else the state could do? There was. Using a borrowed British principle of **parens patriae** the state could step in and act as the "ultimate parent." To be clear—this was not a separate "system" of justice yet for children, in fact it was not seen as a justice system at all but rather as a benevolent intervention. When the parents, in the eyes of the state, were not doing an adequate job of raising their child, the state could step in, without any formal procedure of law, and remove the child from the home and place him or her in the newly founded **House of Refuge**. Because the purpose of the House, again, was to raise the child correctly, a commitment was not a sentence of say 6 months or a year, but rather until age 21. This indeterminate commitment model will be one you see repeated often in the evolution of the juvenile system.

House of Refuge

a house designed to hold youth up until their 21st birthday when the state determined that the youth needed to be removed from his parent's care for proper development

The first such house opened its door in 1825 in New York City. As implied by the name "refuge," the house was to be a safe place where the child could grow and receive proper education and training to become a productive adult. Other large and growing American cities followed suit with Houses of Refuge opening in Pennsylvania, Illinois and Massachusetts.

As you might have guessed, not everyone was happy with this model. Some of those most unhappy were the parents of children who were removed from their care. As noted at the onset of the chapter, many of these youths were the children of recent immigrants from eastern European countries that did not necessarily hold the same values as the Protestant immigrants from England who first settled America. These youth were placed in these institutions so they could be socialized into the prevailing American culture.

Mary Ann Crouse

the youth at the center of the first court case challenging the state's right to place children in such a house if they had not committed a crime. The court sided with the state

The first recorded challenge to this system was by the father of **Mary Ann Crouse** who was committed to the Pennsylvania House of Refuge. Mary Ann's father contested that his daughter was being punished even though she had committed no crime and filed a "writ of habeas corpus" which again literally means to "produce the body." This is a request for the state to explain the basis for holding a person prisoner. In 1938, however, when the Pennsylvania Supreme Court reviewed the case it sided with the state positing that Mary Ann need not commit a crime to be held in the House of Refuge. The House was in their words "charity" and its purpose was "reformation" without which she would have "ended in confirmed depravity." The Court thus affirmed the principle of parens patriae being extended to include the care of children whose parents are alive, but who, in the eyes of the state, are "unworthy."

Daniel O'Connell

the youth at the center of the second case to challenge the placement of a youth in a House of Refuge. In this case, the court sided with the youth/parent

And so this system continued until 1870 when a second formal challenge was brought, this time in the state of Illinois. This case was very similar to the first in which a child, this time a boy named **Daniel O'Connell**, had been committed to the House of Refuge until his 21st birthday. His mother objected and this time the Court took a close look at the actual House of Refuge rather than its mission and decided that living in these conditions was indeed punishment. For example, these were no longer small "houses"; many had instead become large institutions that utilized harsh discipline. The Court also noted that even a criminal had rights before the Court and chances for parole where these youth were sentenced for anywhere from 1 to 15 years depending on their age when taken from the home. The Court deemed "such restraint upon personal liberty" to be "tyranny" and further rejected the argument of parens patriae.

For the Progressives, however, where there was a will there was a way. If they were no longer able to take these youths from incompetent parents and "prevent" them from growing up to be criminals without due process of law, then they would develop a process. This process is what you now know as the juvenile justice system.

The First Juvenile Court

In addition to the O'Connell case severely limiting the ability of the state to intervene in the lives of these wayward youths, two other major factors influenced the origin of the first court. First, was the continued and now unprecedented growth of the American city. For Example, Chicago (Cook County Illinois) grew from only around 5,000 residents at the time it was incorporated in the mid-1800s to over 1.5 million by the turn of the century. With this growth came an ever growing population of youth of immigrant parents who were left to their own devices while their parents worked long hours in factories. When these youth were arrested for crime, however, similar to the situation 75 years earlier in New York, the judges did not want to confine them with adult criminals. So, often, nothing was being done, even in cases where the youths were indeed committing crimes (unlike the cases of Crouse and O'Connell that did not involve commission of a crime). Second, was a greater reliance on medicine and belief in science to cure the ills of society. As noted in Chapter 1, it was around this time that G. Stanley Hall wrote *Adolescence*, bringing attention to this period of life between puberty and adulthood as one of great turbulence during which time the adolescent was in need of much guidance. Add to this the popularity of Darwin's theory of evolution that led many to believe that crime was mainly committed by inferior races that had not yet evolved, and you can see how the problem must have been interpreted. That is, there was an ever-growing population of adolescents in need of guidance and care to become productive adults but many of them came from "inferior" races/ethnicities and were being raised in inferior conditions, by inferior parents. The state needed a way to intervene.

Thus the movement to create the first juvenile court was born. The movement was spearheaded mainly by a group of women, the wives of wealthy and powerful men, who were volunteering their time to charity and witnessing some of the terrible conditions that children faced on the streets of Chicago. Even though the Court had ruled that Houses of Refuge were punishment—surely these conditions were worse. That is to say, while many are critical of the role of the state in trying to intervene in the lives of these immigrant families, there were indeed real problems in the ghettos and slums of Chicago and these women got to experience them firsthand and bring their mission back to their husbands who had the legislative and political power to evoke change.

Remembering the O'Connell decision, the founders of the juvenile court were careful to craft it not as a criminal court that would punish but as a civil **chancery court** that would help children with a variety of remedies not available in adult courts, and less formal procedures. While a full description of the origins of England's Chancery Court system is beyond the scope of your text, let it suffice to say that these courts were used as an alternative to the more formal common law courts to deal with disputes over land or private matters, and matters of infants among others. They were known for being less formal and more liberal than traditional courts. However, the idea here was that the juvenile court would indeed still provide some type of formal process and thus not be seen as tyranny of the state.

The first step of the legislation was to remove children from the jurisdiction of the adult court. To do this, the law's drafters used the principle of mens rea to which you were introduced in the last chapter. The argument went something like this: Children could not commit a crime because they did not have the rational ability to form intent; thus, no criminal court should have jurisdiction over them. Instead, the legislation created a separate juvenile court with a juvenile court judge who would hear the cases of the youth who either committed acts that would be crimes if committed by adults (delinquent acts) or who were wayward and in need of care (dependent acts). Being a chancery court, it also brought back the notion of parens patriae, allowing the state to intervene in the lives of children in place of their parents. This time, the principle would stand up to legal challenges and stand the test of time, remaining, to this day, the underlying justification for a separate system of justice for juveniles.

The Court Today

So just what does this court look like? As noted by Sickmund (1999), our nation does not have a juvenile justice system but rather 51 separate systems of justice that are state specific. It would be too wildly confusing for an introductory student in the area to understand all such nuances, so here I will present to you the "mainstays" of the juvenile system as it originated and the major changes over time that impacted how it is practiced today.

FOCUS ON RESEARCH: Barry Feld

While much of this text will focus on why kids commit delinquent acts, that is, get in trouble, Barry Feld is one of the primary scholars who has studied how the system responds to kids over time. His research has spanned almost five decades of juvenile justice reforms from the 1970s through the current day. Dr. Feld began his research on juvenile justice while obtaining his Ph.D. in Sociology from Harvard. During this time the governor of Massachusetts had ordered the closing of all the state's juvenile training schools, an act touted as one of the most drastic reforms to juvenile justice since its inception. After taking a position at Minnesota Law School, Dr. Feld practiced law, prosecuting in both criminal and juvenile courts, which further spurred his inquiry into juvenile justice. Dr. Feld reports that, while he would try an adult in front of a jury of their peers with attorneys present, he tried the juveniles in "King Arthur's Court" or a "judicial fiefdom" where the judge had all the power and the child no rights. Heavily influenced by the injustices he had seen both inside the juvenile training schools and inside the juvenile courts, Dr. Feld's research was highly critical of the juvenile court—at times even calling for its demise to be replaced with simple mitigated punishments for minors in adult courts. His first book, *Neutralizing Inmate Violence* (1977), he took a close look inside juvenile training schools. He later also attacked the procedural safeguards or lack thereof in the juvenile court in a law review article, "Criminalizing Juvenile Justice" (1984), in which he systematically compared and contrasted the Minnesota court system's rules of procedure for juvenile court to those of adult court and found that: "In promulgating its Rules of Procedure, the Minnesota Supreme Court provided neither procedural safeguards to protect juveniles from the consequences of their own immaturity nor the full panoply of adult criminal procedural safeguards to protect them from punitive state intervention" (p. 274). Thus, just as suggested by the United States Supreme Court in the Gault decision, youth do truly receive the worst of both worlds.

His work extends to be critical of police interrogations and treatment of youth detailed in his book, *Kids, Cops, and Confessions* (2013), and he also tackled the tough issues of racial disparity and disproportionate minority confinement in the system in his book *Bad Kids: Race and the Transformation of the Juvenile Court* (1998). To date he has published over 80 articles and book chapters and 12 books on juvenile justice, and, although nearing retirement at the time of this publication, he remains highly critical of the juvenile justice system—not in philosophy per se, but in practice. He is hopeful that a new generation of scholars will tackle the problems of the current juvenile justice system to provide better safeguards for future generations of children.

INITIAL PRINCIPLES

As noted, the initial juvenile court system was designed as a chancery court with a philosophy of justice that was different than the criminal court. It was based on the idea that the state must step in to parent the child when the family was

Petition

a formal legal document that alleges that a youth is delinquent and asks the juvenile court to take jurisdiction over the caset

Disposition

the final outcome of a juvenile court proceeding after a youth is adjudicated delinquent

not doing so in a way that the state thought was in the best interests of the child. Thus, the child was never punished for wrongdoings because they were not inherently the child's fault—but the result of improper socialization. Therefore the court would not sentence the youth based on the specific act committed but rather would provide rehabilitation, education and a treatment program that was deemed in the "best interests of the child."

This philosophy and practice, while altered a great deal, still hold at the root of the system. While it has become more like a criminal court in recent decades—a phenomenon you will study shortly—it is still not a full criminal court and its practices remain inherently different than the adult system—for better or worse.

FOCUS ON POLICY: The Terminology of Juvenile Justice

If the juvenile court has a different mission than and wants to be viewed separately from a criminal court, then it must come up with language for its procedures that are indeed different from the adult criminal court with which you are familiar. For example, you hear of people being indicted, arraigned, convicted and sentenced in adult court. While the juvenile system has similar processes, each stage has slightly different terminology you should be familiar with, and, for the most part, these terms do reflect key differences in practice. For example, an indictment in adult court means that there is enough evidence to file charges against the accused. In juvenile court that parallel stage would be called the "**petition**." This is where it is decided if there is enough evidence against the youth and if the case is serious enough to warrant bringing it to court. This decision is usually made by a probation officer in juvenile court, and even if not petitioned to court, a youth can be placed on some sort of "informal supervision" which is very different than adult court. The next stage is the arraignment in adult court in which the judge reads the charges against the individual and the defendant enters a plea (e.g., usually "not guilty"). In juvenile court this stage rarely happens, and if it does, there is rarely an attorney present. The next stage in adult court is plea bargain or trial. Most cases in adult court (over 95%) end in a plea bargain, but if they do go to trial there is a defense attorney, a prosecuting attorney, the judge and a jury of peers. Plea bargaining is used in juvenile court, but to a much less extent, so many cases do go to the "adjudicatory hearing" at which time there may or may not be an attorney present and for the majority of states/cases there is not a jury present either. In adult court if the defendant is found guilty he/she is then sentenced. In juvenile court he/she is "given a **disposition** in the best interests of the child." While the terminology may sound different—remember that the actual outcomes may be quite similar—a term of probation or placement in an institution.

THE DUE PROCESS MOVEMENT

The period of the 1960s and 1970s issued in new attention to civil rights. From equal treatment of women and minorities, to protection of minorities from the unyielding power of the state, this time period was marked by a focus on individual rights and a denouncement of government power. As noted in the Focus on Research, Barry Feld and other scholars were critical of the juvenile courts' lack of procedural safeguards for defendants. Similar to the House of Refuge, they would argue that procedural safeguards were important because no matter how benevolent the intention of a juvenile placement, it was indeed punishment and these training schools and institutions were not a substitute for home.

In response to this message, the first official challenge to the court's practice came in 1967 in the case of ***In re Gault***. Gerald Gault was a 15-year-old youth in Arizona who was accused of making an obscene phone call to his neighbor. He and another boy from the neighborhood had been making prank calls, which to them was probably seen as funny, but was offensive to the recipient of the call. When the neighbor called the police and reported that she received the call and that she believed it was the neighbor boy, the police proceeded to arrest Gerald and place him in the youth detention center. He was given no notice of what the charge was, nor were his parents even notified he was arrested. He was not permitted an attorney and at the hearing the neighbor did not even show up to identify him as the boy she heard on the phone. Yet, he was committed to the state training school "until his 21st birthday." With the help of an attorney, his parents challenged the decision and the case went the whole way to the nation's Supreme Court.

In re Gault
in 1967 the first official challenge to the court's practice for procedural safeguards

What you will read next is going to, or should, sound extremely familiar. The decision of the U.S. Supreme Court in this case sounds much like the earlier decision of the Illinois Supreme Court in the decision regarding Daniel O'Connell. Indeed the Court determined that it was of "no constitutional consequence and of limited practical meaning that the institution to which he is committed is called an Industrial School. The fact of the matter is that no matter how euphemistic the title, a 'receiving home' or an 'industrial school' for juveniles is an institution in which the juvenile is incarcerated" (Mennel, 1973, p. 125).

After providing these basic rights to juveniles, a second case was brought before the court that challenged the burden of proof. In adult criminal court the proof for conviction is "beyond a reasonable doubt" which means a reasonable person would have no doubts that the person before them committed that act of which he or she is accused. However, up until this time the burden of proof in the juvenile court remained that of a chancery court, which was "preponderance of the evidence"—this means just slightly more sure the individual committed the act than not—or about 51% sure. In this case, ***In re Winship***, a 12-year-old boy was charged with stealing $112 dollars out of a woman's purse in a store. Even though no one directly saw him do it or found the money on him, a saleslady said she saw the boy dash from the store right before the woman noticed the money missing. A defense witness, however, said the saleslady was in a different part of the store and could not have witnessed anything. At the hearing the boy's attorney specifically brought to the judge's attention that he was not using the standard of "beyond a reasonable doubt" to which the judge replied that the statute said, "preponderance of the evidence." So, in this case the attorney challenged the boy's conviction on the basis that the **adjudication** was similar to a conviction and could result in the youth being taken out of the home. The Supreme Court again sided with the plaintiff noting that the Gault decision had already determined that juvenile placement was punishment and that due process protections applied to youth in the juvenile court. However, this standard was applied only to delinquency cases and not accusations of status offenses.

In re Winship

The Supreme Court decision in which the burden of proof in the juvenile court was changed from preponderance of the evidence to beyond a reasonable doubt

Adjudication

a finding of "guilt." Meaning the judge has enough evidence to determine the youth committed the act in question and is in need of treatment and care

Just one year later another case made its way to the nation's Supreme Court, the case of ***McKeiver v. Pennsylvania***. McKeiver was a 16-year-old boy charged with robbery and larceny and receiving stolen goods for an incident in which he and a large group of youths chased three other youths and stole 25 cents. McKeiver was an adjudicated delinquent and placed on probation. McKeiver's attorney argued that the conviction was invalid because McKeiver had not been tried before a jury of his peers, but rather was convicted solely by the judge. Given the decisions in the past two cases you might predict that the court would agree. But, here they did not. Some argue that it was because you cannot really try a juvenile in front of other juveniles (peers) while others argue it was because it would be too costly. The Court's argument was that this final change would fundamentally change the unique nature of the juvenile court. While they posit the other rights afforded juveniles were to improve fact finding, there was no evidence that juries do a better job of interpreting the facts than a judge. In addition, the Court argued that the adversarial nature of a jury trial could even take away from fact finding and take the focus away from the best interests of the child.

McKeiver v. Pennsylvania

The Supreme Court case in which the Court decided that a youth did not have the right to a trial by a jury of his peers in the juvenile court

However, it should also be noted that between the Gault/Winship decision and the McKeiver decision the makeup of the Supreme Court had changed from a liberal court under Chief Justice Warren to a more conservative court under new Chief Justice Scalia. And indeed, the vote on this case was only 5/4 with all 4 of the justices who voted in favor of extending rights to juveniles in the previous cases again doing so here, but now simply being out-numbered.

THE GET TOUGH MOVEMENT

This change to a more conservative court was accompanied by a more conservative criminal and juvenile justice agenda nationally as President Reagan declared a war on crime in the 1980s. Many are familiar with the mandatory sentences for drug crimes and three-strikes and you're out policies that then prevailed in the adult system, but maybe you are not as familiar with what then happened to the juvenile system. As noted in Chapter 1, the definition of a juvenile delinquent changed from a needy child to a dangerous criminal—in fact even a new breed of criminal that was worse than adults. Thus, many states across the nation altered their juvenile justice systems in response. One of the most sweeping changes was a change in jurisdiction of the juvenile court—that is, which youth were qualified to be considered juvenile, and which youth would be held fully responsible as an adult for their offenses. You see, since the inception of the juvenile court—a court to provide second chances and rehabilitation to maturing youth—there was also a process by which individual youth could be processed in adult court if the judge found the youth unfitting for such benevolence. This process typically referred to as judicial waiver was a decision by the juvenile court judge that the youth was either too serious a criminal, or too mature to be amenable to treatment in the juvenile system. While historically this process was used sparingly, it became much more popular and indeed new pathways were even invented during the get tough era to "help" youth travel from juvenile to adult court.

You learned about the due process movement above, however, one other case heard during this time not yet discussed was the case of Morris Kent. In fact, the first case involving juvenile courts to come to the attention of the United States Supreme Court was that of Morris Kent. However it was not addressing the traditional adjudication hearing, rather it was addressing this unique process by which certain youth could be selectively identified as not appropriate for juvenile justice processing.

In this case, Morris was a youth with a history of serious delinquent behavior and mental illness. When arrested on charges of rape and burglary the District of Columbia decided to waive his case to adult court without a hearing in juvenile court first. Although the judge stated that he had performed a full investigation of the case, there was no such record of an investigation. His attorney appealed this decision arguing that Mr. Kent's due process protections were denied and that the court did not provide a full investigation before waiving Kent to adult court.

In this particular case, the Court ruled that if a state were to have a juvenile court that all youths should be entitled to its protections and that no youth could be waived to adult court without a proper hearing in which the youth was granted the right to an attorney. The case also set forth a list of 8 criteria that the juvenile court judge was to consider at such a hearing including:

1. The seriousness of the alleged offense;
2. Whether the alleged offense was committed in an aggressive, violent, premeditated or willful manner;
3. Whether the alleged offense was against persons or against property with greater weight being given to person offenses;
4. The evidential merit of the complaint (e.g., whether there is enough evidence to expect that a Grand Jury in the adult system would return an indictment);
5. The desirability of handling the trial and disposition of the entire offense scenario in one court when the juvenile's alleged associates in alleged offense are adults;
6. The sophistication and maturity of the juvenile as determined by consideration of home and environmental factors;
7. The prior offending record and previous juvenile court history of the youth including previous contacts with the juvenile court, social service agencies and other law enforcement entities; and
8. The prospects for adequate protection of the public and the likelihood of reasonable rehabilitation if the case is preserved in the juvenile court.

Kent v. United States

The Supreme Court case in which the court gave additional rights to youth facing waiver or transfer to adult court

Statutory Exclusion

when the legislature passes a statute that requires certain youth to be tried as adults based on combinations of age, offense history and current offense

While this original case held only for the District of Columbia as the laws being challenged were specific to this jurisdiction, most states adopted these new rules of law foreseeing challenges of their own if they did not follow suit. However, as the saying goes, for every rule there is an exception. So while the case of Morris Kent (***Kent v. United States***, 1966), set down the rule of law for how a waiver hearing should be held, the get tough movement found many exceptions to this rule. Indeed, states would now enact policies to greatly expand the transfer of juveniles to adult court and bypass many of the safeguards that the Court had attempted to extend to juveniles just a few years earlier (Torbet et al., 1998). These policies, which will be explored in more detail in Chapter 11, are just briefly introduced here. The first were **statutory exclusion** policies that excluded certain children from juvenile court or certain offenses from the definition of a juvenile act. The second set of policies were **direct file** mechanisms that defined certain youth or offenses as having concurrent jurisdiction in both the juvenile and adult court and then allowed the prosecutor the right to decide in which court to file charges. Both of these mechanisms directly skip the waiver hearing. In other cases the waiver hearing was changed from a discretionary waiver to a **mandatory waiver**—that is instead of the judge deciding if the child met the Kent criteria for a waiver, a waiver was mandated if the child was of a certain age and committed one of a list of designated offenses. Thus, the judge's hands are tied in these cases except to confirm that the child was indeed of age and was being prosecuted for a designated offense. A similar but less severe change was to move away from the discretionary waiver to a presumptive waiver in which, instead of the state proving the child should be tried as an adult, it is presumed that he should, and the child's defense attorney must prove that he/she should be kept in the juvenile system.

Another change that took place was a change in philosophy of the system for those youths who remained in the juvenile system (Torbet & Thomas, 1997). Most states had such a change and many even codified it into law, altering the purpose of their juvenile justice system. On last review approximately 25 states had adopted a national model called "**balanced and restorative justice**" that called for recognition of the victim's needs and dispositions that would hold the youths accountable for their actions rather than providing rehabilitation and treatment. Other states went even further—flat out replacing the notion of rehabilitation with that of punishment, as can be seen in Texas's revised juvenile law that states that the purpose of the juvenile court is to protect the public . . . and to . . . promote the concept of punishment for criminal acts." This rather shocking language actually redefines the juvenile as a "criminal" and not as a "delinquent" and specifically calls for "punishment" as an outcome rather than "rehabilitation or care."

Balanced and Restorative Justice
a philosophy of juvenile justice that attempts to balance the needs of the youth with the need to protect the community and repair harm done to a victim

As might be expected, with this change in philosophy came a change in practice that led to a much greater focus on formally petitioning youth to court rather than providing informal sanctions, the greater reliance on pre-adjudicatory detention until the hearing, and, upon adjudication, greater use of out-of-home placements. Overcrowding in detention centers and institutions then became a huge problem in the juvenile system, just as it was in the adult system, and reports started to surface about cases of abuse and even suicide and murder inside these institutions (Purtix & Scali, 1998).

CURRENT PRACTICE

Since the early 2000s there again seems to be a change in juvenile justice policy—this time it is more back to the original emphasis that the child is different than an adult and in need of care. Changes at the Supreme Court level have again rendered some adult punishments, like the death penalty and life without parole, unconstitutional for juveniles. And, many states are questioning their transfer policies that sent so many youths to adult prisons and are revoking or changing these laws. In fact, perhaps the most progressive proposal was recently offered by the governor of Connecticut who in 2015 called to extend the juvenile court up through the age of 21 (Thomas & Pazniokas, 2015), thus placing many more adolescents in juvenile rather than adult court. The details of current practice will be addressed in much more detail in Section 3 of the text; however, for now, just remember that we appear to be in a trend of redefining the juvenile as a child and not an adult criminal and focusing back on the original principles of the juvenile court and the progressives.

Key Words

Adjudication
Balanced and Restorative Justice
Daniel O'Connell
Disposition
Habeas Corpus
House of Refuge
Immigrants
In re Gault
In re Winship
Kent v. United States
Mary Ann Crouse
McKeiver v. Pennsylvania
Petition
Progressive Era
Statutory Exclusion

Chapter Summary

This chapter focused on the development of the formal juvenile justice system as a separate system of justice for youth in the United States. It began with a discussion of some of the key social factors that led to the problems that led to the need for a separate system of justice, which included an influx of immigrants from various countries, industrialization of the economy which led in turn to urbanization and rapid growth of the cities and the formation of our nation's first "slums." In these poor inner-city areas, children, mostly of recent immigrants, gathered without purpose and sometimes without hope.

The House of Refuge was the first attempt to treat these youth differently than adult criminals, and in recognition of their state of development, provide them with education and training rather than harsh punishment like that found in adult jails and prisons. However, these institutions did not live up to the hopes and dreams of their founders, looking remarkably like jails and punishment. So much so, that the Illinois Supreme Court eventually deemed it unconstitutional to hold a youth against his/her will in such an institution without due process of law.

The first juvenile court was then designed to provide such due process, be it less than that of adult court, but more than that of "no process" as had been the case before. Full due process protections were not seen as relevant as the Court and its services were there to help and treat, rather than punish, as set forth in the parens patriae doctrine. However, just as the House of Refuge had come into question so eventually did the practice of the new juvenile system during the 1960s and '70s, a time of great emphasis on individual civil rights. The cases of *In re Gault* and *In re Winship* forever changed the face of juvenile justice by providing basic due process rights in juvenile court. The rights extended by the U.S. Supreme Court in the Gault decision included the right to an attorney, the right to be notified of the charges, the right to cross-examine witnesses and the right to remain silent. The Winship case then altered the burden of proof in juvenile court from a "preponderance of the evidence" to "beyond a reasonable doubt." While the get-tough movement would follow closely on the heels of these changes and seem to eternally alter the practice of juvenile justice, recent times have seen a return to the original philosophies of the juvenile court, and even more progressive stances on emphasizing development over punishment. Similar to the original court that made much of its roots in theories of adolescent psychology and human development, advances in medicine and knowledge about the growth of the adolescent brain and psyche are again behind this change in policy. Where will the juvenile court of tomorrow take us? We will explore this in great detail in Section 3 of your text!

Discussion Questions

1. Compare and contrast the court decisions in the cases of Crouse, O'Connell and Gault. How are they similar? In what ways are they different?
2. What seemed to have changed between the handing down of the decisions in Gault and Winship until McKeiver? What was the rationale for the different outcome?
3. List and define the compatible juvenile justice term for the following criminal court terms: arraignment, indictment, conviction, sentencing. Be sure to note how the terms reflect different and/or similar practices.
4. What were the key social factors that led to the development of the first juvenile court? How would you define a juvenile based on the ideas of that time? How does the idea of the juvenile differ under the more recent get-tough movement? How did this change the juvenile court?
5. The chapter ends with a brief discussion of where juvenile justice seems to be going today. In your opinion based on what you have read in the news or elsewhere, where do you think it is going? Where do you think it should go?

REFERENCES

Bernard, T., & Kurlychek, M. (2010). *The cycle of juvenile justice*. New York: Oxford University Press.

Darwin, C. (1991/1859). *On the origin of species by means of natural selection.* London: Murray.

Feld, B. C. (1977). *Neutralizing inmate violence: Juvenile offenders in institutions. Series on Massachusetts youth corrections reforms*. Harvard: Ballinger Publication Co.

Feld, B. C. (1984). Criminalizing juvenile justice: Rules of procedure for the juvenile court. *Minn. L. Rev.* 69, 141.

Feld, B. C. (1987). The juvenile court meets the principle of the offense: Legislative changes in juvenile waiver statutes. *The Journal of Criminal Law and Criminology (1973–), 78*(3), 471–533.

Feld, B. C. (1988). Juvenile court meets the principle of offense: Punishment, treatment, and the difference it makes. *Bul. Rev. 68,* 821.

Feld, B. C. (1990). The transformation of the juvenile court. *Minn. L. Rev.* 75, 691.

Feld, B. C. (1998). *Bad kids: Race and the transformation of the juvenile court. Studies in Crime and Public Policy*. New York: Oxford University Press.

Feld, B. C. (2013). *Kids, cops, and confessions: Inside the interrogation room.* New York: New York University Press.

Hall, G. S. (1904). *Adolescence: Its psychology and its relation to physiology, anthropology, sociology, sex, crime, religion and education* (Vol. 2). New York: D. Appleton.

In re Gault. (1967). 387 U.S. 1, S. Ct. 1428.

In re Winship. (1970). 397 U.S. 358, 90 S. Ct. 1068.

Kent v. United States. (1966). 383 U.S. 541, 86 S. Ct. 1045.

Markel, H. (2009, December 15). Case shined first light on abuse of children. *The New York Times*: Health. Retrieved from http://www.nytimes.com/2009/12/15/health/15abus.html?_r=0

McKeiver v. Pennsylvania. (1971). 403 U.S. 528, 91 S. Ct. 1976.

Mennel, R. M. (1973). *Thorns and thistles.* Hanover NH: University Press of New England.

Platt, A. M. (1977). *The child savers: The invention of delinquency*. Chicago: Chicago University Press.

Purtix, P., & Scali, M. A. (1998). *Beyond the walls: Improving conditions of confinement for youth in custody.* Washington, DC: U.S. Department of Justice, Office of Justice Programs, Office of Juvenile Justice and Delinquency Prevention.

Snyder, H., & Sickmund, M. (1999). *Juvenile offenders and victims: 1999 national report.* Washington, DC: U.S. Department of Justice, Office of Justice Programs, Office of Juvenile Justice and Delinquency Prevention.

Thomas, J. R., & Pazniokas, M. (2015, November 6). Malloy: Raise the age for juvenile justice system to 20. *The Connecticut Mirror.* Retrieved from http://ctmirror.org/2015/11/06/malloy-raise-the-age-for-juvenile-justice-system-to-20/

Torbet, P., Gable, R., Hurst IV, H., Montgomery, I., Szymanski, L., & Thomas, D. (1996). *State legislative responses to violent juvenile crime*. Washington, DC: U.S. Department of Justice, Office of Justice Programs, Office of Juvenile Justice and Delinquency Prevention.

Torbet, P., & Thomas, D. (1997). *Balanced and restorative justice: Implementing the philosophy*. *Pennsylvania Progress, 4*(3). Harrisburg, PA: National Center for Juvenile Justice.

Measuring and Studying Delinquency

3

"On the morning of May 31, 2014, three 12-year-old girls awoke to a breakfast of strawberries and donuts. It was a Saturday in the sleepy town of Waukesha, Wis. The night before had been a slumber party at Morgan Geyser's house to celebrate her 12th birthday. Morgan didn't have a lot of friends, and the two who stayed over were her closest: Anissa Weier and Payton Leutner, who went by "Bella."

After breakfast, the girls went out to play, first in a nearby park, then in the woods, where Anissa told Morgan, "Kitty, now — go ballistic, go crazy!" and Morgan stabbed Payton 19 times before both girls ran off, leaving Payton for dead."

Source: *New York Post* "Inside Kids' Chilling Slenderman Murder Plot." By Maureen Callahan, January 22, 2017.

Milwaukee Journal Sentinel/Contributor/Getty

Morgan Geyser is brought into court by a sheriff's deputy on Aug. 21, 2015, during the arraignment of the Slenderman stabbing trial in Waukesha County Court in Waukesha, Wis. The court entered a not guilty plea for them and moved to set a trial date in mid-October.

In the book *The Cycle of Juvenile Justice* the authors argue that no matter what else is going on in a society, at all times and in all places people think that there is a juvenile crime wave (Bernard, 1991, Bernard & Kurlychek, 2010). That is, they are under the impression that youth crime is at an all-time high and something must be done about it. It is no wonder in today's society that this would be true. The media saying "if it bleeds it leads" relates to the fact that the most sensational stories gain the most viewers, so the nightly news usually begins with stories of the most horrific crimes of the day. As shown in the crime example above, these crimes seem even more devastating when it is reported that they are committed by youth, leading many older members of society to say, "What is wrong with kids today?"

Well, the fact is that what is wrong with kids today is the same as what was wrong with kids who committed crimes in the past. The youths' behavior generally reflect the social influences to which they are exposed. Whether it be direct exposure to abuse in the home, the witnessing of street violence, or, as in the case above, the exposure to violence and deviant attitudes through the media, the nature and extent of delinquency is a good measure of the other social ills in a society. That is, the levels of juvenile crime go up and down in a society primarily related to other social conditions and ills to which youth are exposed. Sometimes juvenile crime is high, sometimes it is low, sometimes it is more violent, sometimes it is less violent. The question then becomes, how do we know exactly what the juvenile crime rate is, and thus, whether something truly needs to be done about it? Criminologists have several different types of data and methods they can use to answer these questions. In the following chapter you will learn to move beyond popular media depictions of crime and delinquency, and begin to learn how to study juvenile delinquency as a student of criminology.

CHAPTER GOALS

By the end of this chapter you should be able to:

1. Know the major sources of data on juvenile delinquency and delinquents.
2. Understand the strengths and weaknesses of each source of data.
3. Use these data sources to understand current trends in juvenile delinquency and justice.
4. Identify and select an appropriate source of data to answer a particular research question.

Studying Juvenile Delinquency and Juvenile Justice: Sources of Information and Their Uses

As a student studying juvenile delinquency and juvenile justice it is important to know where to find information and how best to use that information. If your instructor asks you "How many crimes were committed by juveniles last year?" Where would you go to find the answer? How would you interpret it? For example, if you found that juveniles committed 500,000 crimes last year, is that a high number or a low number? Is it more or less than years in the past? Although these seem like fairly simple examples, finding the answers to seemingly simple questions like these can be more complicated than it first appears as there are many sources of data on crime and delinquency. Each source has its unique strengths (e.g., things it is good for telling you), and weaknesses (e.g., things it is not so good for telling you). Therefore, it is important to understand the different sources of data and to practice using them to find and interpret answers to specific questions. The goal of this chapter is to introduce you to the major sources of data available for the study of juvenile justice and delinquency and to help you understand which sources might be best for specific tasks at hand.

In the following sections I break the sources of data down into major categories, then present some of the primary data sources within each category, explaining where and how to access and use these data types.

Administrative Data

Administrative Data: often referred to as "official data" because they are reported through official juvenile and criminal justice agencies such as the police, courts, state departments of corrections, and even federal agencies such as the FBI

The first and most commonly used source of juvenile and criminal justice data are **Administrative Data**. These are often referred to as "official data" because they are reported through official juvenile and criminal justice agencies such as the police, courts, state departments of corrections, and even federal agencies such as the FBI. These data sets are most often collected in a manner that is useful to the collecting agency for its purposes and not necessarily for research, which makes it even more important that someone using the data really understand how it was collected and what it represents.

THE UNIFORM CRIME REPORT

Uniform Crime Report

reported annually by the FBI, this data set compiles data from over 97% of police departments in the United States

Violent Crime Index

includes Criminal Homicide, Rape, Robbery and Aggravated Assault

Property Crime Index

includes Burglary/Breaking or Entering, Larceny/Theft, Motor Vehicle Theft and Arson

The largest, oldest and most comprehensive data set for the study of crime in America is the **Uniform Crime Report (UCR)**. Reported annually by the Federal Bureau of Investigation (FBI), this data set compiles data from over 97% of police departments in the United States to report three sets of statistics:

1. Crimes reported to the police
2. Persons arrested for crimes reported to the police
3. Police crime clearance rates

Crimes reported to the police is probably the section of the report most cited and used by individuals studying crime. These statistics are broken down into Part I and Part II offenses. Part I offenses are considered the more serious offenses and are further broken down into the **Violent Crime Index** and the **Property Crime Index** as shown in Exhibit 3.1.

EXHIBIT 3.1

PART 1: VIOLENT CRIMES

Criminal Homicide, which has two categories: 1. The willful killing of one human being by another, and 2. The killing of another person through gross negligence. The second category, manslaughter by negligence, is considered a Part I crime but is not reported as part of the Violent Crime Index and does not include traffic fatalities.

Rape is defined as the "penetration, no matter how slight, of the vagina or anus with any body part or object, or oral penetration by a sex organ of another person, without the consent of the victim." This statistic includes completed and attempted rapes. It does not, however, include statutory rape (rape that may not be forced but is illegal due to the victim being underage to consent).

Robbery is defined as the taking or attempting to take anything of value from the care, custody, or control of a person or persons by force or threat of force or violence and/or by putting the victim in fear.

EXHIBIT 3.1: cont.

Aggravated Assault is defined as the unlawful attack by one person upon another for the purpose of inflicting severe or aggravated bodily injury. Aggravated assault differs from simple assault in that it usually involves a weapon and/or results in more serious bodily injury to the victim.

PART 1: PROPERTY CRIMES

Burglary/Breaking or Entering is defined as the unlawful entry of, or attempt to enter, a structure to commit a felony or a theft.

Larceny/Theft is defined as the unlawful taking, carrying, leading or riding away of property from the possession or constructive possession of another. This category excludes motor vehicle theft.

Motor Vehicle Theft is defined simply as the unlawful taking of a motor vehicle.

Arson is defined as the willful or malicious burning or attempting to burn, with or without intent to defraud, a dwelling house, public building, motor vehicle, or aircraft, personal property of another.

As should be apparent from Exhibit 3.1, these categories are very specific and could easily be misinterpreted if someone did not know the official definition of each as other sources may define these crimes differently.

These crimes are then reported in several ways that may be useful depending on the researcher's purpose. First, the number and type of Part I crimes is broken down by city, county, standard metropolitan statistical area and region. A **statistical metropolitan area**, or SMA as it is often referred to, is an area consisting of a central city and its surrounding suburbs. For example, New York City is a city, but the SMA would include the surrounding boroughs such as Brooklyn, Queens and the Bronx. Regions of the United States are most often reported as Northeast, Southeast, Midwest, Southwest and West. Table 3.1 shows one such breakdown of Part I offenses by region. In interpreting this data it is important to remember that this is not the actual number of crimes committed, but rather the number of those crimes that were actually reported to police.

Statistical Metropolitan Area
an area consisting of a central city and its surrounding suburbs

TABLE 3.1 Crime in the United States (Offense and Population Percent Distribution by Region), 2015

Region	Population	"Violent crime"	"Murder and nonnegligent manslaughter"	"Rape (revised definition)[1]"	"Rape (legacy definition)[2]"	Robbery	"Aggravated assault"	"Property crime"	Burglary	"Larceny-theft"	"Motor vehicle theft"
United States Total[3]	**100.0**	**100.0**	**100.0**	**100.0**	**100.0**	**100.0**	**100.0**	**100.0**	**100.0**	**100.0**	**100.0**
Northeast	17.5	14.7	12.4	13.1	13.3	17.2	13.9	11.9	10.0	12.9	8.0
Midwest	21.1	19.6	21.5	24.2	24.3	18.9	19.2	19.3	19.4	19.6	16.7
South	37.7	41.2	45.9	37.4	36.8	38.6	42.8	42.2	45.2	42.2	35.3
West	23.7	24.5	20.2	25.3	25.6	25.3	24.2	26.6	25.4	25.3	39.9

[1] The figures shown in the rape (revised definition) column were calculated using the revised Uniform Crime Reporting (UCR) definition of rape. See data declaration for further explanation.

[2] The figures shown in the rape (legacy definition) column were calculated using the legacy UCR definition of rape. See data declaration for further explanation.

[3] Because of rounding, the percentages may not add to 100.0.

NOTE: Although arson data are included in the trend and clearance tables, sufficient data are not available to estimate totals for this offense. Therefore, no arson data are published in this table.

Source: https://ucr.fbi.gov 2015 Crime in the United States

HOMICIDE

In general the UCR does not collect information on victims of crimes, just the type of crime reported and any person arrested for that crime. However, in the case of homicide, the most serious crime, data on the victim is collected and stored, including the age, gender and race of the victim and the relationship of the perpetrator to the victim, and type of weapon used in the killing. This allows researchers to better understand the circumstances surrounding murder, and who is most likely to be the victim of certain types of homicides. This information is provided in a section of the report called the "Expanded Homicide Tables" (http://www.fbi.gov/about-us/cjis/ucr/crime-in-the-u.s/2013/crime-in-the-u.s.-2013/offenses-known-to-law-enforcement/expanded-homicide/expandhomicidemain_final) as well as Table 20 of the report (entitled Homicide by Weapon by State).

This section also has tables on justifiable homicides. These are homicides that are not deemed as crimes as the person was acting in self-defense at the time of the killing. Expanded Homicide Table 14 reports justifiable homicides by police officers and Expanded Homicide Table 15 reports justifiable homicides by private citizens.

The second major category reported in the UCR is clearance rates. This is used as a measure of police productivity. A crime is cleared in one of two ways:

1. When at least one person is arrested, charged and turned over to the court for prosecution, or 2. By exceptional means. "Exceptional means" refers to the instance where the police have identified the individual(s) responsible for the crime and have enough evidence to arrest, charge and prosecute; however, due to circumstances beyond their control cannot make an arrest. Examples of this would be if the offender dies or leaves the country and cannot be extradited for arrest. Clearance rates vary greatly by type of crime with murders being the most likely to be cleared (64.1%) and many minor property crimes being significantly less likely to be cleared (13.1% of burglaries).

The third major use of the UCR is to gain estimates on the characteristics of persons arrested for crimes. This includes every time a person is arrested. If a person is arrested 3 times in 2014, he/she will be counted as 3 persons arrested. Moreover, as noted above with clearance rates, not all reports lead to an arrest.

Also, some reports lead to more than one arrest if more than one person committed the offense. All in all, this means that the number of persons arrested is not directly comparable to the number of crimes reported to police or even the number of crimes cleared by police. The diagrams below, in Figure 3.1 and Figure 3.2, attempt to make this point more clear for you.

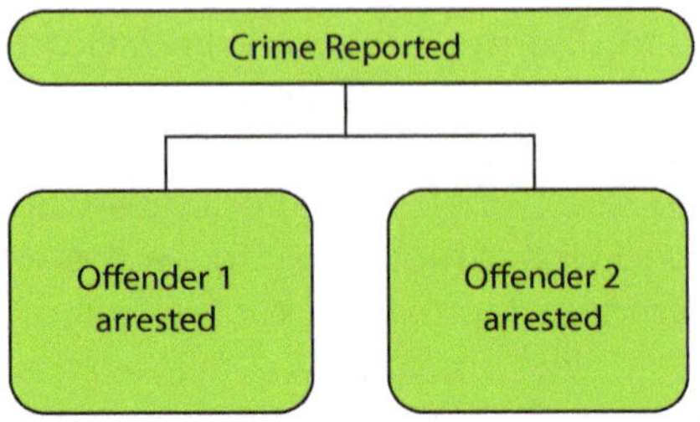

FIGURE 3.1 One Crime Leads to the Arrest of Two People

In this graphic, one crime leads to the arrest of two people. If this were always the case, then the number of crimes would equal half the number of arrestees. Of course, this is not always the case. One crime report can lead to no arrest, to one arrest, or even to three or more arrests. Thus, the number of crimes reported to the police in the UCR does not directly relate to an equal number of arrestees.

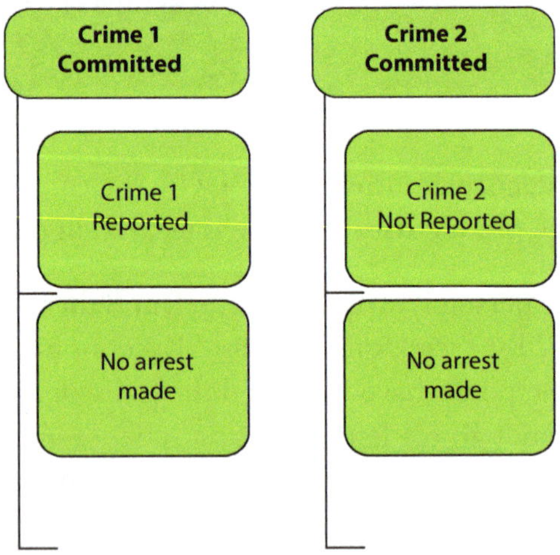

FIGURE 3.2 Two Crimes Committed, Only One Reported

In this second example you also see how the total number of crimes can be undercounted by the UCR. In this simple example, two crimes were committed, but only one of these was reported to the police. Then, for the crime that was reported to the police, there was no arrest ever made. That is, the crime was not "**cleared**" by the police. So for this example there were two actual crimes, but only one would appear as a crime reported to the police in the UCR, and nothing from this incident would appear in the UCR under "persons arrested for crimes" as the crime was never solved.

However, when a crime is cleared, and an arrest made, the UCR breaks down information on persons arrested by age, which does make it a useful source for studying patterns of juveniles arrested for crime. Just be clear in your mind that this is patterns of youth arrested for crime, and does not represent all youth committing crimes as many crimes go undetected, and many also may go unreported to police.

Hate Crime

any crime motivated by biases based on race, gender, gender identity, religion, disability, sexual orientation and/or ethnicity

What exactly is the UCR good for then? I will give several examples. Table 3.2 below demonstrates how the UCR could be used to answer questions such as, how many juvenile arrests were made last year? And was this number higher or lower than in years before?

FOCUS ON POLICY: The Hate Crime Act

The Hate Crime Act **28 U.S.C. § 534§** [Sec. 1.] (a) formally defined a **hate crime** as any crime motivated by biases based on race, gender, gender identity, religion, disability, sexual orientation and/or ethnicity. This act required the Attorney General of the United States to design methods for collecting and reporting national data on incidents of hate crimes to be used for statistical research and law enforcement purposes. This data is now reported annually in a special report released by the FBI called Hate Crime Statistics.

According to Table I of this report, race is still the single-highest motivation for hate crimes, followed by sexual orientation and religion:

- 49.3 percent of the victims were targeted because of the offenders' bias against race.
- 20.2 percent were targeted because of bias against sexual orientation.
- 16.9 percent were victimized because of bias against religion.
- 11.4 percent were victimized because of bias against ethnicity.
- 1.4 percent were targeted because of bias against disability.
- 0.5 percent (33 individuals) were victims of gender-identity bias.
- 0.4 percent (30 individuals) were victims of gender bias.

TABLE 3.2 Five-Year Arrest Trends (Totals, 2011–2015)

[10,685 agencies; 2015 estimated population 217,039,923; 2011 estimated population 211,166,146]

	Number of persons arrested								
	Total all ages			Under 18 years of age			18 years of age and over		
Offense charged	**2011**	**2015**	**Percent change**	**2011**	**2015**	**Percent change**	**2011**	**2015**	**Percent change**
TOTAL[1]	**8,225,888**	**7,213,389**	**-12.3**	**991,398**	**634,718**	**-36.0**	**7,234,490**	**6,578,671**	**-9.1**
Murder and nonnegligent manslaughter	6,968	7,005	+0.5	539	493	-8.5	6,429	6,512	+1.3
Rape[2]	13,168	15,126	-	1,917	2,401	-	11,251	12,725	-
Robbery	67,650	60,085	-11.2	15,037	11,404	-24.2	52,613	48,681	-7.5
Aggravated assault	259,015	246,238	-4.9	26,421	19,008	-28.1	232,594	227,230	-2.3
Burglary	197,756	145,163	-26.6	41,018	23,887	-41.8	156,738	121,276	-22.6
Larceny-theft	855,183	799,643	-6.5	175,433	109,356	-37.7	679,750	690,287	+1.6
Motor vehicle theft	44,336	50,447	+13.8	9,581	9,624	+0.4	34,755	40,823	+17.5
Arson	7,876	6,133	-22.1	3,352	1,914	-42.9	4,524	4,219	-6.7
Violent crime[3]	346,801	328,454	-5.3	43,914	33,306	-24.2	302,887	295,148	-2.6
Property crime[3]	1,105,151	1,001,386	-9.4	229,384	144,781	-36.9	875,767	856,605	-2.2
Other assaults	827,577	727,435	-12.1	127,310	89,835	-29.4	700,267	637,600	-8.9
Forgery and counterfeiting	46,264	36,642	-20.8	1,065	694	-34.8	45,199	35,948	-20.5
Fraud	110,363	90,590	-17.9	3,583	3,246	-9.4	106,780	87,344	-18.2
Embezzlement	10,931	11,011	+0.7	301	426	+41.5	10,630	10,585	-0.4

Stolen property; buying, receiving, possessing	63,792	59,223	-7.2	9,127	6,715	-26.4	54,665	52,508	-3.9
Vandalism	160,380	130,154	-18.8	46,688	29,227	-37.4	113,692	100,927	-11.2
Weapons; carrying, possessing, etc.	99,115	95,803	-3.3	18,665	13,078	-29.9	80,450	82,725	+2.8
Prostitution and commercialized vice	26,777	19,797	-26.1	461	292	-36.7	26,316	19,505	-25.9
Sex offenses (except rape and prostitution)	44,870	34,420	-23.3	8,482	6,048	-28.7	36,388	28,372	-22.0
Drug abuse violations	1,020,875	1,016,402	-0.4	101,191	69,355	-31.5	919,684	947,047	+3.0
Gambling	4,929	3,055	-38.0	618	294	-52.4	4,311	2,761	-36.0
Offenses against the family and children	76,387	65,357	-14.4	2,378	2,335	-1.8	74,009	63,022	-14.8
Driving under the influence	825,909	676,560	-18.1	7,013	4,432	-36.8	818,896	672,128	-17.9
Liquor laws	323,529	181,462	-43.9	63,622	30,876	-51.5	259,907	150,586	-42.1
Drunkenness	361,587	268,115	-25.9	8,185	3,836	-53.1	353,402	264,279	-25.2
Disorderly conduct	382,589	264,528	-30.9	91,752	49,315	-46.3	290,837	215,213	-26.0
Vagrancy	14,587	15,495	+6.2	641	648	+1.1	13,946	14,847	+6.5
All other offenses (except traffic)	2,325,288	2,157,131	-7.2	178,831	115,610	-35.4	2,146,457	2,041,521	-4.9
Suspicion	732	573	-21.7	78	132	+69.2	654	441	-32.6
Curfew and loitering law violations	48,187	30,369	-37.0	48,187	30,369	-37.0	-	-	-

[1] Does not include suspicion.

[2] The 2011 rape figures are based on the legacy definition, and the 2015 rape figures are aggregate totals based on both the legacy and revised Uniform Crime Reporting definitions. For this reason, a percent change is not provided.

[3] Violent crimes are offenses of murder and nonnegligent manslaughter, rape, robbery, and aggravated assault. Property crimes are offenses of burglary, larceny-theft, motor vehicle theft, and arson.

Source: https://ucr.fbi.gov 2015 Crime in the United States/Five-Year Arrest Trends

Limitations of the UCR

The above section introduced you to the basics of the UCR and hopefully demonstrated its value as a resource for research. However, as noted in the beginning of the chapter, each source presented is going to be good for some things and not so good for others. What is the UCR good for? It is the best source of information we have on national crime trends reported to the police, and on the characteristics of persons arrested by police. However, because it collects information only on offenses reported to the police, it is missing all those offenses that are not reported to the police. Some offenses may be so minor that a person does not report them, or they feel nothing could be done. Other times the victim might be too fearful or embarrassed to report the incident, such as has been suggested in the case of domestic violence and rape. Thus it is not a measure of total crime in America. Also, while it collects information on persons arrested, we do not know the characteristics of delinquents who avoid arrest and, other than homicide, it does not gather information on victims of crime. Other issues in validity and reliability of the data that one should be aware of when using the UCR include:

1. *What the report does not include.* Table 3.1 listed all the crimes the UCR records; note that it does not collect information on **victimless crimes**, such that no drug offenses (possession, use, sale, distribution) are included in the UCR. Also, no federal crimes are reported.
2. *How offenses are recorded.* If an offender is charged with multiple crimes at arrest, only the most serious crime per arrest is recorded. For example, if a person broke into a home (breaking and entering), sexually assaulted the resident (rape) and stole significant amounts of jewelry and cash from the home (burglary), only the rape would be reported in the UCR. This is called the **hierarchy rule**. Thus, the UCR may provide an underestimate of many lesser crimes. Also, arrests themselves are counted differently across categories. For example, if a juvenile robbed a group of four other juveniles at gunpoint this would count as one robbery incident. However, if the same juvenile had assaulted each of the juveniles in the group, this would be recorded as four aggravated assaults.
3. *Police department practices.* Some departments are very formalized and professional and strictly follow the UCR guidelines in defining crimes. Others are less formalized or even intentionally underreport crimes.
4. *Individual reporting practices.* Increases in crime rates may actually reflect increases in citizen willingness to report crime and better policing practices. For example, if the number of reported incidents of domestic violence increases, this

Hierarchy Rule

when an offender is charged with multiple crimes at arrest, but only the most serious crime per arrest is recorded could be because of more crime or more willingness of victims to report this crime, or formal policing policies that mandate arrest for all domestic violence reports.

NIBRS

The UCR has been collecting data in much the same way since its inception in 1939. However, in 1982 a five-year redesign effort began to explore better ways of collecting crime information that would allow one to link the specific crime to the person arrested and the victim(s). This process resulted in a new data collection strategy called the National Incident-Based Reporting System (**NIBRS**) that reports and connects all data by criminal incident. In addition, NIBRS has expanded crime categories, including drug offenses, which were not previously captured by the UCR. A researcher using NIBRS can also answer questions such as "are juvenile offenders more likely to offend against other juveniles or older individuals" as it connects that actual person arrested to the characteristics of the victim of the offense. It also includes information on whether the crime can be classified as a hate crime, and whether an arrested offender was under the influence of drugs and/or alcohol when arrested. It should be easy to see that when fully implemented this program will overcome some of the major drawbacks of the current UCR program. This program is currently implemented fully in 22 states with many more working on data collection procedures to allow them to join the NIBRS program. The NIBRS data from these states and charts is available at: https://ucr.fbi.gov/nibrs/2014. (Note that as new years of data become available the last part of this address will switch to /2015, /2016 etc.)

NIBRS
National Incident-Based Reporting System which reports and connects all data by criminal incident

THE NATIONAL JUVENILE COURT ARCHIVE

Even before the UCR began, the federal government had begun collecting information on the cases processed by the nation's juvenile courts. This is a unique source of information for scholars of juvenile justice and it provides not only information on juveniles arrested and petitioned to court, but on the court processes themselves. This program began in 1926 with 100 courts completing a statistical form on each case processed and sending these forms to the Children's Bureau of the U.S. Department of Labor. These data were the basis of early *Juvenile Court Statistics* reports. However, this case-by-case system proved difficult to maintain and expand so efforts were made to ease the process by making it an annual reporting form with only simple counts of number and types of offenses (similar to UCR aggregate statistics).

In 1974 the Juvenile Justice and Delinquency Prevention Act created the Office of Juvenile Justice and Delinquency Prevention within the U.S. Department of Justice to provide oversight and direction for the nation's juvenile justice systems. One of the first major initiatives of this office was to improve the data collection system and awarding a grant to the National Center for Juvenile Justice (NCJJ), the research division of the National Council of Juvenile and Family Court Judges, to take over this initiative. NCJJ found that many states were requiring the juvenile courts to fill out detailed case-specific forms similar to the rich data originally included in the early juvenile court statistical reports. Even though this data collection process varied across states, NCJJ worked with the jurisdictions to develop techniques and procedures to extract a set of commonly defined data elements from these disparate databases. Today the **National Juvenile Court Data Archive** contains over 15 million automated case records. While the information on each case varies across the individual data sets, nearly all records contain demographic information on:

National Juvenile Court Data Archive

contains over 15 million automated case records with nearly all records containing demographic information on age, gender, race, county of residence, offense(s) charged, use of pretrial detention, adjudication, and disposition

- Age
- Gender
- Race
- County of residence
- Offense(s) charged
- Use of pretrial detention
- Adjudication
- Disposition

In addition to producing an annual statistical report, the National Juvenile Court Data Archive makes these data files available to researchers online (http://www.ojjdp.gov/ojstatbb/njcda/asp/guide.asp) and will produce customized analyses upon request.

In addition to these two national administrative data sets (UCR and NJCDA), some agencies readily share their data; others have restrictions or charge fees for the use of their data and it is up to the researcher to navigate these requirements. For example, the Pennsylvania Commission on Sentencing has routinely made its data available to the public. Most data files from this agency are free, with a small fee being charged for judge-specific files. Florida is also a state well known for allowing researchers access to its administrative court and sentencing data sets. Because juveniles are considered a protected population, however, when attempting to access official data on juveniles there may be additional restrictions on access to, and use of, official data and in some cases access can be denied. The best way to collect information from a state is usually to begin with identifying the agency in that state responsible for data collection and making phone calls to introduce yourself and inquire about data availability.

Victimization Surveys

One of the key "flaws" if you will of the UCR is the criticism that not all crimes are reported to the police. Victims can have various reasons not to report a crime and thus we know that the UCR probably underestimates the levels of crime in the United States and probably is a worse estimate for some types of crime than others.

THE NATIONAL CRIME VICTIMIZATION SURVEY

In response to this problem, the **National Crime Victimization Survey (NCVS)** was launched in 1972. It was a multistage cluster sample of U.S. households, with every individual in the household over the age of 12 then interviewed about victimization experiences. Currently, data are obtained from a nationally representative sample of about 90,000 households each year, which consist of nearly 160,000 persons. Each household is interviewed twice during the year.

National Crime Victimization Survey (NCVS)
a representative sample of about 90,000 households each year, which consist of nearly 160,000 persons

Questions included in the NCVS are aimed at assessing an individual's experience with crime from the individual's perspective. If an individual indicates that he/she has been victimized by a certain type of crime, subsequent questions are asked to gain more detail on the incident, including information on the offender when known. Table 3.3 provides sample questions from the current version of the NCVS pertaining to rape and sexual assault. Table 3.4 then provides basic summary statistics from the NCVS gained from answers to these questions.

TABLE 3.3 Sample Questions
Question 43a: Incidents involving forced or unwanted sexual acts are often difficult to talk about. Other than any incidents already mentioned, have you been forced or coerced to engage in unwanted sexual activity by: A) Someone you didn't know B) A casual acquaintance C) Someone you know well.
Follow up questions if subject answers yes to Question 43a.
Question 43b: How many times?
Question 43c: What happened?

TABLE 3.4 Summary of Answers to These Questions			
Rape and sexual assault victimizations against females, by victim characteristics, 1994–1998, 1999–2004, and 2005–2010			
	Rate per 1,000 females age 12 or older		
Victim characteristic	**1994–1998**	**1999–2004**	**2005–2010**
Total	4.2	3.1	2.1
Age			
12–17	11.3	7.6	4.1
18–34	7.0	5.3	3.7
35–64	2.3	1.8	1.5
65 or older	0.1 !	0.2 !	0.2 !
Race/Hispanic origin			
White[a]	4.3	3.1	2.2
Black[a]	4.2	4.1	2.8
Hispanic/Latina	4.3	1.8	1.4
American Indian/Alaska Native[a]	6.4 !	4.8 !	4.5 !
Asian/Pacific Islander[a]	2.5	1.2	0.7!
Two or more races[a]	~	6.6 !	5.1 !
Marital status[b]			
Never married	8.6	6.6	4.1
Married	1.3	0.7	0.6
Widowed	0.8	0.2!	0.8
Divorced or separated	9.0	6.3	4.4
Household income			
Less than $25,000	6.1	5.6	3.5
$25,000–$49,999	3.3	2.7	1.9
$50,000 or more	2.9	2.0	1.8
Unknown	3.5	2.1	1.8
Location of residence			
Urban	5.1	4.0	2.2
Suburban	3.9	2.7	1.8
Rural	3.9	2.5	3.0

Note: See appendix table 5 for standard errors.
! Interpret with caution; estimate based on 10 or fewer sample cases, or coefficient of variation is greater than 50%.
~Not applicable.
[a] Excludes persons of Hispanic or Latino origin.
[b] The NCVS collects information on respondent's marital status at the time of the interview, but it does not obtain marital status at the time of the incident or whether a change in marital status occurred after the incident.

Source: Bureau of Justice Statistics, National Crime Victimization Survey, 1994–2010

As can be seen from Table 3.4, the rich information about the victim of the crime is quite different than the information provided by the UCR. Here we know the age, race, income, marital status and residential area of the victim. The NCVS can also be used to find information on the time of day and day of the week an incident occurred, which helps to detail patterns of victimization. Thus, the NCVS is very good to use for answering questions about who is victimized and whether they know the person who victimized them. Using estimates of crimes provided by the NCVS and comparing them to the UCR, we can also develop an idea of how many crimes go unreported to police. This is often referred to as the "**dark figure of crime**" as it is all the crime that is generally not known about—that is, we are in the dark about it. In general the NCVS shows that many crimes do go unreported to the police. Estimates from comparing the two sources are that only about half of all violent crimes and burglaries are reported to police and fewer than one-third of personal thefts (Langton, Berzofsky, Krebs, & Smiley-McDonald, 2012).

Dark Figure of Crime

crimes that go unreported to the police

More information on the NCVS and its actual full questionnaire can be accessed by visiting the Bureau of Justice Statistics website.

Limitations of the NCVS

It is important to remember that the NCVS is not an official administrative data set as it is not collecting official data, but rather personal accounts from a sample of individuals. This sample is then used to make national estimates about the total number of crime victimizations experienced. This approach has some benefits over the UCR and also some important weaknesses.

While I noted above some things for which the NCVS is good, it is also important to note those things for which it is not so good. First of all, please note that similar to the UCR, it does not collect data on victimless crimes, thus drug crimes are not reported. Also, homicides are not recorded. Other limitations to be aware of when using the NCVS are:

- *Overreporting.* This occurs mainly when an individual thinks a crime happened that did not. For example, a lost cell phone may be reported as stolen. It also can happen because of "telescoping"; this is a phenomenon in which traumatic events that happened in the past seem to the victim as if they happened more recently. Thus when asked about victimization events in the last six months or year, the individual might include events that happened further in the past.

- *Underreporting.* Underreporting can happen simply because a person does not remember all incidents of victimization. More minor incidents are more likely to be forgotten than major crimes. Also, a victim might feel uncomfortable or afraid to report certain experiences. Although the NCVS is worded in ways to try to best illicit responses, it is still likely that some individuals will not be comfortable reporting some information.
- *Sampling error.* Because the NCVS is not a survey of all Americans, it uses the data gained from a sample of households to make national estimates. To the extent that the sample of households is not representative of the U.S. population, its estimates will be biased. In particular, we can easily see that crimes against the homeless will not be found in this survey based on the sampling technique.
- *Question formatting.* Great care has been taken to write and re-write the NCVS questions to make them clear and understandable; however, since the survey is being given to a wide range of people, age, literacy, language and other barriers could impact one's ability to understand and correctly respond to questions.

Self-Report Surveys

Self-Report Surveys

studies that ask individuals to self-report their delinquent behaviors."

Another way to get at the delinquency question is to "get it straight from the horse's mouth"—that is, ask the kids! This type of **self-report survey** was first used in the study of delinquency by Austin Porterfield in 1943 (1943, 1946). In this study Porterfield started by analyzing official records of juvenile delinquents to see for which types of crimes they were most often arrested. He then created a self-report survey and administered it to a group of 337 college students to see if these individuals, who for the most part had no criminal justice system contact, had ever engaged in any of these same activities. He found that for the most part, the college students reported committing the same crimes as the delinquents. This study was one of the first to not only show that individuals were willing to self-report criminal behavior in an anonymous survey format, but that most individuals had committed a crime while they were a teenager, regardless of whether a formal arrest occurred for that behavior.

While this original study was not methodologically sophisticated, it raised interest in this technique. Credit for bringing this methodology to the forefront of the field is usually given to Short and Nye (1957) who "revolutionized ideas about the feasibility of using survey procedures with a hitherto taboo topic" (Hindelang, Hirschi, & Weis, 1981, 23). What distinguished Short and Nye's research was their attention to methodological issues such as selecting an appropriate sample, assessing the reliability and validity of the questions included in the survey and attention to race and class differences (Thornberry & Krohn, 2000). From this time forward the use of self-report studies spread rapidly until this methodology became common in the field (Erickson & Empey, 1963; Akers, 1964; Christie, Andenaes, & Skirbekk, 1965; Elmhorn, 1965; Antilla & Jaakkola, 1966; Gold, 1966, 1970; Buikhuisen, Jongman, & Oving, 1969; Hirschi, 1969; Elliott & Voss, 1974; Klein, 1989; Hagan, 1993).

Another problem for this type of survey is selecting a sample representative of the population of interest. In constructing a self-report survey it is important to take into consideration how to select the sample. That is, do you want to be able to generalize your results to youth in general? Youth in high school? Youth in certain locations?

Also, the wording of questions becomes even more important as the survey is being given to children and thus the questions have to be worded in a way that is age appropriate. Many youth who come into contact with the juvenile justice system are actually behind in development due to other problems in their home or school life, which means their reading level may be significantly below grade level. Also, language barriers must be taken into consideration and perhaps versions of the survey constructed in other languages frequently spoken among the population of interest.

Despite these challenges, this type of data became popular very fast for two reasons. First, it surprisingly revealed that almost everyone had committed a crime at some time in their life, even though only a few were formally arrested and processed by the system. Second, the surveys were able to capture rich personal information about the person committing the crimes, so that this research could be used to develop theories about who commits crimes, what types of crimes they commit, and perhaps, why they chose to commit that crime. Indeed, many of the theories you will learn about in the next section of this text were developed and tested using self-report survey data. While there are too many self-report surveys to review all of them here, below I introduce you to two surveys that are currently being conducted that show two different approaches to collecting such data.

MONITORING THE FUTURE: CROSS-SECTION EXAMPLE

Monitoring the Future is a cross-sectional survey conducted by researchers at the University of Michigan Institute of Social Research. This self-report survey has been administered to a nationally representative sample of high school students since 1978. Today the study surveys 8th, 10th and 12th graders asking questions about delinquency, drug use and other risky behaviors as well as school performance. Similar to early self-report studies, this research confirms that almost everyone breaks the law at some point during their teenage years; however, most popular crimes are the less-serious crimes such as truancy, underage alcohol use, larceny of small amounts (under $50), marijuana use and fighting.

Because this survey is given annually, it provides a great resource for studying trends in offending behavior and types of crimes committed by youth in high schools. However, note that it does not follow the same kids over time; each year it takes a new sample of students in the 8th, 10th and 12th grades. This is why is it called a **cross-sectional survey** because it looks at a cross-section of the population at a given time.

Cross Sectional Survey

looks at a cross-section of the population at a given time

NATIONAL LONGITUDINAL SURVEY OF YOUTH: LONGITUDINAL EXAMPLE

National Longitudinal Study of Youth (NLSY)

a nationally representative sample of approximately 9,000 youths who were 12 to 16 years old as of December 31, 1996

Data Mining

a technique in which researchers are able to literally "mine" a data set created for other purposes to find valuable information related to their research purpose

The **National Longitudinal Survey of Youth (NLSY)** consists of a nationally representative sample of approximately 9,000 youths who were 12 to 16 years old as of December 31, 1996. Round 1 of the survey took place in 1997, interviewing eligible youths and one parent per each youth. Youths were then interviewed on an annual basis thereafter, resulting in a rich data set following the individual from early adolescence through young adulthood. This is called a **longitudinal data set** as it follows the same individuals over time. Created and administered by the United States Department of Labor, the key purpose of this survey is to explore the transition from school to work and into adulthood. However, in addition to schooling and work histories, the survey also collects rich information on demographic and family characteristics, dating and sexual behavior, criminal behavior and alcohol and drug use. Because the survey contains these questions it opens up the opportunity for data mining. **Data mining** is a technique in which researchers are able to literally "mine" a data set created for other purposes to find valuable information related to their research purpose.

FOCUS ON RESEARCH: MINING THE NLSY: Prevalence of Arrest in Young Adults

One recent use of the NLSY that has gained media attention is the work of Brame and colleagues (Brame, Turner, Paternoster & Bushway, 2010; Brame, Bushway, Paternoster & Turner, 2014) to examine the probability of an individual experiencing an arrest by a given age. In the first study, this research team used the self-reported arrest histories of individuals in the NLSY to see how many individuals reported experiencing an arrest by age 23. The answer was perhaps a surprising number with 30% of the sample reporting having been arrested at least once. In the second study the researchers extended their work to further examine patterns of arrest by race and sex. This second study produced two key findings: 1. that males are more likely than females to experience arrest by age 23 and 2. That there is a racial difference in the experience of arrest for males but not females. For example, for white males, only 22% of the sample reported experiencing an arrest by age 23, while 49% of their African-American counterparts reported an arrest by this age.

COHORT STUDIES

A longitudinal study follows the same people over time. A **cohort study** follows a group of people over time that share some common characteristic that makes them a "cohort." For example, everyone born in the year 2012 would be a cohort. Another cohort might be everyone graduating college in 2020. The NLSY study reviewed above is one cohort study because it follows a cohort of individuals who were age 12 in 1997. Similar to the NLSY, most cohort studies are also longitudinal in nature as they follow this selected cohort of individuals over time.

Cohort Study

follows a group of people over time that share some common characteristic

When looking at this history of the study of juvenile delinquency and justice, the most famous early cohort study was a study conducted by Marvin Wolfgang and colleagues in Philadelphia, Pennsylvania in which they followed all individuals born in Philadelphia in 1945 and 1958. This data collection initiative involved combining information from surveys and interviews with official records of arrests, schooling and employment. One of the most lasting findings of this study was that a very small number of individuals were responsible for most of the crime. That is, while almost all kids did at least one thing for which they could be arrested, very few youth went on to have continued contacts with the police. This five percent of the sample was responsible for up to 70% of all the recorded crimes, leading the researchers to coin the term **"chronic offender"** (Tracy, Wolfgang & Figlio, 1990; Wolfgang, Figlio & Sellin, 1972).

Chronic Offender

typically defined as an offender who has had 5 or more contacts with the juvenile and/or criminal justice system

This research method has been repeated with various cohorts over time. Three of the most notable research efforts for the study of adolescent delinquency are the Denver Youth Survey, the Pittsburgh Youth Survey and the Rochester Developmental Study. These research efforts were all funded by the federal government and have been ongoing data collection efforts since the 1980s (Thornberry, Huizinga and Lober, 2004). However, unlike the Wolfgang study that focuses on a birth cohort, these studies focused on a cohort of youth entering a specific grade, or of a specific age at the study origination point. Data from each of these studies has been used to develop theories of crime you will learn about in the next section of the text and is also available for "mining" through the Interuniversity Consortium for Political and Social Research (ICPSR) which can be accessed at: https://www.icpsr.umich.edu/icpsrweb/.

Answering Questions with Imperfect Data

Your head may now be spinning from all the different sources of information introduced, but this variety is actually a good thing. Because each of these methods has weaknesses, we learn a lot sometimes simply by comparing information across sources. Also, it gives the student of juvenile delinquency choices when deciding what questions to ask and how to answer them. While we may never have a perfect measure of the total number of acts of juvenile delinquency committed in a year or the total number of kids committing them, we can answer important questions like those introduced in the beginning of the chapter and know if juvenile crime is increasing or decreasing or even "at an all-time high." The study of this data has led criminologists to note some important patterns in delinquency that persist over time in American society. The next section will highlight these patterns for you.

Juvenile Delinquency Patterns and Trends

Age-crime curve

a pattern in which offending begins to increase in early adolescence, peaks around age 17 or 18, and thereafter declines

AGE AND CRIME

As previously noted, one of the most well-known facts in the study of crime is that young people are responsible for most crime. The **age-crime curve**, as it is usually called, depicts a pattern in which offending begins to increase in early adolescence, peaks around age 17 or 18, and thereafter declines. Most famously debated in Hirschi and Gottfredson's 1983 article, "Age and the Explanation of

Crime", the graphic of the age-crime curve in Figure 3.3 below (from 1977) can be replicated over and over again in various time periods, locations and with different sources of data. It is this invariability of the age-crime curve that has led so many theorists to focus on adolescence as the most interesting time of life when studying the correlates and causes of crime.

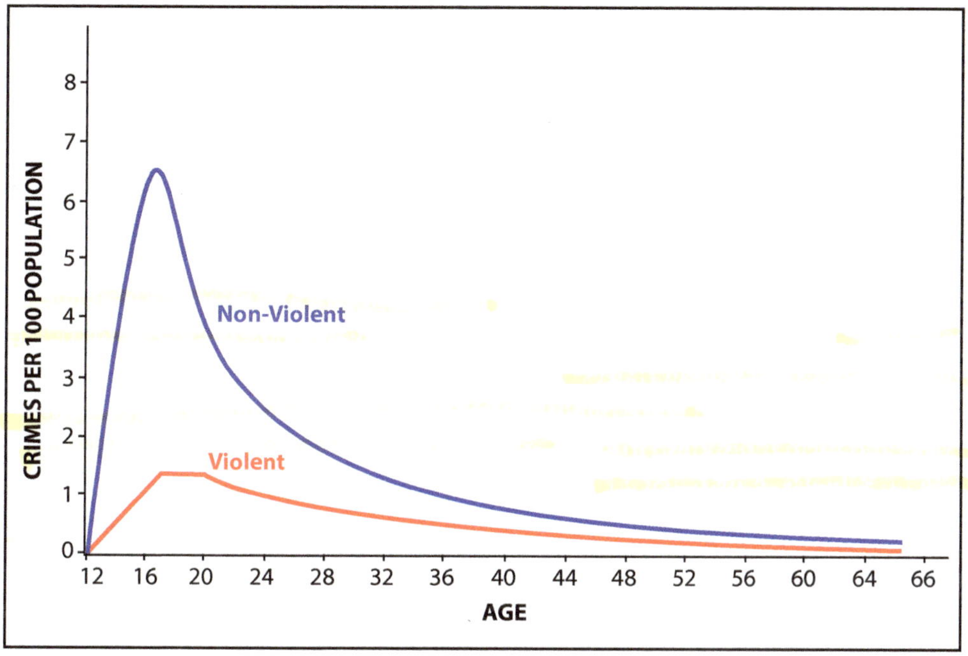

Source: Hirschi, T., and M. Gottfredson. 1983. Age and the explanation of crime. *The American Journal of Sociology 89*(3): 552–584.

FIGURE 3.3 The Age-Crime Curve

Because of this fact the class you are taking now and the theories of, and responses to, juvenile crime you will learn about are of crucial importance not only to the safety of our society, but to the well-being and development of individual youths.

GENDER AND CRIME

Another clear pattern that is observed at almost all times and all places is that males are responsible for much more crime than are females (Bernard & Kurlychek, 2010; Sickmund & Puzzanchera, 2014). This fact that girls offend less often than boys has led to less attention being paid to females in the development of theories of crime and in the treatment responses of the juvenile justice system.

Special attention will be paid to female delinquency in Chapter 9 (theories of female delinquency) and also in Chapter 12 (juvenile treatment and aftercare). For now, note and remember that this is another pattern that persists over time. While female delinquency may rise and fall and change somewhat in nature over time, historically it has always been *less* frequent and prevalent than male delinquency.

RACE AND CRIME

It is an unfortunate fact of American society that minorities, particularly African-Americans and Hispanics, are over-represented in all stages of the criminal justice system (Engen, Steen & Bridges, 2002). Many of the theories of crime you will learn about will highlight how legal policies (e.g., early Jim Crow laws and denial of education), have placed African-Americans at a disadvantage in our society—disadvantage that may leave this population at greater risk for delinquency than their counterparts. Other theories will then point out that current laws and practices also place minority populations at an increased risk of contact with, and formal response from, the juvenile and criminal justice systems regardless of actual risk or behavior. For example, according to the 2010 U.S. Census about 15% of the population under 18 was African-American. However, according to the UCR, about 31% of the youths under the age of 18 arrested were African-American. The disparity becomes greater as one delves deeper into the system, with 38% of youths in juvenile placements and 58% of youths in adult prisons being minority youth (Fagan, 2008).

Disproportionate Minority Contact

occurs when minorities are represented in the criminal justice system at a rate greater than their representation in the general population

This fact has led to a national effort to study, understand and hopefully reduce **disproportionate minority contact** with the juvenile justice system. Disproportionate minority contact means that they are represented in the criminal justice system at a rate greater than their representation in the general population. For example, since you just learned that approximately 15% of the American population is African-American, one would expect 15% of arrests and incarcerations to be for African-American individuals if things were proportionate. But as the figures above demonstrated this is not the case. This is a topic that you will revisit in Chapters 9, 10 and 11 of the text.

Time and Crime

One last trend in juvenile crime that is interesting to learn from these data is the timing of juvenile crime. While most people think of crime as a late night event and juvenile curfews are put in place in certain cities to keep youth off the streets at night, most juvenile crime actually happens in the hours after school from 3 to 6 p.m. In fact, the juvenile violent crime rate peaks between the hour of 3 and 4 p.m on school days as it is during this time that youth are most likely to be out and about, interacting with each other, and it is often the case that parents may still be at work, leading to less supervision of the youth during these hours (Sickmund & Puzzenchera, 2014).

Key Words

Administrative Data
Age-crime curve
Chronic Offender
Cohort Study
Cross Sectional Survey
Dark Figure of Crime
Data Mining
Disproportionate Minority Contact
Hierarchy Rule
National Crime Victimization Survey (NCVS)
National Juvenile Court Data Archive
National Longitudinal Study of Youth (NLSY)
NIBRS
Property Crime Index
Self-Report Surveys
Statistical Metropolitan Area
Uniform Crime Report
Violent Crime Index

Chapter Summary

In this chapter you have learned about several different types of data that criminologists and government officials use to study the phenomenon of juvenile delinquency. These same data and these study results are then used to develop and promote juvenile justice practice and policy. Therefore, understanding the data, what it can and can't tell you, is very important for the practice of juvenile justice.

The first type of data you learned about was administrative data. This type of data is drawn from official police, court and sentencing records. While this is the same data system practitioners have available to them and is usually highly reliable, it is not without faults. For example, it can necessarily only record those cases that come to the attention of the official criminal justice system. The Uniform Crime Report that you learned about, which is compiled annually by the Federal Bureau of Investigation, is the most complete picture of crime in the United States. However, again, it can only record crime reported to police. And, when studying offenders, it can only collect information on those offenders who are formally arrested.

The obvious question then becomes what crimes are not reported to police and how do we gather information on them? The answer to this question is self-report surveys in which individuals are asked to either self-report victimization, offending behavior or both. The most notable victimization survey is the National Crime Victimization Survey (NCVS) which is sponsored by the Department of Justice. This survey, which interviews all individuals over 12 years of age in a sample of households, gathers information on what is known as the dark figure of crime—that is, the crimes that are not reported to police. This survey is also very helpful in gathering information about who is most likely to be victimized by crime, and as you learned not only are juveniles highly involved in committing crimes, they are also highly likely to be victimized by crimes.

Self-report delinquency surveys are probably the most useful source of data for developing and testing theories that attempt to explain why some kids become involved in crime and others do not. In this format, the researcher does not just have information on the crime, but can ask questions about what was going on in the person's life at the time he/she committed the offense as well as a whole host of other questions. Self-report surveys take many forms, including cross-sectional studies that take a cross-section of individuals at a given point in time and longitudinal surveys that follow the same group of people over time. A cohort study is a specific type of longitudinal study that selects the group to be included because they share some given trait or characteristics such as being born in a given year, or entering or graduating from high school in a given year. Some of the main concerns with self-report surveys are questions as to whether individuals will indeed honestly report illegal activity. Over time though many studies have found that self-reports of arrests do seem to line up with official arrests which lends credibility to the claim that individuals will also willingly and accurately report illegal behavior that was not detected and/or did not lead to an arrest. Self-report surveys are therefore perhaps the richest form of information on juvenile delinquency. Several examples of longitudinal self-report studies were provided in this chapter, including the Rochester Youth Development Study and the Pittsburgh and Denver Youth Studies. You will see these names pop up again throughout both the theory and practice sections of this text!

This chapter then ended by providing you a brief overview of how data can be used to study the correlates of delinquency such as gender, race and age. There are many, many more factors that influence the risk of delinquency and in the upcoming chapters you will further explore how these and other factors can increase or decrease the risk of delinquency, and how knowledge of these risks can inform and guide effective juvenile justice policy.

Discussion Questions

1. Your boss wants to know if robbery has been increasing or decreasing over the past five years. Where could you find that information? Also, he wants to know if juveniles are responsible for more or less arrests for robbery than five years ago? How would you answer that question?
2. Both victimization and self-report delinquency surveys ask a person to report about an incident. Discuss some strengths and weaknesses of this approach. What can you learn from this type of survey that you cannot from the UCR?

3. Females are responsible for less crime than males. Imagine you want to understand why. What type of data might you want to query in order to better understand this difference? If you were able to design your own data set, what type of data might you want to collect? For example, would you want to collect official records, create a survey for victims or offenders, create a cohort study?
4. Trends in the data show that minorities are often disproportionately represented in official crime statistics. Do you think this is because minorities commit more crimes? If so, why? Do you think this is because the justice system responds differently to offenses committed by minorities? If so, why?

REFERENCES

Akers, R. L. (1964). Socio-economic status and delinquent behavior: A retest. *Journal of Research in Crime and Delinquency,* 1, 38–46.

Antilla, I., & Jaakkola, R. (1966). *Unrecorded criminality in Finland.* Helsinki: Kriminologinen Tutkimuslaitos.

Bernard, T. J., & Kurlychek, M. C. (2010). *The cycle of juvenile justice* (2nd ed.). New York: Oxford Press.

Brame, R., Bushway, S. D., Paternoster, R., & Turner, M. (2014, April). Demographic patterns of cumulative arrest prevalence by ages 18 and 23. *Crime and Delinquency, 60*(3), 471–486.

Brame R., Turner, M., Paternoster, R., & Bushway, S. D. (2012). Cumulative prevalence of arrest from ages 8 to 23 in a national sample. *Pediatrics, 129*, 21–27.

Christie, N., Andenaes, J., & Skirbekk, S. (1965). A study of self reported crime. *Journal of Scandinavian Studies in Criminology and Crime Prevention, 1,* 86–116.

Elliott, D. S., & Voss, H. L. (1974). *Delinquency and dropout.* Lexington, MA: D.C. Heath.

Elmhorn, K. (1965). A study in self-reported delinquency among school children in Stockholm. *Journal of Scandinavian Studies in Criminology and Crime Prevention, 1.*

Erickson, M., & Empey, L. T. (1963). Court records, undetected delinquency, and decision-making. *Journal of Criminal Law, Criminology, and Police Science, 54*(December), 456–469.

Fagan, J. (2008). Juvenile crime and criminal justice: Resolving border disputes. *The Future of Children: Juvenile Justice, 18*(2), 81–118.

Gold, M. (1966). Undetected delinquent behavior. *Journal of Research in Crime and Delinquency, 3,* 27–46.

Gold, M. (1970). *Delinquent behavior in an American city.* Belmont, CA: Brooks/Cole Publishing Company.

Hagan, J. (1993). The social embeddedness of crime and unemployment. *Criminology, 31*(4), 465–491.

Hindelang, M. J., Hirschi, T., & Weis, J. G. (1981). *Measuring delinquency.* Beverly Hills: Sage Publications.

Hirschi, T. (1969). *Causes of delinquency.* Berkeley, CA: University of California Press.

Klein, M. W. (Ed.). (1989). *Cross-national research in self-reported crime and delinquency.* Los Angeles: Kluwer Academic Publishers.

Langton, L., Berzofsky, M., Krebs, C., & Smiley-McDonald, H. (2014). Victimizations not reported to police: 2006–2010. *Special Report, National Crime Victimization Survey*. Washington DC: U.S. Department of Justice, Office of Justice Programs, Bureau of Justice Statistics.

Nye, F. I., Short, Jr., J. F. (1957). Scaling delinquent behavior. *American Sociological Review, 22*(June), 326–331.

Nye, F. I., Short, Jr., J. F., & Olson, V. (1958). Socioeconomic status and delinquent behavior. *American Journal of Sociology, 63*, 381–389.

Piquero, A. (2008). Disproportionate minority contact. *The Future of Children: Juvenile Justice, 18*(2), 59–79.

Porterfield, A. L. (1943). Delinquency and outcome in court and college. *American Journal of Sociology, 49*(November), 199–208.

Porterfield, A. L. (1946). *Youth in trouble.* Fort Worth: Leo Potishman Foundation.

Short, J. F., Jr., & Nye, F. I. (1957). Reported behavior as a criterion of deviant behavior. *Social Problems,* 5, 207–213.

Short, J. F., Jr., & Nye, F. I. (1958). Extent of unrecorded juvenile delinquency: Tentative conclusions. *Journal of Criminal Law and Criminology, 49*, 296–302.

Sickmund M., & Puzzenchera, C. (2014). Juvenile offenders and victims: 2014 national report. Pittsburgh, PA: National Center for Juvenile Justice.

Thornberry, T. P., Huizinga, D., & Loeber. R. (2004). The causes and correlates studies: Findings and policy implications. Retrieved from https://www.ncjrs.gov/html/ojjdp/203555/jj2.html

Thornberry, T. P., & Krohn, M. (2000). The self-report method for measuring delinquency and crime. *Measurement and Analysis of Crime and Justice,* 4, 33–82.

Tracy, P. E., Wolfgang, M. E., Sellin, T., & Figlio, R. M. (1990). *Delinquency careers in two birth cohorts.* New York: Plenum.

Wolfgang, M. E., Figlio, R. M., & Sellin, T. (1972). *Delinquency in a birth cohort.* Chicago: University of Chicago Press.

Section 2

Understanding Delinquency

4 Birth of the Classical School and Deterrence Theories

©Bonita R. Cheshier/Shutterstock.com

Imagine you are sitting at a high school basketball game. The winning basket is just scored by the home team and the crowd is jumping up and down with excitement. As the bleachers quickly start to empty you notice a $100 bill on the bench in front of you where a gentleman in a suit had just been sitting. Did the $100 fall out of his pocket when he jumped up? Do you pick it up and ask? Do you quickly pick it up and put it in your own pocket? Will anyone see you if you do this? What would the man do if he turned around and saw you taking his money? According to most of the theories of crime discussed in this chapter, you would carefully think through these and other questions as you made the decision of whether or not to commit this crime of theft. Ultimately, your action would be based upon your best rational assessment of what would bring you the most pleasure at the least cost or risk. Hence, these theories are often called "choice" theories. Prior to this approach to crime, however, crime was viewed as a sin—you were either tempted by, or controlled by, outside forces of evil. In other words, if you pick up the $100 it is because the devil made you do it! In this chapter, you will first be exposed to this ancient, yet still present, view of crime before delving more deeply into choice theories.

CHAPTER GOALS

By the end of this chapter, you should be able to:

1. Understand the historical roots of the spiritual approach.
2. Be able to detail the key components of Beccaria's Classical School of Criminology.
3. Discuss the differences between modern day rational choice and routine activity theories as they relate to the Classical School.
4. Identify juvenile justice and crime control strategies that rest upon these theories.

The Spiritual Approach

Perhaps the oldest and still persistent "theory" of crime is the spiritual or supernatural explanation. As long as humans have worshipped deities it has been thought that angering these gods would bring grave consequences upon the offender, and at times, upon the entire civilization. Famine, earthquakes and other natural disasters were often blamed on angry gods and those responsible had to right the situation through rituals and sacrifices—often of their own lives (Newman, 1978).

In medieval society the writings of St. Thomas Aquinas argued that there was a natural order to things based on God's law and that people had a natural tendency to do good. Therefore, people who broke this order broke the natural order of things, upsetting the natural balance of good and evil (Bernard, 1983). This idea was adopted into Roman Catholic thought and quite simply referred to as "the natural law." In some instances it was thought that the offender was weak and gave into temptation by evil; in other instances it was thought that the individual was actually possessed or taken over by evil demons. In either case, however, the outcome was not good for the offender.

Punishments meted out for crimes were designed to save the soul; thus, damage to the outward physical body did not matter as much, with the result that offenders were tortured and often killed in brutal ways. These punishments were designed to "purge the body of a sinner of traces of the devil and thereby restore the body of the community as a whole to its proper relation to God" (Pfohl, 1985, 25). Trial by battle was one popular method that both determined guilt or innocence and provided the ultimate punishment. Most simply, it was believed that God would allow the innocent person to prevail over the guilty so the winner of the battle was innocent and the loser was, well, dead (Bernard, Snipes and Gerould, 2000).

While this view might seem primitive and outdated, it is important to realize that not only did it provide a basis for some of the earliest forms of criminal justice systems, but elements of this perspective remain today both in theory and practice. For example, we maintain trials, even though they are not by battle, and the decision is handed down by a jury of 12 peers—a tradition that evolved from the practice of compurgation set forth by the Pope Innocent III in 1215. Under this system the accused had to gather 12 reputable people who would swear under oath to his or her innocence. Our modern prison system—penitentiaries—is based on the Quaker religious practice of placing someone in isolation with nothing but the Bible to read so that they would be penitent for their sins (Teeters, 1955). Today it is not uncommon to hear individuals in prison say that they have found God or to convert religions while serving their sentences.

Moreover, the saying, "the devil made me do it" is not uncommon and conservative evangelists and even political candidates have blamed recent natural disasters on God's anger at societies or sects of the population. For example, on a September 13, 2001, broadcast of *The 700 Club*, Evangelist Jerry Falwell blames God's anger at America for the 911 terrorist attack on the World Trade Centers as follows:

> "I really believe that the pagans, and the abortionists, and the feminists, and the gays and the lesbians who are actively trying to make that an alternative lifestyle, the ACLU, People For the American Way—all of them who have tried to secularize America—I point the finger in their face and say "you helped this happen."

Although these words might be shocking to some, they are presented here as an example of how and why understanding the historical roots of our criminal and juvenile justice systems is so important. While theories and ideas evolve and change over time, traces of the past remain in our modern day system. And often, changes are brought about in response to displeasure with the status quo. Indeed the choice theories that are discussed in the remainder of this chapter came about in direct opposition to the harsh penalties meted out through this spiritual perspective on crime and justice.

From Spiritualism to Individualism

Although there are traces of the supernatural perspective left in today's criminal justice system, its primary foundation is built upon a perspective that developed during the period of "enlightenment" (approximately, 1620s through, 1780s), also known as the "Age of Reason." It was during this time that great philosophers began to emphasize man's ability to reason and the importance of individual happiness. Thus, thought shifted away from searching for the causes of human behavior in the supernatural, to searching within man himself. As evolved creatures, the human was not controlled by outside or invisible forces, such as demons, but rather by his own intellect. Committing a crime was now seen as an individual choice made by a rational man. But if man is rational one might ask why would he commit crime? The answer to this question is found in what is referred to as the **Classical School of Criminology**.

Classical School of Criminology

the primary theory behind the development of our nation's adult criminal justice system that rests on assumptions of rationality, free will and hedonism

THE CLASSICAL SCHOOL

The Classical School of Criminology is most often linked to the writings of **Cesare Bonesana, Marchese di Beccaria**. Interestingly, Beccaria was not a student of penology or involved in criminal justice in any way, but rather was a student with interests in mathematics, literature and philosophy (Bernard, Snipes & Gerould, 2000). Perhaps it was this last interest, however, that led him to draw on the ideas of some of the great philosophers when writing an essay on penology in response to an assignment he was given. This now classic essay, "On Crimes and Punishments" (Beccaria, 2016, original 1764), brought together the thinking of some of the key philosophers of the time and provided a new approach to criminal justice.

Cesare Beccaria, Marchese d. Beccaria

linked to the Classical School of Criminology. His classic essay "On Crimes and Punishments" brought together the thinking of some key philosophers of the time and provided a new approach to criminal justice

First, rather than being controlled by outside forces, Beccaria would argue that man has free will in determining his destiny. Second, drawing largely on Thomas Hobbes (1588–1679), Beccaria believed that humans were naturally **hedonistic** and would work to serve their own self interests unless otherwise directed. What

Hedonistic

work to serve their own self interests unless otherwise directed

directed humans was their sense of **rationality**, which they would use to make choices that brought them the most benefit at the least cost. Beccaria also drew upon ideas of many great philosophers of this age including John Locke (1632–1704), Montesquieu (1689–1755) and Voltaire (1694–1778) in developing his key ideas, which can be summarized as follows:

Rationality
a human's ability to weigh the cost and benefit of an action before choosing a course

1. Although humans are naturally individualistic and will pursue their own happiness, they are willing to give up certain liberties to live in a society that protects them from harm. This idea was deemed the "social contract" by Hobbes and was further developed in the writings of other philosophers.
2. For the social contract to be successful, society must have some means of enforcing it—hence, government, and some form of justice system.

Given this view of human nature, a new view of the criminal justice system then emerges. This view is one in which the criminal justice system must use the necessary force to ensure individual members of society adhere to the social contract. This is a significantly less severe level of force than that deemed necessary by the spiritualistic approach in which the human must be broken. Here, the individual must only be deterred from violating the contract by having a negative consequence that is proportionally severe to the offense committed. According to Beccaria, it was thus the role of the legislature to determine what an appropriate punishment would be for each violation of the contract. The justice system was then only there to determine guilt or innocence and mete out the punishment already determined by the legislature (Beccaria, pp. 13–14).

There are three key elements to these punishments in order for them to be successful:

1. **Certainty**. Certainty refers to the likelihood that one will actually experience the consequence given he/she commits the offense. According to Beccaria, "The fear of a punishment, even if it be moderate, will always make a stronger impression than the fear of another which is more terrible but combined with the hope of impunity," p. 58–59. Or put in modern-day language, we will fear more a mild punishment that is certain than a more severe one that we think we can avoid. After all, the severity of a punishment matters only if you experience it; thus the chance that you may avoid that punishment inherently mitigates its impact.

Certainty
the likelihood that one will actually experience the consequence given he/she commits the offense

2. **Swiftness**. Swiftness refers to how quickly a punishment is applied to an offender after he/she is caught. According to Beccaria, "The more immediately after the commission of a crime a punishment is inflicted, the more just and useful it will be" (p. 55–56). This is because the human mind must equate

Swiftness
how quickly a punishment is applied to an offender after he/she is caught

the effect—punishment—with its cause—the commission of the crime. The greater the time that elapses between the two the less association one will make between the two events and the less effective the punishment will be in deterring the individual from committing future acts of crime.

3. **Proportional Severity**. This is the most complex of the three components of Beccaria's reasoning and the one upon which he elaborates the most. In general, it means that the punishment should be proportional to the amount of damage the crime inflicted upon the victim and/or society. He also implicitly states that punishments that are too severe actually have the reverse impact. That is, if the punishment does not fit the crime, it reduces the legitimacy of the criminal justice system and the social contract in the eyes of the individual. As put by Beccaria, "For punishment to attain its end the evil which it inflicts has only to exceed the advantage derivable from the crime . . . all beyond this is superfluous and for that reason tyrannical" (p. 62).

Proportionality Severity

the punishment should be proportional to the amount of damage the crime inflicted upon the victim and/or society

In sum, then, the Classical School of Criminology rests on the assumption that man is rational and that he will make the decision to behave in a way that maximizes pleasure and minimizes pain. Thus, the role of the criminal justice system is to deter individuals from committing acts that bring themselves happiness but harm others by ensuring the individual believes he/she will be subject to a certain, swift and proportionally severe punishment upon committing that act.

Today, the Classical School is often referred to as **deterrence theory**, as the primary way in which its policies should reduce crime is through deterring individuals from committing a crime in the first place. There are two types of deterrence: **specific deterrence** and **general deterrence**. **Specific deterrence** refers to the idea that once you as an individual experience a punishment for your offense you will know that the negative consequence outweighs any possible gain and therefore will not commit offenses in the future. **General deterrence** is not based on specific experience but rather general knowledge of possible negative consequences and/or seeing these negative consequences applied to others you know. That is, if in general people believe they will get caught for a crime and a swift punishment will follow, they will choose not to commit the crime in the first place.

Specific Deterrence

the idea that once you as an individual experience a punishment for your offense you will know that the negative consequence outweighs any possible gain and therefore will not commit offenses in the future

General Deterrence

the idea that you will not commit an offense based on general knowledge of possible negative consequences and/or seeing these negative consequences applied to others you know

Other ideas of Beccaria that have made it through the centuries and into modern-day criminal justice in many countries that you might recognize from our own Constitution are the ideas that:

- People should be considered innocent until proven guilty
- People should not be forced to testify against themselves

- People should have the right to counsel and to confront accusers
- People should have the right to prompt and public trials by juries of their peers.

These ideas of Beccaria became the basis for much of the world's criminal justice policy in the 1800s; however, it wasn't until the 1960s when empirical tests of the policies emerged. Gibbs (1968) is credited with the first test of the theory; he assessed the impact of the certainty and severity of a prison sentence for homicide on statewide homicide rates. He found that both the certainty and severity of punishment mattered, but that certainty was more important. A follow-up study by Tittle (1969) extended this assessment to all seven Part I Index Offenses of the UCR (see Chapter 3) and found support for the notion that certainty of punishment deterred crime but did not find severity to matter. In fact, for some offenses, the severity worked in the opposite direction. According to Beccaria's original premise this might indicate that the sentences being handed down were not proportional to the crime and thus, as he predicted, actually increased crime.

Over time, however, additional tests of the theory were not as conclusive and some of its key components came into question. Particularly, Akers (1990) argues that man cannot be truly rational in making a decision when he often only has limited information available. For example, think back to our original example. How certain is the individual that he will be caught if he picks up the $100? How accurately can he really predict this? Moreover, what is the punishment for stealing $100? Does the average individual know exactly what will happen if he/she is caught? Questions such as these led to an increased focus on "perceptions" of risk, rather than actual risk, as the variables to be measured in tests of Classical Theory. A review of this research by Nagin (1998) found that there is a consensus that the consistent negative association found between a person's perceptions of risk and their offending behavior does indeed support deterrence. This research on perceptions further shows that certainty again outweighs the importance of either severity or swiftness of punishment in deterring crime (Nagin & Pogarsky, 2001; Pogarsky, 2002; Pogarsky & Piquero, 2003).

Interestingly though, research by Pogarsky (2002) found that some offenders are deterrable and some simply are not (see Spotlight on Research in this chapter). That is, for some the threat of a criminal justice response does not impact behavior. However, it is unclear if this is because the person does not care about the response or inaccurately assesses the risk of having it applied to themselves. These ideas that people may perceive risk differently and that some individuals simply may not be "deterrable" have interesting applications when applying classical thinking to the deviant behavior of juveniles.

First, regarding adolescents, remember from Chapters 1 and 2 that research has found that the adolescent brain is not fully developed (Lenroot & Geidd, 2006) and that the portion specifically underdeveloped is the portion that controls reasoning and reflective thought (Baird & Fugelsang, 2004). Thus, teenagers are more likely to act on impulse than on thought, which by nature might make them less "deterrable." Second, studies of adolescent decision-making (Steinberg & Cauffman, 1999) suggest that adolescents make decisions differently than adults in three ways. First, their temporal focus is different, which means they place more emphasis on immediate gratification than on long-term consequences. Thus the prospect of receiving a punishment at a later date, no matter how severe, does not outweigh more immediate benefits of an action. Second, they are more susceptible to outside influence such as that of peers. Therefore, while they might know right from wrong when questioned in a clinical setting, the ability to make choices based on this knowledge in a given situation might be highly suspect. And, third, adolescents tend to discount risk. As put by Bernard (1992), they are "invincible," thinking that nothing bad can ever happen to them. In this line, research has also found juveniles to underestimate their probability of getting caught—that is, they feel invincible (Bernard, 1992). Thus, even the certainty of punishment may be less influential in "deterring" juvenile crime.

Carrol (1978) conducted one of the earliest tests of juvenile deterrence, questioning a group of juvenile non-offenders and a group of incarcerated juveniles about the perceived risk of punishment for hypothetical crime opportunities. In this study he found no difference between the groups in terms of the likelihood they would choose to commit the crime. Carroll concluded that juveniles may simply not consider relevant pieces of information when making decisions. More recently, Elizabeth Scott (1992) proposes that adolescent decision-making is different because of different value judgments attached to outcomes in the cost-benefit stage of reasoning. That is, she argues that it is not that adolescents are entirely irrational, but they have less life experience to draw upon when determining possible courses of action, and apply a different calculus to the assessment of cost and benefits of the different outcomes when making a decision.

FOCUS ON RESEARCH: Greg Pogarsky

Pogarsky (2002) provides evidence that young adults do not all respond in the same manner to the threat of punishment. In this study, Pogarsky surveyed a group of 412 college students regarding their willingness to drive after drinking based on different scenarios. In the first scenario the individual was allowed to assess whether he/she would be caught for the offense and the potential sanction was varied between 1 or 12 months of a suspended driver's license—a meaningful potential punishment to young adults. In the second scenario, the certainty was altered so that the individual was told there was NO chance he/she would be caught. Respondents were also asked a series of questions that measured their responses to self and social controls outside of the criminal justice system and their impulsivity.

What was most interesting about this study was that he found two groups of what he called "undeterrable" offenders. The first group was youth who had such strong moral beliefs regarding drinking and driving that they would never engage in this activity even in the second scenario in which there was no chance of getting caught. These youth were instead constrained from the activity by their own beliefs and/or fear of reaction of parents and friends. Thus, the justice system need not deter them. On the other hand, there was a smaller group of incorrigible offenders who would engage in the activity if they wanted to regardless of the certainty or severity of punishment. On average this group of youths was more impulsive than the other youths in the sample.

Given what you have learned so far about juveniles, do you think there may be a subgroup of youths who are undeterrable? What role might impulsivity play in the behavior of immature offenders? What role might fear of peer, family or social disapproval play?

THE NEO-CLASSICAL SCHOOL

Neo-Classical School

introduces mitigating circumstances and individual justice to the original Classical School

One advancement of the original Classical School that may be more applicable to juveniles is the **Neo-Classical School**, which introduces two key new ideas to the model:

Mitigating Circumstances

circumstances beyond the individual's control that may impact his/her ability to make a rational decision

Mitigating Circumstances. **Mitigating circumstances** are circumstances beyond the individual's control that may impact his or her ability to make a rational decision. Potential mitigating circumstances that may make one less culpable for one's actions and less able to understand consequences include mental illness and age. Thus, according to this perspective, being a juvenile by nature makes one less rational.

Individual Justice

recognizes that because people are different and come from different circumstances, the response to crime must be individualistic

Individual Justice. **Individual justice** emerges from the above concept and recognizes that because people are different and come from different circumstances, the response to crime must be individualistic. This might then suggest that the response to a conviction for robbery for a 21-year-old without a mental illness should be drastically different than the response for a 15-year-old with a mental illness. This individualized justice is at the heart of the juvenile justice system which aims consequences at individuals rather than to be "proportional with the crime committed" as would be suggested by original deterrence theory.

RATIONAL CHOICE THEORY

Rational Choice Theory

the emphasis is on understanding why in certain circumstances an individual chooses to commit a crime

Modern-day **Rational Choice Theory** has its roots in Beccaria's writings but also brings into the equation individualized calculus for assessment of risk and benefit. Here, the emphasis is on understanding why in certain circumstances an individual chooses to commit a crime. In this model, a crime is never senseless or irrational—it always makes sense to the individual committing it (Cornish & Clarke, 1986).

According to this approach each crime is both **offense-specific** and **offender-specific** (Cornish & Clarke, 1987). Offense-specific means the individual is considering the benefits of a specific crime. Returning to our opening example, do you pick up the $100 bill? Considerations for this specific event might be things like how likely it is the victim will notice the money missing, how much you perceive the victim might need the money and how likely it is you think someone else or a security camera might catch you taking the money. For example, you might perceive the situation differently if it is a fairly affluent-looking middle-aged man in a fancy suit versus an elderly woman. That is, you might be more willing to take the money if you felt the individual who lost it was not as in need of the money. Offender-specific refers to your assessment of whether or not you can commit the crime and how much you have to gain from the crime. This would include your assessment of how much you need the $100 and whether you think you can nonchalantly pick up the bill without being noticed. This is a fairly easy crime to commit so skill is less of a concern than if our example had been stealing a car or robbing a bank.

Because the crime is always rational to the person committing it and we can't adjust the proportionality of punishment to everyone's individual circumstances at the moment he/or she commits a crime, the justice system application of this form of choice theory shifts the focus to altering circumstances and social situations so the crime simply does not make sense. This is most often called "**situational crime prevention**" (Newman et. al, 1997). **Situational crime prevention** refers to changing the immediate environment to make it less easy for someone to commit the crime. This increases the risk and lessens the possible benefits (Clarke, 1997). Examples include things such as improving lighting or installing security cameras to make a criminal feel more likely to be seen, adding police officers to the patrol force to increase perceptions of certainty of punishment, and even changing environmental design of a building or area to reduce opportunities for crime (Crow, 2004). For example, if there is an abandoned parking lot in which teenagers are hanging out after school and getting into fights or other trouble, this approach might suggest changing that lot into a community garden to make it an inviting space for adults and a less attractive hangout for youth. However, one criticism of this approach is that it will simply **displace** crime to another location, rather than reduce it (Repetto, 1976).

Situational Crime Prevention

changing the immediate environment to make it more difficult for someone to commit the crime

Displace

refers to when a crime-control policy fails to reduce the actual activity but just changes it location from one place to another

ROUTINE ACTIVITIES THEORY

Another extension of this approach focuses more on the actual target of the crime than the individual motivation of the offender. **Routine Activities Theory** (Cohen & Felson, 1979) assumes that everyone could be a motivated offender given the right circumstance. That is, criminals do not commit crime all the time and the average law-abiding citizen could in the right circumstance commit a crime. What better explains crime according to this theory is the **availability of a suitable target** and the **lack of a capable guardian**. We can easily revisit the opening example again and see similarities and differences between the theories. According to this theory, the individual in the stand is an average law-abiding citizen who has just been provided with the **motivation** to commit a crime—financial reward. The availability of a **suitable target**, the $100, has presented itself and the ultimate decision might come down to the lack of a **capable guardian**. That is, will anyone see him pick up the $100? The capable guardian can be the person who lost the $100; that is, how likely are they to turn around or quickly notice it is missing? The capable guardian could also be another individual in the stand or even a security camera on the wall that would record the incident. In order for this crime to occur these three things must converge in time and space (Cohen & Felson, 1979).

Routine Activities Theory

assumes everyone could be a motivated offender given the right circumstance assumes three things must be present for an offense to happen: a motivated offender, a suitable target and the lack of a capable guardian

Another aspect of this theory, and hence its name, is that our daily **routine activities** direct whether and how often these three things converge. The notion of routine activities was first introduced by Hindelang and colleagues (Hindelang,

Gottfedson & Garofalo, 1978). The authors of this theory used it to explain changing crime rates in America during the 1960s and 1970s. Specifically looking at changes in the workforce (increased numbers of women) and the resulting increase in the number of unattended (guarded) homes during the day, the authors seek to explain the increase in home burglaries (Cohen & Felson, 1979). The ideas of this theory have also been expanded to explain patterns of victimization (Hindelang, Gottfredson & Garofalo, 1978). Think for a moment of the patterns of juvenile crime and victimization presented in Chapter 3. Remember that most crime occurs between the hours of 3 and 5 p.m. What is going on in a youth's life at this time? This is the time directly after school when juveniles are most likely to congregate in groups, thus presenting both motivated offenders and suitable targets. As parents may still be at work and not supervising their children, the lack of a capable guardian can be said to exist. This eminent fact of adolescent life then perhaps drives the probability of committing and/or being victimized by a crime during the afterschool hours.

Applications of this theory to juvenile justice on the surface look similar to applications of rational choice theory as they aim to change the immediate situation rather than any motivation of the offender. Increasing supervision of minors is probably the first and simplest ramification—that is, increase the presence of capable guardians. Efforts to reduce school crime provide clear examples of this approach with the addition of metal detectors in many schools and the hiring of school resource officers to police the hallways and unguarded spaces (see Chapter 9 of this text for a more in-depth discussion of policing and juveniles). Second, it also has ramifications for helping one prevent being victimized by crime. For example, if a youth has to pass through a neighborhood in which he or she feels unsafe or is being bullied on the way to and from school, this theory suggests that the correct course of action is to find a different route to school or to take community efforts to "clean up" the route to school, making it safer for all.

POLICY IMPLICATIONS FOR JUVENILE JUSTICE

While the Classical School is at the heart of our modern-day adult justice system, it is less evident in the juvenile justice model described in Chapter 2. The Neo-Classical School's call for individualized justice is much more evident. However, even in applying individualized justice in which it may be acknowledged that juveniles are less rational, or maybe just differentially rational, than adults, the emphasis for most of the system is still not on punishment, but rather on helping the youth develop into a law-abiding citizen rather than an adult criminal. Here, rather than developing a punishment that is proportiontly severe to the crime, the policy is to develop a treatment plan that most reflects the individual's risks and needs as determined by types of assessment instruments discussed further in Chapter 9 of this text. However, many juveniles do find themselves in the adult court, either based on the seriousness of the crime they commit or their prior record, and for such youth, all considerations of immaturity of judgment are removed from the processing phase of the criminal trial. There has lately, however, been attention to the issue of immaturity of judgment and rationality of youth by the United States Supreme Court. In 2002, the Supreme Court determined that it is "cruel and unusual" punishment to subject anyone who was under the age of 18 at the time of their crime to death (*Roper v Simmons*, 543 U.S. 551, 2005). They based this decision on some of the key studies noted above about how adolescents make decisions and the fact that youth are not yet the person who they will develop into. The death penalty is to be reserved for only the most heinous of criminals, and based on the fact that youth are not done developing, the Supreme Court determined that they could not ever fall into this category. More recently, the Court also considered the appropriateness of the use of life without parole for someone who was a juvenile at the time of the crime. In this case, the Court did not place an overall ban on the practice, but rather mandated individualized judgments that would consider such things as the juvenile's role in the crime, his/her culpability for the offense and ultimately his/her ability to understand the consequences of the actions (*Miller v. Alabama*, 567 U.S., 2012). Thus a mandatory sentencing law similar to what Becarria might have supported, such as life in prison for murder, cannot be applied across the board when the offender was under the age of 18 at the time of the crime.

FOCUS ON POLICY: Crime Prevention Through Environmental Design

©michael sheehan/Shutterstock.com

In 1977, C. Ray Jeffery introduced the idea of preventing crime simply by changing the way environments are designed. In general this strategy involves three overarching components: natural surveillance, natural access control and territoriality. **Natural surveillance** refers to improving sight lines so that a would-be offender will feel like he or she will be seen if committing a crime. This can range from reducing the height of overgrown hedges, to installing better street lighting and/or even the installation of surveillance cameras. **Natural access control** refers to ensuring exits and entrances from properties are clearly defined and protected from unwanted entry. **Territoriality** involves methods of noting and clearly denoting the difference between public and private space such as a fence or a row of shrubs at the entrance to one's lawn. A review by Eck (2006) of existing evaluations of variance techniques to defend space found something as simple as improved lighting to be one of the most cost efficient ways of deterring crime. In what ways might improved lighting be implemented to reduce juvenile crime? Think about areas in your neighborhood where crime rates are high; can you think of ways any of these tactics could be used to make people feel more safe from crime in these areas?

©adriaticfoto/Shutterstock.com

Free Will

the belief that man makes his/her own choices and is not controlled by outside forces such as demons

Target Hardening

practices such as adding lighting and locks to make it harder for an individual to commit a "successful" crime

TABLE 4.1 Summary of Theories Covered in This Chapter

	Underlying Assumptions	Cause of Crime	System Application
Spiritual	Controlled by Outside Forces	The Devil/Demons	Harsh Punishment
Classical	Free Will, Hedonistic and Rational	Choice: Benefit outweighs cost	Certain, Swift and Proportionally Severe Punishment
Neo-Classical	Free Will, Hedonistic Not All Equally Rational	Choice: Benefit outweighs perceived cost for that individual	Individualized Justice/Different outcomes based on different levels of rationality
Rational Choice Theory	Free Will, Hedonistic Rationality based on Experience/Circumstance	Choice: Benefit outweighs perceived cost for immediate situation	Situational Crime Prevention
Routine Activities Theory	Everyone Potentially Motivated in Right Circumstance	Convergence of Motivated Offender, Target and Lack of Capable Guardian	Target Hardening Increased Guardianship

Key Words

Certainty
Cesare Beccaria, Marchese d. Beccaria
Classical School of Criminology
Displace
Free Will
General Deterrence
Hedonistic
Individual Justice
Mitigating Circumstances
Neo-Classical School
Proportionality Severity
Rational Choice Theory
Rationality
Routine Activities Theory
Situational Crime Prevention
Specific Deterrence
Swiftness
Target Hardening

Chapter Summary

In this chapter you were introduced to the historical supernatural perspective on crime and how early civilization blamed crime on forces outside an individual's control such as the devil. While one might think that placing the blame outside the individual would lead to less severe consequences, this was not the case with brutal punishments applied and guilt or innocence often determined by one's ability to live through a trial by battle or ordeal. With the period of "enlightenment" and increased emphasis on man's individuality and rationality, the Classical School was born, which placed the cause of crime within the individual. Most simply, a person would choose to commit a crime when he/she rationally determined that the benefits outweighed the costs. Thus, the criminal justice system application of this school of thought is that crime can be deterred by creating certain, swift and proportionally severe punishments that would increase the cost of crime to the point that a rational man would not make this choice. Modern extensions of this theory adopt the notion that not all people are equally rational, and particularly relevant to the study of juvenile justice, that age and maturity of judgment are key components in determining this rationality. While typical models of deterrence that address rational thought may not be equally applicable to juveniles and adults, the policy implications of both Rational Choice Theory and Routine Activities Theory may reduce juvenile crime. For example because both these theories rely on reducing opportunities for crime rather than understanding an individual's rational calculus and motivation for crime they would point to policies that reduce a youths opportunities to commit crime. This could range from **target hardening** practices such as adding lighting and locks to simple "guardianship" over the youth's time ensuring that he does not have too many unstructured and unsupervised hours in a day in which to get into mischief. Another policy implication might focus on ensuring youth are more informed about the possible consequences of their actions and the harm that their actions might inflict on others. Such practices will all be discussed in Section Three of this text that focuses on system responses to delinquency.

Discussion Questions

1. What are some of the ways the Classical School is evident in today's criminal justice system? How are these ideas applied differently in the juvenile justice system?
2. Using the original example of the $100 on the bench, do you think the thought process of deciding whether to pick up the money would differ for an adult and a juvenile? If so, how and why? If not, why not?
3. In the Supreme Court cases discussed in this chapter, the Court determined that the death penalty is never appropriate for a juvenile. Do you agree or disagree? Can you think of other punishments that you think might be cruel and unusual when applied to a juvenile?

Activities

1. First individually, then in small groups, rank the following punishments in order of severity. Did the members of your group all rank the punishments the same? If not, what are some of the considerations that led you to rank them differently? How might this impact your risk calculus when deciding whether or not to commit a crime?

    a. 5 years of probation
    b. 1 year in prison
    c. 6 months at a correctional boot camp facility
    d. 9 months house arrest, followed by 1 year of probation
    e. $10,000 fine and 200 hours community service

2. Online activity. The website for your text has an example of a juvenile crime that the newspapers have portrayed as senseless and "irrational." Review the materials provided online and write a 2-paragraph essay discussing whether you believe this crime could be seen as rational according to any of the theories reviewed in this chapter or whether it is truly an "irrational" crime.

REFERENCES

Akers, R. (1990). Rational choice, deterrence, and social learning theory in criminology. *Journal of Criminal Law and Criminology, 81,* 653–676.

Beccaria, C. (2016/1764). *On crimes and punishments* (5th ed.) (G. R. Newman & P. Marongiu, Trans.). New Brunswick, NJ: Transaction Publishers.

Bernard, T. (1983). *The consensus-conflict debate*. New York: Columbia University Press.

Bernard, T., Snipes, J. B., & Gerould, A. L. (2000). *Vold's theoretical criminology* (6th ed.). New York: Oxford University Press.

Carroll, J. V. (1978). A psychological approach to deterrence. *Journal of Personality and Social Psychology*, 36, 1512–1520.

Clarke, R. V. (Ed.). (1997). *Situational crime prevention: Successful case studies* (2nd ed.). Albany, NY: Harrow and Heston.

Cohen, L. E., & Felson, M. (1979). Social change and crime rate trends: A routine activity approach. *American Sociological Review*, 44, 588–608.

Cornish, D. B., & Clarke, R. V. (Eds.). (1986). *The reasoning criminal*. New York: Springer-Verlag.

Cornish, D. B., & Clarke, R. V. (1987). Understanding crime displacement: An application of Rational Choice Theory. *Criminology*, 25, 933–947.

Crowe, T. (2000). Crime prevention through environmental design (2nd ed.). Woburn, MA: Butterworth-Heinemann.

Eck, J. E. (2006). Preventing crime at place. In. L. W. Sherman, D. P. Farrington, B. C. Welsh, & D. L. McKenzie (Eds.), *Evidence Based Crime Prevention*. New York: Routledge.

Hindelang, M. J., Gottfredson, M. R., & Garofalo, J. (1979). *Victims of personal crime*. Cambridge, MA: Ballinger.

Jeffrey, C. R. (1977). *Crime prevention through environmental design* (2nd ed.). Beverly Hills: Sage.

Lenroot, R. K., & Giedd, J. N. (2006). Brain development in children and adolescents: Insights from anatomical magnetic resonance imaging. *Neuroscience and Biobehavioral Reviews, 30*(6), 718–729.

Nagin, D. S. (1998). Criminal deterrence research at the outset of the twenty-first century. In M. Tonry, (Ed.), *Crime and Justice: A Review of Research*. Chicago: University of Chicago Press.

Nagin, D. S., & Pogarsky, G. (2001). Integrating celerity, impulsivity, and extralegal sanction threats into a model of general deterrence: Theory and evidence. *Criminology, 39*, 865–891.

Newman, G. (1978). *The punishment response*. Philadelphia: Lippincott.

Newman, G., Clarke, R. V., & Shoham, S. G. (Eds.). (1997). *Rational choice and situational crime prevention: Theoretical foundations*. Aldershot, UK: Dartmouth/Ashgate.

Osgood, W. D., Wilson, J. K., O'Malley, P., Bachman, J. G., & Johnson, L. D. (1996). Routine activities and individual deviant behavior. *American Sociological Review*, 61, 635–655.

Pfohl, S. (1985). *Images of deviance and social control: A sociological history*. New York: McGraw-Hill.

Repetto, T. A. (1976). Crime prevention and the displacement phenomenon. *Crime and Delinquency*, 22, 166–67.

Scott, E. (1992). Judgment and reasoning in adolescent decision-making. *Villanova Law Review, 37*(6), 1607–1669. Retrieved from http://digitalcommons.law.villanova.edu/vlr/vol37/iss6/3

Steinberg, L., & Cauffman, E. (1999). The elephant in the courtroom: Developmental perspectives on the adjudication of youthful offenders. *Virginia Journal of Social Policy & the Law*, 6, 389–417.

Teeters, N. K. (1955). *The cradle of the penitentiary: The Walnut Street jail at Philadelphia. 1773–1835*. Philadelphia: Temple University Press.

Biological and Psychological Theories

5

On June 15, 2013, in Burleson, Texas, 16-year-old Ethan Couch was driving illegally with a restricted license when intoxicated. He was speeding and lost control of his vehicle. The vehicle plowed into a group of pedestrians, killing four and injuring nine others. Couch was tried on four charges of intoxicated manslaughter and assault in Tarrant County, Texas with prosecutors seeking the maximum sentence of 20 years in prison.

Ethan Couch

Fort Worth Star-Telegram/Contributor/Getty

However, the defense claimed that the teen was not fully responsible for his actions, as he suffered from a "mental" condition. According to the expert witness for the defense, psychologist G. Dick Miller, the teen was a product of "affluenza" and was unable to link his bad tbehavior with consequences. (Such connections between behavior and consequences were at the heart of the previous chapter on "choice theories" of crime.) Affluenza, according to this expert, was a mental condition in which the boy had not learned right from wrong because his parents taught him instead that wealth buys privilege and that if you have money you do not have to follow the same rules as everyone else. Thus, the boy's mental state was such that he could not determine right from wrong.

Following a court hearing closed to the public, Judge Jean Boyd sentenced Couch to an unspecified lock down rehabilitation facility for an unspecified period of time. Couch was ordered to stay away from drugs, alcohol and driving and was also placed on 10 years' probation. Many were outraged at the apparent leniency of this punishment based on the severity of the crime.

Just what, exactly, is affluenza? Do you believe a "disease" such as this can cause one to commit crime? What about other diseases? Or can someone even be born a criminal? In this chapter we will explore many different proposed biological and psychological explanations of crime. While there is a long historical traditional of looking at biology to explain deviance, many of the early theories were not based on what we would today consider good science. Therefore, in this chapter I will only touch on one or two of the more popular early approaches and focus instead on more modern medical science and what it has taught us about the human body and brain and how these may interact to "cause" delinquency.

CHAPTER GOALS

By the end of this chapter you should be able to:

1. Explain Lombroso's theory of the "atavist" and its connections to phrenology and Darwin's Theory of Evolution.
2. Discuss the nature versus nurture argument with regard to human behavior.
3. Understand the possible connection between the following and delinquency: brain chemistry, the neurological system, the hormonal system and environmental contaminants.
4. Explain the contributions of Freud, Piaget and Kohlberg to the understanding of psychology and delinquency.
5. List the symptoms associated with conduct disorder, oppositional defiant disorder and psychopathology.

6. Explain the elements of the "causal complex" of delinquency as proposed by the Gleucks and relate its importance to the study of delinquency and the nature vs. nurture argument.

Early Biological Theories of Crime

Perhaps the most influential early studies that attempted to link biology with crime come out of the fields of study known as phrenology and physiognomy. While physiognomists studied facial features such as eyes, ears, nose and mouth to try to determine differential features of criminals, phrenologists studied the shape of the skull, looking for abnormalities or bumps that might suggest an underlying defect of the brain. The most famous theory developed from this perspective was Cesare Lombroso's theory of the "**atavist**" (Lombroso, 1876). Heavily influenced by Darwin's writing on the evolution of the species, Lombroso thought that criminals were simply genetic throwbacks—that is, people whose brains had not evolved as much as the rest of the human race. These "atavists," as he called them, were then more animal-like and prone to aggression and violence. Compared to an evolved human, an atavist had stigmatic features such as an asymmetric face, long arms, a large jaw and protruding ears. Because these individuals were simply born inferior, their criminality was not their choice or even their fault. However, the only solution to protect the public from this inherently criminal being was to place him/her in institutions like prisons, much as we keep wild animals in cages at the zoo.

Atavist
a human that is not genetically evolved and thus more animal like

British scholar Charles Goring conducted a formal test of this theory, comparing 43 physical traits of university students to those of known criminals. Finding no differences across the sample, Goring concluded there was no evidence that criminals possessed stigmatic features (Goring, 1913). However, Earnest Hooton, in a re-evaluation of Goring's data, found that he overlooked key findings that would have supported Lombroso's ideas (Hooton, 1939). In later versions of his work, Lombroso expanded his theory to include other types of offenders as well, including "insane" criminals, who were not genetic throwbacks but had other mental disorders, and "criminaloids" who did not have any special physical or mental deficiencies but whose emotional makeup was such that they could engage in criminality in the right circumstances.

As you might guess, there is not much modern support for this notion of a criminal man that is somehow less evolved than the rest of the human race. However, the idea that there are some types of physical or mental deficiencies that may predispose someone to crime is still a central theme in this literature. Today, modern science has allowed us to look inside, rather than merely outside, the body to study human development. With this knowledge of literally what makes the brain work, have come several evolving theories regarding how physical abnormalities can either directly or indirectly lead to greater criminal propensities.

Genetics and Crime

Some of the most well-known studies that search for links between biology and crime assume that there must be something genetic that predisposes an individual to respond in criminal ways. Early research assumed that criminality must be hereditary because it "ran in families." That is, if a parent was in prison, it was likely a child would go to prison. If one child was in prison, it was likely a sibling would also go to prison. More modern research also supports an intergenerational nature to delinquency such that if a father was a schoolyard bully, the son is a schoolyard bully (West & Farrington, 1982) and if the parent demonstrated antisocial behavior as a teen, the child also demonstrates antisocial behavior (Thornberry et al., 2003). However, the simple correlations found by early work, and even the more sophisticated recent analysis of intergenerational data, cannot fully control for the environmental and social influences of a family. For example, if poverty is a social condition that leads to crime then all members of a family living in poverty should be inclined to commit crime, not because of heredity, but because of poverty.

Karl Christiansen developed a unique approach to address the potential hereditary nature of crime by studying sets of identical (monozygotic) and fraternal (dizygotic) twins. Genetically speaking, identical twins come from exactly the same genes, as the embryo splits into two after one sperm fertilizes one egg. However, fraternal twins are the result of two different eggs being fertilized in the womb and thus carry different genetic attributes. If crime is indeed inherited through genes rather than a product of the family/social environment, Christiansen believed he would find a higher concordance of delinquency among identical than fraternal twins. Using the Twins Registery of Denmark, he identified 6000 pairs of twins born between 1881 and 1910. Of the identical male twins, 67 cases had at least one twin registered as a criminal, and 24 of these cases, or 35.8 percent, had the other twin also registered. Compared to this, only 14 or 12.3 percent of the 114 cases of fraternal twins in which one twin was criminal also had the other twin registered as criminal. The difference was even larger for female twins with 3 of 14 cases of identical twins (21.4 percent) having both twins registered as criminal and 1 of 23 cases of fraternal twins (4.3 percent) having both twins registered (Christiansen, 1968, 1974).

Christiansen's work was still scrutinized because one could argue that because identical twins look so similar they are treated more alike than fraternal twins and that this difference could lead to the higher concordance in monozygotic twins. Grove and his colleagues attempted to overcome this difficulty by studying 32 sets of identical twins who were separated shortly after birth. Although the sample was small, as most twins are not separated at birth, it was suggestive of a heredity factor, as has other twin research been since this time (Walters, 1992).

Another method of addressing what is known as the "**nature versus nurture**" argument is the study of adopted children. Hutchings and Mednick provide some of the most convincing evidence in this area in a study of adopted children born in Copenhagen between 1927 and 1941. In this study the authors looked to see first if the youth had a criminal record, and then to see if either the biological and/or adoptive parents also had criminal records. If the youth's criminality had a greater concordance with the biological parent then this would be an argument in favor of "**nature**" or genetics, while if it was more in line with the adopted parent's criminality, it would be supportive of the "**nurture**," or social environment argument. Their research again found some support for a link between biology and crime, although it was not the sole factor. For example, of the boys with a minor criminal record, 37.7% of their biological fathers had criminal records, and of the boys with a more serious criminal record, 48.8% had a father with a criminal record. However, of the boys with no criminal record, still 31.1% of their biological fathers had a criminal record. Thus, while there is a correlation, it is not extremely large. This study also found other factors to be predictive of the boys' criminality, including the socioeconomic status of the adoptive and biological parents, the presence of personality disorders in the biological parents, and the number of placements of the child before the adoption. These correlations, however, only held for property and not for violent offenses (Gabrielli, Mednick & Hutchings, 1984; VanDusen, Mednick, Gabrielli & Hutchings, 1983). For more discussion of the nature vs. nurture debate see the Spotlight on Research.

Nature
genetics/biology

Nurture
social environment

While the overall suggestions of this research are that there might be something inherited that may increase the propensity to commit crime, they do not suggest there is something like a "crime gene" or give any information into how these hereditary processes work. The next sections deal more specifically with the "how" and "why" questions regarding the relationship between biological abnormalities and crime.

Neurophysiological Theories of Crime

In Chapter 2, in discussing the basis for a separate juvenile justice system, it was stressed that one primary reason to treat youth differently is because they are different. Specifically, they are still developing. The emphasis in much recent research in this area has been focused on the development of the brain through both normal maturational processes and abnormalities in development that may influence behavior.

For all teenagers, science has shown that the brain is indeed still developing and does not reach adult functioning until the early 20s. In particular the brain has two cortexes—the subcortex and the cerebral cortex. The subcortex controls most basic functions, such as breathing and heart rhythm, while the cerebral cortex is responsible for higher-level cognition. It is this outer layer, the cerebral cortex, that is indeed still developing and is most related to behavior (Raine, 1993). In the discussion of Choice Theories in Chapter 4, it was noted that the left frontal cortex is not fully developed in adolescence, and, since it is this section of the brain in particular that controls impulses and is responsible for reflective thought, traditional choice theories may not apply as well to the behavior of teenagers as to adults. In addition, research has specifically linked some of the most severe and life-course persistent antisocial behaviors to damage to the frontal lobe, which is thought to be responsible for controlling emotions, sustaining attention, regulating impulses, and allowing an individual to appreciate the consequences of behavior (Raine et al., 2005; Grekin et al., 2001). Raine and Yang (2005) also note that other areas of the brain that may be underdeveloped in adolescents, or to which an impairment may specifically be related to antisocial behavior, include the anterior cingulate, the posterior cingulate, the superior temporal gyrus, the amygdala and the hippocampus. In specific, research has found:

- Reduced cortical blood flow and hypometabolism in the dominant frontal and temporal lobes of repeat violent offenders (Tancredi, 2005)
- Impairment in the pre-frontal lobes, thalamus and medial temporal lobe of the brain in both chronic substance abusers and violent offenders (Raine et al., 2007)
- Low levels of metabolism in the right hypothalamus and decreased correlation between cortical and subcortical brain structures in domestic violence offenders (George et al., 2004)

What does all this complex and highly technical discussion of brain development boil down to? The fact that developmentally there may indeed be something structurally different in the brains of offenders and non-offenders. Some of these differences may be simple developmental stages (e.g., the high prevalence of criminality during adolescence versus later periods of life) and other differences might be more long-lasting. While the goal of this section is certainly not to make you a medical scholar on brain development, it is to open your eyes to the close links between human development and behavior, and how that development can be impacted by the environment. The following sections will thus discuss several known developmental delays, defects of the brain, and interactions between brain development and the environment that may increase the likelihood of delinquency.

ATTENTION DEFICIT HYPERACTIVITY DISORDER

Approximately 11% of children 4–17 years of age (6.4 million) in the United States have been diagnosed with attention deficit hyperactivity disorder (**ADHD**) as of 2011 (Centers for Disease Control, 2016). Boys (13.2%) were more likely than girls (5.6%) to have ever been diagnosed with ADHD. This disorder is diagnosed through its symptoms, which include the inability to pay attention and to sit still for developmentally appropriate periods of time (American Psychiatric Association, 1994). The exact causes of ADHD are still unknown but researchers have suggested it could be related to genetics, reactions to diet and food additives or even emotional turmoil and stress. Perhaps some of the most convincing evidence for a genetic link comes from studies that have documented a particular disorder of the dopamine DR receptor gene (DRD4) to be directly related to the development of ADHD (Faraone et al., 2001).

ADHD
symptoms include an inability to pay attention and to sit still for developmentally appropriate periods of time

Whatever the exact cause, the results are better known, and these include school failure, inappropriate response to discipline, bullying behavior and stubbornness (Stephen Faraone et al., 1993). More and more research is also linking this disorder with delinquency in teenagers, including a variety of antisocial behaviors—from smoking cigarettes, to illicit drug and alcohol use, to arrests for more serious crimes (Moffitt & Silva, 1988). For example, James Satterfield and colleagues compared 110 children with attention deficit disorder (ADD) to 88 without and found that the ADD sample was much more likely to have been arrested for a serious crime, and was 21 times more likely to have been institutionalized for antisocial behavior (Satterfield, Hoppe & Schell, 1982). More recently, Travis Pratt and colleagues conducted a meta-analysis of 20 studies that examined the correlation between ADHD and delinquency and found a consistent and strong relationship between this diagnosis and crime (Pratt et al., 2002).

However, interestingly, parental reports of symptom manifestation show that as children diagnosed with ADHD reach adolescence, while the inattentiveness continues to be an issue, their impulsivity decreases (see Figure 5.1).

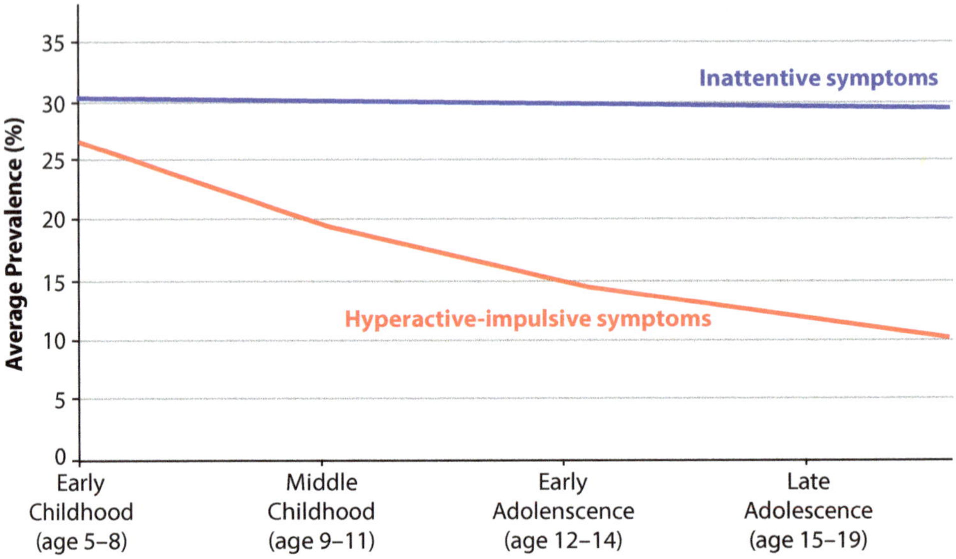

FIGURE 5.1 Persistence of ADHD Symptoms Over Time

This might suggest that attention deficit but not hyperactivity is related to a more permanent trait while hyperactivity could be a developmental delay rather than a life-course persistence disorder.

BIOCHEMICAL THEORIES

While ADHD is one specific disorder that is associated with the dopamine receptor in the brain, this is just one aspect of brain chemistry. As advances in science allow physicians and researchers to better map the functions of the brain, an entire science of brain chemistry is evolving, as well as theories of delinquency known as "biochemical theories." These theories rely on modern medical knowledge regarding the importance of different chemicals and minerals in the brain for normal growth and development. For example, research has shown that as a child grows, proper amounts of potassium, calcium, amino acids and even something as simple as sodium are important for normal brain development (Murata et al., 2004). These effects on crime can be direct, as in the case when a lack of a substance affects immediate behavior, or indirect, through which lack of proper development leads to school failure and other social problems that can lead to delinquency.

Neurotransmitter theory: A growing number of studies are emerging that link a variety of **neurotransmitters** to delinquency. Specifically, low levels of dopamine, gamma-aminobutryic acid (GABA), monoamine oxidase (MOA), norepinephrine and serotonin are linked to various forms of antisocial behavior. Of these chemicals, there is probably the most support for a direct association between MOMA and delinquency. Studies have found that individuals with low levels of this chemical are more likely to be impulsive, to engage in sensation-seeking/risk-taking behavior and to commit both violent and property crimes, and to have worse outcomes when faced with abuse or victimization (Caspi et al., 2002; Lee, 1991; Skondras et al., 2004). Moreover, to further complicate the nature versus nurture argument, research has also shown that prolonged abuse and neglect of children can actually *lead to* biological changes in the way the brain processes and responds to social stimuli (Heide & Solomon, 2006).

Arousal theory: While the link between these specific chemicals and arousal is not directly clear at this time, there is also evidence that people differ in the way they process stimuli from the environment. Some individuals need little stimuli to become aroused and are often overwhelmed by too much stimuli in the environment. Others require a high degree of stimuli to achieve arousal and thus are more likely to engage in risk-taking and sensation-seeking behaviors. It is thought that this latter group, regardless of the reason for the low arousal, is more likely to turn to aggressive and violent behaviors (Lee, 1996). Other studies have further linked these low levels of arousal with lower than normal resting heart rates, particularly in perpetrators of domestic violence and murderers (Raine, 1997).

HORMONES AND CRIME

Hormones: regulatory substances in the human body that influence mood and behavior. Certain hormones have been attached to specific behavioral patterns such as testosterone with aggression

As most parents of adolescents will attest, once puberty begins, behavioral changes ensue. For most this is a normal part of development and in time hormone levels reach a steady level once secondary sex characteristics have reached maturity. However, for some people, fluctuation in hormone levels or sustained higher levels of certain **hormones** can lead to more aggressive behaviors. For example, Booth and Osgood (1993) found a relationship between high levels of testosterone and aggression in male adolescents; however, this relationship was influenced by prior delinquency and the boy's level of social integration.

There is also some evidence that youth who experience early puberty may be more at risk for delinquency than their peers. For males, Felson and Haynie (2002) found that boys who were more physically developed than their peers were more likely to engage in a variety of deviant behaviors from sex and drug use to violence. For girls, it has been found that early puberty can lead to both increased risk of sexually deviant behavior and victimization (Haynie, 2002; Haynie & Piquero, 2006).

However, to return to our nature versus nurture debate, for many of these studies there are implications of environmental factors and influence as well as the possibility of reverse causation. For example, the Booth and Osgood study suggests that the impact of testosterone is mediated by social integration. Moreover, other studies have suggested that partaking in violence or being exposed to violence can increase testosterone, thereby suggesting a reverse causal pattern. Also, the impact of early puberty on girls seems not to be a direct impact of hormones on behavior, but perhaps, others' social responses to the girls based on their appearance. Thus, while there are definite links between hormones such as testosterone and aggression in animals (Brain, 1994), this connection is less direct and observable in humans.

DIET AND CRIME

While we might not have control over our hormones, we do have control over what we eat, and more and more food allergies and additives are being linked to problem behavior in children. Perhaps the number one ingredient parents are warned against is sugar—whether it be in natural or artificial form or the recently vilified "high-fructose corn syrup." Why so much hype about sugar? Most likely it is because of the energy surge it gives to most children and the relationships between sugar and hyperactivity. While hyperactivity itself is not deviant, we have discussed above how it can lead to attention and school problems for children, which may then later lead to delinquency. Also, hypoglycemia (low blood sugar), which can be caused by excess sugar intake, has been shown by some studies to relate to aggressive behavior, although there is not broad support for this particular notion in the field (Kanareck, 1994).

In addition to too much of a good thing causing a problem, on the other end of the spectrum research suggests that not enough nutrition could also be a problem. A 2002 study by Gesch and colleagues documented the behavior of inmates in a maximum-security prison in Great Britain. Half of the inmates were given a vitamin supplement and the other half were given a placebo pill. The inmates receiving the vitamins had a 25% drop in problem behaviors and a 37% drop in assaultive or other violent behaviors. Similar studies here in the United States conducted by Schoenthaler and colleagues on elementary school students, high school students and confined juveniles and adults all show similar findings. That is, improving diet or adding supplements to the diet, particular those rich in omega-3 fatty acids, significantly reduces antisocial, and particularly violent, behavior (Schoenthaler, 2002; Schoenthaler & Bier, 2000). Moreover, Schoenthaler's findings reveal increases in school performances among students given a better diet, and even significant reductions in the diagnosis of learning disabilities. For example in a study of 1.1 million children attending 803 New York City public schools, Schoenthaler found that the academic performance of the students increased 16% after being given a more nutritious diet at school breakfast and lunch and that the number of children labeled as having a learning disability decreased from 125,000 to 74,000. These findings are impressive because of the large sample size of this study, the carefully controlled study procedures that helped to rule out other causes of the changes in behavior and performance, and the magnitude of the effect.

ENVIRONMENTAL CONTAMINANTS AND CRIME

While good nutrition may reduce delinquent behavior, particularly aggression, exposure to contaminants in the environment may actually increase problem behavior. Contaminants linked to problems include cigarette smoke, lead, mercury, and the use of drugs and alcohol. Research does not suggest that exposure to these chemicals directly causes delinquency, but rather that it causes impaired development, reduced intelligence and alters the way the brain reacts to environmental stimuli that in turn place a youth more at risk for problem behaviors.

Perhaps the most well-documented and accepted connection is that between **lead poisoning** and delinquency. Lead poisoning in children leads to a host of problems, from aggression to reduced intelligence, to organ failure, and in extreme cases, even death. Studies of delinquent children in the 1980s found higher concentrations of lead in children resulted in more attention problems, more aggressive behaviors and lower school performance (Denno, 1985; Needleman et al., 2002; Needleman et al., 1996; Nevin, 2007; Wright et al., 2008).

Prenatal exposure to cigarette smoke and drugs/alcohol consumed by the mother have been linked to many developmental issues in children (Mattson & Riley, 1998; Streissguth, Barr & Sampson, 1990; Zuckerman & Bresnahan, 1991). All of these put the child at risk of delayed development, lower IQ, learning disabilities and attention problems and therefore are indirectly linked with later delinquency. Several studies have shown a direct link between this exposure and later delinquency; however, these studies have not adequately controlled for parenting and other potential risk factors over the years to isolate the impact of this exposure. For example, if a child is exposed to alcohol while in the womb and engages in delinquent activity at age 12—there are twelve years of possible influences other than the direct exposure to drugs or alcohol that could be potential causes of that behavior—not the least of which may be that a mother who is willing to smoke, drink and use drugs during pregnancy may also be likely to continue these behaviors or engage in other behaviors that place the child at further risk.

FOCUS ON RESEARCH: Moffit's Taxonomy of Offending

According to Terry Moffit (1993), there are two types of offenders: adolescent limited (AL) offenders and life-course persistent (LCP) offenders. The adolescent limited offenders are basically your typical teens engaging in behaviors that test the limits and rules for a brief period of time as they search for independence and identity. As they mature, they simply age out of this type of behavior. However, the life-course persistent offender starts exhibiting antisocial and problem behavior at a very early age and continues such behavior not only into the teenage years but across the entire lifespan. Moffit's research has linked the emergence of LCPs to a "double whammy." That is, these youth exhibit both biological abnormalities, particularly neuropsychological deficits, as well as being born into adverse social environments. Thus, to place this in our nature and nurture discussion, they got the "short end of the stick" on both fronts.

Empirical studies testing Moffit's taxonomy of offenders has provided initial support for this idea (Blokland, Nagin & Nieuwbeerta, 2005; Cauffman, Steinberg & Piquero, 2005; McGloin, Pratt & Piquero, 2006; Turner, Hartman & Bishop, 2007). For example, Raine et al. (2005) found that boys identified as LCPs had greater deficits in spatial and memory functions as compared with boys identified as ALs or controls, thus providing some support for an underlying neuropsychological link. Another study found that such neuropsychological deficits interact with a disadvantaged home environment in such a way as to allow researchers to predict who is at risk of becoming an LCP (Turner, Hartman & Bishop, 2007). Barnes, Beaver and Boutwell (2011) further suggest that since there is significant evidence that many neuropsychological deficits are genetically inherited, this suggests that there are genetic underpinnings for LCP. They point to three primary reasons to believe there are genetic underpinnings to the emergence of LCP. First, research has shown a strong and distinct relationship between heredity and antisocial behavior with correlations between .41 and .56 indicating that about half of all antisocial behavior can be explained by heredity (Ferguson, 2010; Miles & Carey, 1997; Rhee & Waldman, 2002). Second, they also point out studies that have found strong associations between neuropsychological deficiencies and LCP (Bergen, Gardner & Kendler, 2007; Bouchard & McGue, 1981; Burdick et al., 2007; Dick et al., 2007; Kebir et al., 2009; Plomin et al., 2001; Rowe, Jacobson &Van den Oord, 1999; Savitz, Solms & Ramesar, 2006; Waldman et al., 2006). Finally, they point out that research has also shown great stability in the behavioral patterns of LCPs over time. Indeed one study by Moffit and her colleagues found that about 83% of the stability in such behaviors could be attributed to genetics (similarly, Eley, Lichtenstein & Moffitt, 2003). Barnes and colleagues then further tested this idea with a sample of 2,284 sibling pairs drawn from the National Longitudinal Study of Adolescent Health. The sibling pairs included both monozygotic twins, dizygotic twins, full siblings, half siblings and cousins living in the same household. Their study found that between 56 and 70% of the variance in behavior for LCPs was explained by heredity based on strong correlations of behavior among monozygotic twins. This study also found a strong correlation between behavior and non-shared environments, but no significant influence for the shared environment above and beyond the genetic influences. What might this study suggest about the broader role of genetics and crime? Have criminologists been correct in primarily ignoring biological influences? What might some policy applications of these findings be for juvenile justice?

Psychodynamic Theory

While the previous sections have looked for links between our body and crime, this section takes a closer look at the link between the mind and crime. To be clear, these two are not naturally distinct, as what once was referred to as a "mental disorder" and thought to be part of an individual's personality is now being explained primarily through the brain science already examined. However, I think it is important for you to understand the current state of psychology and its influence on both theories of juvenile delinquency and the resulting practice of juvenile justice.

INTELLIGENCE AND CRIME

French psychologist Alfred Binet is most often credited with creating the first intelligence test. In doing this, he had no theory of what made one intelligent or not; rather he worked with students who were identified by their teachers as either "bright" or "dull" and developed questions that would sort the students into these predetermined categories (Feldman, 2004). Psychologists William Stern and Lewis Tierman built upon the work of Binet and devised a single score from the test to measure intelligence known as the **Intelligence Quotient** (IQ). The IQ is based on a scale such that a score of 100 indicates that an individual is at the appropriate mental capacities for his or her age. Above 100 indicates an advanced individual, and below 100, someone who is behind in mental age.

Intelligence Quotient

based on a scale such that a score of 100 indicates an individual is at the appropriate mental capacities for his/her age

In the United States, H.H. Goddard used the test at the New Jersey Training School for the Feeble Minded at Vineland to determine what "mental age" determined feeblemindedness. Finding none of the admitted individuals to have a mental age over 13, Goddard determined that an adult with the mental age of 12 (IQ of 75) should be determined to be feebleminded. Others then used this standard to administer the test to inmates at prisons to explore for a possible connection between low intelligence and criminality. These studies reported the frequency of "feeblemindedness" among these populations to be anywhere from 28 to 89%. While one might suggest this demonstrates a definite link between IQ and crime, Goddard went so far as to suggest that criminality and feeblemindedness were both aspects of the same degenerate state such that any feebleminded person was a potential criminal. He even went on to suggest that such individuals should be placed in institutions and not allowed to reproduce.

Luckily, modern intelligence tests and their interpretations have come a long way since this time, as have definitions of "feeblemindedness." However, many studies still show a convincing difference in the IQ scores of delinquents and non-delinquents. For example, a 1977 review by Hirschi and Hindelang found that across studies there was an average of an 8-point difference in the IQ of delinquents and non-delinquents. Why then might lower IQ be associated with crime? One idea is that IQ actually represents one's problem-solving ability and is an inborn biological trait. For example, Wilson and Herrnstein suggest that this low problem-solving ability leads youth with low IQs to commit impulsive crimes with immediate rewards (Wilson & Herrnstein, 1985). A second idea is that IQ does not really measure any determined underlying factor, but rather measures what is valued by the dominant culture. Thus, those without these features would themselves be more likely to be labeled delinquent by that culture. A third idea is that IQ measures someone's general abilities, but that these abilities are largely determined by the person's external environment and education rather than any inborn trait, which once again brings us back to the nature vs. nurture argument presented earlier in the chapter. This third idea is probably the most well-accepted notion among criminologists today.

Despite the improvement in the tests, however, most argue that significant cultural biases do still exist. Biases in tests represent those aspects of intelligence that the dominant culture finds important, and thus the test questions do not perhaps capture other aspects of intelligence that may be equally important.

PSYCHODYNAMIC THEORY

Psychodynamic theory is traced back to the early work of Sigmund Freud who proposed that healthy human development occurs through a process of psychosexual development from birth to adulthood (see Table 5.1). The successful completion of each stage is important for the individual to move on to the next stage.

Psychodynamic Theory
from Freud's early work who proposed that healthy human development occurs through a process of psychosexual development from birth to adulthood

Oral **0 to 18 months**	• experience world through mouth • e.g. sucking, biting, chewing
Anal **18 to 36 months**	• focus on bowel and bladder movements • e.g. potty training—control over movements
Phallic **3 to 6 years**	• focus on genitals • coping with incestuous feelings
Latency **6 yers to puberty**	• focus on gender identification
Genital **Puberty onward**	• maturation of sexuality

TABLE 5.1
Source: Megan Kurlychek

In addition, Freud emphasized that a healthy human being had a balanced personality, with the key elements being the **id**, the **ego** and the **superego**. The id, according to Freud, is the most primitive part of the human psyche; it is the part that represents our instincts and is controlled by our desire to seek pleasure at all times (i.e.. the pleasure principle). The two primary instincts that Freud suggests are inborn are aggression and sexual desire. The ego on the other hand refers to the rational part of the personality that controls the id to ensure the human seeks pleasure in socially acceptable ways. A well-developed ego therefore allows a person to delay gratification and suppress aggressive tendencies. Finally, the superego is what you might call your conscience. I like to visualize this as a cartoon in which the actor is trying to decide what to do and the id is the little devil sitting on his shoulder saying "Go ahead and do it!" and the superego is the little angel on the other shoulder saying "No, don't do it, don't do it." The ego, then, balances the two and rationally decides the correct behavior. If any of these components is under- or over-developed it leads to an unbalanced personality and possible delinquency.

Freud's theories are not typically directly used by criminologists today for several reasons including their difficulty to study (e.g., how do I measure your id?) and the advance of more sophisticated theories of childhood and adolescent development. However, they are introduced here as they provided the start of modern examination of the psyche and its relation to behavior. In the next sections we therefore consider both developmental and personality theories that owe their roots to this original work of Freud.

Developmental Theories

Psychological developmental theories typically follow the model of Freud in that they are divided into stages and it is thought that an individual must first successfully complete one stage before moving on to the next. In this section, you will be introduced to two such theories of development that have implications for the treatment of youth who break the law depending on their stage of development.

PIAGET'S THEORY OF COGNITIVE DEVELOPMENT

Jean Piaget was originally employed as a psychologist at the Binet Institute in Paris where he performed IQ tests such as those discussed in the Focus on Research. While administering these tests he realized that children seemed to give the same "wrong" answers and patterns of answers based on age. This finding intrigued him so much that he made the study of how children learn his lifelong passion. Today he is best known for his theory of cognitive development summarized below (Piaget, 1965).

Sensorimotor stage: This is the earliest stage of development. It occurs as infants begin to learn how to manipulate the world around them. They are fascinated by simple things like their toes, and have no idea of their own physical presence as part of a larger society, or even their family. They learn through experience and manipulation of their environment.

Preoperational stage: This stage starts around age 2 when children begin to be able to use words and symbols, instead of physical action, to manipulate their environment. Thus, instead of crying when thirsty the child will ask for "juice" or their "cup." One of the primary aspects of this stage is that the child can only think in one dimension and cannot reason through complex situations. Another characteristic of this stage is egocentrism, or the inability to see other people's points of view. At this stage children cannot even imagine that someone experiences the world differently than they do.

Concrete operational stage: At about age 7, children begin to show the early signs of logical reasoning. However, this reasoning is limited to concrete objects and not to abstract ideas. Thus, their reasoning is based on experience and immediately available stimuli rather than broader principles.

Formal operational stage: At this stage the individual begins to think abstractly about concepts and realizes that ideas can be classified and compared just as inanimate objects can. For example, the individual can understand the use of letters and symbols in formulas to stand for abstract ideas or numbers to be solved. At this stage the individual also begins to be able to deduce rules of behavior in situations and consider multiple aspects of a situation when engaging in problem solving. Thus, before this final stage of development it would be unreasonable to expect a youth to be fully able to understand right from wrong in abstract situations or even, when they know right from wrong, to make the correct choice when confronted with a complex and multifaceted situation.

KOHLBERG'S THEORY OF MORAL DEVELOPMENT

Freud referred to the superego as the conscience that tells a person right from wrong. But how does the conscience develop? How do you know what is right or wrong? Lawrence Kohlberg (1969) presented one of the most well-known theories of moral development in six stages across three levels as follows:

Pre-Conventional Level
avoids punishment and does what is necessary to satisfy needs

Pre-Conventional Level

Stage 1: Avoid punishment. At this stage the young child only seeks to avoid punishment from adults around him/her.

Stage 2: Do what is necessary to satisfy needs. At this stage the individual also recognizes the basic necessities of life and will choose behaviors that satisfy these needs.

Conventional Level
internalize conventional standards of right and wrong with a high regard for authority and maintaining social order

Conventional Level

Stage 3: Win Approval. By around age 9, children usually function at this level, which is where they have begun to internalize conventional standards of right and wrong.

Stage 4: Law and Order. This stage is characterized by a high regard for authority and maintaining the social order.

Post-Conventional Level
realizes laws represent agreed-upon standards and are there for a reason, also realizing there could be a good reason to violate the law. Also the level when people respect differing opinions. Not all people reach that part of the level

Post-Conventional Level

Stage 5: Social order. At this stage law and order are still important but the individual realizes that laws represent agreed-upon standards and are there for a reason. With this recognition also comes the idea that at times there could be a good reason to violate a law.

Stage 6: Universal ethics. This is the highest stage of moral reasoning and is not achieved by most people, according to Kohlberg. It is a universal recognition of the value of human life, dignity and justice. This includes respecting people's differing opinions.

Kohlberg's theory has been influential in that it suggests that before the age of about 13, a child may not be able to address and understand complex situations and problems of crime and delinquency.

Combined, Piaget's and Kohlberg's theories of development are highly suggestive that the younger a child is, the less able he/she is to determine right from wrong and the greater the potential value of education in promoting not only cognitive, but moral development as well. While these theories focus on stages of normal development, most of the following sections of this chapter focus on trying to identify something "abnormal" about the personality of the delinquent.

Personality Theories

Personality theory assumes that individuals are born with inherent behavioral traits that influence the way they respond to their environment. For example, have you ever been described as "shy" or "outgoing"? Or have you ever been asked to come up with adjectives to describe yourself? Some theorists believe these traits are an inborn part of the personality while others think they develop over time. Either way, this strain of theories has sought to determine what is "different" about the delinquent personality.

Personality Theory assumes individuals are born with inherent behavioral traits that influence the way they respond to their environment

One of the first criminological studies of the link between personality and crime was published by Sheldon and Eleanor Gleuck in 1950. In this work, the Gleucks attempted to combine and test many of the growing theories of crime that attributed delinquency to different sources. Their data was taken from a sample of 500 delinquent and 500 non-delinquent young males. Overall, they concluded that there was no one personality factor that led to crime, but that delinquents did tend to have a variety of interrelated personality factors that were different than the non-delinquent sample. These included:

- **Extroversion**—delinquent boys tended to be more outgoing and social than non-delinquent boys. They also tended to be more adventurous and aggressive. Perhaps most notably, however, this study found that more than twice as many delinquents tended to resolve mental conflicts by "extroversion of action" rather than introversion.
- **Hostility, resentfulness and suspicion**—delinquent boys tended to be more suspicious of, and resentful toward, authority and society. They were less likely to submit to authority, perhaps because of their suspicions and resentfulness.
- **Impulsivity**—delinquent boys tended to be more impulsive, thus giving into temptations of the moment and not planning or pre-planning their crimes.
- **Narcissism**—the delinquent boys as a group had a tendency to be more egocentric and less critical of themselves. However, they are also more likely to report feelings of not being appreciated or recognized by others. Thus, their delinquency might be seen as a way of bringing attention to themselves.

Extroversion outgoing and social

Narcissism egocentric and less critical of themselves also likely to report feelings of not being appreciated or recognized by others

The Gleucks' study was very influential because it was the first to really consider the interplay between various factors. However, they in no way suggested that these personality traits were indeed inborn or stable over the life course. They also noted that delinquent boys had many more environmental stressors and conflicts reported than the non-delinquent boys, which taps into the social aspect of delinquency.

The Gleucks' study mainly relied upon the Rorschach test, which you might be more familiar with as the "ink blot" test in which individuals are presented with images and asked to report what they see. Their answers are then analyzed using complex algorithms to detect underlying personality traits (Exner, 1995).

©Sirin_bird/Shutterstock.com

Other personality tests that have evolved over time also take into account the multi-dimensional nature of the human personality. In fact, the most widely used personality test is the Minnesota Multiphase Personality Inventory (MMPI) that uses over 500 questions to assess aspects of the personality across categories. The MMPI-A (A standing for "adolescent" version) has been found to be predictive of violent but not non-violent offending. However, many of the questions relate to social circumstances and past behavior such as past offending, leading to this instrument being highly criticized by psychiatrists and criminologists as not truly measuring "personality" and even being culturally and racially biased (Gynther, 1989; Prichard & Rosenblatt, 1980).

PERSONALITY DISORDERS

In addition to simply measuring personality traits, the fields of psychology and psychiatry have also developed definitions of various personality defects that are more stable sets of traits that disrupt normal social life for the affected individual.

These include such things as paranoia, obsessive compulsive disorder, narcissistic personality disorder, schizoid and antisocial personality disorder. For example, people with schizoid personality disorder have no interest in relationships with other people and become detached from society in general. On the other end people with dependent personality disorder become submissive to others and overly clingy, unable to function on their own. Perhaps of most interest to criminologists has been the notion of **antisocial personality disorder**, which is defined as a disorder in which the individual has a disregard for, and a propensity toward violation of, the rights of others. Individuals with this disorder have no remorse for their behavior when it injures others and continue in such behavior despite threats of social rejection and punishments.

PSYCHOPATHS AND SOCIOPATHS

Closely related to antisocial personality disorder are two terms you are probably more familiar with: psychopath and sociopath. But what exactly do these terms mean? The terms are many times used interchangeably and have varying definitions depending on the source you consult. It seems the term *psychopath* can be traced back to the work of Philippe Pinel who published "A Treatise on Insanity" in 1801. Pinel described the **psychopath** as an individual who did not suffer from hallucinations or delusions, that is, was otherwise in control of their behavior, but exhibited extreme rage and immoral behavior. The more modern understanding of this disorder was presented in Cleckley's 1941 "The Mask of Sanity" which lists 16 features of the psychopath. Some of the more common are untruthfulness and lack of remorse or shame. Today, psychopathy in adults is diagnosed using the PCL-R checklist (Hare, 1991; Hare & Neumann, 2008).

Psychopath
an individual who did not suffer from hallucinations or delusions and was in control of their behavior, but exhibited extreme rage and immoral behavior

While the majority of research has focused on adult psychopaths, some research has been done on juveniles and found that these traits emerge early in life and remain particularly stable. Traits such as being egocentric, lacking impulse control and having little interest in or capability for stable relationships were evidenced by age 10 and persisted into adulthood (Frick et al., 2003).

What then causes this behavior? Psychologists have divided psychopaths into two categories: primary and secondary. The **primary psychopath** is thought to have some brain abnormality that impairs the way he/she processes information and responds to others. The **secondary psychopath** has experienced some great or prolonged trauma such as severe child abuse that leads to these behaviors (Walsh & Wu, 2008). Because the secondary psychopath is more nurture than nature, this is the class that is often referred to as "**sociopaths**." Thus, the symptoms and behaviors are the same, but the causes are different.

Sociopath

an individual who, due to some great or prolonged trauma such as severe child abuse, has extreme rage and immoral behavior

OPPOSITIONAL DEFIANT AND CONDUCT DISORDER

Oppositional defiant disorder (ODD) is not a form of psychosis, but rather a persistent pattern of behavior that defines how an individual interacts with others. Psychologists diagnose this disorder with observed symptoms but there is no agreement on an underlying cause. A person is said to have oppositional defiant disorder if he/she exhibits four or more of the following symptoms consistently over a six-month period:

Oppositional Defiant Disorder

a pattern of behavior that defines how a person interacts with others

- often loses temper
- often argues with adults
- actively refusing to comply with adults' requests or rules
- deliberately doing things to annoy others
- is easily annoyed by others
- blames others for his or her mistakes
- is angry and resentful
- is spiteful and vindictive.

It should be noted that many of these behaviors are typical of teens in general, such as arguing with adults or being easily annoyed; however, this disorder indicates a more severe and consistent pattern of these behaviors. Unfortunately, because this disorder is diagnosed on symptoms, there is not a magic pill or direct cure. In fact, it takes significant counseling and behavioral modification techniques to help these children, and often parents of these children become so frustrated with their behaviors that they tend to ignore some of the minor behaviors as it becomes overwhelming. If not addressed, psychologists propose this disorder can lead to a more serious condition called "conduct disorder." Again, this is a disorder diagnosed by symptoms. The symptoms of **conduct disorder** include those of ODD but also include such things as aggression and bullying, destruction of property, deceitfulness and more serious violations of rules. Unfortunately, many of these "symptoms" can, in and of themselves, be delinquent acts, leading this disorder to fit many delinquents without offering an underlying idea of what causes these behaviors.

Conduct Disorder

symptoms of Oppositional Defiant Disorder along with aggression and bullying, destruction of property, deceitfulness and more serious violations of the rules

POLICY IMPLICATIONS FOR JUVENILE JUSTICE

Sociologists and criminologists for a long time avoided the harsh deterministic biological theories of crime, as suggestions that someone is a born criminal not only do not make sense to most, but also because the recommended social policies would be inhumane—such as genocide and sterilization (see Focus on Policy). However, the more modern social-biological perspectives that combine the nature and nurture arguments into a more realistic vision of how the body and mind interact with the environment provide more hopeful and useful policies for the juvenile justice system.

First, some conditions, such as hormone disorders or brain chemistry disorders, can be treated with medications. For example, Ritalin is a well-tested and useful drug for youth suffering from ADHD. Second, as we now know the possible negative side effects of exposure to environmental **contaminants**, even at the pre-natal stage, efforts have been taken to reduce exposure to these toxins. Third, the research on diet and behavior has led to some sweeping policy changes in our nation's schools, with many now serving breakfast as well as lunch, and even offering summer lunch programs to disadvantaged youth who might otherwise not have nutritious meals. As biological science advances and we learn more and more about the human brain and how genes interact with the environment, this is a particularly interesting area for both research and policy.

Contaminants
strictly defined as a pollutant or poisonous substance. In this case referring to pollutants or poisonous substances in one's environment that delay or impair development

On the psychological front, we also know that some conditions that were once thought to be mental disorders do indeed have medical causes, such as problems with neurotransmitters leading to mood disorders such as depression and anxiety. Also, from the developmental perspective, we have learned that early childhood experiences have the potential to greatly impact adolescent development and behaviors. Thus, intervention at a young age is crucial to help youth avoid such problems. In the medical field, they often say an ounce of prevention is worth a pound of cure and that is truly the case when it comes to preventing developmental problems. See Spotlight on Policy for more discussion on the possible benefits of **early intervention** and prevention.

Early Intervention
intervening at a young age is crucial to help youth avoid problems

Psychological counseling is also one of the greatest tools used by the juvenile justice system to help youth exhibiting problem behaviors. Often, it is believed that behaviors such as aggression, drug and alcohol use and gang joining are ways youth cope with other underlying problems. Individual and group counseling allow youth a chance to express these feelings, perhaps even realize for themselves for the first time how much the feelings are bothering them, and to learn more positive coping strategies.

As may have come to your attention in this chapter, much of the youth's development happens in the home, and you have heard mention of parenting practices. This will be a theme you see throughout many of the remaining theories as they focus on how children learn and grow in interaction with society. Since family and schools are the primary places of socialization for children, they will be a focus of many of the theories of delinquency to come. In fact many of the best youth treatment programs involve the family in counseling and intervention efforts.

FOCUS ON POLICY: Legacy of Biological Theories

Early biological theories of crime were highly deterministic with a focus almost entirely on nature. Individuals were in a way viewed as just products of their biology. The early policies that resulted from these ideas are considered barbaric by today's society. For example, it was common practice at one point to conduct lobotomies on violent criminals to remove the part of their brain thought responsible for their aggression. As recently as the 1950s some mental institutions still routinely involuntarily sterilized their patients so that they could not reproduce and pass on their mental illness (Braslow, 1997). Perhaps the most horrific example of a policy based on the assumption that a certain race or type of individual is inferior is genocide. Genocide was most notably carried out in Nazi Germany where theories of biological inferiority were used to justify the extermination not only of criminals, but of anyone of Jewish or Gypsy descent on the premise that they were genetically inferior (Rafter, 2008).

Because these policies are so brutal, there is a resistance among many criminologists to even consider biological theories of crime despite the advances of modern medicine. However, not all suggested policies were so brutal. For example, phrenologists recommended prison reform to ensure that criminals' "faculties" were put back in balance. The prisoner was never to be subject to any kind of corporal or physical punishment but rather to be provided fresh air, good food and education (Combe & Mittermaier, 1843).

Moreover, today's theories suggest an even larger role for nurture over nature, and the idea that biology might only predispose—not determine—one to be criminal. The policies suggested by today's theories seem much more reasonable and easy to implement, such as medicating a condition such as ADHD that may predispose one to crime, or early identification and intervention strategies for youth with neurological disorders that might predispose them to a life of crime. Other theories suggest even more simple policies such as improving children's diets and ensuring that the environment is free from toxins that can delay or prevent appropriate development.

However, fear of some of the more barbaric early policies keeps many from giving credit to these theories. In addition, there is also a tendency for the media to overemphasize studies of biology, which feeds this fear. For example, research by Adrien Raine (Raine et al., 2000) on a small sample of highly aggressive men found that their brains had a less developed frontal cortex by about 11% as compared to the normal male. This was quickly reduced in the media to a finding that criminals have smaller brains than the rest of us (Rafter, 2008).

Given the nature versus nurture debate and the promise of current theories and policies compared to the legacy of the more brutal and feared policies, do you think there is a place for biological theories of crime in today's society? List out what might be potential harms and benefits of this approach. Which side wins?

TABLE 5.2 Theory Summary Box

	Underlying Assumptions	**Cause of Crime**	**System Application**
Genetics	Behavior is determined by genes	Heredity	Incapacitate, sterilize or even genocide
Neurophysiology	The brain and neurological system control behavior	Chemical imbalance, hormones, diet, contaminants	Diagnose and treat
Intelligence	Intelligence is inborn	Poor decision-making	Used to predict, not prevent, delinquency
Psychodynamic	Development occurs in successive stages	Failure to successfully complete stage	Psycho-therapy/ developmental intervention
Personality	Personality dictates general tendencies for behavior	Personality traits or more severe disorders	Diagnose and treat or identify and incapacitate

Key Words

ADHD
Atavist
Conduct Disorder
Contaminants
Conventional Level
Early Intervention
Extroversion
Hormones
Intelligence Quotient
Narcissism
Nature
Nurture
Oppositional Defiant Disorder
Personality Theory
Post-Conventional Level
Pre-Conventional Level
Psychodynamic Theory
Psychopath
Sociopath

Chapter Summary

This chapter introduced you to a variety of ideas and theories about how biology and psychology might be related to the etiology of delinquent behaviors. Under biological perspectives these theories can be divided into two broad categories: heredity theories and biological abnormality theories. Under heredity theories, crime is the result of an inborn gene or characteristic that is present at birth and affects behaviors. Biological abnormality theories emphasize abnormalities in the neurological or hormonal systems that can be caused either by heredity or the environment, or an interaction of the two.

You were also introduced to several varieties of psychological theories, including developmental theories that focus on the development of thinking strategies and morals over time and personality theories. Developmental theories stress the importance of successfully navigating stages of development so that the youth appropriately moves on to the next stage. Personality theories, on the other hand, focus more on what are considered inborn traits or tendencies such as extroversion and impulsiveness.

The chapter ends with a discussion of various psychological abnormalities, such as conduct disorder, oppositional defiant disorder and psychopathology. While these last topics are considered some of the most sexy and are the topic of many TV shows and more sensational stories of crime, I pointed out several problems with these diagnoses that make them less useful than some of the other theories in addressing juvenile delinquency. First, these disorders are diagnosed mostly on symptoms and there is no known underlying cause to treat. Second, many of the symptoms used to diagnose these disorders include illegal behaviors. This confuses the cause with the outcomes. That is, it is tautological to say most delinquents suffer from some type of conduct disorder when the "symptoms" used to "diagnose" conduct disorder include destruction of property, dishonesty, theft and aggression—all of which are behaviors that can lead to arrest.

What do these theories in general then suggest for juvenile justice? They suggest that some risk factors can be inborn and some develop in early childhood. Therefore, early detection and prevention and intervention efforts are crucial to reducing problem behaviors in adolescents. Modern medicine also holds much promise for helping us better understand the relationship between the body and crime and how medications that address chronic health problems may reduce the risk of delinquency.

Discussion Questions

1. We began the chapter with a discussion of a supposed disease called "affluenza." After reading this chapter, do you believe this should be classified as a psychological disease? What criteria should courts use to determine "disease"?
2. This chapter discussed various ways in which exposure to environmental contaminants and poor diet can lead to developmental, learning and ultimately behavioral problems. In Chapter 3 of this text you learned about the statistical relationship between socio-economic status and crime. How might these two findings be connected?
3. Similar to arguments about cultural bias in intelligence tests, many argue that standardized tests such as the SAT and ACT, which you may have had to take to get into college, are biased against certain minority groups. Some colleges are now not using these tests at all, or making them optional. What do you think about standardized tests? Can we truly capture someone's innate potential and intelligence in one test? How else might we measure intelligence and/or potential?
4. The media is captivated with some of the most rare and severe crimes that involve the popular notion of the Psychopath/Sociopath, particularly serial killers. View this link: https://www.sociopathicstyle.com/psychopathic-traits/ and discuss the traits as they relate to some real life psychopath/sociopaths you can find online such as Josef Mengele and Jeffrey Dahmer as well as fictional character versions such as Hannibal Lecter in the *Silence of the Lambs*. Do you think these media representations accurately represent what is known about personality and crime? How common do you think such a severe condition might be?

REFERENCES

Barnes, J. C., Beaver, K. M., & Boutwell, B. B. (2011). Examining the genetic underpinnings of Moffitt's developmental taxonomy: A behavioral genetic analysis. *Criminology, 49*(4), 923–954.

Bergen, S. E., Gardner, C. O., & Kendler, K. S. (2007). Age-related changes in heritability of behavioral phenotypes over adolescence and young adulthood: A meta-analysis. *Twin Research and Human Genetics, 10*, 423–33.

Booth, A., & Osgood, W. D. (1993). The influence of testosterone in adulthood: Assessing and explaining the relationship. *Criminology, 31*, 93–117.

Blokland, A., Nagin, D. S., & Nieuwbeerta, P. (2005). Lifespan offending trajectories of a Dutch conviction cohort. *Criminology, 43*, 919–54.

Brain, P. (1994). Hormonal aspects of aggression and violence. In A. J. Reiss, Jr., K. A. Miczek, & J. A. Roth (Eds.), *Understanding and Preventing Violence: Biobehavioral Influences* (Vol. 2, pp. 173–244). Washington DC: National Academic Press.

Braslow, J. (1997). *Mental ills and bodily cures: Psychiatric treatment in the first half of the twentieth century* (Vol. 8). Univ of California Press.

Bouchard, T. J., & McGue, M. (1981). Familial studies of intelligence: A review. *Science*, 212, 1055–1059.

Boutwell, B. B., & Beaver, K. M. (2008). A biosocial explanation of delinquency abstention. *Criminal Behaviour and Mental Health, 18*, 59–74.

Burdick, K. E., Funke, B., Goldberg, J. F., Bates, J. A., Jaeger, J., Kucherlapati, R., & Malhotra, A. K. (2007). COMT genotype increases risk for bipolar disorder and influences neurocognitive performance. *Bipolar Disorders, 9*, 370–376.

Caspi, A., McClay, J., Moffitt, T. E., Mill, J., Martin, J., Craig, I. W., . . . Poulton, R. (2002). Role of genotype in the cycle of violence in maltreated children. *Science, 292*, 851–854.

Cauffman, E., Steinberg, L., & Piquero, A. R. (2005). Psychological, neuropsychological and physiological correlates of serious antisocial behavior in adolescence: The role of self-control. *Criminology*, 43, 133–176.

Centers for Disease Control. (2016). Retrieved from http://www.cdc.gov/ncbddd/adhd/data.html

Christiansen, K. O. (1968). Threshold of tolerance in various population groups illustrated by results from the Danish criminologic twin study. In A. V. S. de Reuck & R. Porter (Eds.), *The Mentally Abnormal Offender* (pp. 107–116). Boston: Little Brown.

Christiansen, K. O. (1974). Seriousness of criminality and concordance among Danish twins. In Roger Hood (Ed.), *Crime, Criminology and Public Policy* (pp. 63–77). New York: Free Press.

Cleckley, H. (1941). *The mask of sanity.* St. Louis: C.V. Mosby.

Combe, G., & Mittermaier, C. J. A. (1843). On the application of phrenology to criminal legislation and prison discipline. *Phrenological Journal, 21*, 1–19.

Darwin, C. (1859). *On the origin of the species*. London: John Murray.

Denno, D. (2007). Sociological and human developmental explanations of crime. *Criminology*, 23, 711–741.

Dick, D. M., Aliev, F., Kramer, J., Wang, J. C., Hinrichs, A., Bertelsen, . . . Edenberg, H. J. (2007). Association of CHRM2 with IQ: Converging evidence for a gene influencing intelligence. *Behavior Genetics, 37*, 265–272.

Ellis, L. (1991). Monomine oxidase and criminality: Identifying an apparent biological marker for antisocial behavior. *Journal of Research in Crime and Delinquency*, *28*, 227–251.

Exner, J. E. (1995). *The Rorschach: A comprehensive system. Vol 1: Basic foundations*. New York: John Wiley and Sons.

Faraone, S., Doyle, A., Mick, E., & Biederman, J. (2001). Meta-analysis of the association between the 7-repeat allele of the DRD4 gene and ADHD. *American Journal of Psychiatry, 158,* 1052–1057.

Feldman, R. S. (2004). *Child development*. Upper Saddle River, NJ: Prentice Hall.

Felson, R., & Haynie, D. (2002). Pubertal development social factors and delinquency among adolescent boys. *Criminology, 40,* 967–988.

Ferguson, C. J. (2010). Genetic contributions to antisocial personality and behavior: A meta-analytic review from an evolutionary perspective. *Journal of Social Psychology,* 150, 1–21.

Frick, P., Kimonis, E., Dandreaux, D., & Farell, J. (2003). The four year stability of psychopathic traits in non-referred youth. *Behavioral Sciences and the Law, 21,* 713–736.

Gesch, B., Hammond, S. M., Hampson, S. E., Eves, A., & Crowder, M. J. (2002). Influence of supplementary vitamins, minerals and essential fatty acids on the antisocial behaviour of young adult prisoners: Randomized, placebo-controlled trial. *British Journal of Psychiatry*, 181, 22–28.

Grekin, E., Brennan, P., Hodgins, S., & Mednick, S. (2001). Male criminals with organic brain syndrome. Two distinct types based on age at first arrest. *American Journal of Psychiatry, 158,* 1099–1104.

Goddard, H. H. (1914). *Feeblemindedness: Its causes and consequences*. New York: Macmillan.

Goring, C. (1913). *The English convict*. London: His Majesty's Stationary Office.

Gynther, M. D. (1989). "MMPI comparisons of Blacks and Whites: A review and commentary." *Journal of Clinical Psychology, 45*(6): 878–883.

Hare, R. D. (1991). *The hare psychopathy checklist revised*. Toronto: Multi-Health Systems.

Hare, R. D., & Neumann, C. (2008). Psychopathy as a clinical and empirical construct. *Annual Review of Clinical Psychology, 4,* 217–246.

Haynie, D. (2002). Contexts of Risk? Explaining the link between girls' pubertal development and their delinquency involvement. *Social Forces,* 82, 355–397.

Haynie, D., & Piquero, A. (2006). Pubertal development and physical victimization in adolescence. *Journal of Research in Crime and Delinquency,* 43, 3–35.

Heide, K., & Solomon, E. (2006). Biology, childhood trauma and murder: Rethinking justice. *International Journal of Law and Psychiatry,* 29, 220–233.

Hirschi, T., & Hindelang, M. (1977). Intelligence and delinquency: A revisionist review. *American Sociological Review, 42,* 572–87.

Hooton, E. (1939). *Crime and the man.*

Ishikawa, S., & Raine, A. (2003). Prefrontal deficits and antisocial behavior. In B. Lahey, T. Moffitt, & A. Caspi (Eds.), *Causes of Conduct Disorder and Juvenile Delinquency* (pp. 277–304). New York: Guilford Press.

Kanarek, R. B. (1994). Nutrition and violent behavior. In A. J. Reiss Jr., K. A. Miczek, & J. A. Roth (Eds.), *Understanding and Preventing Violence: Biobehavioral Influences* (Vol. 2, pp. 515–539). Washington DC: National Academic Press.

Kebir, O., Tabbane, K., Sengupta, S., & Joober, R. (2009). Candidate genes and neuropsychological phenotypes in children with ADHD: Review of association studies. *Journal of Psychiatry and Neuroscience,* 34, 88–101.

Kohlberg, L. (1969). *Stages in the development of moral thought and action*. New York: Holt, Rinehart and Winston.

Lombroso, C. (1876). *The criminal man*. Milan, Italy: Hoepli.

Mattson, S. N., & Riley, E. P. (1998). A review of the neurobehavioral deficits in children with fetal alcohol syndrome or prenatal exposure to alcohol. *Alcoholism: Clinical and Experimental Research*, *22*(2), 279–294.

Miles, D. R., & Carey, G. (1997). Genetic and environmental architecture of human aggression. *Journal of Personality and Social Psychology*, 72, 207–217.

McGloin, J. M., Pratt, T. C., & Piquero, A. R. (2006). A lifecourse analysis of the criminogenic effects of maternal cigarette smoking during pregnancy: A research note on the mediating impact of neuropsychological deficit. *Journal of Research in Crime and Delinquency*, *43*, 412–426.

Moffitt, T., & Silva, P. (1988). Self-reported delinquency neuropsychological deficit and history of attention deficit disorder. *Journal of Abnormal Child Psychology*, 16, 553–569.

Moffitt, T. E. (1993). Adolescence-limited and life-course persistent antisocial behavior: A developmental taxonomy. *Psychological Review*, *100*, 674–701.

Moffitt, T. E. (2005). The new look of behavioral genetics in developmental psychopathology: Gene-environment interplay in antisocial behaviors. *Psychological Bulletin*, *131*, 533–554.

Needleman, H., McFarland, C., Ness, R. B., Fienberg, S. E., & Tobin, M. J. (2002). Bone lead levels in adjudicated delinquents. *Neurotoxicology and Teratology*, *24*, 711–7171.

Needleman, H., Riess, J., Tobin, M., Biesecker, G., & Greenhouse, J. (1996). Bone lead levels and delinquent behavior. *Journal of the American Medical Association*, *275*, 363–369.

Nevin, R. (2007). Understanding international crime trends: The legacy of preschool lead exposure. *Environmental Research*, *104*, 315–336.

Murata, K., Weither, P., Buditz-Jorgensen, E., Jorgensen, P. J., & Grandjean, P. (2004, February). Delayed brainstem auditory evoked potential latencies in 14-year-old children exposed to methylmercury. *Journal of Pediatrics*, *144*(2), 177–183.

Piaget, J. (1965). *The moral judgment of the child*. New York: Free Press.

Plomin, R., Hill, L., Craig, I. W., McGuffin, P., Purcell, S., Sham, P., . . . Owen, M. J. (2001). A genome-wide scan of 1842 DNA markers for allelic associations with general cognitive ability: A five-stage design using DNA pooling and extreme selected groups. *Behavior Genetics*, *31*, 497–509.

Pratt, T., Cullen, F., Blevins, K., Daigle, L., & Unnever, J. (2002). The relationship of ADHD to crime and delinquency: A meta-analysis. *International Journal of Police Science and Management*, *4*, 344–360.

Prichard, D. A., & Rosenblatt, A. (1980). Racial bias in the MMPI: A methodological review. *Journal of Consulting and Clinical Psychology*, *48*(2), 263.

Rafter, N. (2008). *The criminal brain. Understanding biological theories of crime.* New York: New York University Press.

Raine, A. (1993). *The psychopathology of crime: Criminal behavior as a clinical disorder*. San Diego: Academic Press.

Raine, A. (2008). From genes to brain to antisocial behavior. *Current Directions in Psychological Science*, *17*, 323–328.

Raine, A., Lencz, T., Bihrle, S., LaCasse, L., & Colletti, P. (2000). Reduced prefrontal gray matter volume and reduced autonomic activity in antisocial personality disorder. *Archives of General Psychiatry*, *57*(2), 119–127.

Raine, A., Moffitt, T., Caspi, A., Loeber, R., Stouthamer-Loeber, M., & Lynam, D. (2005). Neurocognitive impairments in boys on the life-course persistent antisocial path. *Journal of Abnormal Psychology*, *114*, 38–49.

Rhee, S., & Waldman, I. (2002). Genetic and environmental influences on antisocial behavior: A meta-analysis of twin and adoption studies. *Psychological Bulletin*, *128*, 490–529.

Rowe, D. C., Jacobson, K. C., & Van den Oord, E. J. C. G. (1999). Genetic and environmental influences on vocabulary IQ: Parental education level as moderator. *Child Development, 70,* 1151–1162.

Satterfield, J., Hoppe, C., & Schell, A. (1982). A prospective study of delinquency in 100 adolescent boys with ADD and 88 normal adolescent boys. *American Journal of Psychiatry, 139,* 795–798.

Savitz, J., Solms, M., & Ramesar, R. (2006). The molecular genetics of cognition: Dopamine, COMT, and BDNF. *Genes, Brain and Behavior, 5,* 311–328.

Schoenthaler, S. (2000). *Intelligence, academic performance and brain function.* California State University: Stanislaus.

Schoenthaler, S., & Bier, I. (2007). The effect of vitamin-mineral supplementation on juvenile delinquency among American schoolchildren: A randomized double-blind placebo controlled trial. *Journal of Alternative and Complementary Medicine: Research on Paradigm, Practice and Policy, 6:* 7–18.

Skondras M., Markiano, M., Botsis, A., Bistolaki, E., & Christodoulou, G. (2004). Platelet monoamine oxidase activity and psychometric correlates in male violent offenders imprisoned for homicide or other violent acts. *European Archives of Psychiatry and Clinical Neuroscience, 254,* 380–386.

Streissguth, A. P., Barr, H. M., & Sampson, P. D. (1990). Moderate prenatal alcohol exposure: Effects on child IQ and learning problems at age 7 1/2 years. *Alcoholism: Clinical and Experimental Research, 14*(5), 662–669.

Turner, M. G., Hartman, J. L., & Bishop, D. M. (2007). The effects of prenatal problems, family functioning, and neighborhood disadvantage in predicting life-course-persistent offending. *Criminal Justice and Behavior, 34,* 1241–1261.

Waldman, I. D., Nigg, J. T., Gizer, I. R., Park, L., Rappley, M. D., & Friderici, K. (2006). The adrenergic receptor α-2A gene (ADRA2A) and neuropsychological executive functions as putative endophenotypes for childhood ADHD. *Cognitive, Affective, & Behavioral Neuroscience, 6,* 18–30.

Walsh, A., & Wu, H.-H. (2008). Differentiating antisocial personality disorder, psychopathy and sociopathy: Evolutionary, genetic, neurological and sociological considerations. *Criminal Justice Studies, 21,* 135–152.

Wilson, J. Q., & Herrnstein, R. J. (1985). *Crime and human nature.* New York: Simon and Schuster.

Zuckerman, B., & Bresnahan, K. (1991). Developmental and behavioral consequences of prenatal drug and alcohol exposure. *Pediatric Clinics of North America, 38*(6), 1387–1406.

Social Structure and Strain Theories

© Sascha Burkard/Shutterstock.com

"Mama's favorite question was, "Boy, why you so bad?" I tried many times to explain to Mama that I wasn't "so bad." I tried to make her understand that it was trying to be good that generally got me into trouble. I remember telling her that I played hookey to avoid getting into trouble in school . . . When I stole things, it was only to save the family money and avoid arguments or scoldings whenever I asked for money."

—Claude Brown. 1965. Manchild in a Promised Land, p. 13. New York: Touchstone.

The past two chapters have presented theories of delinquency and crime that focus on the individual. Choice theories emphasize the individual's free will and choice to commit a crime, and biological and psychological theories focus more on the individual's internal make-up and factors that "make" someone be delinquent. In this chapter you will discover the roots of social theories of crime that begin to look outside the individual and to factors of society that might influence crime and deviance. Specifically, this chapter is dedicated to social structure theories of crime that are divided into two categories: 1) Social Ecological Theory and 2) Strain Theories.

CHAPTER GOALS

By the end of this chapter you will be able to:

1. Describe the changes in America that led to the beginning of the sociological tradition of the study of crime and deviance.
2. Explain the three primary factors of urban neighborhoods that were associated with the original Social Disorganization Theory.
3. Discuss the major changes that have occurred in the social disorganization perspective over time.
4. Contrast the roots of Strain Theory to that of Social Disorganization Theory as they relate to the role of society.
5. Give examples of strain at both the societal level and the individual level.
6. Define and discuss the idea of a subculture and how this developed into various theories of criminality.

The Chicago School

In Chapter 2 you learned about the origins of the first juvenile court which was established in Cook County, Illinois (e.g., Chicago, Illinois) in 1899. What was not presented in Chapter 2 were some of the other key social changes going on in Chicago during this time and the early 1900s. For example, when the City was first established in 1833 its population was slightly over 4,000 people. Around the turn of the century when the court was established Chicago was a city of about 1 million people, and by 1910 it had doubled to over 2 million people (Palin, 1981). As the city grew so rapidly, so did the social ills of poverty and crime. But why did the city grow so fast? And what were the problems that ensued?

One primary reason for the city's growth was the major change in the American economy from primarily agricultural to industrial. Large numbers of people flocked to the cities in search of work in the new factories. However, the work they found was perhaps not what they expected. Long hours, 7-day workweeks, poor working conditions, and low pay greeted most of those flocking to the cities in search of the American dream (Palin, 1981, p. 64).

As hard as it was for the rural resident to assimilate to the city, conditions were worse for the rash of immigrants coming to America to escape oppression and famine in their home countries and the large number of migrant African-Americans fleeing the segregation and oppression of the southern states to seek a new life in northern cities. This population faced literacy and language barriers as many of the immigrants did not speak English and the African-Americans had, for the most part, been denied an education based on oppressive Jim Crow laws in the southern states enacted after the Civil War. But still the immigrants came in flocks, and African-Americans from the South flooded northern cities such as New York, Philadelphia and Chicago in hopes of finding a better life. Indeed the excerpt given in the introduction of this chapter is from an autobiography written by a young African-American male whose parents were among this wave of relocating to the North in hopes of the "Promised Land" where there was endless opportunity and African-Americans would be treated as equals.

However, coming on the heels of Social Darwinism and the early biological theories of crime studied in Chapter 5, many blamed some inferiority in the biology or evolution of different races/ethnicities of people for crime in the city. Not everyone accepted these views. The Progressives (remember, the same group responsible for the development of the juvenile court in Chicago) represent one essential force who believed otherwise. They believed it was not the people but the environment that met them in the city that led to crime.

This same perspective was to be taken by sociologists studying and researching at the University of Chicago as they studied the growth of the city itself, the patterns of immigration and migration to the city, and the development of rapid crime in some city neighborhoods. Because most of the research was done through researchers affiliated with the University of Chicago, this tradition of looking at the environment rather than the individual to explain crime has been coined "The Chicago School."

The first name associated with this "School" is Robert Park. Park (1928) was in fact not originally a scholar but rather a newspaper reporter. During his 25 years as a reporter, he spent much of his time investigating and documenting the growth of Chicago and its problems. In doing so, he related the growth of the city to terms and ideas he borrowed from plant ecology. This might seem strange to you at first, but remember America was changing from an agricultural society to an urban industrial society, so this point of reference made sense.

How do plant "communities" grow? The first concept that Park borrowed from the study of plant ecology was that plants grow in "communities." That is, plants in a given habitat tend to have much in common and are able to live better together than alone. This process, referred to as **symbiosis**, means that the species provide mutual benefits to each other; thus they live together as a larger ecosystem or "superorganism." Park related this to the growth of the city, as certain groups of people tended to live together. Particularly, immigrants coming from other countries would tend to clump together as they sought to be around something familiar. Thus, natural pockets of the city such as Little Italy or Chinatown emerged. In fact, if you are from or have traveled to the nation's large cities you might be well aware that such areas still exist. The second important notion brought forth from plant ecology by Park was the idea of how these areas change. Through processes of **invasion**, **domination** and **succession**, new plant communities can form. For example, **invasion** is the process by which a new species of plant begins to grow in an area previously occupied by a different plant. **Domination** occurs when this new species or plant overtakes the area, making it no longer a friendly habitat for the original plant. **Succession** occurs when the area stabilizes with a new balance of plants.

Symbiosis
a relationship between two organisms living in close proximity to each other (be it plants or people) that provides mutual benefits

Invasion
process by which a new "species" comes into an area

Domination
when the new species overtakes the area

Succession
when the area stabilizes with a new balance

These shifts in the city of Chicago involved new groups of immigrants coming into areas once occupied by an earlier group as well as the growth of business and industry into areas that used to be residential. This latter point was further developed by a colleague of Park's at the University of Chicago, Ernest Burgess (1925, 1967). Burgess's key contribution was the recognition that cities grew mainly from the inside out. That is, he noted that cities grow in patterns of concentric circles out from the central business district. The center circle, referred to as **Zone I**, is the central business district or heart of the city. Surrounding this is **Zone II**, or the **zone of transition**, that separates business from more residential housing. **Zone III** is then the first zone of stable working men's homes followed by **Zone IV**, a more affluent residential area, and finally **Zone V**, which is the outer edges surrounding the city that are still somewhat rural—referred to by Burgess as the Commuter Zone.

Zone of Transition
Zone II which separates business from more residential housing

Because of this pattern of growth, what was once Zone II will eventually become Zone I, what was once Zone III will then become Zone II and so on. Of particular interest for the study of crime was Burgess's notion that Zone II would be an area of dilapidated homes that would be allowed to deteriorate further in anticipation of the area being invaded by business. As such, only the poorest people unable to afford to live anywhere else would occupy this area. As is the case with

American history, the poorest people are often the most recent immigrants who have yet to establish a foothold in American society.

According to this model, the low rent apartments and dilapidated buildings of this area provided housing to the waves of immigrants coming to the city who could not afford decent housing. In the book "Manchild in the Promised Land" from which your opening quote comes, the author also describes coming home to his apartment after being sent away for while. In this description he notes:

"The hallway looked smaller, but it was still the same, the way it was supposed to be looking on Sunday morning. Somebody had gotten cut the night before, and blood was still in the hall. And somebody had pissed on the stairs, and it was still there, just like it should have been. . . . On the landing just before ours, somebody had vomited." (page, 43). Is this indeed the American dream or the Promised Land? Is this the apartment to which you would long to come home? Or is it an area any one of us would want to leave behind in search of something better?

The concentrated poverty and poor living conditions in the area were hypothesized to contribute to crime. If this is true, then if one were to plot crime in the city, it would not be occurring all over the city, but it would be highly concentrated in this area. This idea would be put to the test by two fellow researchers at the University of Chicago, Clifford Shaw and Henry McKay.

Do you remember again that Chicago was home to the first juvenile court? It just so happens that with this, Chicago also kept data on all juvenile arrests and school truancy. Shaw and McKay took painstaking efforts to plot each of these arrests on a map of the city for decades of data. In doing so they found support for Burgess's

FIGURE 6.1 Provides an example of how these zones would have looked coming off of Lake Michigan in Chicago.

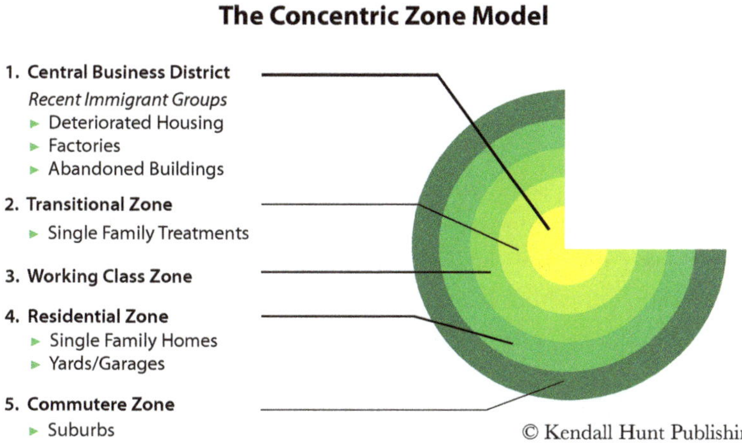

hypothesis that the greatest concentration of crime happened in **Zone II**, the proposed zone of transition, and that crime steadily and rapidly decreased as you moved outward through the proposed zones (Shaw, 1929; Shaw & McKay, 1941).

Perhaps the most important contribution of this theory at the time was that Shaw and McKay's research revealed that high crime was always located in this area immediately surrounding the central business district regardless of the race or ethnicity of the population. For example, at the beginning of the time period they were studying, Zone II was mainly populated with German and Irish immigrants, while later it was Polish and Italian immigrants (Remmie, 1978).

Poverty

defined as living with an income below that needed to survive in a society. Today that figure is $30,750 in America for a family of four

But Shaw and McKay did not stop with testing this hypothesis; instead they took the important step of developing these early ideas into the Social Disorganization Theory of Crime, which would attempt to explain exactly "why" crime was concentrated in these areas. According to this theory there are three primary characteristics of this area that make it a hotbed for criminal activity.

Residential Mobility

refers to people moving in and out of an area quickly. The longer someone stays the more ties and commitments are made to the neighborhood

Racial Heterogeneity

refers to how many different races/ethnicities and types of people live in an area. The more people are alike the more they share common values. The more they are different, the greater the potential for their values to conflict

1. **Poverty**: People with low incomes are forced to live in these low rent and run-down properties. This brings a lot of poverty-stricken people into a small physical area. These people do not for the most part even have the basic necessities needed for survival; thus the temptation to earn money illegally or steal goods would be greater among this population.
2. **Residential Mobility**: This is obviously not a desirable area to live in and these people are living here out of necessity—not choice. Thus, as soon as they gain a financial foothold and can move out of this area, they will. Thus people are constantly coming and going from this area. This prevents people from getting to know each other and from developing any sense of community.
3. **Racial Heterogeneity**: As new immigrant groups flock to the city, this area becomes populated with a variety of people from different cultures who even may speak different languages. Similar to issues with residential mobility, this leads to people not developing a sense of community nor knowing their neighbors. In addition, it may often even lead to distrust of others in the community as cultural differences cause conflict.

In addition to this large-scale research on Chicago cities, Shaw in particular became interested in a more microscopic look at what made a delinquent "tick," so to say. He began studying the individual life histories of delinquents through interviews and following these youths over time. These ethnographies turned into classic books such as *The Jack-Roller* (1930) and *Brothers in Crime* (1938). From these studies, Shaw made the following key observations that are directly related to the remaining theories of delinquency you will be learning about in this text:

1. Delinquents are not different than non-delinquents "with respect to intelligence, physical condition or personality traits." Thus, he directly rebutted accounts of criminality proposed by early biological and psychological theories.
2. In the areas that had high rates of delinquency "the conventional traditions... through which neighborhoods usually affect control over the behavior of children, were largely disintegrated." In this way Shaw was the first to highlight the importance of family and schools and other social institutions in the life of children and the development of juvenile delinquency.
3. The neighborhoods with high delinquency rates also provided ample opportunities for crime. This notion set forth the importance of community as well as family and schools not only for preventing delinquency, but perhaps, in some ways encouraging delinquency through providing opportunities for crime.
4. Delinquent activities often started very early in life, resulting from early childhood play groups collecting on the streets of the city. In this way Shaw also highlighted the role of peers in the emergence of delinquency, another notion that is incorporated into many later theories of delinquency—most notably Differential Association Theory that is discussed in detail in the next chapter.
5. In the high delinquency areas a type of culture of delinquency emerged that was handed down from older youth to younger youth thus creating a type of subculture of crime. Shaw and McKay referred to this as **cultural transmission** of values and it is incorporated into many of the subcultural theories of crime you will be learning about later in this chapter.
6. If someone remained delinquent for a long period of time, he/she eventually incorporated the idea of being a criminal or delinquent into his/her identity. This came through both long-term associations with other criminals and experiences with the juvenile and criminal justice systems. These notions are explored further in Chapter 7 that discusses social reaction to deviance and the impact of labeling and stigma on a youth.

Cultural Transmission
the process through which a culture of delinquency is handed down from older youth to younger youth creating a subculture of crime

Thus, although the Social Disorganization Theory itself did not receive a lot of scholarly attention after the 1940s, almost all of its key observations and notions were built into more individualistic theories of crime that dominated the field of criminology from the 1950s through the 1980s. Then, in the 1980s and 1990s, several scholars began to revisit the original theory and extend it to more modern-day applications.

SAMPSON'S THEORY OF COLLECTIVE EFFICACY

Perhaps the scholar who did the most to revitalize the original work of Shaw and McKay was Robert Sampson. Sampson was inspired by the notion that social disorganization was indeed the other side of social control. To Sampson social disorganization is merely the end result of broken social controls; thus the focus should be on how these social controls work to prevent delinquency. While many scholars at the time were examining control at the individual level (Briar & Piliavin, 1965; Hirschi, 1969; Toby, 1957), Sampson, like Shaw and McKay, was more interested in how this worked at the **macro-level**, or community level. He was particularly interested in how forms of **informal social control**, such as those exerted by families, schools and community members, could shape the extent and nature of delinquency in a community. In particular he extended the ideas of **Systemic Theory** (Kornhauser, 1978; Bursik & Grasmick, 1993) that viewed neighborhoods as an interrelated group of **social networks**. In this model such things as poverty and residential mobility still matter, but the focus is not as much on these macro-level factors as how they break down the relationships between people that are important for exhibiting social control. So in addition to those three factors considered by Shaw and McKay, Sampson's tests of the systemic model of social control included variables such as local friendship networks, the community's ability to control local teenage groups and participation in community organizations (Sampson & Groves, 1989).

Informal Social Control
controls exerted by families, schools and community members rather than the formal justice system

Systemic Theory
viewed neighborhoods as an interrelated group of social networks

Social Networks
a person's network of relationships. That is, the other people with whom one interacts on a regular basis

Perhaps most famously, Sampson then went on to create his own theory of **collective efficacy** (Sampson, Raudenbush & Earls, 1997), defining this term to be the ability of members of a community to come together to achieve a common goal. In this particular case, the main goal of the community is to socialize its children properly and to prevent delinquency and disorder. For example, think about the typical high delinquency neighborhood described by Shaw and McKay, with high levels of residential mobility and racial heterogeneity; the members of the community do not have the ability to form strong connections between each other. Also, stressed by individual and collective poverty, they do not have the resources to draw on outside institutions or strengthen community institutions to help them raise their children. Thus, collective efficacy in these communities is low. Thus, collective efficacy describes the process through which variables such as poverty and residential mobility lead to social disorder and crime.

Collective Efficacy
ability of members of a community to come together to achieve a common goal

Similar to Shaw and McKay, Sampson also put his theory to the test using empirical data. Sampson and his colleagues (Sampson et al., 1997) interviewed 8,762 people living across 343 Chicago neighborhoods. Controlling for person-level characteristics of the individuals interviewed, this research found that collective efficacy was a strong and robust predictor of differing levels of violence across these neighborhoods. More specifically, as the level of collective efficacy went down, the level of violence went up. (For more detail on this research see the Spotlight on Research below.)

FOCUS ON RESEARCH: Robert Sampson and Project on Human Development in Chicago Neighborhoods

In 2012, Robert Sampson launched the Project on Human Development in Chicago Neighborhoods (PHDCN) as an interdisciplinary study of how families, schools and neighborhoods all combine to impact child and adolescent development. The project, influenced by Sampson's theory of collective efficacy and the long-standing Social Disorganization Theory of Shaw and McKay, collects detailed information on Chicago's various urban neighborhoods, including not only the people who reside there but the community institutions and resources. Information collected on the neighborhoods included the social, economic, organizational, political and cultural structures of the neighborhoods and any changes in these over the time period of the study.

However, departing from the primarily macro-level nature of past tests of these theories, this project also seeks to advance individual-level understanding of the developmental pathways into juvenile delinquency, adult crime, substance abuse and violence. This second component then followed over 6,000 randomly selected children, adolescents and young adults to examine the changing circumstances of their lives and the personal characteristics that might lead them toward or away from a variety of antisocial behaviors.

The results of this study have led to many new insights into the mechanisms by which societies, particularly our local communities, impact the socialization of youth. Sampson's book, *The Great American City: Chicago and the Enduring Neighborhood Effect*, shows how the community within which we live can influence everything from daily acts of altruism, to teenage births and delinquency rates, to our navigation of larger social events. Perhaps most influential, the book also shows how the patterns that emerge in inner-city neighborhoods actually work to reproduce the very inequalities that lead to the original social disadvantage.

From *The Great American City: Chicago and the Enduring Neighborhood Effect* by Robert J. Sampson. Reprinted by permission of University of Chicago Press.

Concentrated Poverty: From Social Disorganization to Social Isolation

Remember that American cities were growing at astonishing rates at the time of the original writing of Shaw and McKay, as was the industry and inner-city businesses sector of the American economy. While Shaw and McKay's theory centered on three aspects: racial heterogeneity, residential mobility and poverty, perhaps only one of these remains at the heart of inner-city problems today: Poverty. The chances for upward mobility and for people to gain a foothold in a growing American economy simply did not keep pace with immigration, reproduction and demand for these jobs. Thus, a segment of our society has to some extent become left behind in these inner-city neighborhoods. James Julius Wilson has conducted some of the most extensive research on this notion of concentrated poverty and suggests that the mere grouping together of people without individual resources leads to even greater problems. Imagine, if your family is poor, but you live in a neighborhood where most of the families are not. In this case, income and tax revenue from the other families who are not in poverty can help to ensure good schools, recreational leagues and other community resources. Community members who have more can donate and help out those who have less. But what happens when all your neighbors are as poor as you, or have even less? According to Wilson (1987), this **concentrated poverty** causes problems all of its own as it decreases quality of schooling, access to positive role models for youth and access to jobs and even marriage partners. According to research by Sampson and Wilson (1990), this is the plight of many African-American families today who have been left behind by the development of the American economy and left most vulnerable to social ills. Transformation of the inner city in recent decades has resulted in increased concentration of the most disadvantaged segments of our society—primarily poor, female-headed, black families. Thus many of the regional and demographic patterns of crime discussed in Chapter 3 can be related not to where crime-prone individuals live, but what happens to individuals living in crime-prone neighborhoods.

Concentrated Poverty

when all of your neighbors are as poor as you or have even less. It causes decreases in quality schooling, access to positive role models for youth and access to jobs and even marriage partners

Policy Applications for Juvenile Delinquency

Finally, in addition to contributing to a new perspective on crime, and providing the foundations for many additional theories of delinquency, Shaw and McKay took their theory one step further and developed a program, "The Chicago Area

Project," designed to reduce deviance in these troubled neighborhoods. The project originally started in 1932 in three Chicago neighborhoods and eventually grew to over a dozen communities by the 1950s (Kobrin, 1959). The approach was three pronged: 1) first, have local community residents take pride in their community by helping them improve its appearance, 2) second, create recreational and other opportunities for youth to be involved in pro-social activities and 3) and finally, when a youth did get in trouble, intervene on his/her behalf with the school or justice system trying to keep them from further trouble. In its over 60 years of existence the project has brought both much criticism and praise. Some have criticized the program for not addressing the structural factors in our economy that perpetuate continued inequality (Snodgrass, 1976) while others herald the program as consistently reducing levels of juvenile delinquency and helping communities to self-organize (Schlossman, Hellman & Shavelson, 1984)

FOCUS ON POLICY: Broken Windows

In 1982, James Q. Wilson and George Kelling proposed a slightly different model of why disorganization in a community might matter. While Shaw and McKay were focused on the socialization of youth, or lack thereof, in these disorganized neighborhoods, Wilson and Kelling proposed that the disorganization provided opportunity for crime. Their basic example was that if a house had a broken window and the owner immediately fixed it, this was a sign that the owner was present and cared about the property. However, if the broken window remained, this sent a message that it was ok to vandalize the property as the owner did not care about the building. To Wilson and Kelling these "broken windows" were outward signs of social disorganization and could include many things such as gatherings of rowdy teens, graffiti, panhandlers and drunks just as some examples. When these signs of "incivility" are allowed to prosper in an area, decent citizens will be fearful of these areas and avoid them by either staying in their own homes or even moving out of the neighborhood. This slightly different perspective on disorganized neighborhoods has a very different policy focus: policing of these areas. Because the citizens could not do this themselves it would be the responsibility of the police to rid these areas of drunks, panhandlers, rowdy teens and the like. Studies of "Broken Windows" policing efforts have found primarily favorable results. An evaluation of New York City Police Departments, efforts to follow this model and aggressively police even minor forms of disorder found that this model led to a decrease in crime and violence overall (Kelly & Coles, 1996). Others suggest, however, that the interplay between crime and disorder is more complicated and may even work in the reverse order in which the crime and violence lead to the disorder (Harcourt, 2001).

Cultural Transmission and (Sub)Cultural Theories of Crime

Remember the notion of cultural transmission proposed by Shaw and McKay? This idea was that as delinquency remained concentrated in these areas over time, the older youths in the area would transfer their delinquent ideas and values to younger or new youth entering the community. Thus, instead of the youth being socialized by traditional law-abiding adults in the community or through strong social institutions such as the church or the school, they are be socialized on the streets! This notion has been studied and documented by many scholars and has resulted in the development of several cultural theories of crime. These theories, while not positing that there is something biologically different or wrong with delinquents, do posit that delinquents are different than other people because they have learned different goals, norms or values. These theories are central to the study of one of the key concerns in juvenile delinquency today: street gangs. One of the earliest theorists, who like Shaw was interested in the young male play group, was **Walter Miller**.

Miller's Focal Concerns Theory

Walter Miller (1958) was an anthropologist who argued that lower socioeconomic class communities had a long-standing culture all of their own. Much of this he argued was due to family disruption in which many young males were growing up in homes without a father figure or male role model. Thus, they looked to their peers on the street to figure out exactly what it meant to "be a man" so to speak. He argued that their values emphasized six key "focal concerns."

Trouble
being able to cause trouble without getting caught, or into trouble

Trouble: While many lower-class youth resort to criminal activity such as stealing to get things they cannot afford, they also value staying out of formal trouble with the law. Thus, the more acts you can commit without getting into "trouble" the better your credentials!

Toughness
ability to physically dominate other males

Toughness: Survival of the fittest may be the best way to render this concern. The male who is the strongest, and the best fighter and gets the most girls wins! He relates this concern back to the fact that these young males are being raised in mainly matriarchal households without a male role model; thus they value being as "masculine" as possible.

Smartness: While formal schooling is not important to this population, the capacity to outfox, outwit or con others is a necessity of street life. Also, you must be able to avoid having these things done to you as well.

Excitement: The search for excitement is a central focus of lower-class life according to Miller. With little money and little opportunity in their neighborhoods, the youth may fight, gamble or have sex simply for the excitement of doing something they know they are not supposed to be doing.

Excitement
risky activities that break up the monotony of everyday life

Fate: There is a belief that life and its circumstances is to a large extent beyond their control. It is a result of fate or luck and perhaps good luck can come and change their plight. This is evidenced by obsessions with gambling and playing "the numbers" among inner-city populations.

Fate
a belief that life and its circumstances are largely beyond our control

Autonomy*:* On the other hand, because they feel much is out of their control and/or they are being controlled by others with higher status for much of their life, the need to achieve autonomy is still important. According to Miller this means that not succumbing to the authority of police, teachers or even parents becomes important to lower-class male youth.

Autonomy
not succumbing to authority, particularly authority by of police, teachers or even parents

Combined, these "focal concerns" become the goals or norms that are handed down through the process of cultural transmission. As the text progresses you will be exposed to several other subcultural theories of crime that tie the ideas of Shaw and McKay to the ideas of later theorists. Each subcultural theory will be presented as it relates both to this original work, and to the work of later theorists that expanded notions of how such subcultures might emerge.

Strain Theories

The second set of theories that focus on society or the individual as he/she is situated in society are called **strain theories**. Rather than being centered on the growth of cities, however, these theories are more deeply rooted in the concept of American capitalism. The American dream of capitalism tells us that everyone can succeed and be anything they want if they just work hard enough. Going back to the opening of this text, do you remember since a young age people asking you what you want to be when you grow up (such as President, a Princess or Batman)? Or perhaps people telling you that you can be anything you want to be if you just work hard? While strain theorists do not argue that America promises

Strain Theories
focus on society or the individual as they are situated in society. It is deeply rooted in the concept of American capitalism with some at a disadvantage

us these goals, they proclaim that the deck is stacked. That is, not everyone is dealt the same opportunity to achieve these goals. Some have to work harder than others to succeed, and some are placed in positions that, no matter how hard they work, will never achieve these goals. This is the basis of Strain theories.

The origins of Strain Theory can be traced to Philadelphia sociologist Robert Merton. In 1939 Merton wrote the now classic article "Social Structure and Anomie" that drew off the philosophies of French sociologist Emile Durkheim. While we will not delve deeply into the theories of Durkheim here, it is important to note that the origins of Merton's writings borrowed from Durkheim the notion of anomie which was defined as a state of normlessness. This could happen to a society at times of great change—either economic downturns or upward mobility—when society failed to communicate to an individual the limits on what was to be defined as success.

Legitimate Means
approved avenues for achieving success such as education and employment

In American society Merton altered this idea slightly to be defined not as true normlessness, in which there is no definition of success, but rather as a disjunction between what society sets as the "norm" or success goal and the **legitimate means** society provides for an individual to achieve this goal. That is, in America we are taught that you can become anything you want as long as you work hard. But, our capitalist economy provides some individuals with more "means" to achieve this goal than others. For example, think about your own college search. Were there schools that were simply financially out of reach for your family? How could you attend college without money or access to loans? Do you know any of your friends who could not attend the college of their choice, or maybe not attend college at all? For Merton, this situation was very real as he was able to attend college and move up in life, while many of his childhood friends did not have the means to do so.

What happens when you are told you should be doing something, achieving something, and then are denied the opportunity to do so? According to Merton you feel a great deal of frustration and/or strain, which makes you feel separated from the norms of society—or his version of anomie. Since this is obviously not a desired state of mind, you then must find some way to adapt to this situation so that you do not remain in a constant state of strain. Merton offered five modes of adaptation that are summarized in Figure 6.2.

FIGURE 6.2 Merton's Five Modes of Adaptation to Strain

	Goals	Means
Conformism	+	+
Innovation	+	-
Retreatism	-	-
Ritualism	-	+
Rebellion	+/-	+/-

Conformist
conforms to both society's goals and their means for achieving them

Innovator
has the goals instilled but not the legitimate means to achieve them so they must make, or innovte, up their own means

Retreatist
separated from society no longer holding goals of success. They may suffer mental illness or turn to drugs or alcohol to ease their strain

Rebellion
can be criminal or related to progress of a society as some goals and things should be changed

The **conformist** is perhaps the lucky individual who holds society's goals of success and has the means to achieve them. The **innovator** on the other hand has the goals instilled but not the legitimate means to achieve them. Thus, he or she must make up his/her own means. According to Merton, youths who find themselves in this situation may resort to stealing or selling drugs or other illegal items to gain monetary success. The **retreatist** on the other hand has kind of given up. He or she is totally separated from society—no longer holding goals of success. These individuals, according to Merton, may suffer mental illness and/or turn to alcohol and drug abuse to ease their strain. The **ritualist** is in kind of the funny situation of not really buying into the success goals society has set, but since he/she has the means to achieve them kind of goes along anyway. This mode of adaptation releases stress because the individual no longer stresses the success goal for him/herself but rather gains self-worth by going through the motions and plugging away at the societally accepted means. Finally the **rebel** denies the goals of society and attempts to change them, or at least sets alternative means for achieving them. **Rebellion** can be criminal or it can be related to progress of a society as perhaps some of the goals and means are things that should be changed. For example, Martin Luther King, Jr. can be thought of as a rebel as he rejected the given social structure of America that blocked opportunities for success to African-Americans. In his time, he was labeled a criminal by many and in fact went to jail over 20 times for his efforts to change society. In the end, he became a hero of the Civil Rights Movement; but in his time, he was viewed differently by many. Not all rebels, however, have such a noble cause in mind. Many, are just frustrated and angry with society and rebel in criminal and violent ways and/or even form criminal subcultures such as gangs. Two specific sets of theories have used Merton's Strain Theory as the starting block for the examination of these types of criminal subcultures and the formation of youth gangs.

Albert Cohen's Delinquent Boys

In 1955, Albert Cohen's book *Delinquent Boys: The Culture of the Gang* shone the spotlight for the first time on the role of greater societal structure in producing gangs. According to Cohen, lower-class boys were constantly judged on an unfair standard: A standard he called the "**middle-class measuring rod**." Focusing on young boys, Cohen's work shows how young males are expected to behave and achieve in school according to middle-class standards. According to Cohen these standards include such things as ambition, achievement, rationality, courtesy, likeability, low physical aggression and mild temperament. When they do not meet these expectations set by their middle-class teachers, they experience strain, which he deems "**status frustration**." Here, the goal is different than Merton's emphasis on monetary success; it is approval of others such as teachers and peers. Unable to achieve status according to these middle-class standards, the boys form their own definition of "status" and acceptance by their fellow lower-class peers that often "spits in the face" of middle-class standards. To most these actions seem purely malicious and irrational, but to the delinquent the alternative standard of behavior serves its own purpose of receiving the approval and acceptance of fellow peers. Cohen called this seemingly irrational, malicious hostility toward the middle class "**reaction formation**." The subculture of the gang then stresses short-term pleasures and does not seek long-term success in American society. Rather, success is often judged by harm done to the middle class or anyone seen as disrespecting the youth's rightful status.

Middle-Class Measuring Rod
the middle class standard to which all students are typically held in American schools

Status Frustration
the feelings of frustration that occur when one is not able to meet these middle class definitions of success

Reaction Formation
alternative behaviors that emerge to deal with the inability to achieve traditional measures of success

Opportunity Theory

Richard A. Cloward and Lloyd E. Ohlin bring together ideas of both Merton and Cohen. From Merton, they accept the fact that society sets goals for us and then does not distribute the means to achieve these goals equally. From Cohen, they adopt the idea that delinquent cultures can form. Their primary new contribution was the idea that even "illegitimate" means to achieve goals are not distributed equally. That is, one can have both legitimate and illegitimate opportunities blocked. According to Cloward and Ohlin, it is this illegitimate opportunity structure that influences the formation of a delinquent subculture and the nature of youth gangs.

Criminal Subculture
A culture that values criminal means to achieving goals rather than the traditional legal means in a society

Criminal Subculture. This is the subculture that develops when there are illegitimate means available to reach society's monetary goals. For example, drug dealing, fencing stolen items and/or motor vehicle theft rings emerge to help youth reach these goals. Younger youth learn to admire the wealth and success of older criminals and thus adopt their ways and beliefs about the appropriate means to achieve these goals. Why work hard at a minimum wage job when you can earn much more selling drugs?

Conflict Subculture. This particular subculture is most in line with Cohen's version of the gang in which the youths simply rebel against everything middle class. According to Cloward and Ohlin, this type of subculture emerges when illegitimate opportunities to achieve success (defined as monetary wealth) are blocked. Thus the youth form their own definitions of success that often center on violence and defending the territory of the gang and one's own status within the gang.

Conflict Subculture
youths rebel against everything middle class and form their own definitions of success that often center on violence and defending their territory

Retreatist Subculture. This subculture may also emerge when illegitimate opportunities are blocked. But, instead of reacting with violence as in the conflict subculture, these youths retreat in the typical fashion described by Merton: drugs and alcohol. These youth spend most of their time hanging out together and just getting high. The high, in a real sense, becomes the goal.

Retreatist Subculture
a type of subculture that develops when both legitimate and illegitimate means are blocked. This subculture revolves around escaping society, perhaps through drugs and alcohol, rather than trying to achieve within it

General Strain Theory

A final version of Strain Theory that is important for the study of juvenile delinquency is Robert Agnew's General Strain Theory. Like Cohen, he is focusing more on the types of strain faced by adolescents. Unlike Cohen, however, he maintains the individualized focus of Merton rather than trying to explain group delinquency. According to Agnew's book *Pressured into Crime* there are three main sources of strain that exert pressure on youth to commit crime:

Failure to Achieve Positively Valued Goals. This notion includes the traditional strain that Merton describes when one cannot meet or achieve **goals** that he or she has been taught to value because one simply does not have the means to do so (i.e., disjunction between aspiration and expectation). In addition, Agnew addresses strain that may occur if you actually expect to achieve something but do not (a disjunction between expectation and actual achievement) and a disjunction between what one might perceive as a fair outcome and the outcome experienced, which is produced when one cannot achieve that which is expected of one. For example, imagine there is a test coming up in chemistry. You aspire to achieve an A but you do not really expect to because the class has a lot of math in it for which you were not prepared. Your friends all have math or chemistry tutors, but your family could not afford one. You perform significantly below the level of your friends on the exam. You would feel strain because you did not have the means provided to them to achieve the same level of success. This is the traditional "strain." In Agnew's model you could also feel strain if you felt you were doing very well in chemistry, and studied hard for the exam. You truly expected to earn an A on the exam but found it more difficult than you expected and only earned a C. This would be the second form of strain—a disjunction between your actual achievement and what you had expected to achieve. Finally, envision the scenario that the chemistry teacher handed out a review sheet and you studied it very hard and knew absolutely everything on that sheet. But, when you took the exam, it seemed to have nothing to do with the review sheet and you received a C. In this instance you might feel it was very unfair of the teacher to put questions on the exam that were not related to the review sheet. This is an example of the third kind of strain—the disjunction between a just outcome and the outcome you received.

Removal of Positively Valued Stimuli

a strain occurs when something that is valued is taken away

Removal of Positively Valued Stimuli. Another totally different kind of strain that Agnew introduced was that which occurs when something we value is removed from our lives. For an adult it might be a job or a spouse. For an adolescent it could be loss of friends due to changing schools, loss of a parent through death or divorce, or even loss of a loved pet. These life events are stressful.

Introduction of Negative Stimuli

strain happens when a negative new factor is introduced

Introduction of Negative Stimuli. This is again a new source of strain not discussed in other versions of strain theory. It involves what happens when a negative new factor comes into our life. Perhaps your favorite chemistry teacher left midyear and the new teacher does not respond well to you. Or, in the case your parents divorced (loss of positive stimuli) and your mother remarries a person whom you do not like and who does not, at least in your mind, treat you right. This would be the introduction of negative stimuli.

Agnew does not argue that any one of these things or even that one of each of these things alone is the "formula" for delinquency. Rather, he is noting that there are many different types of strain that adolescents experience, and that if they experience too much strain it will have negative outcomes. In specific, he argues that the process through which strain leads to delinquency is when too much strain leads someone to live in a constant negative emotional state. Such states can include the state of anger, fear, depression or even hopelessness.

Tests of General Strain Theory have shown a direct link between various measures of strain and delinquency (Agnew & White, 1992; Paternoster & Mazerolle, 1994; Hoffman & Miller, 1998; Hoffman & Cerbone, 1999; Mazerolle et al., 2000; Piquero & Sealock, 2000). However, Agnew notes that even under excess strain not everyone "copes" through delinquency. Thus elaborations of his theory have looked at what might determine a delinquent or non-delinquent response to strain. It is here that this theory, like many others, becomes intertwined with many other theories of crime. For example, things that might determine a delinquent adaptation include lack of social bonds, lack of social control, opportunity for crime, low self-control and prior learning of criminal attitudes. All of which are concepts to which you have already been introduced or you will read about at length in the following chapter.

In summary then, Agnew's theory's main contribution is the elaboration on the types of strain that an adolescent might face and how they may lead to negative emotive states. The exact process, however, that leads one person to adapt in a delinquent way and another to adapt in a non-delinquent way is not defined, much like Merton's theory.

POLICY APPLICATIONS FOR JUVENILE JUSTICE

Perhaps the most straightforward application of any of the versions of strain theories described would be to expand equal opportunities for all. However, this is much easier said than done. Perhaps most noted were the efforts of Cloward and Ohlin in the Mobilization for Youth (MFY) program. Indeed Cloward was chosen to be the director of research for the MFY. This program drew heavily on Merton's version of Strain Theory by setting up programs to help youth gain education and employment. MFY also tapped into the social disorganization perspective, building stronger community organizations. Moreover, this strategy evolved to go beyond working with the youth, by trying to change the very opportunity structure of American society through lawsuits against slumlords, boycotts of schools and efforts to increase voter registration, and by such, the political voice of this population. However, it was this latter part of the program that led to its downfall. It was criticized by many for these efforts to the extent that the program and its leaders were even accused of being communist (Liska, 1981, p. 52). Thus, attempts to reduce delinquency through changing society were primarily abandoned, many leaders of the program, including Cloward, resigned, and efforts were again refocused on "reforming" delinquent youth instead of the neighborhoods and opportunity structures from which they came.

Current programs you might know of that stem from this perspective and the goal of expanding opportunities are the Head Start pre-K program that strives to help disadvantaged youth be ready for traditional school and the Job Corps program which strives to teach youth job readiness skills and place them in meaningful employment upon the completion of an education.

The following summary box (Figure 6.3) presents some of the key ideas of each theory:

FIGURE 6.3 Theory Summary Box			
Theory	**Key Concepts**	**Cause of Crime**	**System Application**
Social Disorganization	Poverty Residential Mobility Racial Heterogeneity	Breakdown in Social Institutions and Community Relations	Improve Social Institutions
Collective Efficacy	Collective Efficacy Social Capital	Inability of Community to Socialize Youth	Improve Social Networks and Trust
Anomie	Disjuncture between Goals and Legitimate Means	Adaptation to Strain	Increase Access to Legitimate Means
General Strain	Negative Stimuli Removal of Positive Stimuli	Excessive Strain Negative Affective States	Reduce Stressors Intervene with Troubled Youth

Key Words

Autonomy
Criminal Subculture
Collective Efficacy
Concentrated Poverty
Conflict Subculture
Conformist
Cultural Transmission
Domination
Excitement
Fate
Informal Social Control
Innovator
Introduction of Negative Stimuli
Invasion
Legitimate Means
Middle-Class Measuring Rod
Poverty
Racial Heterogeneity
Reaction Formation
Rebellion
Removal of Positively Valued Stimuli
Residential Mobility
Retreatist
Retreatist Subculture
Social Networks
Status Frustration
Strain Theories
Succession
Symbiosis
Systemic Theory
Toughness
Trouble
Zone of Transition

Chapter Summary

In this chapter you were introduced to two primary ways in which society may contribute to its own problem of delinquency. The first, the human ecological tradition and theories of social disorganization, focused on society as it is organized in cities, and in neighborhoods within these cities. The second, strain theories, focused on the greater structure of society and its role in both setting goals for members of society and unequally providing means to achieve these goals.

The human ecological tradition, as set forth as "the Chicago School," has had a lasting impact on sociological study of crime as it focuses so specifically on the macro-level explanation of crime, or why crime rates vary across cities and neighborhoods. While the original forces such as poverty, residential mobility and racial heterogeneity applied well to the growth of the American city at that time, more recent renditions of the theory that focus on concentrated poverty and the lack of social networks or collective efficacy in these perpetually disadvantaged communities may apply more directly today to the life of the American teenager.

The various versions of strain theories presented are then micro-level theories that look and how and why an individual may adapt to feelings of strain and frustration in different ways. While

Merton's original Theory of Anomie focused on the greater social structure, Agnew's more recent General Strain Theory focuses on individual life circumstances and daily sources of strain that may be experienced by teenagers. The last new thing you were introduced to in this chapter is the idea of the study of group or gang delinquency and its relation to the subcultures that may exist in society that hold different values than the normative culture. Miller's Focal Concerns Theory explained how young males growing up in communities lacking father figures and male role models would band together to form their own definition of what it "means" to be a man. Similarly, Cohen's study of delinquent boys focused on how lower-class boys, unable to achieve "middle-class" measures of success, would in groups redefine success in ways achievable to them—such as fighting. Cloward and Ohlin took this one stop further, looking at the opportunity structure of both legitimate and illegitimate means to success to define different possible types of gangs that might form. Chapter 13 will provide a more comprehensive look at the nature of peers and gang delinquency today.

Discussion Questions

1. What was so unique about Chicago that led to the extensive study of crime in this city? Why was the focus on juvenile delinquents?
2. Collective Efficacy Theory focused on the role of the community in socializing youth. This theme is the topic of Hillary Clinton's book *It Takes a Village*. Why do you think it takes a community or village to socialize youth? What is the role of the family? Think about your own teenage years and what social institutions and/or people influenced your growth.
3. Merton's Theory of Anomie assumes that everyone has the same goals. Do you think this is true? Try to list goals you have that you think are generalizable to everyone in America. Then list goals that are more specific to you. Now do a similar activity for "norms" or social rules. What are norms that you think everyone in America generally holds? What norms might be specific to you based on where you grew up or what you were taught?
4. Everyone has stress or strain in their lives at various times. Compare the strain theories you learned about and how or why they suggest one person or one situation might lead to crime while another situation of strain may not. Do the theories do a good job of this? What is left that they do not explain?

REFERENCES

Agnew, R. (1985). A revised strain theory of delinquency. *Social Forces, 64,* 151–167.

Agnew, R. (1992). Foundation for a general strain theory of crime and delinquency. *Criminology, 30,* 47–87.

Agnew, R. (2006). *Pressured into crime: An overview of general strain theory*. Los Angeles, CA: Roxbury.

Agnew, R. (2013). When criminal coping is likely: An extension of general strain theory. *Deviant Behavior, 34,* 653–670.

Braga, A. A., & Weisburd, D. L. (2012). The effects of focused deterrence strategies on crime: A systematic review and meta-analysis of the empirical evidence. *Journal of Research in Crime and Delinquency, 49,* 323–358.

Briar, S., & Piliavin, I. (1965). Delinquency, situational inducements, and commitment to conformity. *Social Problems, 13*(1), 35–45.

Brown, C. (2011/1965). *Manchild in a promised land.* New York: Touchstone.

Burgess, E. W. (1967/1925). The growth of the city: An introduction to a research project. In R. E. Park, E. W. Burgess, & R. D. McKenzie (Eds.), *The City* (pp. 47–62). Chicago, IL: University of Chicago Press.

Bursik. R. J. Jr. (1986). *Ecological stability and the dynamics of delinquency in communities and crime.* A. J. Reiss & M. Tonry (Eds.). Chicago: University of Chicago Press.

Cloward, R., & Ohlin, L. (1960). *Delinquency and opportunity: A theory of delinquent gangs.* New York, NY: Free Press.

Cohen, A. K. (1955). *Delinquent boys: The culture of the gang.* New York, NY: Free Press.

Durkheim, E. (1951/1897). Suicide: A study in sociology. New York, NY: Free Press.

Empey, L. T. (1982). *American delinquency: Its meaning and construction.* Homewood, IL: Dorsey.

Harcourt, B. E. (2001). *Illusions of order: The false promise of broken windows policing.* Cambridge, MA: Harvard University Press.

Kobrin, S. (1959). The Chicago area project: A 25-year assessment. *Annuals of the American Academy of Political and Social Science,* 322, 19–29.

Liska, A. E. (1981). *Perspective on deviance.* Englewood Cliffs, NJ: Prentice Hall.

Mazerolle, P. (1998). Gender, general strain, and delinquency: An empirical examination. *Justice Quarterly, 15,* 65–91.

Mazerolle, P., Burton, V. S., Jr., Cullern, F. T., Evans, T. D., & Payne, G. (2000). Strain, anger and delinquent adaptations: Specifying general strain theory. *Journal of Criminal Justice, 28,* 89–101.

Mazerolle, P., & Maahs, J. (2000). General strain and delinquency: An alternative examination of conditioning influences. *Justice Quarterly, 17,* 753–778.

Mazerolle P., & Piquero, A. (1997). Violent responses to strain: An examination of conditioning influences. *Violence and Victims, 12,* 323–343.

Miller, W. B. (1958). Lower class culture as a generating milieu of gang delinquency. *Journal of Social Issues, 14,* 5–19.

Palin, J. J. (1981). *The urban world* (3rd ed.). New York, NY: McGraw Hill.

Park, R. E. K., Burgess, E. W., & McKenzie, R. D. (1928). *The city.* Chicago: University of Chicago Press.

Rennie, Y. (1978). *The search for criminal man.* Lexington, MA: Lexington Books.

Sampson, R. J., & Groves, W. B., (1989). Community structure and crime: Testing social-disorganization theory. *American Journal of Sociology, 94,* 774–802.

Sampson, R. J., Morenoff, J. D., & Earls, F. (1999). Beyond social capital: Spatial dynamics of collective efficacy for children. *American Sociological Review, 64,* 633–660.

Sampson, R. J., & Wilson, W. J. (1995). Toward a theory of race, crime and urban inequality. In J. Hagan and R. D. Peterson (Eds.), *Crime and Inequality* (pp. 36–54). Stanford, CA: Stanford University Press.

Schlossman, S., Hellman, G., & Shavelson, R. (1984). *Delinquency prevention in South Chicago: A fifty-year assessment of the Chicago area project.* Santa Monica, CA: RAND.

Shaw, C. R. (1929). *Delinquency areas.* Chicago: University of Chicago Press.

Shaw, C. R. (1930). *The Jack-Roller 1938. Brothers in Crime.*

Shaw, C. R. (1930). *The Jack-Roller: A delinquent boy's own story*. Chicago, IL: University of Chicago Press.

Shaw, C. R., & McKay, H. D. (1941). *Juvenile delinquency and urban areas*. Chicago: University of Chicago Press.

Shaw, C. R. (with H. D. McKay & J. E. MacDonald). (1938). *Brothers in crime.* Chicago, IL: University of Chicago Press.

Snodgrass, J. (1976). *Clifford Shaw and Henry McKay*. In J Short Jr. (Ed.), *Delinquency, Crime and Society.* Chicago: University of Chicago Press.

Toby, J. (1958). Social disorganization and stake in conformity: Complementary factors in the predatory behavior of hoodlums. *Journal of Criminal Law Criminology & Police Science, 48,* 12.

Wilson, J. J. (1987). *The truly disadvantaged: The inner city, the underclass and public policy.* Chicago: University of Chicago Press.

Wilson, J. J. (1996). *When work disappears: The world of the new urban poor.* New York: Alfred A. Knopf.

Wilson, J. Q., & Kelling, G. L. (1982). Broken windows: The police and neighborhood safety. *Atlantic Monthly, 249*(3), 29–38.

Social Learning and Social Process Theories

Here's the thing, if you talk to some thieves, they take pride more or less in being a thief, much like an honest man in his work does. Many thieves define themselves as thieves, as good thieves—at least, they wanna think that way and have others see them that way. Say, there are five thieves at the bar. I walk in and they say, "There's a helluva safe-cracker." It would be like Reggie Jackson walking into a place, and they say, "Boy, can he hit a home run."

Quote from *The Fence* by Darrell Steffensmeier. 1986. Totowa, NJ: Rowman and Litterfield. p. 57.

In the previous chapter you learned about how the structure of a community, and even overall society, can influence crime and delinquency. In this chapter we turn more toward individual experiences and what it is that motivates a person to commit a crime, or keeps someone, who might otherwise be motivated to commit a crime, from doing so. This chapter is called social process theories because the theories discussed herein look at the development of crime in an individual as the individual interacts with the environment. Thus, you will not be breaking entirely from social structures learned in the previous chapter, but rather focusing in more directly on the individual as he/she grows and develops in this environment.

This chapter will cover three main types of theories: social learning theories, social control theories and labeling theories. The first set of theories, social learning theories, focus on how individuals learn to either follow society's norms, or to accept and follow different values that would be considered delinquent by the majority of society. These theories assume everyone is born equally capable of committing crime, and whether or not they do so basically depends on how they are taught to behave. The quote above from ***The Fence*** was taken from a professional thief who was the subject of an ethnography by criminologist Darrell Steffensmier. This book follows one individual's journey into a life of crime and shows how he learned the particular beliefs he held. While primarily set in social learning theories, the experiences of this thief named "Sam" also show how his ties to general society break down over time and how he comes to define his own self-worth through his criminal activity. This leads us to the remaining theories covered in this chapter: Social Control and Labeling theories.

Social control theories take a bit of a different approach toward delinquency than one would traditionally assume. These theories assume that not only are we all born capable of committing crimes, but that we all would do so if something did not stop us. What stops us? According to these theories it is how society controls us that matters. The final set of theories, labeling theories, assume that not only are we all capable of deviance, but that most of us actually **are** deviant at some point in our lives. What matters then, is not this initial act of deviance, but how others respond to it and to the individual committing the act. Thus, if one accepts the deviant label and define himself that way, like "Sam" he would be happy to be referred to as a "helluva safe-cracker."

CHAPTER GOALS

By the end of this chapter you will be able to:

1. List and explain the nine postulates of Edwin Sutherland's Differential Association Theory.
2. Compare and contrast the subcultural values proposed by Miller's "Focal Concerns Theory," Anderson's "Code of the Streets" and Wolfgang and Ferracuti's "Culture of Violence."
3. Identify the key individuals contributing to social control theories.
4. Describe the four elements of the social bond as proposed by Travis Hirschi and how they relate to delinquency.
5. Define primary and secondary deviance.
6. Explain the difference between integrative shaming and reintegrative shaming and give an example of a policy that reflects each.

Social Learning Theories

As noted in the introduction, this is a set of theories that assume criminal behavior is learned. This does not seem like it should be a novel idea as we learn all kinds of things, but when the first social learning theory of crime was proposed by Edwin Sutherland in the early 1900s it was indeed a novel idea. Receiving his Ph.D. from the University of Chicago in 1913, Edwin Sutherland was highly influenced by the social ecological model and the impact of community on individuals, but he was also very interested in how one person came to commit a crime while another did not. Moreover, he noted that crime was often very specific. Criminals do not simply go around committing crime all the time or committing every type of crime. How is it then that a person defines a situation as appropriate for committing a certain type of crime? According to Sutherland, this is simply something that we learn (Sutherland, 1947).

People, according to Sutherland, are pretty much born blank slates. We have no preconceived notions of right from wrong or legal and illegal. These are things that are taught to us by those around us.

Imagine the following scenario. A young boy is being picked on at school by his classmates. His school has a policy that violence against another person is never acceptable and the school holds assemblies to teach this message and posts signs around the school. However, the boy's father tells him that it is ok to use violence to defend yourself and you are not a man if you do not. Which definition will he adopt? How will he behave if he is again confronted with this same situation?

I present this scenario as it is perhaps these mixed messages that are the heart of Sutherland's theory. That is, we are not necessarily taught that it is ok to break every law all of the time, but we are given messages that sometimes it is ok or justifiable, and the messages we receive may vary from person to person. Sutherland called these "**differential associations**"; they are, most simply, our associations with other people that give us these various messages. Which do we choose to adapt and act upon? According to Sutherland this depends on various factors that he outlines in the nine postulates of his theory. These postulates are as follows:

Differential Associations

our associations with other people that give us various messages about the appropriateness of rules and laws

1. Delinquency behavior is learned.
2. Delinquency behavior is learned in interaction with others through communication.
3. Learning occurs in intimate groups.
4. Learning includes the techniques for committing crime as well as the motives, attitudes and rationalization.
5. The specific direction of motives and drives is learned from definitions of the legal code as being favorable or unfavorable.
6. A juvenile becomes delinquent because of an excess of definitions favorable to violation of a specific law.
7. The learning of delinquency will be affected by the frequency, duration, priority and intensity of the learning experience. **Frequency** refers to how often a person is exposed to a message. **Duration** is for how long. **Priority** refers to how early in life one receives the message and **intensity** focuses on how much we care about the person giving us the message.
8. Learning delinquent behavior involves all the same mechanisms involved in any other learning.
9. Criminal behavior and noncriminal behavior are expressions of the same needs and values; thus these needs and values cannot be used to explain delinquency.

Frequency

how often a person is exposed to a message

Duration

how long a person is exposed to a message

Priority

how early in life a person receives a message

Intensity

how much a person cares about the person giving him/her the message

Some of this theory is so simple that you are probably saying to yourself, "of course," and "that makes sense," while other parts seem a bit vague or confusing. For example, of course we learn things through communicating with others, but what the heck is a motivation or rationalization for crime? Here what Sutherland is referring to is the idea that it may be ok to perform certain acts in given situations, but not in others. For example, your parent might communicate to you that it is ok to use violence to defend yourself or someone else but not just because you are angry with someone. Thus, your choice to use violence will depend on your definition of the situation of one of defense rather than one of aggression. In the situation discussed above it was a teacher giving the child one definition and the parent another.

Sutherland's theory has been very influential in the study of career criminals who spend most of their life emerged in crime as an occupation such as that detailed in his book *The Professional Thief* and also for the study of crime committed by others within their "legitimate" career. For the latter, he is also known for coining the term "white-collar crime" and beginning the study of crime in organizations and businesses. However, for the study of juvenile delinquency, what may be most relevant is this theory's focus on the role of peers on delinquency. Studies by Mark Warr have found support for the influence of friends on adolescent delinquency, particularly for youths who make delinquent friends early (priority), which in turn increases their duration (length) and frequency of exposure to these influences. Warr (1998) coined the term "sticky" friends to exemplify how once an individual became involved in a delinquent peer group these friends tended to "stick" throughout adolescence and increase each other's delinquent behaviors. A more formal evaluation of the theory conducted by Ross Matsueda (1988), concluded that overall the empirical research found great support for Sutherland's ideas, including the role of delinquent friends, the definitions of some situations as appropriate for violating a specific law and the overall balance of definitions favorable or unfavorable to violating the law.

Another key element of the theory that is not spelled out in the original nine postulates is the idea of **differential social organization**. Remember I said Sutherland was influenced by the Chicago School. However, rather than agreeing with Shaw and McKay that certain areas of society were disorganized, in Sutherland's final version of his theory published in 1949 he coined the term differential social organization to mean that these communities were simply organized around a different set of norms and values. Thus, if you live in these areas, you will be exposed to different definitions of right and wrong than in mainstream society. In this way, Sutherland's theory contributed the evolution of various theories we know as "subcultural" theories of crime, several of which you were already introduced to in the previous chapter.

Differential Social Organization

communities that are organized around a different set of norms and values

FOCUS ON RESEARCH: Elijah Anderson's Code of the Streets

Elijah Anderson conducted extensive ethnographic research in the city of Philadelphia, exploring the ways in which living in poor, crime-ridden communities impacted the residents, particularly the youth. In this research he found that there were two major ways in which people might adapt to these trying circumstances. "Decent values," as he defined them, represented families who adopted middle-class standards and who still valued education and hard work regardless of their personal situation. "Street values" on the other hand represented families and people who had given up on mainstream America and realized the need to survive within their violence-ridden communities. For these individuals the primary value is that of respect. Having not much else in life, having the respect of others takes center stage. Respect, or "juice" as it is referred to, means that one does not have to constantly fight for survival because others will not challenge or "diss" (disrespect) you. Ways to gain respect are to be aggressive and to act with violence first so that others know you are ready to kill or be killed and are not afraid of them. Otherwise you become easy "prey." While youth from families with "decent values," as Anderson calls them, maintain hope for a better future, they also know the code and can act appropriately when needed. For example, they would know how not to disrespect someone and thus put themselves in danger, and they would know when they need to act aggressively, even violently, to survive. Anderson referred to this as "code switching." Overall Anderson's ideas have been well received by the criminological community and shine a new light on the plight of poor families growing up in some of the nation's poorest neighborhoods.

Anderson, Elijah. 2000. *Code of the Street: Decency, Violence and the Moral Life of the Inner City.* New York: Norton. Anderson, Elijah. 1998. Violence and the inner-city street code. In *Violence and Children in the Inner City,* Joan McCord (ed.) New York: Cambridge University Press. Anderson, Elijah. 1994. The code of the streets. *Atlantic Monthly* 273:80–94.

Despite Sutherland's broad influence, his theory also received strict criticism for not really explaining the way it is in which people learned. Indeed his postulate just says that we learn crime the same way we learn everything else. Well, how exactly is that? In fact one of the greatest criticisms of Sutherland's theory was that he didn't really address this very much.

Classical Conditioning

a person learning to associate an outcome with a stimulus

Here, we have to reach outside of criminology and into psychology and cognitive development to understand how people learn. Psychologists often talk about classical and operant conditioning. **Classical conditioning** is best represented by Pavlov's famous study with dogs. In this experiment Pavlov capitalized on natural instincts. That is, when a dog smells food, it will naturally salivate. Pavlov would then ring a bell when introducing food. Eventually just the sound of the bell was enough to make the dog salivate as the animal then associated the sound with getting food. Thus, classical conditioning refers to a person learning to associate an outcome with a stimulus.

Operant Conditioning
learning is based on rewards and punishments

Operant conditioning adds a more active component on the part of the individual and bases learning on experiences of rewards and punishments. B. F. Skinner, often referred to as the "father of behavioral psychology" proposed that behavior is "caused" by its consequences and that learning occurs by trial and error (Skinner, 1938; Skinner, 1953). For example, Piaget's work with pigeons showed how these birds would learn to tap a lever to reveal food—a reward. According to behavioral theorists, humans learn in similar ways as animals, just at a higher level (Skinner, 1938); thus by studying how animals react to rewards and punishments in their environment we can understand how humans learn and behave as well. Therefore we can expect humans to behave in a manner that will gain the most rewards and limit punishments in any particular situation. This particular model of learning is very relevant for juvenile justice and is incorporated into a broad array of treatment programs, known as behavioral modification programs, that will be discussed more in Chapter 10. In general, these programs start working with troubled youth by giving them rewards for even the smallest positive pro-social behaviors, in hopes that over time gaining rewards for such behaviors will help these youth internalize the value of behaving in these ways.

Imitation
mimic behaviors of those around us

A third way that people learn is through **imitation**. This simply means that we mimic the behaviors of those around us. Psychologist Albert Bandura refers to this process as "observational learning." This component of learning also has direct applications when thinking about the development of delinquent behaviors as well as programs to help prevent delinquency. For example, if you are exposed to people who act in delinquent ways or hold delinquent values, you are likely to mimic these behaviors, particularly if those engaging in such behaviors are people you value. Many programs addressing juvenile delinquency look at the possible influence of negative peer associations—that is associating with peers who are delinquent, or in growing up in communities without positive role models.

AKERS' SOCIAL LEARNING THEORY

While these studies find substantial support for the role of differential associations in the development of delinquency, as mentioned, one of the greatest critiques of the theory was that it failed to address how learning actually occurred. Ron Akers has set forth the most profound extension of Sutherland's original Differential Association Theory. Akers' Social Learning Theory has four central concepts:

1. *Differential Association:* Similar to Sutherland's original theory, this is defined as the process through which an individual is exposed to definitions either favorable or unfavorable to violating the law.
2. *Imitation:* This refers to the third type of learning discussed above and is the simple fact that a person engages in behavior after observing others engage in that behavior.
3. *Definitions:* Are a person's own attitudes and beliefs that are adopted and internalized. These can be both general ideas about right and wrong, and also very specific notions about when a particular behavior is ok or not ok (for example, it is bad to fight, but it is ok to fight if you are protecting someone else, like a younger sibling).
4. *Differential Social Reinforcement:* This refers to another type of learning presented above—operant conditioning in which one learns to repeat certain behaviors and avoid others based on the rewards and punishments received for the varying behaviors.

Overall, Akers suggests that definitions are learned through one's differential associations with others. In these associations, people both imitate the behavior of those around them, and respond to the rewards or punishments they receive for performing such behaviors. It is this last piece that Akers proposes determines whether the individual continues to engage in crime. If upon performing a delinquent act, the youth receives rewards, he/she will continue committing such acts.

Akers provided the first test of his own theory using self-report measures from 3,065 adolescents in grades 7 through 12. In this study he found that the four factors in his theory could account for about 55% of the variation in alcohol use and over 68% of variation in marijuana use among these teenagers. Overall, other studies have also found strong empirical support for the role of social learning in adolescent delinquency (Akers, Ronald L., Marvin D. Krohn, Lonn Lanza-Kaduce, & Marcia Radosevich, 1979, Akers, Ronald L., & Gang Lee, 1996). Similar to the earlier study by Warr cited above, more recent research also suggests that the number of delinquent friends is the top predictor of criminal involvement (Warr, 2002; Wright & Cullen, 2000; Akers, 1999). Moreover a recent meta-analysis of 133 studies revealed consistent support for this theory (Pratt et al., 2010).

Policy Implications for Juvenile Justice

Of the theories discussed so far, none has perhaps had as much influence as social learning theory. Programs based on this theory include the very popular behavioral-modification programs that focus on a simple reward/punishment structure to rehabilitate juveniles. These programs are often referred to as "token-economies" where within the program the youth can earn rewards by exhibiting positive behaviors. Rewards can be something small like a dessert or something larger like an extra home visit or freedoms within the facility. In addition, cognitive-behavioral interventions are on the rise. These programs aim to change behavior by first changing definitions (e.g., antisocial values) and reduce the influences of negative peer associations. These latter programs have been shown to be highly effective in reducing recidivism (Cullen & Gendreau, 2000; Cullen, Wright, Gendreau, & Andrews, 2003; Lipsey, Chapman & Landenberger, 2001; McKenzie, 2006).

Social Control Theory

Social control theories ask a slightly different question than did social learning and differential association theories. Whereas these theories asked why some youth became and stayed involved in criminal activities, control theories ask instead, "why don't all youths engage in delinquency?" From this perspective, it is normal for people to look out for themselves and to try to get all they can without regard for others. Our society is filled with influences that might push or pull someone towards crime (e.g., motivations for crime). Criminal behavior is not abnormal; rather it would be the norm if we were not controlled from committing such acts.

So the question then becomes what controls us and makes us suppress this natural instinct?

There are several key players in the development of Social Control Theory during the 1950s including Ivan Nye, Walter Reckless and Albert Reiss. Reiss, in writing his doctoral dissertation as a student at the University of Chicago in the late 1940s, defined delinquency as "the failure of personal and social controls" (Reiss, 1951). According to Reiss, personal controls are the norms and beliefs a person internalizes and his/her ability to conform behavior to these norms. This latter part relied on the notion of the "ego" as discussed in Chapter 5 under psychological theories. Social controls, on the other hand, were those controls exerted by others over the individual to ensure compliance, even when the individual might not have enough personal control to prevent deviance. The primary form of social control focused on by Reiss was the family.

Similarly, Ivan Nye, working at the University of Michigan in the 1950s, placed much emphasis on the role of the family developing what he called a family-focused theory of social control (Nye, 1958). According to Nye, the family worked in four ways to ensure that a youth did not deviate. First, the family is responsible for fulfilling the youth's immediate needs such as shelter and food. Second, the family is who teaches the youth moral values, thus helping the youth to develop a conscience and have internal control. Third, because the youth is cared for by the family, he/she has an affectual connection to the family and is indirectly then controlled by their norms and values even if they have not yet been internalized. That is, maybe the youth does not commit a delinquent act because he/she does not want to disappoint a parent. Finally, the family has direct control over the youth through the ability to monitor the youth's behavior and punish him/her for inappropriate behaviors.

Walter Reckless devised one of the earliest formal control theories which he called "Containment Theory." His theory in a way mirrored Reiss's early idea of personal and social control redefining these constructs as "inner" and "outer" containment. However, he expanded considerably on these notions. Inner containment to Reckless was more than just one's conscience. It also involved the notion of one's self-concept or self-esteem. Self-concept was important to Reckless because it is this strength of one's belief in the self that allows one to be true to one's moral ideals when faced with pulls or pushes to deviate. Moreover, **inner containment** is also related to goal orientation. Goal orientation is defined as one's desire to achieve legitimate goals (such as an education and a job). If one has such goals, one will be involved in behavior that leads one toward this goal, which by definition would be normative, not deviant, behavior.

Inner Containment

more than just one's conscience, also involves the notion of one's self-concept or self-esteem

Outer containment on the other hand reaches beyond the family as proposed by Reiss and Nye and more to the general social environment of the individual. It includes such things as consistent presentation of moral norms, consistent reinforcement for normative behaviors, the provision of a meaningful role for the individual in the environment and opportunities for acceptance and belonging to the broader group/society. Here you can probably see some elements of learning and strain theories only presented in the opposite direction. For example, exposure to consistent norms is in a way the opposite of the notion of differential association in which one will be exposed to definitions both favorable and unfavorable to violating the law. Similarly, having a meaningful role in society and a sense of belonging would be the opposite of a feeling of anomie, or normlessness, in which one feels separated from society.

Outer Containment

reaches beyond the family and more to the general social environment of the individual

Perhaps, however, the most influential social control theory was to be proposed by Travis Hirschi in 1969, known as Social Bond Theory.

HIRSCHI'S SOCIAL BOND THEORY

In 1969, Travis Hirschi published *Causes of Delinquency*, which quickly became the most influential social control theory. Hirschi's primary argument, in line with the control perspective, was that we are "all animals and thus all naturally capable of committing criminal acts." His theory argued that those of us who do not commit criminal acts refrain because of our close social bonds with family, friends and social groups. He then further specified four specific elements of the social bond as follows:

Attachment

the emotional connection that you have with others in their lives

Attachment. **Attachment** in this theory is specifically the emotional connection that youths have with others in their lives. The most important attachment studied by Hirschi was that to parents, but teachers and friends were also explored. It is through this emotional attachment that parents are able to exercise indirect social control over their children. That is, even when a parent is not present to supervise the child, he/she will not behave in a certain way because it would upset the parent. Parents also of course have direct control through supervision over children's behavior, but Hirschi found this to be of little theoretical interest.

Commitment

how committed you are to traditional beliefs and behaviors

Stakes in Conformity

what you have to lose by committing a delinquent act

Commitment. The social bond of **commitment** was based upon the earlier notion of Jackson Toby who proposed "**stakes in conformity**" (Toby, 1957). That is, a person will choose not to commit a crime when they have too much to lose. The more a person has invested in a normative goal, the more he or she would have to lose by violating the rules. According to Hirschi, then, this is the "rational" component of the social bond in which the individual "must consider the costs of this deviant behavior, the risk he runs of losing the investment he has made in conventional behavior" (p. 20).

Involvement

the more time spent in conventional settings, the less time there is to be deviant

Involvement. The social bond of **involvement** is then the time component of the social bond. The more time one spends in conventional activities, the less time he/she has to be deviant. You may have heard the old saying, "idle hands are the devil's workshop."

Belief

beliefs about right and wrong

Belief. The social bond of **belief** is then the attitudinal component. It is not a deep psychological concept such as the "id" as proposed in prior theories though; it is more impressions and opinions that have been learned. Hirschi also notes the connection of the deep-rooted nature of beliefs to attachments to those teaching the beliefs; thus, in a way, bringing his theory full circle.

Hirschi tested his theory using a self-report survey of 4,000 junior and senior high school students from the San Francisco Bay area. His findings overall found the most support for the component of attachment. In particular he found that, regardless of other factors, boys who were more closely attached to their parents were less likely to engage in delinquency. The fact that this finding held regardless of the delinquency of friends was in direct conflict with Differential Association Theory and other theories that supported the role of social learning and delinquent associations in the emergence of delinquency. Also, he found support for the notion of commitment to goals as a constraint from committing delinquency. However, he found less support for his last two components—involvement and beliefs. Other scholars have also devised tests of his theory and the findings, for the most part, remain consistent. That is, there is strong empirical support for the components of attachment and commitment, but less so for the bonds of involvement and beliefs (Costello & Vowell, 1999). The main criticism of Hirschi's theory, however, was that his measure of delinquency included only very minor behaviors to which an adolescent would openly admit, making it more questionable whether this theory of social control would apply to more serious forms of delinquency such as robbery, rape and/or murder. In specific, his measure of delinquency asked students if they had stolen anything worth less than $2, between $2 and $50, and over $50, as well as whether or not they had "beaten up on anyone or hurt anyone on purpose," "taken a car for a ride without the owner's permission" or "banged up something that did not belong" to them (Hirschi, 1969).

DELINQUENCY AND DRIFT

David Matza, who was studying crime and delinquency in the 1960s as well, took a slightly different approach to how norms and beliefs shape behavior than either learning or control theories. According to Matza, delinquency is even more "normal" than perhaps proposed by Hirschi. That is, almost everyone does it during their teenage years. He also proposed, however, that almost everyone outgrows this stage as they mature. He also took affront to theories such as strain that assume that once a youth is delinquent, the youth will continue to be delinquent most, if not all, of the time. According to Matza, delinquents do not really hold subcultural values (as proposed in the section on subcultures above) or hold different beliefs than everyone else (as would be proposed by Hirschi's Social Bond Theory). Rather, they know right from wrong and behave in the "right" way most of the time. But dependent on the situation they can "drift" in and out of delinquency as situations present themselves. He further elaborated on these ideas with his colleague Gresham Sykes, developing "**techniques of neutralization**," which are, put most simply, ways to neutralize one's conscience (Sykes & Matza, 1957). That is the individual knows at heart an action might be wrong, but in this situation he/she can rationalize why it is the "right" thing to do. Sykes and Matza summarized these techniques as:

Denial of Responsibility. In this instance, the youth knows that overall the behavior is wrong, but rationalizes that it really wasn't his/her fault. The youth blames the delinquency on a force outside his/her control such as an abusive family member or a non-caring teacher.

Denial of Injury. In this situation, the action is only bad because it causes someone injury. So, if the injury can be denied, then the act itself is not so bad. For example, if I break into your home and steal your TV but you have homeowner's insurance that will replace your TV, I really did not cause you any harm.

Denial of Victim. In this case, the victim is seen as "asking for it." For example, when teaching in class I often use the example of showing up to a bar in Boston right after the Red Sox lose to the Yankees wearing my Yankee cap. In the case of juvenile delinquency it might be something as simple as walking on the rival gang's territory when you know you were not supposed to be there, or sitting at the wrong table at lunch.

Condemnation of the Condemner. This occurs when the youth blames the police or other authority figures themselves for causing the problem. Statements such as "those cops are crooked anyway" and "my parents drink alcohol so who are they to tell me not to" would be examples of this reasoning.

Appeal to Higher Loyalties. In this situation the individual knows an action is wrong, but must partake in that action to protect someone else. Perhaps punching a bully to protect a younger sibling, or even shooting a rival gang member to protect a "brother" in his own gang.

Matza's theory is interesting in that it incorporates learning of these techniques of neutralization (Learning Theory) and how one neutralizes controls (Control Theory) and it also addresses why most kids do not commit delinquent acts most of the time, but most do in certain situations. The downside of this theory is that it is extremely difficult to test because of its transient nature of the youth drifting in and out of delinquency, rather than it being a constant factor that can be measured over time.

THE GENERAL THEORY OF CRIME

Later in Travis Hirschi's career he was to develop a different version of Control Theory with colleague Michael Gottfredson. In this version, the focus is more specifically on the family as the primary socializing force on the child. According to this theory, the General Theory of Crime, it is during early life within the family that a child learns to control impulses and act in socially appropriate ways. Thus, ineffective parenting early in life, according to this theory, would lead to a youth never developing this sense of internal **self-control**. If this sense of self-control was not instilled by age 8, the individual would be in a way doomed to go through life more likely to engage in all types of delinquency and antisocial behavior as opportunities present themselves.

Self-control

to control impulses and act in socially appropriate ways

Policy Implications for Juvenile Justice

The policy implications of social control/social bond theories are perhaps some of the most straightforward to understand. These theories suggest that the more closely one is bonded to others and to society, the less likely he/she is to become delinquent. Thus, our programs should promote and support such pro-social connections. This includes working with the family to ensure family stability, keeping the youth in the home and community whenever possible, and programs to help youth remain in and succeed in school. Since Hirschi's social bond theory also addresses involvement, this would suggest that having youth enrolled in structured activities also helps to keep them out of trouble—this could involve boy/girl scouts, boys/girls clubs, sports teams and the like. Finally, since a pro-social bond is often experienced at a personal level, this theory would also be supportive of mentoring programs such as big brothers/big sisters that help to match at-risk youth with others. I would like to take just one moment to note here that as you continue to learn about theory you will start to see more and more overlaps between the theories and perhaps suggested policies. While this might be a bit confusing at times, in the end it is perhaps a good thing because it means that particular programs address various causes of delinquency (as proposed by various theories). For example, here is one overlap. Deterrence theory (from the Classical School) assumes you will not commit delinquency if the costs outweigh the benefits. Jackson Toby's notion of stakes in conformity suggests you will not commit delinquency when you have a lot to lose. Thus, the more social bonds you have, the more you have to lose and thus perhaps the greater the "costs" of committing an act of delinquency.

Labeling Theory and Stigma

The last of the three social process perspectives considered in this chapter takes it even a step further than Hirschi's assumption that everyone will naturally commit criminal acts if not controlled. This next theory assumes that there really is no deviance unless society defines an act that way and that everyone, at some point in their lives, will most likely do something that goes against these rules and norms set by society. What matters then is which acts a society defines as unacceptable, and what happens to people who are caught committing these acts.

These ideas are deeply rooted in a sociological tradition called "symbolic interactionism." While a full discussion of this perspective is beyond the purpose of this text, to understand these theories you need to be acquainted with some basic premises of this perspective. First, is that there is no objective reality. Reality only exists in the minds of those defining the situation. Thus, there is no such thing as a "crime" unless someone defines it as such. Second, these definitions are constantly evolving and changing as people interact with each other over time. And, thirdly, these definitions include not only definitions of objects and of acts, but of ourselves as individuals as well. For example, take a moment and pick three adjectives that describe yourself. Now, pick three adjectives that might have described you five years ago. Are they the same? What about adjectives your parents might use to describe you? Hopefully, from this brief exercise you can see how your idea of self and how others perceive you might evolve and change over time.

This idea of defining the self was probably best described by George Herbert Mead (1930, 1934) who called it the "looking glass self." That is, we might have one opinion of ourselves, but as we see others respond to us, we change that opinion. This in particular is at the core of the labeling perspective on delinquency.

One of the earliest renditions of Labeling Theory was presented in 1938 by Frank Tannenbaum. In his book, *Crime and the Community*, Tannenbaum objected to the dichotomy that delinquents and non-delinquents were two different types of kids. He called this the **dualistic fallacy**. According to Tannenbaum, kids (i.e., juveniles) are often at odds with the adults in their community for things as simple as playing music too loud or hanging out. As conflicts between kids and adults grow, the adults tend to think of the children themselves as bad instead of just disapproving of the things they do. A term I particularly like that he uses to describe this is "**dramatization of evil**," which means that instead of seeing the act as evil or bad, they see the kids as evil or bad.

Dramatization of Evil

instead of seeing the act as evil or bad, the person committing the act is seen as bad or evil

It was Edwin Lemert, however, writing some 13 years later, who brought forth the first formal "labeling" theory of delinquency. Lemert proposed that for a variety of reasons, be it social, biological or psychological, most people at some point violate a social norm and/or the law. This is called "**primary deviance**." It may be more than one time and it can be something as minor as shoplifting an eyeshadow or something as major as robbing someone at gun point. **Secondary deviance** occurs, however, when someone internalizes the label of delinquent or evil put upon them by society and then commits delinquent acts in response to this label. What is unique about this perspective is that it does not focus on the motivation for those first acts of primary deviance; rather it focuses on how society and society's response to an individual can actually increase rather than decrease delinquency.

Primary Deviance

a deviant act one commits, whether serious or minor, as a normal part of growing up

Secondary Deviance

an act of deviance that occurs after someone internalizes the label of delinquent

Howard Becker, writing in the 1960s, furthered this perspective in his elaboration of how one becomes deviant. Similar to the earlier labeling theorists, he assumes that no act is inherently deviant and that youth will engage in a variety of behaviors, some of which are bound to deviate from adult norms. What matters is when the juvenile is caught and labeled "delinquent." This person, labeled by others, is then the first suspect when a new deviant act occurs—when police round up suspects for questioning, this youth is now on their radar as a "bad kid" and is likely to be questioned. At some point, Becker contends, this stigmatization by others can lead to the label of delinquent actually becoming a master status for the individual that "takes precedence over all other statuses or characteristics of the individual" (Curran & Renzetti, 2001, p. 174).

Overall there has been consistent support that labeling minor delinquents can indeed lead to negative outcomes for these youth. Gary Sweeten found that high school students who are formally processed for offenses are more likely to drop out of school than similar youth who are arrested but not formally processed (Sweeten, 2006). Ted Chiricos and colleagues conducted a study of almost 100,000 youths in Florida who were convicted of felony offenses. Based on policy, some of these youths were formally convicted and thus bore the label of delinquent while others had the conviction and label withheld as they successfully completed a specialized deferred sentence. Consistent with the premises of Labeling Theory, this study found that those youths formally tagged with the felon label were more likely to be rearrested within two years than those who were offered the diversionary sentence.

Research has also provided support for the notion that not everyone committing a deviant act is equally as likely to be caught and labeled. In particular, work by John Hagan and Holly Foster examined a national sample of youth to see if and how race impacted system response to drug use among adolescents. This research found that while a significant number of privileged white youths admitted to using drugs and partying, they were not likely to be detected by the system or arrested for this activity. On the other hand, while a smaller number of African-American youth reported using illicit drugs, they were much more likely to be caught, arrested and formally processed for these activities (Hagan & Foster, 2006).

However, other research has not been as supportive of the idea that the youth actually accepts a new identity based on these system outcomes (Thomas & Bishop, 1984; Foster, Dinitz & Reckless, 1972; Hepburn, 1977). In particular, a study by Charles Thomas and Donna Bishop that examined the competing assumptions of deterrence theory and labeling theory (1984) found no evidence that being arrested and sanctioned pushed youth to think of themselves as delinquent. Thus, while research overall is supportive of the notion that **labels** and **stigma** can lead to further delinquency and that labels may not be applied equally across social groups and classes, there is less support for the actually proposed "**identity reformation**" process through which labeling theory suggests the label becomes a self-fulfilling prophecy.

Identity Reformation
the process through which labeling theory suggests the label applied by others can become a self-fulfilling prophecy

Policy Applications for Juvenile Justice

Reintegrative Shaming

doing something but ensuring that the consequence keeps the youth connected to society and recognizing his/her own potential to be a good person in the end

Disintegrative Shaming

not only punish a youth for their action, but applying the unmistakable and inescapable label of delinquent upon the youth

From a pure labeling perspective, some sociologists would then suggest that most delinquency laws are unnecessary and actually do more harm than good. Thus, a policy of "radical nonintervention" (Schur, 1973) might be best. That is, for most acts of delinquency that are minor and not necessarily aggressive or directly harmful to others, the system should simply not intervene in the life of the youth as the label of delinquent and its resulting stigma will do more to create than prevent criminality. Another policy implication is that of "**reintegrative shaming**" discussed below which, instead of doing nothing, involves doing something but ensuring that the consequence keeps the youth connected to society and recognizing their own potential to be a good person in the end. Here again we can see some overlap between theories. Remember above you learned that social control/bond theories imply we should help to build and maintain youths ties to society. One reason labeling is "bad" is because it can break such ties—reintegrative shaming works to maintain or restore such ties during and after sanctioning for delinquent acts.

FOCUS ON POLICY: Reintegrative Shaming

The most recent, and perhaps currently most influential, form of Labeling Theory is an extension of the theory proposed by John Braithwaite in his theory of "**reintegrative shaming.**" In this context, Braithwaite suggests that radical nonintervention might not be the way to go as youths do need to know that their actions have consequences. However, he proposes that the system react with "reintegrative" rather than "**disintegrative shaming.**" Disintegrative shaming refers to much of the current practices of the justice system that punish a youth for his/her action and instill the unmistakable and inescapable label of delinquent upon the youth. Reintegrative shaming, on the other hand, allows for adults and the community to disapprove of the youth's actions and apply some sort of sanction, but insists that the sanction be followed by a form of forgiveness or acceptance that helps the youth leave the label of deviant or delinquent behind and feel that he/she is part of the community.

Current policies in the juvenile justice system that reflect this theory include restorative justice practices in which a victim and offender are brought together through a mediator to discuss the crime. Upon learning of the impact of the crime on the victim, the young offender is then given steps to take to remedy the harm, and at the end of the process receives a notion of forgiveness from the victim. Other practices include such things as the use of community restorative justice boards instead of formal court proceedings. Such practices will be further elaborated in Chapter 12.

FIGURE 7.1 Theory Summary Box			
Differential Association	All behavior learned	Excess of definitions favorable to violating law	Reduce exposure to delinquent definitions
Differential Reinforcement	Crime learned through rewards/ punishments and imitation	Learned rewards for behavior	Behavioral modification
Social Bond	Crime natural behavior if not controlled	Lack of social bonds	Strengthen social bonds
General Theory of Crime	Self-control instilled by parents	Lack of self-control/ Bad parenting	Improve parenting early in life
Delinquency and Drift	Delinquents hold same values as non-delinquents	Rationalization/ Neutralization of values	
Labeling	No behavior inherently deviant, just labeled as such	Self-fulfilling prophecy/Response to label/Stigma	Radical non-intervention
Reintegrative Shaming	People controlled through integration to society	Stigma/Ostracization	Reintegrative shaming

Key Words

Attachment
Belief
Classical Conditioning
Commitment
Differential Associations
Differential Social Organization
Disintegrative Shaming
Dramatization of Evil
Duration
Frequency
Identity Reformation
Imitation
Inner Containment
Intensity
Involvement
Operant Conditioning
Outer Containment
Primary Deviance
Priority
Reintegrative Shaming
Secondary Deviance
Self-control
Stakes in Conformity

Chapter Summary

In this chapter you were introduced to three different perspectives on how social processes can lead to crime. These processes were: 1) social learning, 2) social control/bonding and 3) labeling (which might even be called social ostracization). Each of these theories assumes to some extent that we are all capable of committing acts of deviance—there is nothing inherently different about the delinquent as was suggested by the biological and psychological perspectives. Also, each theory assumes that while individuals might have some choice in committing crimes, this is not an entirely free choice as assumed by Deterrence Theory and the Classical School. Instead juveniles are learning from and reacting to the environment around them.

First, according to learning theories, crime, like any other behavior, is learned. We learn in a variety of ways, including classical and operant conditioning as well as imitation. Sutherland's Differential Association Theory really focused on our learning of definitions of the law and whether or not violating the law is favorable in given situations. Learning for Sutherland occurred mainly in small intimate groups, including both the motivation for committing the crime (the why) and the technique for committing the crime (the how). Finally it was also influenced by our exposure to these definitions in frequency (how much), duration (how long), intensity (who from) and priority (how early in life). Akers' Reformation of Learning Theory focused more specifically on how we learn with a special emphasis on rewards and punishments (operant conditioning) and imitation of behavior of those whom we admire.

Next, we considered social control theories that suggest crime need not be learned—it is as natural as Calvin pounding those nails into the table in the cartoon. Why do we commit crime? Because we can. Why do we not commit crime? Because something stops us. What stops us, according to Hirschi, is our social bonds with others, and there were four primary types of bond: attachment, commitment, involvement and beliefs. Matza on the other hand suggests that delinquents have these same bonds but, in some circumstances, can rationalize away or neutralize their influence. Finally, in Hirschi's later work with colleague Michael Gottfredson, he focuses more specifically on self-control, which is instilled in the child by parents in early childhood—as the key control that prevents one from simply engaging in a variety of antisocial behaviors.

Finally we turned to social reaction theories that posit that maybe it is not the behavior itself that matters, but how society responds to the individual committing the act. In this part of the chapter you specifically learned about Labeling Theory, which suggests that all of us mess up at some point in time; this is known as **primary deviance**. Most of us simply grow out of this type of behavior. Some people, however, get caught by the system and labeled a delinquent. If this label leads to stigma and blocked opportunity and/or the consequences are too severe, the individual may then decide to accept this label as "deviant" and act accordingly. Thus, **secondary deviance** ensues.

These theories have some similar and some different policy applications to be considered by the juvenile justice system. Learning Theory suggests that it is important to give children rewards for positive behavior and punishments for negative behavior. However, it also might suggest that it is inherently unwise to group delinquents together, particularly minor delinquents with more serious offenders, as the more serious offenders will only teach the others more criminogenic ways. Control theories on the other hand suggest that we need to work within the family and school to increase a youth's bonds to society. The more he or she has affectional bonds toward these social institutions and spends his/her time dedicated to conventional norms and goals, the more he/she will have to lose by committing an act of deviance. Finally, labeling theory might suggest that the best approach may be at times to simply do nothing, thereby ensuring that we do not decrease or weaken social bonds, and that when punishment is necessary that we ensure it is "**reintegrative**" instead of ostracizing.

Discussion Questions

1. Try to think back to your earliest memory. What is the first thing you remember learning from your parents? Maybe the alphabet? Or colors? Do you think you learned these concepts in a different way than you would learn to steal? Use drugs?

2. Children who do well in school are less likely to be delinquent. What does Social Learning Theory say about this relationship? What about Social Bond Theory and labeling theories? Which of these approaches do you think best explains the relationship between school failure and delinquency?
3. Hirschi and Gottfredson's General Theory of Crime has gained strong empirical support. What are the policy implications of this theory? What should the system do with a 16-year-old offender? A 12 year old?
4. One policy suggestion of Labeling Theory is radical non-intervention. Can you think of an instance in which such policy seems appropriate? What about when it might not be appropriate? Are there people and/or delinquent acts for which non-intervention should not be an option?
5. Online activity. Go to prisonexp.org. Click on the link for "the story." Read the material and view the short video clips of the Zimbardo prison experiment provided here. Using this new information, how do you think labeling someone might change or not change their identity and behavior?

REFERENCES

Akers, R. L. (1996). Is differential association/social learning cultural deviance theory? *Criminology, 34,* 229–247.

Akers, R. L., Krohn, M. D., Lanza-Kaduce, L., & Radosevich, M. (1979). Social learning and deviant behavior: A specific test of a general theory. *American sociological review*, 636–655.

Anderson, E. (1994). The code of the streets. *Atlantic Monthly, 273,* 80–94.

Anderson, E. (1998). Violence and the inner-city street code. In Joan McCord (Ed.), *Violence and Children in the Inner City*. New York: Cambridge University Press.

Anderson, E. (2000). *Code of the street: Decency, violence and the moral life of the inner city.* New York: Norton.

Becker, H. (1963). *The outsiders.* New York: Free Press.

Braithewaite, J. (1989). *Crime, shame and reintegration*. Cambridge, UK: Cambridge University Press.

Burkett, S., & Hickman, C. (1982). An examination of the impact of legal sanction on adolescent marijuana use: A panel analysis. *Journal of Drug Issues, 12,* 73–87.

Chiricos, T., Barrick, K., Bales, W., & Bontrager, S. (2007). The labeling of convicted felons and its consequences for recidivism. *Criminology, 45*(3), 547–581.

Cullen, F. T., & Gendreau, P. (2001). From nothing works to what works: Changing professional ideology in the 21st century. *Prison Journal, 81,* 313–338.

Cullen, F. T., Wright, J. P., Gendreau, P., & Andrews, D. A. (2003). What correctional treatment can tell us about criminological theory: Implications for social learning theory. *Social learning theory and the explanation of crime: A guide for the new century. Advances in criminological theory* 11 (pp. 339–362). New Brunswick, NJ: Transaction.

Curran, D., & Renzetti, C. (2001). *Theories of crime* (2nd ed.). Boston: Allyn and Bacon.

Foster, J., Dinitz, S., & Reckless, W. (1972). Perceptions of stigma following public intervention for delinquency behavior. *Social Problems, 23,* 202–209.

Gresham M., & Matza, D. (1957). Techniques of neutralization: A theory of delinquency. *American Sociological Review, 22*(6).

Hagan, J., & Foster, H. (2006). Profiles of punishment and privilege: Secret and disputed deviance during the racialized transition to American adulthood. *Crime, Law and Social Change, 46,* 65–85.

Hepburn, J. (1977). *The impact of police intervention on juvenile delinquency. Criminology, 15,* 235–262.

Hirschi, T. (1969). *Causes of delinquency*. Berkeley: University of California Press.

Lemert, E. M. (1951). *Social pathology*. New York: McGraw-Hill.

Matsueda, R. L. (1988). The current state of differential association theory. *Crime and Delinquency, 34,* 277–306.

Matza, D. (1964). *Delinquency and drift*. New York: Wiley.

Mead, G. H. (1930). Cooley's contribution to American social thought. *American Sociological Review, 35,* 693–706.

Mead, G. H. (1934). *Mind, self and society.* Chicago: University of Chicago Press.

Reckless, W. C. (1961). A new theory of delinquency and crime. *Federal Probation, 24,* 42–46.

Reiss, A. J. Jr. (1951). Delinquency as the failure of personal and social controls. *American Sociological Review, 16,* 196–207.

Schur, E. (1973). *Radical nonintervention*. Englewood Cliffs; NJ: Prentice-Hall.

Sutherland, E. H. (1947). *Principles of criminology*. Philadelphia: J.B Lippincott.

Sykes, G. M., & Matza, D. (1957). Techniques of neutralization: A theory of delinquency. *American Sociological Review, 22,* 664–70.

Sweeten, G. (2006). Who will graduate? Disruption of high school education by arrest and court involvement. *Justice Quarterly, 23*(4), 462–480.

Tannenbaum, F. (1938). *Crime and the community*. Boston: Ginn.

Thomas, C., & Bishop, D. (1984). The effect of formal and informal sanctions on delinquency. *Journal of Criminal Law and Criminology, 75,* 1222–1245.

Toby, J. (1957). Social disorganization and stake in conformity: Complementary factors in the predatory behavior of hoodlums. *Journal of Criminal Law, Criminology and Police Science, 48,* 12.

8 Developmental and Integrated Theory

The case of *Roper v. Simmons* (543 U.S. 551, 2005) has become famous because it was in this case that the United States Supreme Court ruled that it was illegal to execute someone who was under the age of 18 at the time of his/her crime. Previous cases (*Thompson v. Oklahoma* 487 U.S. 815, 1988; *Stanford v. Kentucky* 492 U.S. 361, 1989) had already outlawed such penalty for 15 and 16 year olds respectively. Other than the fact that this case changed the use of the death penalty in the United States there are two reasons that I bring it up at the beginning of a theory chapter. First, much of the accounts of the case focus on the childhood of the defendant, Christopher Simmons, and understanding how he came to commit this crime. If you search his name in the "Murderpedia," an online encyclopedia of murderers, you will find, along with information on the case, this information on his childhood.

Christopher Simmons

Source: www.washingtonpost.com (accessed Jan. 9, 2010)

CHRISTOPHER SIMMONS SUFFERED PHYSICAL AND MENTAL ABUSE

According to testimony, Simmons' stepfather, Bob Hayes, was an alcoholic who was both physically and emotionally abusive to Christopher during his childhood. It was reported that Hayes would scream at young Christopher and severely beat him. In one documented incident, Hayes had tied the toddler to a tree so that he could fish without being bothered to supervise the youth. This scenario was reported by Bob Hayes himself in an interview with Dr. Robert Smith, a clinical psychologist who evaluated Christopher Simmons after he was sentenced to death.

ALCOHOL AND DRUG ADDICTION

It is also reported that Christopher was exposed to alcohol at an early age. His maternal aunt reported seeing him being served alcohol at his mother's wedding. Other incidents include a report that when Christopher was four, his father took him to a bar and gave him alcohol for the amusement of others. By the time Christopher was a teenager he was drinking hard liquor and smoking marijuana almost daily. He also reported that on occasion, he would use hallucinogens such as mushrooms, LSD, and cocaine. Moreover, when the abuse at home became severe, Christopher would use his neighbor's trailer as an escape. The neighbor, a 28-year-old man, would provide drugs and alcohol to neighborhood children and often require the youth to commit various crimes for him to "pay" for their drugs.

POSSIBLE MENTAL ILLNESS

According to Dr. Smith, given the environment in which Simmons was raised and his family's prior generational history of psychiatric illnesses and substance abuse, he was predisposed to having a mental illness. Thus, it is no surprise that in addition to all these social ills, Dr. Smith testified that Christopher suffered from schizotypal personality disorder. This disorder is distinguished by a pervasive pattern of social and interpersonal deficits. In particular, this disorder includes acute discomfort and a reduced capacity for close relationships and cognitive and perceptual distortions. Finally, Dr. Smith also reported that the lack of a loving and supportive male role model in his life contributed to his problems, including low self-confidence, lack of self-esteem, and "distorted" views about relationships with others.

From this description of Simmons' childhood you can see that it was not just one thing that was impacting his development, but rather a host of risk factors that together led to the tragic day when, at the age of 17, Christopher Simmons would commit a heinous murder. Because many youth are subject to multiple factors that put them at risk of delinquency (e.g., bad family environment, negative influences in the neighborhood, access to drugs and alcohol, mental illness, etc.) it is sometimes hard to select which theory of delinquency might fit best when examining a case. Thus, in recent years, many criminologists have attempted to integrate theories to account for this multi-faceted nature of delinquency. Moreover, as is noted above, the process by which Christopher Simmons became a murderer did not start when he was a teenager; in fact it perhaps started as early as two years of age when his stepfather admitted to tying him to a tree so he would not have to watch him. This leads to the second focus of this chapter, which is developmental theories of delinquency that, instead of focusing on just the teenage years (when most crime occurs), focus on the broader life course from birth through adulthood.

In this chapter you will notice that we will bring together a lot of the ideas you have already learned into some of the most modern and currently influential theories of criminology. The first thing that will be discussed is "integrated theories," which are theories that attempt to tie together some of the key components of many of the theories you have learned into a more comprehensive explanation of delinquency. The second thing you will explore are developmental theories that look at delinquency across the life course from its beginnings, sometime in early childhood, until its end, sometimes early in adolescents, and other times not until later in adulthood. These two ideas are not mutually exclusive, as many developmental theories integrate ideas from other theories as well. Finally, we will consider one modern approach to juvenile justice which focuses less on theoretical causation of delinquency and more on just knowing what risk factors are correlated with delinquency, in order to help those working in the system to better identify and provide early treatment and prevention to at-risk youth.

CHAPTER GOALS

By the end of this chapter you should be able to:

1. Define and differentiate what is meant by a developmental and an integrated theory of delinquency.
2. Recognize and point out the overlap in many of the theories learned in the prior four chapters.
3. Discuss the importance of the family, the school and the community environment on development and how these influences may differ across the lifespan.
4. Identify and differentiate risk and protective factors that contribute to or reduce delinquency.
5. Be prepared to apply these principles to the application of juvenile justice and recognize the connections between theory (presented in this and the previous four chapters) and juvenile justice practice (presented in the following four chapters.)

Integrated Theory

Integrated Theory takes ideas or components from other theories and ties them together into one broader theory

As might be obvious from the title, an **integrated theory** is one that takes ideas or components from other theories and ties them together into one broader theory. For example, Social Learning Theory posits that we learn in small intimate groups from those to whom we are closest. Social Bond Theory talks about the importance of attachment to one's parents. One could take these two ideas and say that we learn more definitions from our parents when we have a close personal attachment to them. This is a simple example of connections that can be made across theories. Some theorists have taken this further and developed what are considered fully integrated theories of delinquency. Here I will present two of the most popular such theories and walk you through where each of the components comes from and how the theorists tie the ideas together.

One of the first noted integrated theories was offered by Elliott, Ageton and Cantor in 1979. In their theory they explicitly state components of three theories you have already learned about: Strain Theory, Social Control Theory and Social Learning Theory. First, these authors posit that the main premise of Strain Theory is that delinquency occurs in response to actual or anticipated failure to achieve desired goals (such as money, power, or even social status). This should sound familiar to you. Second, they note that the probability of delinquency as a response to strain is increased when one also has low levels of social control. Moreover, since social control includes community elements such as social disorganization, they note that living in a socially disorganized area can both reduce social control and increase levels of strain. Next, the authors bring in elements of social learning theory, particularly within adolescent peer groups. Here the authors deviate a bit from traditional control theory that assumes all bonds are good, and note that bonds to delinquent peers promote delinquent attitudes and reward delinquent behaviors. Figure 8.1 below adopted from a later version of the theory visually demonstrates the causal pathway to delinquency proposed by this integrated theory:

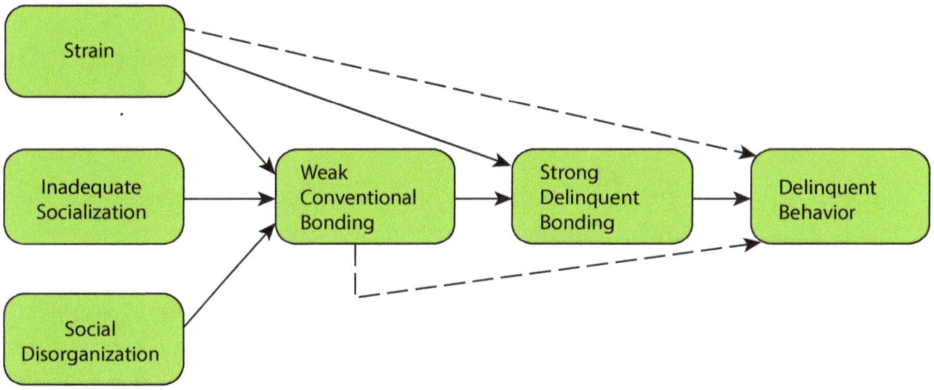

FIGURE 8.1 The Causal Pathway to Delinquency Proposed by Integrated Theory

Republished with permission of SAGE Publications, from *Explaining Delinquency and Drug Use*, Delbert S. Elliot, © 1985; permission conveyed through Copyright Clearance Center, Inc.

One important thing to note here is that the authors do not simply say, "Strain and control theories together cause delinquency." Instead they talk specifically about points made in each theory and integrate those ideas. They also note when their approach deviates at all from one of the original theories (e.g., the idea that bonds to delinquent friends are bad, which is in line with social learning theories but contradictory to social control/bond theory).

A second popular and more recently proposed integrated theory is Thornberry's Interactional Theory that also combines elements of social control and social learning theory (Thornberry, 1987). Specifically, Thornberry lays out the elements from each theory he will integrate. From Hirschi's version of Social Bond Theory he specifically takes:

- Attachment to parents
- Commitment to school
- Beliefs in conventional values

From Sutherland's Differential Association Theory he then combines:

- Association with delinquent peers
- Adoption of delinquent values

After spelling out these factors, Thornberry notes that his main emphasis is on the social control factors—that is, it is the weak bonds that provide the opportunity for delinquency. Once such opportunity exists, the delinquent peers provide the exposure to the delinquent values that then provide the motivation for delinquency. His theory is "interactional" in that he proposes that these two ideas—control and learning—are reciprocal. That is, weak attachment to parents and low commitment to school can lead to bonding with delinquent peers. This bonding with delinquent peers and adoption of delinquent values then serves to further weaken pro-social bonds and so on.

Another important element of Thornberry's theory is that he proposes that these influences may differ in importance based on age and proposes three distinct periods: 1) early adolescence, ages 11 to 13; 2) middle adolescence, ages 14 to 17 and 3) late adolescence, ages 18 to 20. He suggests that attachment to parents matters the most in early adolescence as this might then influence commitment to school and selection of peers. During middle adolescence, these things matter less as peers now take on a more significant role in the teenager's life and it is the social learning through peers that is center stage. Then, in late adolescence social control begins to matter more again with new factors coming in such as commitment to other pro-social institutions such as college and/or work.

There have been many tests of Thornberry's theory, particularly growing out of the Rochester Youth Development Study (RYDS) which you learn more about in this chapter's Focus on Research. This unique longitudinal data set has provided the opportunity to study the middle and later adolescent aspects of the theory. Tests of the period of early adolescence found strong causal support for the notion that attachment to parents led to both a decrease in delinquency and an increase in commitment to school (Thornberry, Lizotte, Krohn and Farnworth, 1991). Tests of middle to late adolescence then have found more causal evidence of delinquency as a result of delinquent peers and the reciprocal relationship between delinquent peers and the adoption of delinquent values (Thornberry, Lizotte, Krohn and Farnworth, 1991). This may not be surprising as Thornberry proposed that attachment to parents mattered more at earlier ages (RYDS began interviewing youth at age 14, middle adolescence) and delinquent peers in middle adolescence (Jang, 1999; Thornberry et al., 1994). Overall, Thornberry concludes that a true understanding of delinquency can only be accomplished through the use of longitudinal data sets that follow youth over time and incorporate not only the variety of influences in their lives, but the reciprocal relationships between these concepts.

I selected Thornberry's Interactional Theory as the second integrated theory to present to you for one important reason. Specifically, it suggests that different factors may work differently across the life course. This focus on influences over the life course is a key underlying component of the developmental theories to be discussed next. In fact, some texts identify this theory as an integrated theory, as I did here, while others place it under developmental theories. There is a very thin line, and the classification is not as important as the understanding of the concepts. Here, my focus was to emphasize that integrated theories specifically draw out components of other theories and explain why and how they work together to promote or prevent delinquency. In the next section on developmental theories, the focus is on at what point in the life course delinquency develops and/or ends.

Developmental Theories

Developmental Theory
focus on an aspect or multiple aspects of development over time

Developmental theories are specifically theories that focus on an aspect of development or perhaps multiple aspects of development over time. Some focus more on early childhood, some on later adolescence, but most on the entire developmental process. In fact in this text you have already been introduced to several theories that might be classified as developmental theories.

First, in Chapter 5 when you learned about neurological deficiencies and crime you were introduced to the research of Terrie Moffitt (1993). Her taxonomy of offenders into adolescence-limited (those who succumb to peer pressure and acting out behavior during adolescence) and life-course-persistent offenders (those who develop problem behaviors early on due to biological factors and persist in anti-social behavior throughout life) is considered by many to indeed be a developmental theory of crime. For the adolescence-limited offender her theory focuses on those life influences that are particularly salient during adolescence and are for the most part a natural occurrence (for example, wanting to test the limits and break away from parents to form a unique identity and to begin experimenting with "adult" behaviors). This part of the theory explains why so many teenagers get in trouble as compared to other age groups. On the other side, her notion of a life-course-persistent offender focuses on factors that are present since birth, such as a neurological problem that impacts how the child interacts with the environment, and also discusses how this problem manifests over time.

Another theory you have learned that some consider a developmental theory is the General Theory of Crime by Gottfredson and Hirschi (1990). This theory focuses on early childhood and the development of self-control that encompasses environmental factors, parenting and personality traits. Others, including myself, would argue that this is a "latent" trait theory rather than a developmental theory since, according to the theory's authors, once self-control is developed or not, the path is set for the individual by about age 8. Thus, it leaves little room for later "development."

DEVELOPMENTAL PATHWAYS TO CRIME

Perhaps one of the earliest development theories of crime was created by Rolf Loeber. Using a sample of youths entering the first, fourth and seventh grades in Pittsburgh, Pennsylvania in 1987, this longitudinal study was able to follow the children forward in time and capture the onset of delinquency and continuation of delinquency, particularly for the youth in the youngest sample (i.e., entering first grade). Based on the study of these youth, Loeber and colleagues (1991) proposed that there were three different pathways that a child could follow into delinquency and that these pathways prescribed, at least to some extent, the types of delinquency in which the youth would become involved.

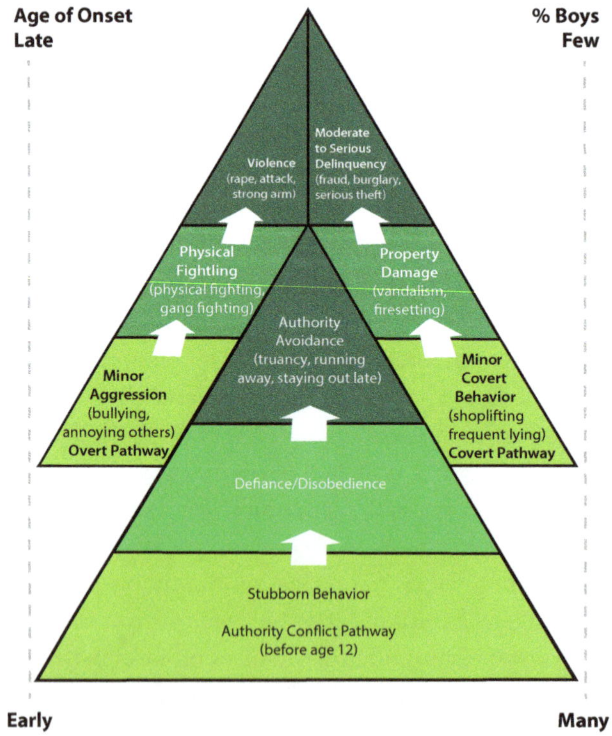

FIGURE 8.2 Pathways to Boys' Disruptive Behavior and Delinquency
https://www.ojjdp.gov/jjbulletin/9805/offenders.html Serious and Violent Juvenile Offenders, *Juvenile Justice Bulletin,* May 1998.

The first pathway is the authority **conflict pathway**. This path begins with simple stubborn behavior, which then leads to defiance of authority and eventually avoidance of any authority. These youth engage in behaviors such as staying out after curfew, running away from home, and skipping school.

Conflict Pathway

begins with simple stubborn behavior which leads to defiance of authority and eventually avoidance of any authority

The second pathway is the **covert pathway**, which begins with simple lying. From there the behavior may escalate into shoplifting, fraud and other types of theft and property crimes.

Covert Pathway

begins with simple lying but may escalate into shoplifting, fraud and other types of theft and property crimes

The final pathway is the **overt pathway**. These youth exhibit problem behavior such as bullying in school. Their behaviors escalate into violence such as assault and robbery and these youth are more likely than others to join a gang.

Overt Pathway

begins with problem behavior such as bullying in school which escalates into violence such as assault and robbery

Loeber notes that not every child who exhibits the early minor behaviors goes on to a life of crime, and that some children enter more than one of these pathways—that is, they are not mutually exclusive. The research also further divided each pathway into three stages from early exhibition of the behaviors, through later escalation of behavior. Research using these stages helps to further define what Loeber and colleagues (LeBlanc, Cote & Loeber, 1991; Loeber, Stouthamer-Loeber & Green, 1991; Loeber, Keenan & Zhang, 1997) called experimenters or persisters in crime as follows:

- Persisters will be more likely than experimenters to enter a pathway at its first stage.
- Experimenters will be more likely than persisters to enter a pathway at the second or third stage.
- Persisters will be much more likely than experimenters to follow the sequence of stages in a pathway, thereby developing different manifestations of disruptive behavior more predictably.

Again, here some clear connections can be seen between this theory and Moffitt's, showing that some youth enter delinquency and problem behaviors early and that these youth are the most likely to persist while others experiment more briefly and often less seriously with delinquency.

THE AGE-GRADED THEORY OF INFORMAL SOCIAL CONTROL

The most well-known developmental theory is the Age-Graded Theory of Informal Social Control (also often called the Age-Graded Theory of Crime) developed by Robert Sampson and John Laub (1993). This theory in particular could also be considered an integrated theory as the diagram in Figure 8.3 shows it

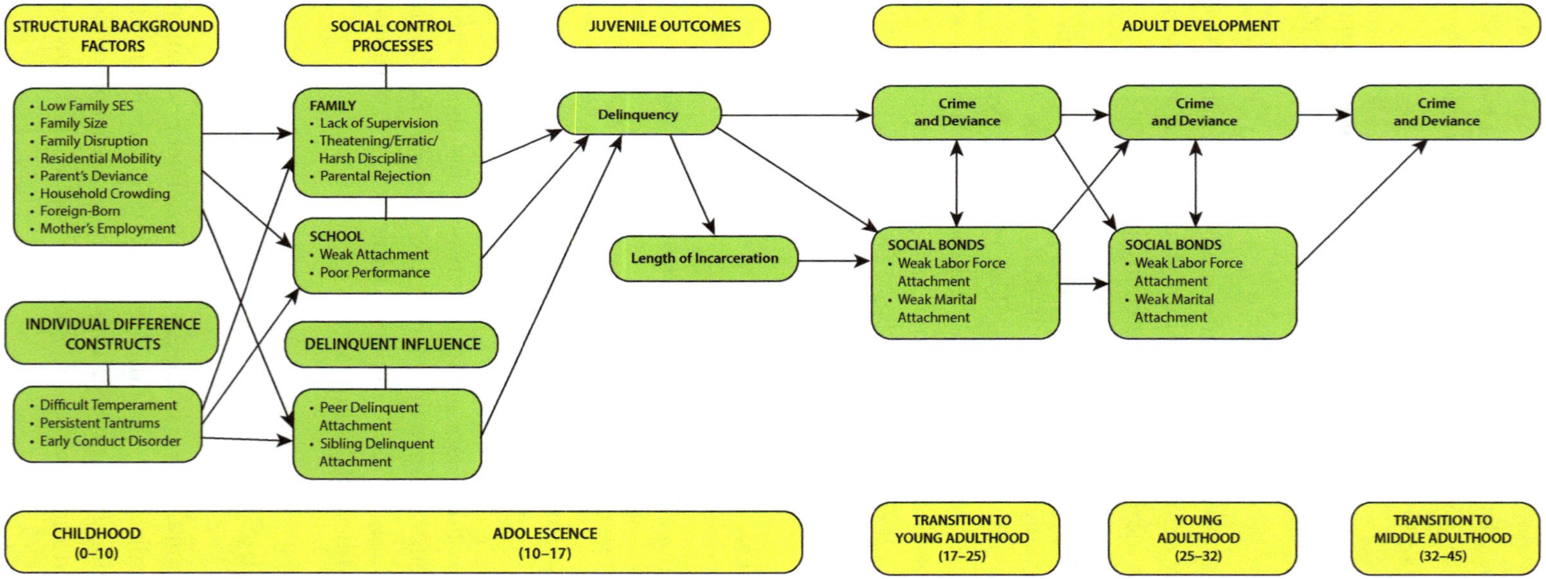

FIGURE 8.3 Age-Graded Theory of Informal Social Control

Diagram of Theory from Robert Sampson and John Laub. Crime in the Making: pathways and Turning Points through Life. 1993 pp 244-245. Republished with permission of SAGE Publications, from *Explaining Delinquency and Drug Use,* Delbert S. Elliot,© 1985; permission conveyed through Copyright Clearance Center, Inc.

begins with considerations of structural factors that include components of Social Disorganization Theory, such as poverty, residential mobility and family disruption. It also includes key concepts from Social Bond Theory, such as weak attachments to parents and school, and, although not directly stated, elements of Social Learning Theory through the influences of delinquent peers.

The theory also adds some new and important considerations from other disciplines that have become important and respected tenets in criminology. These ideas are those of trajectories, transitions and turning points (Rutter, 1996). A **trajectory** is the path a person is following (Nagin, 1999). It could be a good path, such as doing well in preschool, succeeding in elementary school, making honors and taking AP classes in high school and moving on to college and a good career. Or, it could be a negative path such as entering kindergarten unprepared, acting out in elementary school, dropping out of high school and joining a gang. A **transition** is a time in life when things are changing. For example, leaving high school and starting college is a big transition for many youth. Transition can also be considered to be "on-time" such as starting college when you are 18 or 19, or off-time, perhaps returning to college when you are 40. Another example is having a baby. An on-time transition would be having a baby that is planned when you are in your '20s or '30s. An off-time transition would be a teenage pregnancy. Off-time transitions are considered to be more difficult to navigate successfully than on-time transitions.

Trajectory

the path a person is following

Transition

a time in life when things are changing

This leads to an important concept in this theory. A transition can be navigated without changing the life trajectory, or it can provide for a **turning point** (Abbott, 1997). Moreover, turning points can be either good or bad. For instance, from the first example above, take the youth who succeeded all through school, but perhaps when he got to college the party scene was too inviting and he became involved in alcohol and drug use and started failing classes and then was arrested for possession of drugs on campus. This could be a negative turning point. On the other hand for the other youth, if after dropping out of school he was arrested and assigned a youth mentor, this mentor could provide a turning point for the youth encouraging him to complete his GED and to go on to college.

Turning Point

when a transition leads to a change or turn in a developmental trajectory--either for better or worse

Another unique component of Sampson and Laub's theory is the idea of "adult social bonds" serving as positive turning points to lead a youth out of delinquency. The key social bonds they focus on are employment, as work and a career replace the importance that school held during adolescence, and marriage, as the forming of a new bond/family replaces the family of origin.

Research on the Age-Graded Theory of Crime is mixed, but overall has been generally supportive. In particular research supports the notion that people do really change over the life course and what might be predictive of delinquency in adolescence is not so in adulthood (Paternoster & Brame, 1997). Research also supports the notion that life trajectories can be improved if life conditions improve. For example, Macmillan and colleagues found that children of mothers who were originally living in poverty but were able to improve their circumstances were no more likely to develop behavior problems than children who never lived in poverty (Macmillan, McMorris & Kruttschnitt, 2004). Research on the adult social bonds of employment and marriage has been slightly more mixed, but the overall consensus seems to be the stable work and good relationships (marriage or cohabiting) do reduce delinquency, while part-time work and unstable or abusive relationships do not (Horney & Osgood, 1995; Laub, Nagin & Sampson, 1998; McCord, 2001; Sampson & Laub, 1996).

RYDS
Rochester Youth Development Study where 1,000 inner-city youth were studied beginning in 1987 and continues today (2018) looking at the influence of the inner-city on their development over the life course

FOCUS ON RESEARCH: RYDS

In 1987 a team of researchers from the University at Albany School of Criminal Justice started a project known as the **Rochester Youth Development Study (RYDS)**. These three colleagues, Drs. Terence Thornberry, Alan Lizotte and Marvin Krohn, received funding from the National Institute of Drug and Alcohol Abuse to begin a study of 1,000 youth growing up in inner-city Rochester, New York. The original sample of 1,000 youths was selected to over-represent youth exposed to risk factors for delinquency to allow for a closer study of how these factors influence development over the life course. The original sample of youths were 13 or 14 years old in 1987 and were interviewed every six months until their 19th birthday. Thereafter, they were interviewed annually. In addition to these youths, the study also included interviews with their parents, and continues today in 2018—now tracking the original subjects and their children as well.

In addition to the interviews with parents, children and now the children's children, this research also collected official education, police and social service reports to provide a more complete picture of the youths' developmental environment. This type of study, known as longitudinal research (Chapter 3), tracks the same individuals across time and helps researchers better understand what leads a child into and even out of delinquency.

To date, this project has resulted in over 150 publications that span topics from parental attachment, school achievement, gang involvement, and drug and alcohol addiction to peer influences on delinquency. Research from this project was influential in the development of Thornberry's Interactional Theory, to a better understanding of peer influence on delinquency and in particular to the nature of gang involvement, including gang entering, gang exiting and the long-term influence of gang membership on life outcomes. Most recently with the children of the original participants now entering adolescence, the study is beginning to be able to track intergenerational transmission of attitudes and behaviors. As criminologists become more and more interested in how delinquency develops and desists over the lifespan, these long-term studies become more and more important to the study of delinquency. Other studies you might want to look up online are:

- The Pittsburgh Youth Study (Principal Investigator Rolf Loeber)
- The Denver Youth Study (Principal Investigator, Delbert Elliott)
- The National Longitudinal Survey of Youth (U.S. Department of Labor)
- The National Longitudinal Study of Adolescent to Adult Health (Carolina Population Center)

Partial List of Publications:

Thornberry, Terence P., Marvin Krohn, Alan Lizotte, and Deborah Chard-Wierschem. 1993. The role of juvenile gangs in facilitating delinquent behavior. *Journal of Research in Crime and Delinquency 30*(1): 55–87.

Thornberry, Terence P., Alan J. Lizotte, Marvin D. Krohn, Margaret Farnworth, and Joon Jang. 1994. Delinquent peers, beliefs and delinquent behavior: A longitudinal test of interactional theory. *Criminology 32*(1): 47–83.

Smith, C., A. J. Lizotte, T. P. Thornberry, and M.D. Krohn. 1995. Resilient youth: identifying factors that prevent high-risk youth from engaging in delinquency and drug use. *Current Perspectives on Aging and the Life Course 4*: 217–247.

Thornberry, Terence P., David Huizinga, and Rolf Loeber. 1995. The prevention of serious delinquency and violence: Implications from the Program of Research on the Causes and Correlates of Delinquency. In Rolf Loeber and David P. Farrington (eds.) *Serious, Violent, and Chronic Juvenile Offenders: A Sourcebook*. Thousand Oaks, CA: Sage Publications.

Krohn, Marvin D., Alan J. Lizotte, Terence P. Thornberry, Carolyn Smith, and David McDowall. 1996. Reciprocal causal relationships among drug use, peers, and beliefs: A five wave panel model. *Journal of Drug Issues 26*(2): 405–428.

Weerman, Frank M., Peter J. Lovegrove, and Terence Thornberry. 2014. Gang membership transitions and its consequences: Exploring changes related to joining and leaving gangs in two countries. *European Journal of Criminology 12*(1): 70–91.

Thornberry, Terence P., and James H. Burch II. 1997. Gang members and delinquency behavior. *Bulletin*. NCJ 165154, Washington, DC: United States Department of Justice, Office of Justice Programs, Office of Juvenile Justice and Delinquency Prevention.

For a full list visit of publications please see: https://www.icpsr.umich.edu/icpsrweb/ICPSR/biblio/series/00566/resources?collection=DATA&archive=ICPSR&sortBy=1

Risk and Protective Factor Approach

Not all researchers or practitioners buy into the idea that one theory, even if it is integrated and developmental, can ever describe all delinquency. Some criminologists and practitioners adhere to a more direct approach of identifying the **risk factors** that we know delinquency. That is, we know youths growing up in poverty are more likely to turn to crime than youths growing up in families with more money. From a risk factor approach it does not matter if poverty causes crime by putting the individual under strain, or by disorganizing the community, we just know that individuals living in poverty are more crime prone, so we work to address poverty.

Risk Factor
things such as poverty that increase the probability of delinquency

This approach is appealing as most youths who come into the juvenile justice system do not present with just one problem. Rather they have a host of problems. This is often referred to as the **comorbidity** of risk factors. Think back to the example provided at the beginning of the chapter. This particular youth, Christopher Simmons, did not just have a bad home life, but also suffered from potential mental illness, and was influenced by the community (e.g., a neighbor who provided drugs and alcohol). Such problems often cluster together in the lives of youths, making them particularly prone to delinquency.

This particular approach to juvenile delinquency is adopted from the public health sphere rather than criminology. Farrington (2000) calls this recent movement toward the public health model the "risk factor paradigm." The basic idea here is to identify the key risk factors a youth or community is facing, and design programs to address these risk factors rather than try to theoretically connect why these risk factors might matter (Farrington, 2000, p. 1).

The U.S. Surgeon General defines a risk factor as "anything that increases the probability that a person will suffer harm" (Office of the Surgeon General, 2001, chapter 4). Pollard, Hawkins, and Arthur (1999, pg. 146) note that "protective factors are those factors that mediate or moderate the effect of exposure to risk factors, resulting in reduced incidence of problem behavior."

However, researchers disagree about what constitutes a **protective factor**. Protective factors "have been viewed both as the absence of risk and something conceptually distinct from it" (Office of the Surgeon General, 2001, chapter 4). The former view looks at risk and protective factors as opposite ends of a continuum. For example, excellent performance in school might be considered a protective factor because it is the opposite of poor performance in school—a known risk factor. The second view of protective factors sees them as "characteristics or con-

Protective Factor
the absence of risk and characteristics that interact with risk factors to decrease delinquent behavior

ditions that interact with risk factors to reduce their influence on violent behavior" (Office of the Surgeon General, 2001, chapter 4). Thus, while poor school performance might be a risk factor, having a positive connection to a teacher, coach or other influential adult might serve as a "protective" factor that mediates the impact of the poor school performance.

The risk and protective factors are also often envisioned as occurring across domains such as the individual level (e.g., for Christopher Simmons this would be his own mental illness), the family level (e.g., for Christopher Simmons this would be the abusive stepfather), and the community level (e.g., the presence or access to drugs and alcohol etc.). The following chart (Figure 8.4) from the U.S. Surgeon General provides one such depiction of risk and protective factors.

FIGURE 8.4 U.S. Surgeon General's Risk Factors for Youth Violence

Risk Factors	Definition	Adolescent Substance Use	Young Adult Substance Use
Individual/Peer			
Early initiation of substance use	Engaging in alcohol or drug use at a young age.	✔	✔
Early and persistent problem behavior	Emotional distress, aggressiveness, and "difficult" temperaments in adolescents.	✔	
Rebelliousness	High tolerance for deviance and rebellious activities.	✔	✔
Favorable attitudes toward substance use	Positive feelings towards alcohol or drug use, low perception of risk.	✔	✔
Peer substance use	Friends and peers who engage in alcohol or drug use.	✔	✔
Genetic predictors	Genetic susceptibility to alcohol or drug use.	✔	✔
Family			
Family management problems (monitoring, rewards, etc.)	Poor management practices, including parents' failure to set clear expectations for children's behavior, failure to supervise and monitor children, and excessively severe, harsh, or inconsistent punishment.	✔	✔
Family conflict	Conflict between parents or between parents and children, including abuse or neglect.	✔	✔
Favorable parental attitudes	Parental attitudes that are favorable to drug use and parental approval of drinking and drug use.	✔	✔
Family history of substance misuse	Persistent, progressive, and generalized substance use, misuse, and use disorders by family members.	✔	✔

Risk Factors	Definition	Adolescent Substance Use	Young Adult Substance Use
School			
Academic failure beginning in late elementary school	Poor grades in school.	✔	✔
Lack of commitment to school	When a young person no longer considers the role of the student as meaningful and rewarding, or lacks investment or commitment to school.	✔	✔
Community			
Low cost of alcohol	Low alcohol sales tax, happy hour specials, and other price discounting.	✔	✔
High availability of substances	High number of alcohol outlets in a defined geographical area or per a sector of the population.	✔	✔
Community laws and norms favorable to substance use	Community reinforcement of norms suggesting alcohol and drug use is acceptable for youth, including low tax rates on alcohol or tobacco or community beer tasting events.	✔	✔
Media portrayal of alcohol use	Exposure to actors using alcohol in movies or television.	✔	
Low neighborhood attachment	Low level of bonding to the neighborhood.	✔	
Community disorganization	Living in neighborhoods with high population density, lack of natural surveillance of public places, physical deterioration, and high rates of adult crime.	✔	
Low socioeconomic status	A parent's low socioeconomic status, as measured through a combination of education, income, and occupation.	✔	
Transitions and mobility	Communities with high rates of mobility within or between communities.	✔	

From Office of the Surgeon General. 2001. *Youth Violence: A Report of the Surgeon General.* Washington, DC: U.S. Department of Health and Human Services, Office of the Secretary, Office of Public Health and Science, Office of the Surgeon General. Retrieved from www.surgeongeneral.gov/librar/youthviolence

As you might imagine, this approach is semi-controversial as many believe you must understand the causes, not just the correlates, of delinquency to address it. However, I present it here as this approach is currently very influential in the practice of juvenile justice and it provides you with useful knowledge before delving into the final section of the text where we address the actual current practice of juvenile justice.

FOCUS ON POLICY: Youth Violence as a Public Health Problem, the Centers for Disease Control's Approach

The Centers for Disease Control has identified youth violence as a public health problem since the 1980s. Recent statistics released by the CDC reveal that:

- 4,828 young people aged 10 to 24 were victims of homicide—an average of 13 each day—in 2010.
- Over 707,000 young people aged 10 to 24 years had physical assault injuries treated in U.S. emergency departments in 2011—an average of 1,938 each day.
- In a 2011 nationwide survey, about 33% of high school students reported being in a physical fight in the 12 months before the survey.
- About 5% of high school students in 2011 reported taking a weapon to school in the 30 days before the survey (Centers for Disease Control and Prevention, 2011).

Moreover, the CDC estimates that this violence costs the U.S. over $16 billion per year in health care and lost earnings (Centers for Disease Control and Prevention, 2012).

The CDC approach to attacking youth violence includes four steps as follows: defining the problem, identifying risk factors, developing and testing prevention programs and ensuring widespread adoption of such programs. The CDC has also released many publications specific to combatting various forms of youth violence such as school bullying and gang joining. Throughout all of these publications the risk/protective factor approach discussed previously in this chapter can be seen, which is reflective of the medical model of prevention.

Thus a child with multiple risk factors might fare better in terms of not engaging in delinquency or violence if one or more protective and promotive factors are present. As we cannot always "cure" risk factors, such as poverty, then, it is important to introduce to the greatest extent possible protective and promotive factors to reduce violence.

JUVENILE JUSTICE POLICY APPLICATIONS

Integrated and developmental theories have perhaps some of the most influential and interesting direct and indirect applications to juvenile justice. First, as might be obvious from integrated theories, they suggest that it is not enough to look at just one aspect of a juvenile's life, such as the family or peer relations. Instead, these theories show that all these factors matter for a youth. For example, while social disorganization theory promoted programs to organize the community, integrated and developmental theories would also consider these important. However, they would not assume that any one such approach might "fix" the problem. Instead, in addition to addressing problems in the community, these theories suggest one must also look at the individual youth, the family, the youth's peers and any other immediate influences on development.

Also, with the focus on development, many of these theories start early in life—way before the typical "juvenile justice system" becomes involved with a youth. Thus, there is a focus on early identification of problem behavior and on prevention and intervention efforts that begin well before a youth might find him/herself at the mercy of a juvenile or adult court judge. If delinquency is the end result of a multitude of developmental challenges ranging from biological to social, then the earlier the intervention begins the better the outcomes for the individual youth, the family, the community and ultimately the safety of society. Thus, early identification and prevention of problem behaviors becomes a crucial part of a juvenile justice system that was designed to deal with teenagers. In the next chapters that deal more directly with the juvenile justice system, you will see that most of the system does indeed deal directly with adolescents. However, the Federal Juvenile Justice and Delinquency Prevention Act passed in the 1970s does indeed include a focus on "delinquency prevention," which opens the door for the system to consider, develop and implement a variety of programs that are not merely aimed at adolescents, but that reach back to the social welfare roots of the child saver's movement (Chapter 2) and place a strong emphasis on treating the child in the home, school and local community (the social context of development) rather than removing the child and placing him or her in any type of placement, unless it is a last resort. In the final section of this book I will be referring back to all of the theories you have learned thus far as they relate to the different components and treatment options utilized in the past and today by this nation's juvenile justice system.

FIGURE 8.5 Theory Summary Box			
	Underlying Assumptions	**Cause of Crime**	**System Application**
Integrated Theory	Ideas from Social Control and Strain	Actual or anticipated failure and lack of social control	Increase social control for youth experiencing strain
Interactional Theory	Ideas from Social Control and Differential Association	Low social control and bonds with delinquent peers	Increase social control and reduce exposure to delinquent peers
Pathways Theory	Ideas from Biological and Learning Theories	Different causes for different pathways	Identify problem behavior early before progression on pathway
Age-Graded Theory	Ideas from Biological, Social Control, Labeling, and Social Structural	Focus on trajectories, turning points and desistance	Provide potential turning points and pro-social bonds

Key Words

- Conflict Pathway
- Covert Pathway
- Developmental Theory
- Integrated Theory
- Overt Pathway
- Protective Factor
- Risk Factor
- RYDS
- Trajectory
- Transition
- Turning Point

Chapter Summary

In this chapter you have learned some new ideas, but mostly you have learned about new ways of packaging and combining old ideas to create innovative approaches to the study of juvenile delinquency. Integrated theories cover a broad variety of theories that integrate ideas or concepts from other theories. While there are many of these theories in existence, in this chapter I chose to focus on two of the most popular and to outline for you their approach to integrating theory. This approach is important as it shows that in order to incorporate theories, you must first understand each theory and then decide which components of the theories, and how, they will be combined. For example, in Elliott et al.'s approach they clearly note that two of the theories they are combining have different notions about bonds with friends. Social Control Theory states that such bonds are positive, while Differential Association Theory suggests that bonds with delinquent peers promote delinquency. The authors thus clearly note that in their combination of ideas from these theories they select the differential association assumption about how and why ties to delinquent peers matter in the formation of delinquency.

Thornberry's Interactional Theory then not only combines aspects of theories, but notes how they have reciprocal relationships over time and how influences from different sources (family, school, peers) may vary by age. For example, while family is of primary importance in childhood, by middle adolescence peers have taken over as the key influence in a juvenile's life. This theory provided a nice lead in from integration of theory to developmental theory that looks at crime and delinquency across the life course.

The Pathways Theory presents three trajectories that youth can follow into delinquency that start early in life with minor behaviors and that can escalate over time. They are the overt, the covert and the authority conflict pathways. These pathways are not, however, mutually exclusive and entry into one does not always mean that a youth follows through to the worst possible outcome. Instead the theory incorporates various factors that can either help or hinder a youth's positive social development.

The second developmental theory you were introduced to is probably the most influential theory of crime today. The Age-Graded Theory developed by John Laub and Robert Sampson, built off of the data started by the Gleucks decades before (Chapter 5). They followed these juvenile delinquents into adulthood and looked for factors that helped them either desist from crime, or continue on a criminal trajectory. The theory can easily be seen as an integrated theory as there are notions of structural factors, personality traits, social bonds, and differential associations as well as even labeling by the system. I classify it here, however, as a developmental theory, as its main focus is on what allows an individual to either continue on a given trajectory over time, or to alter this trajectory through a developmental turning point and change their life course.

This ability of people to change as they develop was indeed key to the U.S. Supreme Court decision in *Roper v. Simmons* that you were introduced to in the beginning of the chapter. In fact one of the requirements in the implementation of the death penalty is that it be reserved for only the most heinous offenders. The U.S. Supreme Court determined in this case that a juvenile offender can NEVER be classified as such since the individual was a youth and thus the behaviors exhibited were not necessarily indicative of the adult he/she was to become. In the beginning of this text you saw that the progressives, so many years ago, fought for separate institutions for youth and ultimately a separate system of justice because they believed juveniles were fundamentally different than adults in that they were developing into the adults they would one day become (Chapter 2). Then, in Chapter 5, you learned much about the brain development of youth and how modern day science has indeed confirmed that juveniles are different than adults. In this chapter you have now learned that developmental theories address these differences over time from early childhood all the way through adulthood, and that such development can be and is the foundation of legal regulations regarding the treatment of juveniles in both the adult and juvenile justice system.

This concludes our journey into the world of theories of delinquency; in the next section you will learn how today's juvenile justice system actually operates and the real-world consequences of the theories you just studied.

Discussion Questions

1. The analysis of Christopher Simmons's childhood was drawn from the "murderpedia" online. Go to this source and identify another murderer (child or adult) and see if you can come up with a list of developmental challenges and risk factors that may have led to this individual becoming a murderer. Can you connect them with any theories you have learned so far? If so, which ones?

2. Integrated theories draw on already posited theories, and rather than creating a new theory, combine elements of existing theories. Some individuals think this is not a good approach as the various theories make different assumptions about how individuals think and choose to act or are pushed into actions by society. Are there particular theories that you think seem to integrate well based on their underlying assumptions? What theories might not integrate well because they are too different?
3. Thornberry's Interactional Theory suggests that different things might matter more at different times in the life course. Think back through your own life up to today. At what times did family matter most? Are there times you were more influenced by your peers than your family? What influences matter most to you today?
4. Entering college could be considered a major life transition. Using Sampson and Laub's theory discuss what things might help you continue on your current life trajectory toward academic success. Can you identify challenges college students face that might make it hard to navigate this transition? Give an example of what could alter a positive life trajectory.

REFERENCES

Abbott, A. (1997). On the concept of turning point. *Comparative Social Research,* 16, 85–105.

Centers for Disease Control and Prevention. (2010). National center for injury prevention and control. Web-based injury statistics query and reporting system (WISQARS). Retrieved from www.cdc.gov/injury/wisqars

Centers for Disease Control and Prevention Youth Risk Behavior Surveillance—United States, 2011. (2012). *MMWR, Surveillance Summaries 2012, 61*(SS-4).

Centers for Disease Control and Prevention. Fact sheet, understanding youth violence. Retrieved from www.cdc.gov/youthviolence//pdf/yv_factsheet2012-a.pdf

Elliott, D., Ageton, S. S., & Cantor, R. (1979). Integrated theoretical perspective on delinquent behavior. *Journal of Research in Crime and Delinquency, 16*(1), 3–27.

Elliott, D. S., Huizinga, D., & Ageton, S. S. (1985). *Explaining delinquency and drug use*. Beverly Hills, CA: Sage.

Farrington, D. P. (2000). Explaining and preventing crime: The globalization of knowledge—The American Society of Criminology 1999 presidential address. *Criminology, 38*(1), 1–24.

Glueck, S., & Glueck, E. (1930). *500 criminal careers*. New York: A.A. Knopf.

Glueck, S., & Glueck, E. (1940). *Juvenile delinquents grown up*. New York: The Commonwealth Fund.

Glueck, S., & Glueck, E. (1943). *Criminal careers in retrospect*. New York: The Commonwealth Fund.

Glueck, S., & Glueck, E. (1950). *Unraveling juvenile delinquency*. New York: The Commonwealth Fund.

Glueck, S., & Glueck, E. (1968). *Delinquents and nondelinquents in perspective*. Cambridge, MA: Harvard University Press.

Gottfredson, M. R., & Hirschi, T. 1990. *A general theory of crime*. Stanford, CA: Stanford University Press.

Horney, J., Osgood, D. W., & Marshall, I. H. (1995). Criminal careers in the short-term: Intra-individual variability in crime and its relation to local life circumstances. *American Sociological Review, 60*, 655–673.

Huizinga, D., Loeber, R., & Thornberry, T. P. (Eds.). (1993). *Urban delinquency and substance abuse: Technical report.* Washington, DC: U.S. Department of Justice, Office of Justice Programs, Office of Juvenile Justice and Delinquency Prevention.

Jang, S. J. (1999). Age varying effects of family, school and peers on delinquency: A multilevel model test of interactional theory. *Criminology, 37*(3), 643–686.

Laub, J. H., Nagin, D. S., & Sampson, R. J. (1998). Trajectories of change in criminal offending: Good marriages and the desistance process. *American Sociological Review, 63*, 225–238.

Le Blanc, M., Côté, G., & Loeber, R. (1991). Temporal paths in delinquency: Stability, regression and progression analyzed with panel data from an adolescent and a delinquent male sample. *Canadian Journal of Criminology* (January), 23–44.

Loeber, R. (1991). Questions and advances in the study of developmental pathways. In D. Cicchetti and S. Toth (Eds.), *Rochester Symposium on Developmental Psychopathology: III.* Rochester, NY: Rochester University Press.

Loeber, R., Keenan, K., & Zhang, Q. (1997). Boys' experimentation and persistence in developmental pathways toward serious delinquency. *Journal of Child and Family Studies, 6*, 321–357.

Loeber, R., Stouthamer-Loeber, M., & Green, S. M. (1991). Age at onset of problem behavior in boys, and later disruptive and delinquent behaviors. *Criminal Behavior and Mental Health, 1,* 229–246.

Macmillan, R., McMorris, M. J., & Kruttschnitt, C. (2004). Linked lives: Stability and change in maternal circumstances and trajectories of antisocial behavior in circumstances and trajectories of antisocial behavior in children. *Child Development, 74,* 205–220.

McCord, J. (2001). Understanding desistance from crime. In Michael Tonry (Ed.), *Crime and Justice: A Review of Research* (Vol. 28, pp. 1–69). Chicago: University of Chicago Press.

Moffitt, T. E. (1993). Adolescence-limited and life-course persistent antisocial behavior: A developmental taxonomy. *Psychological Review, 100,* 674–701.

Nagin, D. S. (1999). Analyzing developmental trajectories: A semi-parametric, group-based approach. *Psychological Methods, 4,* 139–157.

Paternoster, R., & Brame, R. (1997). Multiple routes to delinquency? A test of developmental and general theories of crime. *Criminology, 35,* 49–84.

Office of the Surgeon General. (2001). *Youth violence: A report of the surgeon general.* Washington, DC: U.S. Department of Health and Human Services, Office of the Secretary, Office of Public Health and Science, Office of the Surgeon General. Retrieved from www.surgeongeneral.gov/library/youthviolence

Pollard, J. A., Hawkins, D., & Arthur, M. W. (1999). Risk and protective factors: Are both necessary to understand diverse behavioral outcomes in adolescence? *Social Work Research, 23*(3), 145–158.

Rutter, M. (1990). Psychosocial resilience and protective mechanisms. In Jon Rolf et al. (Eds.), *Risk and Protective Factors in the Development of Psychopathology* (pp. 181–214). Cambridge: Cambridge University Press.

Rutter, M. (1996). Transitions and turning points in developmental psychopathology: As applied to the age span between childhood and mid-adulthood. *International Journal of Behavioral Development, 19,* 603–626.

Sampson, R., & Laub, J. (1993). *Crime in the making: Pathways and turning points through life.* Cambridge, MA: Harvard University Press.

Sampson, R., & Laub, J. (1996). Socioeconomic achievement in the life course of disadvantaged men: Military service as a turning point, circa 1940–1965. *American Sociological Review, 61,* 347–367.

Thornberry, T. P. (1987). Toward an interactional theory of delinquency. *Criminology, 25,* 863–91.

Thornberry, T. P., Lizotte, A. J., Krohn, M. D., & Farnworth, M. (1991). Testing interactional theory: An examination of reciprocal causal relationships among family, school, and delinquency. *Journal of Criminal Law and Criminology, 82*(3), 3–35.

Thornberry, T. P., Lizotte, A. J., Krohn, M. D., Farnworth, M., & Jang, S. J. (1994). Delinquent peers, beliefs and delinquent behavior: A longitudinal test of interactional theory. *Criminology, 32*(1), 47–83.

Section 3

Practicing Juvenile Justice

9 Entering the Juvenile Justice System: Police, Diversion and Detention

© Robert Nickelsberg/Contributor/Getty

The juvenile justice system is just that—a system of processing that sets different priorities, rules and goals from the moment a youth comes into contact with a police officer, to the moment he or she exits the system. Imagine a scenario in which four friends are drinking alcohol in a parking lot after a high school football game. The four youth are all seniors at the high school "celebrating" after the last home football game of the season with a few beers one of the boys has stolen from his parents' refrigerator. A police officer sees the gathering of boys as the parking lot clears and approaches them to determine if there is a situation that requires police intervention. Two of the boys are 17 years old, defined as juveniles in the jurisdiction in which the police officer works. The other two boys are 18, defined as adults in the jurisdiction in which the police officer works. Although the boys look quite similar in appearance and are close friends in the same grade in high school, what happens next to the boys will differ drastically dependent on this age difference at the time of the encounter.

In the following chapter we will discuss in detail the difference in the front end processing of cases for which the youth is defined as a juvenile rather than an adult. While much of the focus in adult criminal justice is on what happens in the courtroom and prisons, you will find that much of the true action in the juvenile system happens before these stages with only a portion of youth who come into contact with the system making it to these later stages.

CHAPTER GOALS

By the end of this chapter you should understand:

1. How police contact and arrest of a youth defined as a juvenile is different than an adult arrest.
2. The intake role of juvenile probation officers.
3. The front-end diversionary tactics of the juvenile justice system, including both how they work and why they are so important.
4. The role of pre-adjudicatory detention as part of the juvenile justice system.

Also, throughout this chapter you will see some of the theories and concepts you have already learned come to life in the day-to-day practices of the juvenile justice system. As each state operates its own version of a juvenile justice system, this chapter will provide a basic summary of the most common practices and use specific state examples of policies and practices to help drive points home. We begin where each youth's experience with the juvenile system would most likely begin: police contact.

The Initial Encounter: Policing Juveniles

The most recent estimates are that police arrest approximately 1.3 million youth under the age of 18 a year (Puzzanchera, 2015). However, these arrests are only part of the picture. Every day, police come into contact with juveniles in a multitude of situations and many times these contacts do not lead to an arrest. Sometimes the officer merely warns the youths about the behavior and lets them go, other times the officer takes the youths home or calls the parents to the police station and releases them to their parents with no formal arrest. In some cases, police departments offer special programs for youths such as police/youth athletic leagues to help keep youths off the streets and out of trouble. What determines whether or not there is a formal arrest? Police have a large amount of **discretion** in their work as they are making decisions "on the spot" and trying to assess all the information being presented in a short period of time to determine whether an arrest is warranted. Factors that often influence the use of discretion in making an arrest decision include both **legal factors** and **extra-legal factors**. **Legal factors** refer to those factors specifically related to the crime, including the seriousness of the crime and the presence of a victim or witness. They also include an individual's prior record—with an officer more likely to proceed formally with someone already known to the system than to a first time offender.

Discretion

police have the freedom to decide what the best course of action is in a situation

Legal-Factors

factors specifically related to the crime, including seriousness of the crime and the presence of a victim or witness

Offense seriousness. Offense seriousness may be the single most important predictor of whether or not an arrest is made. Indeed an early study that reviewed the outcome of 9,000 juvenile contacts with police officers revealed that the seriousness of the offense was the single best predictor of whether a formal arrest would be made (Terry, 1967). Similarly, Black and Reiss found that arrests were *twice* as likely when the offense was classified as a felony rather than a misdemeanor (Black and Reiss, 1970). However, as noted in Chapter 3, (The Extent and Nature of Delinquency), most juveniles come into contact with the system for minor offenses. Indeed, in the Black and Reiss study noted above only about 5% of the instances were for felonies.

Prior Record. A juvenile's past conduct and contact with the system may also influence the police officer's decision. For example, perhaps the officer has come into contact with this youth before and has let him go home with just a warning. On a second occasion, the officer took the same youth to the station and called his parents but then released the youth to the parents without a formal arrest. Now, on this third contact, the youth is a known entity to the police even though he or she has no formal record and the police probably feel as if they have already given the youth leniency, and for this third contact, regardless of seriousness, a formal arrest is made. Returning to our original example of the four teenagers drinking underage, imagine that one of the two youths had a prior record for simple assault for fighting on school property. Research suggests that even though the current event is trivial, this youth would be more likely to be arrested than the 17-year-old standing right beside him engaging in the exact same drinking behavior (Cicourel, 1995).

However, it is important to note that the prior record itself is often thought to be linked to extra-legal factors and can thus introduce bias or discrimination into the system under the cover of legally valid arresting criteria. **Discrimination** occurs when an individual receives a different and more severe outcome than another individual based on uncontrollable factors such as one's race, age or gender. Factors such as these are often referred to in the literature as **extra-legal factors**.

Discrimination

when an individual receives a different and more severe outcome than another individual based on uncontrollable factors such as race, age or gender

Extra-Legal Factors

factors such as race, age or gender not related to the crime

Race: There is much data to show that African-American youth are more likely to be arrested and referred on to juvenile court than white youths. The first look at the role of race in juvenile court processing was provided by Goldman (1960) who reported that while only 34% of white youths who were arrested were referred to court rather than diverted, 65% of African-American youths were referred to court. Over the years similar results have been reported over and over again across jurisdictions. While some studies indicate that much of this difference can be accounted for by prior record and seriousness of the offense (Black & Reis, 1970; Fox and Zawitz, 2006), other studies challenge this finding, showing race itself to be a primary predictor of formal processing (Engel, Calnon and Bernard, 2002; Harris, 2003; Leiber and Johnson, 2008). Indeed this concern has become so great that the 1994 re-enactment of the **Juvenile Justice and Delinquency Prevention Act** (to be discussed further in the following chapter) added a core requirement for states to address and report on **disproportionate minority contact** with the juvenile justice system starting with police contacts and continuing through arrest, court referral, detention and placement stages of the system.

Disproportionate Minority Contact

minority youth are more likely to be arrested and referred on to juvenile court than white youths

Gender: As you previously learned, most delinquency is committed by males; however, an increasing number of females are becoming involved in delinquency and even serious violent crimes. Historically, studies have noted that police tend to be more lenient with females (Elliot and Voss, 1974; Armstrong, 1977; Chesney-Lind, 1970; Teilmann and Landy, 1981) and this has been noted as the "chivalry" hypothesis (Chesney-Lind). However, some studies show that police are more likely to arrest young girls for crimes that seem out of character or violate society's standards for young females (e.g., such as sex offenses) (Elliot and Voss, 1974; Visher, 1983). In addition, some research suggests that females are also treated more harshly for minor status offenses such as running away from home (Krohn et al., 1983). A greater discussion of female delinquency is presented in Chapter 12, "Special Topics in Juvenile Justice."

Age: While in general, we are discussing a rather young group of individuals when we refer to juvenile justice, the age range of youths coming before the juvenile court still varies considerably. Many states, about two-thirds, have no lower limit for arrest and referral to court, while other states set lower limits as follows: 11 states set 10 as the youngest age, 3 states set 8 as the lower limit, 5 states set 7 as the lower limit and 1 state, North Carolina, sets 6 as the lower limit for juvenile court prosecution (National Juvenile Defender Center, 2016). Studies have found that police are particularly lenient with youths under the age of 10 who are brought to their attention, making the arrest and referral to court of such youth unlikely. While it was originally thought that the different response of police might be related to lack of a prior record or minor nature of offenses, studies have found that the leniency toward younger youth persists even when controlling for these factors. Indeed the study by Terry (1967), previously noted for finding offense seriousness to be the single most important legal factor in determining arrest, also found age to be the single most important extra-legal factor in determining police response to juveniles.

Demeanor: An additional extra-legal factor that one has more control over than one's race, age or gender is the juvenile's **demeanor**. In this context, **demeanor** refers to a person's attitude toward and response toward the police officer. Again, returning to our introductory example, imagine the police officer approaches the youths and they immediately become nervous and apologetic and hand the alcohol over to the officer. Studies suggest this type of attitude and response is more likely to lead to less severe sanctions than if the juveniles begin to mouth off to the officer or, worse yet, run away, making the officer chase them. Piliavin and Briar (1964) systematically recorded data for juvenile contacts with police officers, classifying the juvenile's response as either "cooperative" or "uncooperative." Of the 21 juvenile encounters classified as "uncooperative," 66% resulted in arrest as compared to only 4% of the encounters classified as "cooperative." This study also suggested that reaction to police might be tied to race with minorities being more distrusting of the police and thus less cooperative and that this difference in response to police may account for part of the race differential in the outcome of police-juvenile contacts noted above.

Demeanor

a person's attitude toward and response toward the police officer

Parental Involvement: An additional extra-legal factor that comes into play when policing juveniles is the attitude and wishes of the parent. The last point is one in which the area of policing juveniles may differ the most from adult justice. As an adult it is assumed that you are fully responsible for your behavior and the formal justice system is really the only means of control over deviant behaviors. However, for youth, it is assumed that they are still growing and learning right from wrong so a warning or diversion may help the youth to learn. Also, parents can provide an extra layer of protection for society, exerting social control over the youth through punishment and restrictions in the home, thus making formal justice system intervention unnecessary for many minor behaviors.

Sometimes, however, it is the parents themselves who ask for justice system involvement in the case in which the parents cannot control the child or may even feel threatened or in danger from the child. Thus the role of the parent in either preventing or requesting an arrest is a factor unique to juvenile justice.

The Arrest and Interrogation Process: Rules for Policing Juveniles

Probable Cause
the set of facts known to the police officer at that time that would lead a reasonable person to conclude that a crime has occurred and that the person being arrested had committed it

Miranda Warning
a formal statement of the accused's constitutional rights including the right to remain silent and the right to an attorney that police must read to all individual's upon arrest

Exclusionary Rule
excludes any evidence from court that is not collected according to constitutional search and seizure rules

Some of the rules for policing juveniles are the same as for policing adults. For example, to make an arrest the officer must have probable cause. **Probable cause** means that the set of facts known to the police officer at that time would lead a reasonable person to conclude that a crime has occurred and that the person being arrested had committed it. Upon arrest, similar to an adult, the juvenile will be read the **Miranda Warning** (*Miranda v. Arizona*, 1966) and evidence must be collected in accordance with rules for search and seizure set forth by the 4th Amendment to the U.S. Constitution or the evidence is not admissible in a juvenile court, just as it would not be admissible in an adult court under the **Exclusionary Rule** set forth in the *Mapp v. Ohio* decision (1961).

However, there are important differences in policing juveniles, particularly when it concerns the rules and restrictions that come into play for booking, interrogation and holding of a youth during an arresting procedure. At booking an adult is photographed (the mug shot we often see on TV), fingerprinted and DNA samples can be taken. Juveniles traditionally have not been subject to these procedures to avoid stigmatizing the youth. However, during the 1990s many states changed the rules so that a youth could be fingerprinted and photographed if the alleged crime was a serious violent felony and to allow DNA samples to be taken in cases of sex offenses (Torbet, Gabel, & Montgomery, 1996).

According to the Juvenile Justice and Delinquency Prevention Act of 1974 (JJDP Act), a youth has the right to have a parent present during questioning, and the police must not physically restrain a juvenile (e.g., hold in handcuffs or prevent him/her from leaving the station) for more than six hours. The youth also cannot be held in a holding cell with adult arrestees; in fact, the juvenile is not even supposed to see or hear adult arrestees under the "sight and sound" separation clause of the Juvenile Justice and Delinquency Prevention Act of 1974.

Connections: These requirements are closely linked to both **labeling** and **differential association theories** you learned about in previous chapters as well as **developmental theories** that suggest such actions toward a minor may indeed do more harm than good.

One controversial topic in the interrogation stage of juveniles is when, and under what circumstances, a juvenile can waive the right to have a parent present and, more importantly, waive the right to have an attorney present. To date the most prominent standard has been the **totality of circumstance** rule set forth by *People v. Lara* (1967), which says that a youth can only waive the right to an attorney if it can be determined that the youth fully understood his or her rights before waiving them. Factors such as age and the ability to consult with a parent or family member before making the decision might be considered as part of the totality of the circumstance in judging whether the youth did indeed understand the consequences of waiving a right. However, advocates of juveniles, such as David Schwartz of the Juvenile Law Center, suggest that a juvenile should never have the right to waive an attorney, as youth simply do not have the maturity and capacity to understand the future consequences of such a decision. In fact some scholars go so far as to say permitting a juvenile to waive the right to an attorney is essentially denying them the right to an attorney (Berkheiser, 2002).

Totality of Circumstance

states a youth can only waive the right to an attorney if it can be determined that the youth fully understood his or her rights before waiving them

As you can see the "rules of the game" are different for police when approaching a juvenile, as opposed to an adult. Moreover, the lines are often blurred between these two statuses, which makes the police role even more confusing and complicated. In our opening example, two of the four friends would fall under the procedures defined above for juveniles and two of the friends would not; they would be handled as adults. Even more complicated, in many states a youth under the age of adulthood can be considered an "adult" for certain criminal charges but not for others. Imagine a youth is arrested for robbery of an occupied building and breaking and entering. Breaking and entering is a juvenile offense and robbery is an adult offense in the given state. What procedures should the police officer follow? Juvenile or adult? Is a parent contacted? Do the six-hour rule and sound and sight separation rule apply? As you can see, while it is easy on paper to describe the difference in arresting procedures for juveniles and adults, in the real world police officers face many challenges that are not so simply defined. Many jurisdictions indeed operate special **juvenile units** within the police department in which officers are specially trained in federal, state and local rules for the handling of youths defined as minors to ensure that correct decision making and processing occur.

Connections: You learned in Chapter 2 that the juvenile justice system started with a push for separate placement facilities for youths, at the time called Houses of Refuge. These same developmental concerns led to the development of an entire court system of justice for juveniles, and in recent years these different policing techniques operate in recognition of the immaturity and malleability of youths.

Regardless of the complexity of the encounter, however, at the end of the day, the possible outcomes can be divided into two major categories: Diversion or Formal Arrest. Recent estimates are that about 22% of juvenile arrests are handled within the police department and not referred on to the next stage of processing. Police departments vary drastically in the measures they use to informally divert a youth—primarily dependent on the type of police philosophy used and services available in their community. The following section discusses some general police styles or strategies and how they may impact juvenile/police encounters.

Police Styles

Community-Oriented Policing

relies on a mutual sense of trust between community members and the police

Community-Oriented Policing: This style of policing returns to the basic roots of the police function, which relies on a mutual sense of trust between community members and the police. The police work to understand the concerns of community members and to solve problems through systematic analysis (Giacomazzi and Thurman, 1994). Some tactics that are commonly used with community policing include using small community-based patrol offices that are accessible to the public, holding routine community-police forums where information and concerns are shared between the community members and the police and having the police officers patrol on foot or bicycle or even a Segway instead of in a car to encourage more interpersonal interactions. As you can see, each of these tactics works to improve communication lines between the police and the community they are sworn to serve. If police have good relations with youths in the community they might be more effective in warning youths away from trouble, thus leading to greater diversion and less reliance on a formal arrest.

Problem-Solving Policing

a tactic in which police work proactively to reduce the factors in a community that lead to crime rather than reacting to the crime after it happens

Problem-Solving Policing: This is a police style that can be used along with community-oriented or other police models. It refers to a tactic in which police work proactively to reduce the factors in a community that lead to crime rather than reacting to the crime after it happens. This could be something as simple as helping to create a community garden in what once was a vacant lot that would attract gatherings of teens at night or creating an athletic league to give youths something to do other than simply hang out on the streets after school. Departments employing this type of tactic might be more likely to divert a youth to a service that might "solve his/her problem" than formally arrest the youth and refer to court for processing.

Broken-Windows Policing

focuses on making the streets of the community unattractive for crime and making the citizens feel safe again

Broken-Windows Policing: This type of policing draws directly from the social structure and social disorganization theories you learned about in Chapter 6. According to this idea, areas that are rundown or broken create fear in law-abiding citizens, leading them to avoid such areas and provide attractive places for crime to occur. The idea of broken-windows policing is thus to focus on making the streets of the community unattractive for crime and making the citizens feel safe again. Again, this is not necessarily a stand-alone police model but can be used in conjunction with community policing or problem-solving policing. Indianapolis, for example, uses this strategy in conjunction with community-based policing and has found great success; while St. Petersburg has combined it with a problem-solving approach (Paoline, Myers and Worden, 2000). On the other hand, broken-windows policing can be used as an approach to "clean up the streets," which, unlike the two previously discussed models, would actually encourage more formal arrests over diversion.

Hot-Spots Policing

focuses police presence in areas known to have high crime rates

Hot-Spots Policing: Similar to broken-windows policing in that it targets certain areas, hot-spots policing refers to a strategy that focuses police presence in areas known to have high crime rates. Unlike the proactive strategies noted above, however, this is a reactive strategy that reacts to where the crime is happening rather than trying to prevent it. This strategy has been highly successful in reducing crime rates in cities such as Seattle, Washington, DC and Jersey City, New Jersey (Weisburd and Mazerolle, 2000). This type of model is linked more directly with Deterrence Theory and Routine Activities Theory (Chapter 4), as it is meant to increase the certainty that one will be caught and reduce the availability of suitable targets and victims. As such, this police style would also favor formal arrest over diversion for criminal activity in these hot spots.

FOCUS ON POLICY: Police Encounters with Minority Juveniles

One of the current biggest controversies in policing is the use of force, particularly deadly force, by police. Questions arise about when this force is warranted and when police use excessive force, particularly when engaging in encounters with minority populations. The recent shooting and killing of unarmed minority youth such as Michael Brown in St. Louis and Freddie Gray in Baltimore have fueled the fire for many peaceful and some not so peaceful protests and what has now become known as the larger "Black Lives Matter" movement. While these cases may be what draws media and popular attention to police and minority community member interactions, it is just one of many stages in which minority youth seem to experience what may be seen as unfair or biased treatment by the system.

One of the earliest policing studies of excessive use of force toward youth was conducted by Albert Reiss in 1980. This study, however, focused more on abusing language and treatment of youths, and found police were more aggressive in their language in interactions with black youths. This type of minor harassment continues to be reported by youth with a 1994 study finding 10 percent of white youth and almost half of surveyed minority youth (46.6%) reporting they had been personally harassed by police.

Minorities are also more likely to report being illegally or legally stopped and searched. Stop-and-frisk policies have made pedestrian stops a common experience among black and brown citizens in many American locales. For example, New York City Police Department (NYPD), stop-and-frisk policies allowed police to "temporarily detain," question and search pedestrians for a wide variety of crimes on the grounds of "reasonable suspicion" (Spitzer, 1999). Multiple complaints have been levied against police departments, and the NYPD, in particular, for perceived discriminatory practices toward African American and Hispanic citizens who complain that police harass them on the street (Spitzer, 1999) and use aggressive stop-and-frisk tactics (see *Kelvin Daniels et al. v. City of New York*, 2004).

Recent research supports citizens' concerns about the NYPD's stop-and-frisk policies. Gelman, Fagan and Kiss (2007) found that African Americans and Hispanics were disproportionately represented among citizens who are stopped and frisked in New York City with African Americans representing 53% of stops and Hispanics representing 33% of stops. When compared to whites, African Americans and Hispanics were stopped 23% and 39% more often, respectively. This pattern held even when controlling for characteristics of the precincts where the stops occurred and across offense types for which the stop was initiated.

Moving to physical force, studies have also long documented, again, a difference in white and black youths' experience with the police. While national surveys report that police use of force in encounters is actually not very common, occurring in only about 1% of incidents

(Langan et al., 2001), studies seem to suggest it is more likely to be used in encounters involving juveniles. Borrero (2001) interviewed 132 youths in Hartford, Connecticut and found that combined they reported over 400 negative contacts with police officers, including 39% reporting physical encounters such as hitting and the use of force resulting in physical injury.

The use of deadly force is even more rare; however, it is what makes our national news coverage and what may taint many individual's opinions about police behavior. While each individual police department will have its own training on the use of force, and states may have somewhat varying policies, the U.S. Supreme Court set down at least some national guidelines in the case of *Tennessee v. Garner* (1985). In this case the Court ruled that it is constitutional for a police officer to use deadly force to prevent the escape of a suspect when the suspect poses a threat of serious physical harm, either to the officer or to others. However, it is not constitutional to use deadly force to prevent the escape of a suspect simply based on the seriousness of the alleged conduct (Walker, 2010).

Because this is obviously a controversial topic and police work in potentially dangerous situations on a daily basis and have to make spur of the moment decisions, there has perhaps not been as much research in this area as is needed. One reason that it has gained more national attention recently is the increase in the use of social media, cell phone recordings and body cameras worn by police officers. Combined these are letting the average American citizen see in more detail what actually occurs in some encounters between minority citizens and the police. On one hand this is a good thing, as it is bringing attention to a needed area. However, on the other hand, it is important to remember that such instances are still rare and that most police officers do not intentionally stereotype or discriminate against minorities and that the police do provide a valuable and important function in American society. Perhaps more attention to these issues will lead to more research, and ultimately better and more informed policy that will benefit both policing and citizens.

Police in Schools

Police have also taken on innovative roles in the prevention of delinquency and much of this activity has occurred in our nation's schools, perhaps because this is the environment in which youths spend much of their time. In fact, you may yourself have participated in or be familiar with some of the examples provided below.

DARE
a curriculum taught by police officers to middle and high school children to help them understand the dangers of illegal drugs and learn tactics to resist peer pressure to engage in illegal drug use

DARE. **Drug Abuse Resistance Education (DARE)** is a curriculum taught by police officers to middle and high school children to help them understand the dangers of different illegal drugs and to learn tactics to resist peer pressure to engage in illegal drug use. While initial assessments of DARE found it to be ineffective in reducing overall drug use (Dejong, 1987; Dukes, Ullman and Stein, 1996; Ennet et al., 1994; Sherman et al., 1997; Zagummy and Thompson, 1997) it was found to improve youths' attitudes and relationships with police. Despite the lack of research indicating program effectiveness it is still operated in many schools today.

Connections: This program is in line with social learning theories that you learned about in Chapter 7 as it focuses on teaching youths definitions unfavorable to the use of drugs and to provide them with strategies for making good decisions rather than punishing them after the fact.

School Resource Officers

police officers stationed in schools to increase safety

SRO. **School Resource Officers (SROs)** are police officers stationed in schools. While it may be thought that the officers are there to arrest students who break the law while at school, it is actually thought that having an officer present will prevent students from engaging in activities that might lead to an arrest and disrupt the educational setting. For example, students may be less willing to bring drugs or weapons into school if they know a resource officer is present and could detect such contraband. Also, students might be hesitant to start a fight in the hallway or cafeteria knowing that a police officer rather than just a teacher might witness that fight (e.g., the resulting punishment might be a formal arrest rather than afterschool detention).

Connections: This use of police in schools is in line with **Deterrence Theory**, which you learned about in Chapter 4.

From Arrest to Intake

Intake Units

units in which officers are assigned to ONLY conduct intake assessments and are responsible for all front-end decision making regarding a case

One of the most unique aspects of the juvenile system is the intake process in which almost every youth is assigned an intake officer who assesses not just the warrants of the case, but the actual youth. Some juvenile probation departments have special **intake units** in which there are officers assigned to *only* conduct intake assessments. They are responsible for all the front-end decision making regarding a case, but do not follow the youth through the system. In other departments one juvenile probation officer is assigned to a youth and that officer remains with the youth throughout the case processing, including intake, any diversionary supervision ordered, any court proceedings, and any post-adjudication probation, placement or aftercare supervision. Regardless of which method is used, the responsibilities of the intake stage remain the same, which are to:

1. Assess whether there is reason to believe the youth committed the accused behavior;
2. Determine if the youth is in need of treatment by the juvenile justice system;
3. Determine if the youth poses an undue risk to the community and society if left in the home.

Intake probation officers use many tactics in conducting these assessments, including interviews with the youth and his/her family, calls to high schools to determine attendance, grades and behavior in school, and interviews with any other significant individuals who might be working with the youth at the time such as a coach, pastor or social worker. While this process has traditionally been informal, it is becoming more and more popular for intake officers to use official assessment instruments to guide the questions they ask, and to determine how to use this information in making decisions about a youth. In a few states the district attorney or local prosecutor makes the next decision rather than a juvenile intake officer. In these states the focus is less on treatment and needs of the youth than on seriousness of the charge and strength of evidence to move forward with prosecution.

ASSESSING YOUTH: THE ROLE OF RISK ASSESSMENT INSTRUMENTS

If the overall goal of the juvenile system is to treat and rehabilitate a youth, then it is of critical importance that those responsible for making decisions about the youth understand the root causes of the behaviors. Often, for minor acts of delinquency, it is just that the youth is experimenting or acting out and these behaviors are not indicative of deeper-rooted problems. These youth are ideal for diversion. However, other youths may be experiencing troubles at school, conflict or even abuse in the home, and/or mental health problems that require more significant intervention. Table 9.1 on the following page displays the sites and risk assessments evaluated for inter-rater reliability and validity table.

Risks
problems the youth is facing that make him or her more likely to continue in delinquency and anti-social behaviors

Needs
areas of a youth's life in which his or her needs are not being met, regardless of whether they directly contributed to the behavior at hand

These are just some examples, as there are many different assessment instruments that have been developed across the states to help intake officers and social workers properly determine a youth's risks and needs. **Risks** in general refer to those problems the youth is facing that make him or her more likely to continue in delinquency and anti-social behaviors. **Needs** refer to those areas of a youth's life

TABLE 9.1 Sites and Risk Assessments Evaluated for Inter-Rater Reliability and Validity

Site Agency	Risk Assessment Instrument	Who completes risk assessment protocol?	What decisions does it inform?
Florida Department of Juvenile Justice (DJJ)	Positive Achievement Change Tool (PACT)	Probation officers	Supervision levels, services
Georgia Department of Juvenile Justice (DJJ)	Comprehensive Risk/Needs (CRN) assessment, an early derivative of COMPAS Youth	Probation/commitment assessment specialists	Supervision levels, commitment and placement decisions
Nebraska Department of Health and Human Services, Office of Juvenile Services (OJSJ)	YLS/CMI for youth in secure commitment	OJS evaluation coordinators	Supervision levels, commitment decisions
Nebraska Office of Probation Administration	YLS/CMI	Probation officers	Supervision levels, case planning
Oregon Juvenile Justice	Juvenile Crime Prevention (JCP) assessment developed for youth referred to juvenile justice system	Probation officers, detention workers, and prevention workers	Direct service supervision, case plan
Solano County, California	Gender-specific risk assessments in JAIS for youth referred to probation	Probation officers	Risk informs supervision and service intensity, needs assessment case plan
Virginia Department of Juvenile Justice (DJJ)	Youth Assessment and Screening Instrument (YASI) for youth on probation, facility or parole	Probation officers and facility staff	Supervision levels, number of probation contacts, case plan

Source: Baird et al., National Council on Crime and Delinquency, A Comparison of Risk Assessment Instruments in Juvenile Justice, page iii, 2010.

in which his or her needs are not being met, regardless of whether they directly contributed to the behavior at hand, such as inadequate health care or lack of food in the home. More recent assessment instruments also aim to diagnose a youth's strengths. **Strengths** refer to those things a youth is particularly good at and which can be used to help him or her succeed in life (Bonta & Andrews, 2007).

Strengths
things a youth is particularly good at and which can be used to help him or her succeed in life

Connections: Many of the risks and needs measured in these assessments relate to the factors you learned about in Chapter 8 and developmental theories of delinquency.

Pre-Adjudicatory Diversion

Pre-adjudicatory diversion refers to any effort made to informally adjust a youth without formal court processing and adjudication. **Informal adjustments** in general refer to the handling of a juvenile's case outside of the formal court system. This process is usually reserved for first-time or less serious offenders and requires agreement by the juvenile and the parents or guardian. The simplest version of such a diversion is when the police do what they call a **station adjustment**. This is simply when the police officer makes the decision to take the juvenile to the station, but then decides not to proceed with a formal arrest and releases the youth to his/her parent or guardian with just a warning.

Informal Adjustments

the handling of a juvenile's case outside of the formal court system, usually reserved for first-time offenders or less serious offenders

Station Adjustment

when a police officer makes the decision to take the juvenile to the station, but then decides not to proceed with a formal arrest

The next simplest version of diversion is when a youth is simply warned by a probation officer about the consequences of his or her behavior if it continues, and then the case is dismissed. Another version of this would be to include in the warning a condition that the youth not get into any more trouble for 3 or 6 months. After that time passes, the case can be dismissed without the youth having a formal record or more system intervention.

Other times the intake officer might want the youth to have more supervision or to receive some services, but does not yet want to burden the youth with a formal juvenile record. Almost every juvenile probation department offers an option of **informal probation** (also referred to as an informal adjustment) in which the youth, upon admitting to the behavior, is placed on probation supervision for a short period of time. During this time the probation officer continues to monitor the youth's behavior, such as school attendance or attendance at counseling if required. If the youth meets the conditions of the informal probation term, the case is again dropped and the youth has no formal juvenile record.

Informal Probation

a period of probation supervision agreed upon by the youth, the youth's family and the probation officer but not formally ordered by a judge

Other diversionary tactics are more localized and the services an intake officer orders will depend on not only the youth's needs, but the services available in his/her community. While a list of all programs used across the nation is impractical, some examples of more popular practices are given below.

Community Review Boards: Community review boards are boards made up of volunteer community members who hear the cases of youth being diverted from formal court processing. The youth and the youth's parents must agree to this option. The case is then heard by the Board and they assign a course of action for the youth to take to be accountable for his/her actions and any harm that has come from them. In some cases this can be as simple as writing an apology letter to the victim, in others it might involve researching and writing an essay

Community Review Boards

volunteer community members who hear the cases of youth being diverted from formal court processing on the dangers of a particular activity, or it may involve a form of community service or payment of damages to a victim.

Teen Courts

a program through which the case is heard by a jury of the teens peers rather than being sent to the formal juvenile justice system

Teen Courts: Teen courts are similar to community review boards except instead of adult community members hearing the case, it is heard by a jury of the teen's actual peers. Outcomes of teen court are usually similar in nature to the methods used by community review boards noted above. In addition, often a youth served by such a court is required to later serve on the court him/herself.

Multi-Systemic Family Therapy: In addition to being placed on informal probation, conditions can be set on the probation that might require the youth and his/her family to obtain counseling. One particularly popular method of counseling used with juveniles is called multi-systemic family therapy as this approach involves not only the youth, but the family, the school and even the community in which the youth lives to address a variety of risks or needs of the youth.

Connections: While these programs differ in intensity, length and specific goals, they all share one important goal: keeping a youth from acquiring a formal juvenile justice system record. This goal, different from the treatment goal, derives primarily from concerns expressed in earlier chapters regarding *labeling of youth* and *stigma*. As noted in the earlier discussion of Labeling Theory, most youth act out or commit some form of primary deviance as teenagers, but few will go on to become adult criminals. By burdening a youth with a formal juvenile record, the system could indeed have the reverse effect of its intentions: that is instead of rehabilitating youth, it could lead youth to further delinquency. In addition to concerns brought forth from labeling youth, aspects of social learning theories also drive decisions. If a youth has a positive home and school environment then this is the best environment for the youth to learn law-abiding behaviors. If such a youth is removed from the home and placed in a detention center or treatment facility where he or she is instead surrounded by other delinquent youths, again, the system could have unfavorable consequences. Thus, even the mission of many states' juvenile justice systems formally states that the goal is to keep the youth in the home whenever possible. This mission applies not only to intake, but we will see it again when we discuss dispositions used by juvenile court judges after formal adjudication.

Prior to the get tough era it was accurate to say that most youth who came into the system would be handled through one of the diversionary tactics noted above.

However, since the 1990s, a youth is slightly more likely to receive formal than informal processing. The most recent figures available nationally estimate that in 2010, 23% of all formal arrests involving juveniles were handled within the law enforcement agency, 68% were referred on to juvenile court and 8% were transferred to adult court. The remaining 1% were either referred to a social welfare agency or transferred between jurisdictions (Sickmund & Puzzanchera, 2014).

For those youth who are being referred to court for formal processing there is one other pre-adjudicatory decision to be made: whether or not the youth should be held in a detention center until the court hearing. In the following section we discuss the issue of **pre-adjudicatory detention**.

FOCUS ON POLICY: Using Risk Assessments to Divert Youth

The risk assessment instruments, such as the YASI mentioned before, are used to determine the level of service and the type of services that might best help a child. Recently, instead of these instruments being used later in system processing, there has been a push to use them up front when a police officer or probation officer is considering the use of pre-adjudicatory detention. This push came about for two main reasons. First, during the 1980s and 1990s, detention centers across the country were literally bursting at the seams with youth sleeping in cots in hallways and living in unsafe circumstances due to the overcrowding. Second, research began to come to light that youth who were sent to detention were then much more likely to be sent to placement by the judge at disposition. Thus, this early decision to send a youth to detention had the possibility of influencing later decision points in the system. Some speculated reasons for this relationship were the fact that someone had already made the decision to remove the youth from his/her home, thus the judge was not removing the youth from a home to placement but from a detention center to placement. Second, youth in detention centers typically show up at in court in their correctional system jumpsuit with handcuffs and shackles. Compare in your mind the image this portrays to the judge compared to the youth who walks in in a clean suit with a fresh haircut with his parents at his side. Which youth "looks" more like a criminal?

Many states and local jurisdictions experimented with a variety of risk score instruments for this purpose with YASI itself offering a specific Detention Screening Instrument. This instrument was implemented by Suffolk County, New York (i.e., Long Island area), in 2010 to see if it was effective in identifying the correct youth to send to placement. In addition, the county received grant funding from the state to place probation officers "on call" in the evening and overnight hours so that if a police officer arrested a youth he/she thought needed detention, the probation officer would meet the youth at the detention center and perform the **screening** before admitting the youth to the detention center.

The county solicited a formal external evaluation of this initiative in 2012 to see if it had indeed been effective in reducing detention placements. The evaluators determined that effectiveness should include two parts. First, as might be expected, fewer youth should be being admitted to the detention center. Second, those youth who were "diverted" should not pose an undue risk of a new arrest while in the community. To perform this evaluation the researchers therefore collected data on the population of youth coming into the system the year before the initiative (i.e., a comparison group), and the first year of the initiative. The findings revealed that the program was effective in greatly reducing the numbers of youth being sent to detention, and that the youth diverted from placement did not pose a risk to society (Kurlychek & Fowler, 2012). This suggests that risk assessment instruments can be a valuable tool at the detention decision stage.

Pre-Adjudicatory Detention

Pre-Adjudicatory Detention

holding a youth in a detention facility while awaiting a formal hearing. Traditionally used to prevent the youth from absconding or to protect the community or the youth

For some youth, the intake officer will decide it is necessary to petition the case on to court. Now, another decision must be made: Can the youth return home until such time or must he/she be removed from the home? **Pre-adjudicatory detention** refers to holding in a facility intended for short-term care. Unlike treatment programs and case management plans mentioned above, the role of the detention center is to house the youth until the adjudication hearing if the youth is seen as either posing a risk of flight before the hearing or posing an undue safety risk to the community or to him/herself if left in the home.

Youth subject to pre-adjudicatory detention have another set of rules and procedures that apply to them that varies in formality by jurisdiction but follows the same general pattern.

1. Upon arrest a police officer can take a youth to a juvenile detention center if the officer cannot reach parents or guardians to take responsibility for the youth or if the officer believes the youth is at high risk.
2. Upon reaching the detention center a probation officer or intake officer at the detention center will perform an assessment of the youth to determine if they believe the detention is warranted and a juvenile court judge will be contacted to approve admittance.

3. A formal detention review hearing must be held in front of the judge within a certain time frame—typically 24 to 72 hours—at which time the youth, in most cases, may have an attorney present. The judge will then decide if the youth must stay in detention until the adjudication hearing.
4. If the youth is remanded to detention, there are then special time limits that apply to scheduling the hearing. In most states the hearing must be held within 30 days, and in some even as little as 10 days.

These procedures noted above were not in place in the original court, and have evolved over time as system workers and youth advocates have become more and more aware of the dangers of placing youth in detention centers. In fact there has been a great movement away from using detention in the past decades. In the 1990s it would not have been uncommon to visit a detention center and see rows of cots in the hallways as these centers were mainly operating above capacity during what we have discussed as the "get tough" era. However, after several key studies documented the dangers of such placement both on the courts and on developmental outcomes for youth, there has been a movement away from use of such centers. In 1994, the study, *Conditions of Confinement: Juvenile Detention and Correction Facilities*, found that less than half the facilities reviewed met standards for basic needs such as living space, health care and food, clothing and hygiene requirements (Parent et al., 1994). In addition, widespread deficiencies were reported in the control of suicidal behavior and safety and security. While there were a few facilities that had deficiencies in almost all areas, the major finding of this study was probably that most facilities suffered from at least some deficiencies and that these were primarily linked to overcrowding. Since this time states have made consistent efforts to reduce the use of pre-adjudicatory detention, primarily through increased use of formal intake assessment instruments and more formal criteria for determining which youth require such detention.

Today, pre-adjudicatory detention remains an important component of the juvenile justice system as there are some youth who truly pose a risk to society if they are released prior to receiving treatment; however, its usage has greatly decreased, partly due to the use of the assessment risk instruments discussed above that help intake officers to identify only the most risky cases for placement in such centers.

Another interesting note about juvenile detention is that historically a placement in detention meant you stayed there until your adjudication hearting—there was not "bail" to set like in adult case processing. Today several states do operate a potential system of bail for juveniles; however, reports are that in practice it is hardly ever used, and instead states rely on the reduced time to trial policies as noted above to ensure the youth are not spending extended unnecessary stays in detention centers. After all, these centers are primarily for holding youth and not for treating them, and the primary goal of the juvenile system is to treat those youth in need of such services.

Shelter or Respite Care

another type of pre-adjudicatory holding of a youth that is used when it is unsafe for the juvenile to return home. This type of facility is traditionally less secure than a formal detention center

For some youth, while formal detention might not be warranted, there could be reasons it is unsafe for the youth to return home, particularly if there is conflict or violence occurring in the home or if the youth is actually arrested for running away from home. Another type of care commonly known as either **shelter or respite care** is reserved for these youths. This type of facility is less secure than a detention center. True to the roots of the juvenile justice system that is ever striving to keep youth away from influences that might drive them further down the path to delinquency, the availability of such services provides immediate shelter and care for youths who need such care without mingling them with a population of youths who have evolved into more serious and dangerous behaviors (e.g., those held in the secure detention center). Also, in line with the mission of the juvenile justice system, this type of care is to be used sparingly as it is most often the mission to keep a youth in the home and family environment whenever possible.

Whether held in detention or not, the next step for a youth referred to juvenile court is the adjudication hearing. The formal court process is the topic of the next chapter.

Key Words

Broken-Windows Policing
Community Review Boards
Community-Oriented Policing
DARE
Demeanor
Discretion
Discrimination
Disproportionate Minority Contact
Exclusionary Rule
Extra-Legal Factors
Hot-Spots Policing
Informal Adjustments
Informal Probation
Intake Units
Legal-Factors
Miranda Warning
Needs
Pre-Adjudicatory Detention
Probable Cause
Problem-Solving Policing
Risks
School Resource Officers
Shelter or Respite Care
Station Adjustment
Strengths
Teen Courts
Totality of Circumstance

Chapter Summary

In this chapter you moved from learning about theories of delinquency to the actual juvenile justice system. The focus here was on the early stages of system contact and processing, starting with policing. Police are the primary gatekeepers to the juvenile justice system as this is the way most youth come into contact with the system. You also learned that whether or not a police contact leads to an arrest can be influenced by many factors such as the seriousness of the crime itself, the youth's prior system contacts, age, race, gender and even the demeanor of the youth when responding to police.

Another factor that can influence arrest is the policing strategy being used in a given precinct or community. For example, community-oriented policing and problem-oriented policing are strategies that focus more on preventing crime and strengthening community-police relationships whereas hot-spots policing and broken-windows policing are policies that emphasize arrest.

One of the key controversies of our present time is the police use of force in arrest, particularly with minority youth. Recent incidents of police shootings of unarmed youth have brought this issue to the national forefront and spurred the "Black Lives Matter" movement, which emphasizes the right of the citizen to be protected from the use of excessive and deadly force by police officers.

In some ways the policing of juveniles is similar to policing of adults, as police must read the youth his/her Miranda warning and follow search and seizure procedures set forth by the U.S. Constitution and case law. However, in other ways it is quite different with police required to follow special rules when interacting with youth. These include such things as keeping the youth out of sight and sound contact with adult offenders and not being allowed to detain the youth for more than six hours.

Another way the system processing of youth is different than adult court is that after the initial police contact, the next step in the process is most often the assignment of a probation or intake officer to the case. This is a unique function of the juvenile justice system as the probation officer comes into play at the "front end" of the system rather than being assigned after sentencing. This is because the probation officer is responsible for many key decisions for the youth, including whether or not the youth is eligible for diversion programs or will be petitioned to court for formal processing. At this stage the probation officer may use any of a variety of risk assessment instruments to help him/her make decisions about the appropriate next steps for the youth.

One of the most influential decisions at this point is the decision to keep a youth in pre-adjudicatory detention or not. This is important as it requires removing a youth from his/her home and has been found to then lead to later outcomes of extended periods of out of home placement. While detention is warranted for some youth, there has been a movement away from routine use of placement and to the reliance on more formal risk screening instruments to identify only the most severe or risky youth for such placement.

Discussion Questions

1. Compare and contrast the following policing styles: Community-Oriented Policing, Problem-Solving Policing, Broken-Windows Policing, Hot-Spots Policing. Which of the approaches do you think might be most effect in combating youth crime? Is this different than the answer you might have for adult crime? Why or why not?
2. List at least three ways that policing of juveniles is similar to the policing of adults. Next list three ways in which it is different. Do these similarities and differences reflect the overall mission of the juvenile justice system you learned about in Chapter 2? Why or why not?
3. What is the unique role of a probation officer in the juvenile justice system? List some key decisions that a probation officer might make regarding the case of a youth accused of committing a delinquent act.
4. In this chapter you learned about the use of risk and needs assessment instruments that help juvenile justice practitioners make decisions about a youth's case. What are risk factors that you think should lead to more formal processing of youth? In what cases is pre-adjudicatory diversion more appropriate?

REFERENCES

Armstrong, G. (1977). Female under the law-protected but unequal. *Crime and Delinquency, 23,* 109–120.

Berkheiser, M. (2002). The fiction of juvenile right to counsel: Waiver in juvenile courts. *Florida Law Review, 54,* 577–650.

Black, D., & Reiss, A. (1970). Police control of juveniles. *American Sociological Review, 35,* 63–77.

Bonta, J., & Andrews, D. A. (2007). Risk-need-responsivity model for offender assessment and rehabilitation. *Rehabilitation, 6,* 1–22.

Borrero, M. (2001). The widening mistrust between youth and police. *Families in Society: The Journal of Contemporary Human Services, 82,* 399–408.

Chesney-Lind, M., & Shelden, R. (1992). *Girls, delinquency and juvenile justice.* Pacific Grove, CA: Brooks/Cole Publishing.

Dejong, W. (1987). A short-term evaluation of Project DARE (Drug Abuse Resistance Education): Preliminary indicators of effectiveness. *Journal of Drug Education, 17*(4), 279–294.

Dukes, R. L., Ullman, J. D., & Stein, J. A. (1996). Three year follow-up of drug abuse resistance education. *Evaluation Review,* 20, 49–66.

Engel, R., Calnon, J., & Bernard, T. (2002). Theory and racial profiling. *Justice Quarterly, 19,* 247–273.

Elliott, D., & Voss, H. (1974). *Delinquency and dropout.* Lexington: MA: Lexington Books.

Ennett, S. T., Tobler, N. S., Ringwalt, C. L., & Flewelling, R. L. (1994). How effective is drug abuse resistance education? A meta-analysis of Project DARE outcome evaluations. *American Journal of Public Health, 84*(9), 1394–1401.

Gelman, A., Fagan, J., & Kiss, A. (2007). An analysis of the New York City police department's "stop-and-frisk" policy in the context of claims of racial bias. *Journal of the American Statistical Association, 102*(429), 813–823.

Giacomazzi, A., & Thurman, Q. C. (1994). Cops and kids revisited: A second-year assessment of a community policing and delinquency prevention innovation. *Police Studies, 17,* 1–20.

Harris, D. (2003). The reality of racial disparity in criminal justice. *Law and Contemporary Problems, 66,* 71–97.

Horowitz, R., & Pottieger, A. (1991). Gender bias in juvenile justice handling of seriously crime-involved youth. *Journal of Research in Crime and Delinquency, 28,* 75–100.

Kelvin Daniels et al. v. City of New York. (2004). Stipulation of settlement, 99 Civ 1695 (SAS), Ordered January 9, 2004; filed January 13, 2004.

Krohn, M., Curry, J., & Nelson-Klinger, S. (1983). Is chivalry dead? *Criminology,* 21, 417–439.

Kurlychek, M. C., & Fowler, E. (2015). Evaluation of the Nassau County's detention diversion initiative: Final report. Report to the New York Division of Criminal Justice Services. Albany, NY.

Langan, P. A., Greenfield, L. A., Smith, S. K., Curose, M. R., & Levin, J. J. (2001). *Contacts between police and the public: Findings from the 1999 national survey.* Washington, DC: U.S. Department of Justice.

Paoline III, E. A., Myers, S. M., & Worden, R. E. (2000). Police culture, individualism, and community policing: Evidence from two police departments. *Justice Quarterly, 17*(3), 575–605.

Parent, D. G., Lieter, V., Kennedy, S., Livens, L., Wentworth, D., & Wilcox, S. (1994). *Conditions of confinement: Juvenile detention and corrections facilities.* Boston, MA: Abt Associates Incorporated.

Piliavin, I., & Briar, S. (1964). Police encounters with juveniles. *American Journal of Sociology, 70,* 206–214.

Pope, E. H., & Snyder, H. (2003). *Race as a factor in juvenile arrests.* Washington DC: United States Department of Justice.

Puzzanchera, C. (2015). *Arrests of juveniles*. Pittsburgh, PA: National Center for Juvenile Justice.

Reiss, A. J. Jr. (1980). Police brutality. In R. J. Lundman (Ed.), *Police Behavior: A Sociological Perspective* (pp. 274–296). New York: Oxford University Press.

Sherman, L., Gottfredson, D., MacKenzie, D., Eck, J., Reuter, P., & Bushway, S. (1997). *Preventing crime: What works, what doesn't, what's promising*. Washington, DC: U.S. Department of Justice, Office of Justice Programs.

Sickmund, M., & Puzzanchera, C. (2014). *Juvenile offenders and victims: A national report.* Washington DC: Office of Juvenile Justice and Delinquency Prevention, U.S. Department of Justice.

Spitzer, E. (1999). *The New York City police department's "Stop and frisk" practices*. Albany, NY: Office of the New York State Attorney General.

Teilmann, K., & Landry, P. (1981). Gender bias in juvenile justice. *Journal of Research in Crime and Delinquency, 18*, 47–80.

Terry, R. (1967). Discrimination in the handling of juvenile offenders by social control agencies. *Journal of Research in Crime and Delinquency, 4,* 218–230.

Visher, C. (1983). Gender, police arrest decisions, and notions of chivalry. *Criminology, 21,* 22–23.

Walker, J. T. (2010). *Tennessee v. Garner.* In R. del Carmen and C. Hemmens (Eds.), *Criminal Procedure and the Supreme Court: A Guide to the Major Decisions on Search and Seizure, Privacy, and Individual Rights* (p. 285). Lanham, MD: Rowan and Littlefield.

Weisburd, D., & Green Mazerolle, L. (2000). Crime and disorder in drug hot spots: Implications for theory and practice in policing. *Police Quarterly, 3*(September), 331–349.

Zagumny, M. J., & Thompson, M. K. (1997). Does D.A.R.E. work? An evaluation in rural Tennessee. *Journal of Alcohol and Drug Education, 42,* 32–41.

Juvenile Court Processing: After the Petition

10

©ggw/Shutterstock.com

In Chapter 2 you learned about the origins of our nation's juvenile justice system, which was based on the premise that youth are indeed different from adults and can, given the right treatment, be saved from a life of crime. Thus, the movement leading up to the nation's first juvenile court is often called the "child saving" movement. Because the juvenile court was designed to save and not punish, the original court did not focus on due process rights for defendants as does our adult system. Yet, the reality is that the juvenile court does, regardless of intention, in some ways punish youth for their behaviors. That is, the court can require youth to follow formal conditions of probation, to pay costs, fines and restitution to victims, and can even remove youths from their homes and place them in detention or treatment facilities. These facts were recognized by the nation's Supreme Court in the series of court cases you learned about in Chapter 2 that gave juveniles some, but not all, of the same due process rights as adult defendants. What is left is a system of justice somewhere between its original benevolent social welfare roots and its predecessor, the retributive adult criminal justice system. To make the picture even more complicated, each state has its own rules about who is considered a juvenile before the eyes of the law, including variations in the maximum age of juvenile court jurisdiction and a myriad of policies that allow some youths to be transferred to adult courts.

In the following pages you will learn about how these differences unfold on a daily basis and what they mean for youth, both in the juvenile court and those finding themselves transferred or otherwise within the jurisdiction of the adult criminal justice system. As every state has slightly different procedures, I will try to focus on the most generalizable knowledge, pointing out states that depart from the traditional in special examples.

CHAPTER GOALS

By the end of the chapter you should:

1. Be familiar with juvenile court terminology as it differs from adult court terminology.
2. Be able to discuss the key practical differences between an adjudication hearing and an adult conviction hearing.
3. Be able to discuss the key practical differences between a dispositional hearing and an adult sentencing hearing.
4. Be able to define the purpose of the federal Office of Juvenile Justice and Delinquency Prevention and the core tenets of the Juvenile Justice and Delinquency Prevention Act.
5. Understand the various mechanisms by which youth can be processed in adult courts and what research tells us about the later outcomes for these youths.

After the Petition

Remember from the last chapter that in most cases the intake decision is made by a probation officer or a specialized probation officer called an intake officer. After reviewing the specifics of the case this officer decides if the youth is right for pre-court diversion or whether the youth should be petitioned to court for formal processing. A **petition** is a formal legal document that alleges that a youth is delinquent and asks the juvenile court to take jurisdiction over the juvenile, or, in some cases, to transfer the juvenile to adult court.

Petition
a formal legal document that alleges that a youth is delinquent and asks the juvenile court to take jurisdiction over the case

After a **petition** is filed there can be several hearings. The first is usually a **preliminary hearing** at which the judge explores the nature of the case and decides if it should proceed further. The judge must also make sure that the juvenile and the parents understand the charges against the youth and decide if it is safe for the child to stay in the home or if the youth needs to be placed either in a secure detention center, a non-secure detention center (often called residential or respite care) or in a foster home. If the judge decides there is merit to the case and it should move forward an **adjudication** hearing is scheduled.

Preliminary Hearing
the first hearing before a judge in which he/she determines if the case has merit. Similar to arraignment in adult court

If the youth has already been placed in pre-adjudicatory detention by the police or intake officer, as you learned in the last chapter, a **detention review hearing** is also held. Most states require that such hearings be held within a short period of time (such as 48 hours) as being held against your will is a deprivation of liberty. The hearing is held before a judicial officer, most often a juvenile court judge. At such a hearing the youth does not have a constitutional right to an attorney, but many states do allow them. The youth does, however, have the right to be present, to have a parent or legal guardian present, to be informed of the charges against him/her, have his/her legal rights explained and in some states to request bond. There are three reasons that a youth should be held in detention according to the *Shall v. Martin* decision. These are:

Detention Review Hearing
a hearing, usually held within 24 to 72 hours of pre-adjudicatory detention placement in which the judge decides if the placement is warranted. Similar to a bail hearing in adult court, however, most states do not set bail for youth

- The youth is a threat to himself
- The youth is a threat to others
- The youth poses a risk of **absconding**

Absconding means running away or otherwise failing to show up for later hearings. So for example a youth with a history of running away from home or who has failed to appear before the court on other issues would be deemed to pose such a risk.

Absconding
running away and/or failure to appear for a scheduled hearing

If at this hearing the judge or juvenile court official determines the youth must stay in detention, there is a time limit placed on the amount of time that can pass before the adjudication hearing. This is because most states do not provide bail/bond for juveniles and the juvenile is being held against his/her will. The time frame can range from 7 to 60 days (Sickmund & Puzzanchera, 2014). While 60 days may sound like a long time, remember during this time the prosecution and defense both have to prepare their cases and background information on the youth and his/her family is also being collected to inform the court about the child.

Whether or not the youth is held in detention, if the case is formally processed and a plea deal is not arranged the next stage is an **adjudication hearing**. The **adjudication hearing** is centered on the facts of the case and it is at this stage where the judge is concerned with determining whether or not the juvenile did or did not engage in the alleged delinquent behavior. As you learned in Chapter 2, the youth has the right to an attorney at the adjudication hearing as determined by the decision *in In re Gault* if a possible outcome of the case is that the youth can be placed outside the home. Because attorneys are costly and alter the nature of the process, some jurisdictions have chosen to divide cases into those more minor cases that cannot result in placement outside of the home and those more serious cases that can result in placement outside the home. For the first set of cases, attorneys are not used and often a **quasi-judicial hearing officer** referred to as a "referee" or "master" presides over the case (Rubin, 1998).

Status Offense

a behavior that is only illegal because of one's status as a juvenile

Delinquent Offense

an act that would be a crime if committed by an adult

Another important distinction between cases is the nature of the alleged offense. If the alleged offense is a **status offense**, the burden of proof is lower than for a **delinquent offense**. Remember, a **status offense** is a behavior that is only illegal because of the youth's "status" of being under age such as skipping school (i.e., truancy), running away from home or drinking alcohol. A **delinquent offense** is behavior that is illegal for adults to engage in as well. Because a status offense is less severe and the potential penalties are not as great as for a delinquent offense, the burden of proof in these cases is a preponderance of the evidence. For a delinquent offense, however, the *In re Gault* decision set the burden of proof as "beyond a reasonable doubt," which is the same as adult court.

In reality, however, most juveniles admit to the behavior, or at least some wrong-doing, and a formal hearing where the attorneys argue the facts of the case is rare. While *In re Gault* also gave juveniles the 5th Amendment right against self-incrimination, the fact is that most juveniles admit to the behavior during questioning. In fact estimates are that only 5% of all cases ever make it to a formal adjudication hearing with attorneys battling it out to determine guilt or innocence (Rubin, 1989; Bernard & Kurlychek, 2010).

While this might seem disturbing at first, one benefit of admitting to the behavior is that the defense attorney can negotiate a plea bargain that reduces the charges or the possible outcome. Often the defense lawyer will attempt to have the actual charge lowered as the final charge can impact other outcomes for the youth. For example, if the original charge is a sexual assault, the defense lawyer might argue for aggravated assault, which then avoids state sex offender registry laws and the stigma of having a sex offense on record. Similarly, while the original juvenile court kept all records confidential, many states now make the names and records of juvenile felony offenders public. Thus, the defense attorney might argue to have a felony charge reduced to a misdemeanor charge (Sanborn, 1993).

> **Connections:** Working to reduce such social stigma is in line with several of the theories of delinquency you have previously studied, including **Labeling Theory** and **Age-Graded Theory**.

One might ask what the prosecutor has to gain from agreeing to a plea bargain as it would seem to only benefit the defense. The truth is most public prosecutors, especially those assigned to juvenile courts, have such high caseloads that they simply do not have time to take every case to a hearing. Studies show that prosecutors are often open to plea bargains due to large caseloads and the desire to push cases through the system in an efficient manner. Thus, they may be less concerned with the outcome of any one case than with meeting the demands of their overall caseload (Alschuler, 1968; Smith, 1986). The problem that arises with the juvenile plea bargain is that it bypasses the disposition hearing and perhaps even a pre-dispositional review, which are important steps in crafting a disposition that is in the best interests of the child such as is called for by the mission of the juvenile court. You will read more about pre-dispositional reviews and disposition hearings below.

In the rare instance that the youth denies the charges and a plea is not reached, then the formal adjudicatory hearing is held. However, even in these cases the estimates are that to this day most youth enter the courtroom unrepresented by legal counsel. Early studies in the 1970s immediately after the *Gault* decision found that judges often failed to inform youths of their right to an attorney and to appoint attorneys to indigent youth (Bortner, 1982; Lefsteink, Stapleton & Teitelbaum, 1969; Scholossman, 1977). An indigent youth is one whose family cannot afford a private attorney, and indeed these youth make up most cases before the courts.

While more youth are represented by attorneys today than in the past, there is still not consistent representation. Some states reported to have high representations rates are California and Pennsylvania in which over 80% of youths do receive an attorney, but other states with low rates still have fewer than half of youths being represented by an attorney. There can also be a difference between urban and rural areas, with urban youth more likely to receive an appointed attorney than rural youth, and differences based on the seriousness of the crime, with youths facing more serious charges being more likely to be represented by an attorney (Feld, 1999; Puritz et al., 1995).

If attorneys are present the case proceeds much like what you envision in the typical adult courtroom with the state presenting evidence to prove the youth is the one who committed the alleged behavior and the youth's attorney dispelling the evidence and offering proof that he/she did not. However, remember that in the *McKeiver v. Pennsylvania* decision, the U.S. Supreme Court denied juveniles the right to a trial by jury so juries are not usually present. A state can still elect to allow a jury, the Supreme Court did not forbid this, it is just not a guaranteed right as is the right to an attorney. At the time of the writing of this text only 4 states had statutes that specifically allow juveniles the right to request a jury trial, while 13 other states allow for a jury trial in specific circumstances (e.g., when an adult sentence might be a final outcome through blended sentencing procedures). Even in those states that allow for jury trials, however, it appears they rarely happen. However, trials by jury actually happen fairly rarely in adult courts as well, with over 96% of all cases in adult court being settled through a plea bargain rather than a jury trial, so this difference between the systems is not as large in practice as it appears on paper.

Pre-Disposition Report

a report that outlines the youth's situation including risks, needs and strengths and makes a recommendation to the judge for a disposition

Connections: Much of the juvenile court process you are learning about in this chapter is guided by the series of Supreme Court cases you learned about in Chapter 2, including *In re Gault, In re Winship* and *McKeiver v. Pennsylvania*.

If the youth is adjudicated delinquent at the hearing, a **pre-disposition report** is often ordered. It is here that one best sees the traditional juvenile court at work.

At this time a court worker, often a specialized probation officer, conducts an in-depth evaluation of the youth. Similar to the intake interview process, the youth's home and school environments are examined, and further risk and needs assessments done. In many states it is the job of the probation officer to conduct this report and recommend a disposition to the judge that truly meets the identified needs of the youth. Of course, the prosecutor can ask for a different outcome, and/or the judge can craft an outcome that he/she sees fit after reviewing all the information, but in many cases it is the probation officer's recommendation that carries the most weight in determining the final outcome (Torbet, 1996).

Disposition Hearing

the hearing at which the judge hands down the final outcome of the case such as a term of probation or placement in a residential facility

The **disposition hearing** is then this final stage at which the juvenile court judge or quasi-judicial hearing officer determines the final outcome of the case. You learned about the McKeiver decision and that the juvenile court was not required to provide a trial by jury in that case, but what you did not yet learn was the logic behind that decision. The U.S. Supreme Court in its decision in this case noted that juveniles do not need equal protection under the law as adults because the juvenile court offers a "compensating benefit." That benefit is the right to treatment and a disposition crafted in the best interest of the child. That is specifically why the adjudicatory hearing is to be held separately from the disposition hearing with the first focusing only on the facts of the case (i.e., due process of the law) and that latter focusing on the best interests of the child (i.e., parens patriae). To put it most simply, in adult court the punishment is to fit the crime. In juvenile court the disposition is to fit the needs of the juvenile, regardless of the actual crime committed. For example, a youth who is adjudicated delinquent for aggravated assault but has no other history of problems with the justice system or in the home or school could receive a much less serious outcome than a youth adjudicated delinquent for a simple theft who presents with a history of fights in school, drug addiction and family problems. If you remember nothing else from this chapter (or even this entire text) I would ask you to remember this—the disposition is to fit the needs of the child—that is the cornerstone of the juvenile justice system and if it is eroded or taken away then the juvenile court will indeed just become a miniature adult court, or perhaps disappear altogether.

Figure 10.1 on the following page summarizes the process from petition to disposition to help you visualize the flow of cases through the system.

The most severe sanction ordered in more than 55,000 adjudicated delinquency cases (13%) in 2010 was something other than residential placement or probation, such as restitution or community service

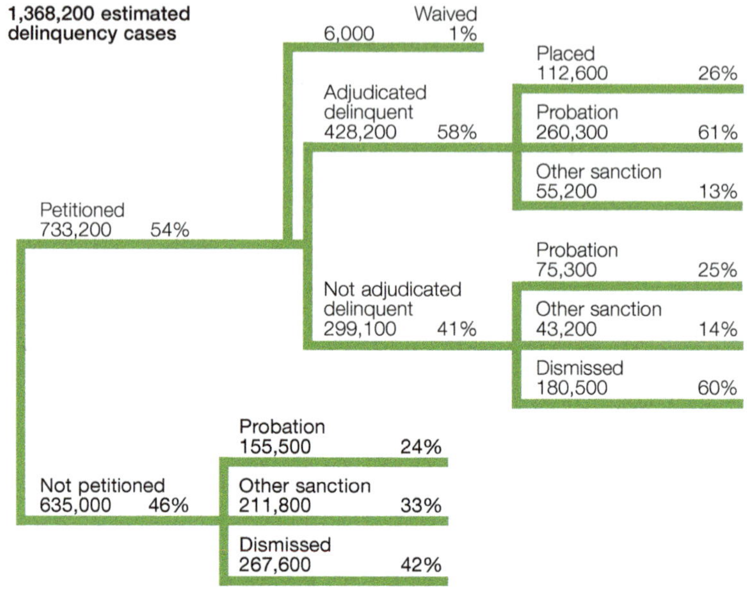

Adjudicated cases receiving sanctions other than residential placement or probation accounted for 40 out of 1,000 delinquency cases processed during the year

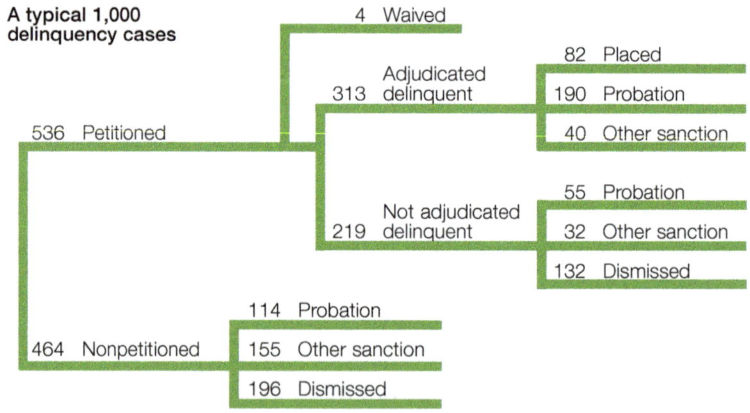

Notes: Cases are categorized by their most severe or restrictive sanction. Detail may not add to totals because of rounding. Annual case processing flow diagrams for 1985 through 2010 are available online at ojjdp.gov/ojstatbb/court/faqs.asp

Source: Authors' adaptation of Puzzanchera et al.'s *Juvenile Court Statistics 2010.*

Figure 10.1 The Juvenile Court Process
Source: National Center for Juvenile Justice, December 2014. Juvenile Offenders and Victims: 2014 National Report/2014, page 170.

The Office of Juvenile Justice and Delinquency Prevention

While most of the information provided above is generalized as states do things very differently, there are federal efforts to maintain some consistencies in the treatment of youth across states and to protect youth from harm. Most federal policy regarding juvenile justice comes from the **Office of Juvenile Justice and Delinquency Prevention** (OJJDP), which was created in 1974 through the Juvenile Justice and Delinquency Prevention Act. Since its inception the Office has worked to fund local juvenile justice policies through a variety of funding streams such as Bryne Memorial Funds and Juvenile Block Grants just to name a few. States are required to comply with basic rules and regulations put out by OJJDP in order to be eligible for these funds. The basic requirements are called "**Core Mandates**" and there are currently four such mandates.

Office of Juvenile Justice and Delinquency Prevention (OJJDP) the federal office in charge of setting rules and regulations for state juvenile justice policy and providing funding for juvenile justice services

1. *Deinstitutionalization of Status Offenders*: this means that youths accused only of a status offense and not a delinquent offense should not be held in juvenile detention and placement centers.
2. *Sight and Sound Separation*: juveniles should at no time during their arrest, processing or later placement be able to see or hear adult criminals who might further corrupt the youths.
3. *Removal of Juveniles from Adult Jails and Lockups*: juveniles should at no time be held in adult jails and lockups. Again, this is to keep these youths away from the corrupting influence of more sophisticated criminals.
4. *Addressing Disproportionate Minority Contact*: as minorities are over-represented at all stages of the juvenile justice system from police contacts and arrests, to detention and placement confinements, states are required to document this over-representation and develop formal plans and efforts to alleviate this apparent discrimination in the system.

Beyond these core requirements, the Office of Juvenile Justice and Delinquency Prevention also funds many programs, program evaluations and other research efforts to help us learn more about the phenomenon of juvenile delinquency and to develop best-practice programs to address the needs of youths before the court. Much of the information you are learning about in this chapter and the next in fact comes from reports and research commissioned by OJJDP. Take a moment and visit their website at OJJDP.US.Gov and search on some of the key words from these chapters to see all the information available for the study and practice of juvenile justice.

FOCUS ON POLICY: Balanced and Restorative Justice

Philosophy of the court. In Chapter 2 you learned that the original mission of the juvenile court was to save youths from growing up to be adult criminals. Thus, from its very beginnings the juvenile court has maintained a focus on helping or "saving" children rather than merely punishing them. The court evolved as a civil rather than criminal court to maintain this basis, gaining its legal foothold in the doctrine of "parens patriae" or state as parent.

In 1959 the Standard Juvenile Court Act was proposed by the National Council of Juvenile Court Judges, the National Probation and Parole Association and the U.S. Children's Bureau. This model act embodied this original spirit, stating that the purpose of a state's juvenile justice system should be to give every child coming before it the "care, guidance and control that conduce to his welfare."

While states varied of course in their adaptation of this language, it is safe to say that nationally each state's unique system maintained a similar focus until the time of the get tough movement you have been learning about. At this time, states began to question whether such a benevolent philosophy was the best approach for youth, particularly those committing violent crimes. In addition to transferring many youth to adult court (which you will also learn about in this chapter) the policies that came out of the get tough movement also changed the philosophy of the juvenile justice system in many states, thus impacting those youth who remained in the juvenile courts as well.

Some states adopted a modest approach known as "balanced and restorative justice" that attempted to balance the needs of the youth with the needs of the victim and community impacted by the juvenile's crime (Maloney, Roming & Armstrong, 1988). This model originated as a philosophy for probation in Oregon proposed by Denis Maloney, a probation officer in that state, and gained national attention. Soon the philosophy grew from one just for probation, to a more system-wide approach. For example, in 1995, Pennsylvania changed the purpose clause of its juvenile justice act to incorporate this philosophy as follows:

"Consistent with the protection of the public interest, to provide for children committing delinquent acts programs of supervision, care and rehabilitation which provide balanced attention to the protection of the community, the imposition of accountability for offenses committed and the development of competencies to enable children to become productive members of the community" (42 Pennsylvania Consolidated Statutes § 6301(b)2.

You can see in this language some of the original purpose of the court—that is providing programs of supervision, care and rehabilitation and also enabling children to grow up to become productive and law-abiding adults. However, the new part is balancing this goal with the new mission of imposing accountability for the offense and protecting the public and community from any other offenses a youth might commit. The question then becomes what does it mean to hold a youth accountable? And what needs to be done to protect the community? In response, in 1997, the Office of Juvenile Justice and Delinquency began the Juvenile Accountability Block Grant program to assist states in implementing programs that aimed to meet these goals and to provide for the evaluation of such programs. A plethora of research on this topic then followed (Beyer, 2003; Cooper, 2001; Crowe & Sydney, 2000; Decker, 2000; Gramckow & Tompkins, 1999; Kurlychek, Torbet & Bozynski, 1999; Roush & McMillen, 2003).

Not all states bought into the BARJ philosophy, however, and some further changed the mission of their juvenile courts to reflect a more adult-like, criminalized court. Several states went further, incorporating the words "criminal" and/or "punishment" into their new philosophies. One such state is Texas whose juvenile justice act now calls upon the juvenile court to "promote the concept of punishment for criminal acts" (Texas Family Code, Title 3 Chapter 51-60).

Juveniles in Adult Court

WHO GOES TO ADULT COURT?

The idea of juveniles being processed in adult courts seems to be a fundamental contradiction to the creation of the juvenile court in the first place. If juveniles are different than adults and thus deserve differential treatment before the law, then why would any juvenile ever be processed in adult court?

The answer is that the juvenile court was indeed created for youth who were seen as still developing and amenable to treatment. However, if a youth under that age of majority displays characteristics of a more mature adult, then this individual could be singled out for transfer to adult court via a **judicial waiver**. Judicial waiver policies have indeed been around as long as there has been a juvenile justice system. They were, however, first regulated in 1966 when the Supreme Court heard the case of *Kent v. the District of Columbia*. In this case one might be hard pressed to not agree that this youth might deserve to be processed in an adult court. By the time Morris Kent, Jr. was transferred to adult court he had accumulated quite the history of juvenile court involvement, including charges for housebreaking and purse snatching. After being placed on probation for these charges he was arrested for breaking into a woman's apartment, stealing her wallet and raping her.

Judicial Waiver
a decision by the juvenile court judge to "waive" a youth to adult court. This indicates the judge believes the youth is not treatable as a juvenile and requires punishment

Kent's lawyer was quick to file a motion requesting a hearing about possible waiver to adult court as he assumed, given the serious manner of the charges, that the judge and/or prosecuting attorney might request a transfer. He, however, wanted to argue against transfer at such a hearing as Kent was diagnosed by a psychiatrist as having severe psychopathology and he thought the youth would be better served by a mental health hospitalization than placement in an adult prison. The judge, however, never held such a hearing and simply transferred Kent on to adult court for processing. Kent's attorney appealed and eventually this case was heard by the same Supreme Court that would later rule in the Gault case.

What was and is unique about the Kent decision is that it did not require states to operate a juvenile justice system, but rather said that if they did choose to operate such a system all youths were eligible for the benefits of such a system and that no youth could be deprived these benefits without a proper hearing. It also set forth some basic principles regarding what such a waiver hearing should look like and what factors the judge should consider, which included the maturity of the youth, his/her amenability to treatment, the youth's prior record and the seriousness of the alleged charge.

Presumption Waiver Hearing

a hearing at which the law presumes the youth should be treated as an adult, but the judge retains some discretion to retain the youth in juvenile court if he finds the youth amenable to treatment

Connections: In Chapter 2 you learned about the differences between juvenile and adult court philosophies, but also that, since the inception of the juvenile court, there was also a mechanism by which juveniles could end up in adult court. These ideas are revisited in this chapter as the waiver process is an important juvenile court hearing in and of itself.

ON POINT: Pennsylvania's Juvenile Court Judge's Commission gives examples of checklists to be used at different types of hearings. An example of the checklist for a Transfer Hearing follows.

Mandatory Waiver Hearings

a hearing at which it is mandatory for the juvenile court judge to waive a youth to adult court if the facts are confirmed such as the youth's age, prior record and severity of offense

These discretionary waiver hearings were the lay of the land for the most part until the get tough movement of the 1980s/1990s that you read about in Chapter 2 when states invented many new ways by which youth could end up in adult court. In addition to these discretionary judicial waiver hearings, states added **presumption waiver hearings** in which the presumption was that the youth should be transferred and the defense had to prove that the juvenile was indeed amenable to treatment, and **mandatory waiver hearings** in which the judge really had no authority other than to review the youth's prior record and

Transfer Hearing Checklist

Present:

In all cases:

- ❍ Juvenile
- ❍ Juvenile's parent, guardian or caretaker
- ❍ Attorney for the juvenile
- ❍ Attorney for the Commonwealth
- ❍ Juvenile probation officer

As necessary:

- ❍ Police Officer
- ❍ Victim, victim's parent/guardian, victim advocate
- ❍ Interpreter

Before Starting the Hearing:

- ❍ Appoint counsel, if necessary
- ❍ Provide juvenile/guardian/attorney with copy of the written allegation
- ❍ Inform juvenile/guardian of the right to remain silent as to delinquency allegations

Issues to Be Resolved:

- ❍ Is detention required to protect the person or property of others?
  — Does juvenile meet minimum offense threshold for public safety detention? (See § 5-6)
- ❍ Is detention required to ensure attendance at hearing?
  — Does juvenile have a recent demonstrable record of willful failure to appear? (See § 5-7)
- ❍ Is detention required to protect the juvenile?
  — Has juvenile submitted written request to be detained?
- ❍ Do extraordinary and exceptional circumstances justify detention?
- ❍ Have alternatives to detention been considered and found unsuitable?

Required Findings:

- ❍ Probable cause to believe that the juvenile
  — has committed the acts alleged
  — is within the court's jurisdiction
- ❍ Necessity of detention for public safety reasons, to protect the juvenile, to ensure attendance at hearing, or due to extraordinary circumstances
- ❍ IV-E eligibility findings:
  — Contrary to the juvenile's welfare to leave him at home
  — Removal without services was "reasonable due to the emergency nature of the situation, safety considerations, and circumstances of the family."

Things to Remember:

- ❍ "When the admission of a child to a secure detention facility is being considered, preference should be given to non-secure alternatives which could reduce the risk of flight or danger to the child or community." (See § 5-5)
- ❍ If juvenile is detained after the hearing in a case involving new allegations of delinquency, a petition must be filed within 24 hours or on the next court business day.

Statutory Exclusion

when the legislature passes a statute that requires certain youth to be tried as adults based on combinations of age, offense history and current offense

Direct File

a situation in which the decision to file charges in either juvenile court or adult court is left in the hands of the prosecutor instead of the judge

the seriousness of the charge and declare that they met the criteria for transfer. **Statutory exclusion** provisions also became popular in which certain youths were just not defined as juveniles any more based on a combination of their age, prior record and offense charge. And finally a handful of states enacted **direct file** policies that removed the decision making from the hands of the juvenile court judge and placed it instead with the prosecuting attorney. A summary of state transfer laws is provided in Figure 10.2.

What these changes meant was that a lot more youths were being processed in adult courts than ever before. However, it looks like recently these trends are changing with a new emphasis on keeping youths in juvenile court. For example, from 1985 to 1994, the height of the get tough movement, the number of delinquency cases waived to criminal court climbed 132% from 5,700 cases to 13,300 cases. More recent numbers, however, show that by 2010, the number of waived cases was 55% below the 1994 peak, for an overall change between 1985 and 2010 of only 4% (Sickmund & Puzzanchera, 2014).

In addition to understanding the sheer numbers of youth being processed as adults, researchers are also interested in exactly which youth end up in adult court and for what reasons. Early research in this area found that older youths with more extensive juvenile court contacts were most likely to be transferred, particularly youths with a long history of property crimes. However, after the get tough movement the profile of waived youth changed such that it was youth who committed a violent or person offense, regardless of prior record, who found themselves before the adult court judge (Sickmund & Puzzanchera, 2014). This is interesting because it suggests that before this movement the judge was considering the history of the youth with the juvenile court as an indicator of amenability to treatment and to select youth who were more mature and not appropriate for juvenile rehabilitation and that after the get tough movement the focus has shifted to the seriousness of the immediate offense as an indicator of maturity.

Research also found evidence of gender and racial differences. For example, a 2002 study found that males charged with a violent offense were six times more likely than females charged with similar crimes to be waived to criminal court. Also, studies have found that black youths are more likely to be waived to adult court for drug crimes than other races (Sickmund & Puzzanchera, 2014). Overall, minority males are the most likely to be waived to adult court regardless of offense type and individuals accused of violent crimes are the most likely to be waived to adult court over other types of offenses (e.g., drug, property offenses). These trends are summarized in Figure 10.3 on page 230.

Most states have multiple ways to impose adult sanctions on offenders of juvenile age

State	Judicial waiver: Discretionary	Judicial waiver: Presumptive	Judicial waiver: Mandatory	Prosecutorial discretion	Statutory exclusion	Reverse waiver	Once an adult/ always an adult	Blended sentencing: Juvenile	Blended sentencing: Criminal
Number of states	45	15	15	15	29	24	34	14	17
Alabama	■				■		■		
Alaska	■	■			■			■	
Arizona	■			■	■	■	■		
Arkansas	■			■		■		■	■
California	■	■		■	■	■	■		■
Colorado	■	■		■		■		■	■
Connecticut			■			■		■	
Delaware	■		■		■	■	■		
Dist. of Columbia	■	■		■			■		
Florida	■			■	■		■		■
Georgia	■		■	■	■	■			
Hawaii	■						■		
Idaho	■				■		■		■
Illinois	■	■	■		■		■	■	■
Indiana	■		■		■		■		
Iowa	■				■	■	■		■
Kansas	■	■					■	■	
Kentucky	■		■			■			■
Louisiana	■		■	■	■				
Maine	■	■					■		
Maryland	■				■	■	■		
Massachusetts					■			■	■
Michigan	■			■			■	■	■
Minnesota	■	■			■		■	■	
Mississippi	■				■	■	■		
Missouri	■						■		■
Montana				■	■	■		■	
Nebraska				■		■			■
Nevada	■	■			■	■	■		
New Hampshire	■	■					■		
New Jersey	■	■	■						
New Mexico					■			■	■
New York					■	■			
North Carolina	■		■				■		
North Dakota	■	■	■				■		
Ohio	■		■				■	■	
Oklahoma	■			■	■	■	■		■
Oregon	■				■	■	■		
Pennsylvania	■	■			■	■	■		
Rhode Island	■	■	■				■	■	
South Carolina	■		■		■				
South Dakota	■				■	■	■		
Tennessee	■					■	■		
Texas	■						■	■	
Utah	■	■			■		■		
Vermont	■			■	■	■			
Virginia	■		■	■		■	■		■
Washington	■				■		■		
West Virginia	■		■						■
Wisconsin	■				■	■	■		■
Wyoming	■			■		■			

■ In states with a combination of provisions for transferring juveniles to criminal court, the exclusion, mandatory waiver, or prosecutorial discretion provisions generally target the oldest juveniles and/or those charged with the most serious offenses, whereas younger juveniles and/or those charged with relatively less serious offenses may be eligible for discretionary waiver.

Note: Table information is as of the end of the 2011 legislative session.

Source: Authors' adaptation of OJJDP's *Statistical Briefing Book* [online].

FIGURE 10.2 A Summary of State Transfer Laws

Source: National Center for Juvenile Justice, December 2014. Juveline Offenders and Victims: 2014 National Report, page 100.

Racial differences in case waivers stemmed primarily from differences in person and drug offense cases

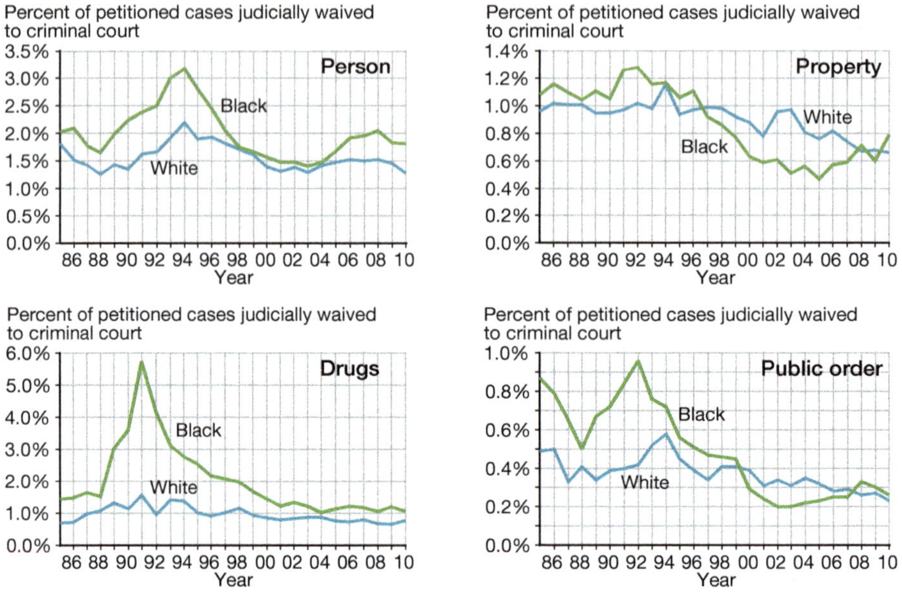

- For most of the period from 1985 to 2010, the likelihood of waiver was greater for black youth than for white youth, regardless of offense category. These data, however, do not control for racial differences in offense seriousness within the general offense categories or differences in the seriousness of juveniles' offense histories.

Source: Authors' adaptation of Puzzanchera et al.'s *Juvenile Court Statistics 2010.*

FIGURE 10.3 Trends in Juveniles Waived to Adult Court
Source: National Center for Juvenile Justice, December 2014.
Juvenile Offenders and Victims: 2014 National Report, page 174.

WHAT HAPPENS TO YOUTH TRANSFERRED TO ADULT COURT?

With the increased transfer of youths after the get tough movement, scholars also began to investigate the immediate and long-term outcomes of transferred youth. For example, the purpose of transfer to adult court was to provide more severe punishment, but the research on whether or not this is what actually happens is quite mixed with some studies finding that transferred youths suffer more severe outcomes than their counterparts maintained in juvenile court (Eigen, 1981; Meyers, 2001) while others suggest that juveniles retained in the juvenile system actually received more severe outcomes—e.g., they were more likely to be placed in a treatment facility and to remain there for a longer period of time than juveniles processed in adult courts (Bortner, 1986; Champion, 1989; Clement, 1997; Klein, 1998; Hamparian et al., 1982). Bernard (Bernard & Kurlychek, 2010) referred to this phenomenon as a "forced choice" in which an adult court judge, faced with the alternative of doing something too severe (i.e., adult jail or prison), or doing nothing at all, would pick "doing nothing." Thus, youths processed in adult courts may receive no punishment because judges feel confinement in adult jails and prisons is too severe while youths retained in the juvenile system may be sent to juvenile placement/treatment facilities that are seen as being uniquely designed to treat and rehabilitate youths.

Another line of inquiry in this area has thus questioned whether juveniles retained in the juvenile system are the correct comparison group when assessing whether or not juveniles in the adult system actually receive "adult" punishment. Kurlychek and Johnson (2004) argue that not only do the two systems of justice have different underlying philosophies, but that they also have very different practical resources available to them at the time of disposition/sentence. That is, this research argues that placement in a juvenile treatment facility may reflect both a different judicial philosophy (treatment versus punishment) and provide a very practical different experience for the youth than placement in an adult jail or prison. In two studies in Pennsylvania (Kurlychek & Johnson, 2004) and in Maryland (Kurlychek & Johnson, 2010) these authors compare the sentencing outcomes of transferred youths to those of similarly situated young adult offenders ages 18 to 21, and in both studies find that the transferred juveniles actually receive more severe sentences than similar young adults and label this effect as the "juvenile penalty." Additional research by Steiner (2009) comparing transferred juveniles to young adults (age 29 years or younger) in 37 urban counties across the United States finds similar outcomes. This study examines both bail and incarceration (but not sentence length) and finds evidence that juveniles are slightly more likely to be held on bail and substantially more likely to be imprisoned compared to young adult offenders.

Another interesting line of inquiry that has focused specifically on New York courts has found that judges in this jurisdiction may actually recreate some components of the juvenile court *within the adult court* when they are faced with processing minors. First proposed by Singer and colleagues (Singer, Fagan & Liberman 2000), in their chapter entitled "The Reproduction of Juvenile Justice in Criminal Court: A Case Study of New York's Juvenile Offender Law," this idea has been reproduced and extended in several more recent studies. Kupchik (2006) specifically examines the outcomes of young juveniles (ages 13 to 15) statutorily excluded from juvenile court in New York state based on the seriousness of the crime committed. In New York, such youths are referred to as Juvenile Offenders (JOs) and are processed in a special youth part of the adult court. On the very surface this system exemplifies the contradicting statuses of adults being transferred to adult court and minors being processed in a separate part of the court specifically designed for youths. Kupchik assesses the process in these courts as one of "sequential" justice in which the first stage (fact finding and conviction) is based on traditional adult court concerns such as strength of evidence, followed by a second stage of sentencing in which the judges return to a juvenile justice model with a focus on rehabilitation. Indeed, Kupchik concludes that "Criminal court decision makers view transferred youths as adolescents who are less culpable for their offenses than adults, and they reintroduce elements of juvenile justice to criminal court case processing" (Kupchik, 2006, p. 130). This process harkens back to the Supreme Court decisions of the late 1960s and 70s in which youths in juvenile court were granted access to an attorney and other due process rights during the adjudication/fact finding process, but were denied such rights at disposition (i.e., sentencing) indicating that such an adversarial atmosphere would be counterproductive to crafting a disposition in the best interests of the child (Bernard & Kurlychek, 2010, p. 151).

More recently, Barrett (2013) provides a qualitative analysis of how one judge's philosophy and practice in a youth part of New York's adult court system maintains a traditional juvenile court philosophy. In this book the author details the dialogue used by the judge as he interacts with the youth and their families. Highlighting practices such as addressing the youths by first name and asking family and friends for information on the youth's behavior are indicative of the informal and child-focused nature of the juvenile rather than the adult criminal justice system. Similar to Kupchik's findings above, Barrett also finds that while the judge may verbally admonish the youth's behavior, he or she also often comments on the youth's ability to change and provides a sentence that focuses on rehabilitation rather than punishment. Barrett summarized her overall impression of this court as a criminal court that "in its day to day handling of cases, it harkened back to the early Progressive era *parens patriae*-style justice" (Barrett, 2013, p. 89).

Blended Sentencing

As if the practice of selecting some or all juveniles for processing in adult court was not confusing enough, there is another practice adopted by some states that further blurs the lines between juvenile and adult status. This practice, called "**blended sentencing**," allows a juvenile court judge in some cases to give an adult sentence and an adult court judge in some cases to give a juvenile sentence. That is, for a juvenile tried in juvenile court, adult jail or prison is not a usual possible outcome, but in some states with blended sentencing laws it is. And, for a juvenile tried in adult court, placement in a juvenile rehabilitation/treatment center is not usually a possible outcome, but again, in some states with blended sentencing laws it is. There are five types of blended sentences defined below.

Blending Sentencing
a policy that "blends" sentences from the juvenile and adult court allowing the judge to use options from either or both systems

Juvenile Exclusive. The word juvenile here means the case is tried in juvenile court. The word *exclusive* means that the juvenile court judge has the authority to order either a juvenile or adult court outcome—but not both. The judge must pick which system's outcomes best suits the juvenile.

Juvenile Inclusive. The word *juvenile* here means that the case again is tried in juvenile court. In this instance the judge can actually use possible sanctions from both systems such as a week in an adult jail followed by juvenile probation. Research has found that in these instances the judge usually uses the adult sentence as a threat. That is, the youth is sentenced to say a year in prison, but is placed on juvenile probation instead. The adult sentence is "suspended" and only kicks in if the juvenile messes up on probation. Thus, it is kind of a carrot and stick approach where the juvenile sentence is the carrot and the adult sentence the stick.

Juvenile Contiguous. In this case you should now guess that juvenile means it is tried in a juvenile court. The juvenile court traditionally has authority to sentence a youth only up to a given age—for example the 21st birthday in most states. However, if a state has a juvenile contiguous policy the juvenile court judge can sentence the youth for longer. When the youth reaches the maximum age of juvenile court jurisdiction for holding in a residential placement facility, the juvenile will be taken from the juvenile facility to an adult jail or prison to finish the remainder of the sentence.

Criminal Exclusive. This is exactly the same as the juvenile exclusive mechanism stated above except that the case is heard in adult court; thus the word *criminal* instead of *juvenile*. In this case, upon conviction, the adult court judge decides if an

Recidivism is the commission of a new crime after an initial crime is committed. This is usually measured by a new arrest, but could be measured by self-report data, conviction data or placement data as well

adult sentence (i.e., jail or prison) or a juvenile disposition (i.e., juvenile probation or residential placement) is the best outcome for the youth.

Criminal Inclusive: Criminal, again, means the case is heard and decided by an adult court judge. Upon conviction the judge can craft a sentence that has elements of both juvenile and adult court outcomes. Similar to the juvenile inclusive sentence described above, the adult court sentence is usually suspended and only comes into play if the youth "messes up" serving the juvenile sentence.

FOCUS ON RESEARCH: Does Transfer Work?

The answer to this question depends on what you believe the purpose of transfer is. If it is to punish the youth then the research by Kurlychek, Johnson and Steiner would indicate that yes, perhaps it works because the youth do receive punishment. However, if you believe the purpose is to make society safer, then other things need to be considered; in particular, which system reduces crime better. There is a plethora of studies that investigates the recidivism outcomes of youth processed in the adult system versus the juvenile system, and, while the findings are somewhat mixed, the overall consensus seems to be that youth processed in the adult system fair worse. That is, they go on to become adult criminals.

Most early studies seemed to suggest that juveniles punished in adult courts did indeed fare worse in terms of likelihood of future criminality (Goodstein & Sontheimer, 1987; Fagan, 1991, 1996; McNulty, 1996; Bishop et al., 1996; Winner et al., 1997). However, on the surface, it is easy to argue that this is simply because more serious or chronic offenders are targeted for waiver/transfer. Researchers have employed several creative techniques, however, to overcome this problem. For example, Fagan (1991), compared youth ages 15–16 adjudicated originally in juvenile court in New Jersey to those adjudicated originally in adult court in New York. This is a unique comparison because New York simply defines all 16 year olds as adults rather than having a select few transferred to adult courts. In this study, Fagan found lower recidivism rates for youths processed in juvenile court.

Another set of convincing studies comes from a group of researchers studying juvenile transfer in Florida. The earliest study by this group (Bishop, Frazier, Lanza-Kaduce & Winner, 1996) found that juveniles retained in juvenile court recidivated less than a matched pair of juveniles transferred to adult court in terms of prevalence and incidence. Additionally, the adult sample was arrested more quickly on average than the juvenile sample. Related studies by this group found that those juveniles waived to adult court recidivated more often than those retained in juvenile court within a two-year follow-up period (Winner, Lanza-Kaduce, Bishop & Frazier, 1997), but that the recidivism rates tended to converge over time, with the transferred youths having a 42% chance of re-arrest in five years and the youths retained in the juvenile system a 43% chance. However, the authors still concluded that juvenile court processing was preferable, as this effect was driven mainly by property offenses, with youths retained in the juvenile system still being less likely to be re-arrested for serious felonies and having longer times to recidivism.

Two more recent studies provide some of the most convincing evidence, however, that juvenile court processing is preferable to adult court processing for most youth. Lanza-Kaduce and colleagues (Lanza-Kaduce, Frazier, Lane & Bishop, 2002), again examining transferred youth in Florida, used sophisticated propensity score matching techniques to compare youth across the systems, making sure the youth they were comparing were actually similar. They found that while only 35% of the youths processed in juvenile court were re-arrested after age 18, 50% of the youths processed in adult court were re-arrested.

Kurlychek and Fowler (2017) also found much lower rates of **recidivism** for youth processed in juvenile rather than adult court. **Recidivism** is the commission of a new crime, usually measured by a new arrest, but sometimes measured by a new conviction or a new incarceration. While all of the studies above focused on a new arrest, this study examined recidivism as both a new arrest and a new conviction. What is interesting about this study is that it was an evaluation of Connecticut's "Raise the Age" law which changed the maximum age of juvenile court jurisdiction for the entire state. That is, up until 2009 all 16 and 17 year olds in Connecticut were defined as adults and processed in the adult courts. That all changed on January 1 of 2010 when 16 year olds were included in the definition of juveniles and were all processed in juvenile court. The evaluation of this change found that while the 16 year olds processed as adults in 2009 had a recidivism rate of 42% for new arrests and 46% for new convictions, the 16 year olds processed in the juvenile system the following year had a recidivism rate of only about 36% for new arrests and 26% for new convictions (Fowler & Kurlychek, 2016).

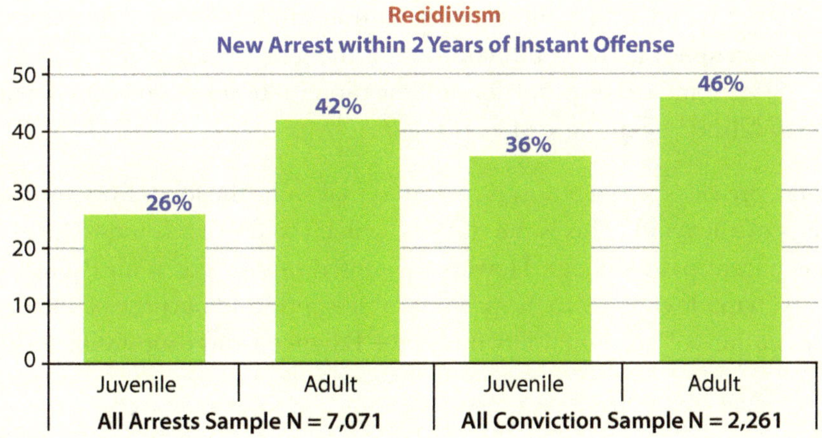

Courtesy Megan Kurlychek.

Key Words

Absconding
Blending Sentencing
Delinquent Offense
Detention Review Hearing
Direct File
Disposition Hearing
Judicial Waiver
Mandatory Waiver Hearings
Office of Juvenile Justice and Delinquency Prevention (OJJDP)
Petition
Pre-Disposition Report
Preliminary Hearing
Presumption Waiver Hearing
Recidivism
Status Offense
Statutory Exclusion

Chapter Summary

In this chapter you learned more in detail about what happens to a youth once they are petitioned to juvenile court or waived or otherwise transferred to adult court. These processes were set up to be different from adult court so that much of the attention remains focused on the youth instead of the actual act committed. However, since the due process movement and the resulting court cases and the later get tough movement, the juvenile court of today in many ways resembles its adult counterpart perhaps more than its original form.

While the terminology is a bit different than what you might be familiar with in the adult court, much of the process is the same. The petition, as you learned, is the formal document requesting the youth come before either the juvenile or adult court. Once petitioned to court, a preliminary hearing is held to determine if there is enough evidence to move forward with the case. If the case is moving forward the youth may be held in secure detention with or without bail. At the adjudicatory hearing the judge determines if the youth committed the alleged act or not *and* if he or she is in need of treatment. The standard of proof for adjudication is "beyond a reasonable doubt," similar to adult court as established by the case of *In re Gault.*

After adjudication a pre-disposition report is prepared that shifts the focus from the facts of the case to the best interests of the child. This is the stage at which the process is most like its original roots and maintains the parens patriae focus. However, as noted in the "Focus on Policy" section above, many states have even made changes to the primary philosophy and purpose of their juvenile justice systems to bring in notions of accountability under the Balanced and Restorative Justice philosophy.

While this text is focused on the juvenile justice system, it is important to also remember that not all youths, in the end, are processed in this system and that every state in the nation maintains some mechanisms, if not multiple mechanisms, by which youths can be transferred to, found guilty and sentenced in the adult criminal justice system.

While research findings on the impact of these waivers and transfers are mixed, it appears that in general the findings show that the sentencing received in adult court might vary by the type of youth who is transferred and by the transfer mechanism itself. The plethora of research on later recidivism outcomes seems to suggest that juvenile justice system processing is preferable to adult criminal justice processing when looking at both the developmental outcomes of the youth and the overall safety of society.

Discussion Questions

1. In this chapter you have been told several times that all states do things just a little bit differently from each other, making broad statements about juvenile justice difficult. In 2005 the National Center for Juvenile Justice published a comprehensive guide that summarized each state's policies and practices. Go to the following website to download this publication: http://www.ncjj.org/pdf/1State_Juvenile_Justice_Profiles_2005.pdf. Find your home state and read the summary of its profile. Then, select another state, perhaps where you are attending college, or have relatives, and read that state's summary. How are the states similar or different? What is the biggest difference you can find?
2. You learned about several types of hearings that are held in juvenile court in this chapter. How do these hearings/stages seem similar or different than adult court? Compare the terminology of the two systems. In which ways are the terms similar and in which ways are they different?
3. The federal Office of Juvenile Justice and Delinquency Prevention (OJJDP) was established in 1974 by the Juvenile Justice and Delinquency Prevention Act to provide some basic federal guidance and regulation to the nation's juvenile justice system. What are the core requirements of this Act? In what ways does OJJDP support and enforce these requirements?
4. So far you learned about the original mission of the juvenile court and how some states revised their mission statements. Pretend you were asked to draft a mission statement for the ideal juvenile court. What would it say? Compare your answer to your classmates' answers.
5. While every state in the nation maintains policies to transfer some youth to adult court, or to process entire populations of youth below the age of majority in adult courts, there is no consistency across states as to which court will adjudicate which youth. Do you think it is right for a youth to ever be prosecuted and sentenced as an adult? If so, which youth? What criteria should be used to select those youths who should be treated as adults?

REFERENCES

Alschuler, A. W. (1968). The prosecutor's role in plea bargaining. *The University of Chicago Law Review*, *36*(1), 50–112.

American Bar Association, Criminal Justice Section, Juvenile Justice Center.

Bernard, T., & Kurlychek, M. (2010). *The cycle of juvenile justice (2nd ed.)*. New York: Oxford University Press.

Beyer, M. (2003). *Best practices in juvenile accountability: Overview*. Washington, DC: US Department of Justice, Office of Justice Programs, Office of Juvenile Justice and Delinquency Prevention, Juvenile Accountability Incentive Block Grants Program.

Bortner, M. A. (1982). *Inside a juvenile court: The tarnished ideal of individualized justice*. New York: New York University Press.

Cooper, C. S. (2001). *Juvenile drug court programs*. Washington, DC: US Department of Justice, Office of Justice Programs, Office of Juvenile Justice and Delinquency Prevention, Juvenile Accountability Incentive Block Grants Program.

Crowe, A. H., & Sydney, L. (2000). *Developing a policy for controlled substance testing of juveniles*. Washington, DC: US Department of Justice, Office of Justice Programs, Office of Juvenile Justice and Delinquency Prevention, Juvenile Accountability Incentive Block Grants Program.

Decker, S. H. (2000). *Increasing school safety through juvenile accountability programs*. Washington, DC: US Department of Justice, Office of Justice Programs, Office of Juvenile Justice and Delinquency Prevention, Juvenile Accountability Incentive Block Grants Program.

Feld, B. (1999). *Bad kids, race and the transformation of the juvenile court*. New York: Oxford University Press.

Gramckow, H. P., & Tompkins, E. (1999). *Enabling prosecutors to address drug, gang, and youth violence.* Washington, DC: US Department of Justice, Office of Justice Programs, Office of Juvenile Justice and Delinquency Prevention, Juvenile Accountability Incentive Block Grants Program.

Kurlychek, M., Torbet, P., & Bozynski, M. (1999). *Focus on accountability: Best practices for juvenile court and probation*. Washington, DC: US Department of Justice, Office of Justice Programs, Office of Juvenile Justice and Delinquency Prevention, Juvenile Accountability Incentive Block Grants Program.

Lefstein, N., Stapleton, V., & Teitelbaum, L. (1989). In search of juvenile justice: Gault and its implementation. *Law and Society Review*, *3*, 491–562.

Puritz, P., Burrell, S., Schwartz, R., Soler, M., & Warboys, L. (1995). A call for justice: An assessment of access to counsel and quality of representation in delinquency proceedings. Washington DC: Office of Juvenile Justice and Delinquency Prevention.

Roush, D., & McMillen, M. (2000). *Construction, operations, and staff training for juvenile confinement facilities*. Washington, DC: US Department of Justice, Office of Justice Programs, Office of Juvenile Justice and Delinquency Prevention, Juvenile Accountability Incentive Block Grants (JAIBG) Program Bulletin.

Rubin, H. Ted. The juvenile court landscape. In Albert R. Robert (ed.) *Juvenile Justice*. Chicago: Dorsey Press.

Sanborn Jr, J. B. (1993). Philosophical, legal, and systemic aspects of juvenile court plea bargaining. *NCCD News*, *39*(4), 509–527.

Sanborn, J. (1993). Philosophical, legal and systematic aspects of juvenile court plea bargaining. *Crime and Delinquency*, 39(1993), 509–527.

Schlossman, S. (1977). *Love and the American delinquent: The theory and practice of "Progressive" juvenile justice.* Chicago: University of Chicago Press.

Sickmund, M., & Puzzanchera, C. (2014). *Juvenile offenders and victims: A national report.* Washington, DC: Office of Juvenile Justice and Delinquency Prevention.

Smith, D. A. (1986). The plea bargaining controversy. *The Journal of Criminal Law and Criminology*, *77*(3), 949–968.

Steiner, B., 2009. The effects of juvenile transfer to criminal court on incarceration decisions. *Justice Quarterly*, *26*(1), pp.77–106.

Torbet, P. (1997). Juvenile probation: The workhorse of the juvenile justice system. In D. W. Thomas & P. McFall Torbet (Eds.), *Juvenile Probation Administrators Desktop Guide* (p. 13). Pittsburgh, PA: National Center for Juvenile Justice.

After the Disposition: Treatment, Placement and Aftercare

©2p2play/Shutterstock.com

©carroteater/Shutterstock.com

The above picture depicts a home like living environment similar to what the original child savers had in mind. That is when removing youth from the home, the state was to become the parent and provide a loving environment in which the child could develop normally into an adult. However, this has not been the model maintained over time. Rather many youth detention and placements centers more resemble an adult jail or prison like that one pictured on the right. Think about the difference between growing up in an environment such as your own home, the picture on the top or the picture on the right. How might just this physical environment impact your emotions and development?

Obviously, the approach on the right is not what the child savers had in mind when they developed a separate system of justice and placements for youths. In fact, many facilities have been shut down over the years due to youth suicides and other injuries. Massachusetts was the first state to take a wholesale approach against such facilities when in the Governor simply closed all juvenile facilities. Another, less drastic approach was taken by Missouri over 30 years ago when the state switched away from large placement facilities and designed a system around small, cottage-style homes that keep youths close to their families and provide a truly rehabilitative environment in the least secure setting possible.

While state's continue to struggle with the dilemna between the need to lock up some youths to keep the public safe and the needs of the youth to have caring and enriched environments for development, the Missouri model has perhaps provided the most hope in obtaining such a balance. This model is being promoted as a national model for change by the Annie E. Casey Foundation (a non-profit organization dedicated to improving the lives and safety of children) as well as being recognized for its achievements by the federal Office of Juvenile Justice and Delinquency Prevention. Several other states, including Hawaii and Connecticut, also operate similar systems.

I use the stark contrast above to remind you of the notion that our nation has 51 different systems of juvenile justice (each state and the District of Columbia). Thus, while the programs and approaches described below are generalizations, there are many variations on the theme of juvenile justice.

Disposition

the phase of the juvenile justice system that would be similar to "sentencing" in adult court. It is the final outcome after an adjudication of delinquency has been made

This is important in studying the **disposition** stage of the juvenile system in particular as this is where "the rubber hits the road." Remember that disposition is that phase of the juvenile justice system that would be similar to "sentencing" in adult court. It is the final outcome after an adjudication of delinquency has been made. It is at this point that the theory and knowledge we have collected about youths and why they become delinquent can and should be used to design appropriate treatment options. The disposition stage comes after it is determined that a youth has committed a delinquent act and that upfront diversion (in line with labeling and differential association theories) are not suitable. In such cases the court must craft a final disposition that is both in the best interests of the child and that protects public safety. In order to craft a disposition that is indeed in the best interests of the child, the judge must understand what led the youth into delinquency in the first place. Was it lack of attention or other problems in the home? Was it failure in school or association with delinquent peers? Does the youth have more serious risks such as drug or alcohol addiction or a mental health disorder that may have led to the delinquency? These are all questions the juvenile court judge will want answered before crafting a disposition.

Notice that I have used the word "crafting" several times here rather than "handing down" a sentence as is often the terminology in adult court. Remember the goal of the adult court is to assign a sentence or punishment that is proportional to the crime committed. That is not the case in juvenile court. The disposition is designed to rehabilitate the juvenile so that he or she will not grow up to be an adult criminal. Thus, the disposition should be carefully designed to meet the needs of the youth committed, which may or may not be reflected in the type of crime committed.

Disposition options range from providing services while keeping the youth in the home to placement in adult jails and correctional facilities.

CHAPTER GOALS

The goals of this chapter are for you to:

1. Articulate why and how a disposition is different than an adult court sentence.
2. Have a clear understanding of the variety of diversion options still available to a judge even after adjudication.
3. Understand the difference between different types of juvenile treatment facilities and how a judge might determine the appropriate placement for a youth.
4. Be able to define and discuss aftercare as part of the juvenile system.
5. Be able to critically debate the processing of youths in adult courts.
6. Understand important challenges before the system at the disposition stage, including disproportionate minority confinement and the need for gender-specific services.

Disposition versus Sentencing

While some texts might use these terms of sentencing and disposition interchangeably, I want to remind you here again about the origins and the philosophy of the juvenile court that you learned about in Chapter 2. Remember the first challenge to the use of the House of Refuge as a separate place of placement for youths was in the case of Mary Ann Crouse. In this case, before a juvenile court even existed, it was determined that it was constitutional to remove a youth from his/her home even if proof of a crime was not exhibited if it was thought to be in the best interests of the child. Based on the parens patriae philosophy you have learned about, the idea was that the state could indeed step in and raise the child if it was thought the parents were not doing so adequately. This was later questioned, however, in the O'Connell case in which the Illinois state court decided that any time a youth is removed from the home it does indeed constitute "punishment" because, despite any good intentions, the facilities in which these youths are housed are not the same as being raised at home.

Although the mission of the juvenile court remains to save children from a life of crime, not all programs and services are equal. The juvenile court judge has many options before him/her at the time of the disposition and is faced with the challenge of designing a disposition that hopefully reforms the youth in the realization that many of the facilities in which a youth may be placed can have negative effects as well. In the sections below you will learn about a variety of the options available and research assessing the effectiveness of these programs.

> **Connections:** Just as many of the theories learned suggest that diversion from the system might be a good idea for minor offenders, many theories suggest that when formal intervention is needed, limiting this intervention to the least amount possible is equally beneficial. For example, if services can be provided in the home this prevents the youth from being in a facility where he/she only associates with other delinquents and it maintains family bonds and community bonds.

In addition, I would like to note that although the U.S. Supreme Court cases of the due process movement (Chapters 2 and 10) outlined a process by which the adjudication phase would focus on fact finding and the disposition stage on treatment, with treatment being the "compensating benefit" that allows the juvenile justice system to operate without the full protections of the adult criminal justice system, the Supreme Court stopped short of mandating that the juvenile system actually provide such treatment. Thus, treatment is the goal of the juvenile justice system in most instances, but it is not a requirement.

COMMUNITY-BASED SERVICES: DIVERSION AFTER ADJUDICATION

Dispositions that maintain youths in their home community are the most popular dispositions utilized in the juvenile justice system. Because the hope is to help the youth grow into a positive adult, it is thought that the home environment is usually the best context for this to occur. In the following sections you will learn about a variety of different options a juvenile court judge might have. The judge could impose only one of these options, or could impose multiple options when crafting the disposition.

POST-ADJUDICATORY PROBATION

In previous sections you learned that the role of a juvenile probation officer is in many ways different than that of an adult probation officer. That is because, in the juvenile system, the probation officer is usually the main actor gathering information on the case before the court, interviewing the youth and family, and helping to determine the best disposition for a youth. Such activities are not traditionally part of an adult probation officer's job responsibility. However, one possible disposition available to the juvenile court judge upon adjudication is to assign the youth to formal **probation supervision**. In fact, formal probation supervision is the most popular intervention used by the juvenile court, accounting for about 60% of all formal dispositions (Puzzanchera, Adams & Hockenberry, 2012). In this particular role, the juvenile probation officer is much like an adult probation officer in that his/her role is to ensure that the youth adheres to all conditions placed upon him/her by the judge and attends any and all treatments ordered. Probation officers may also be responsible for collecting restitution and fine monies if so ordered by the judge.

Probation Supervision
a period of formal court ordered supervision of a youth during which the juvenile probation officer, much like an adult probation officer, ensures that the youth adheres to all conditions placed upon him/her by the judge

The idea of probation as an outcome dates back to 1841 when John Augustus, a Boston shoemaker, would work with the court to take responsibility for offenders, often letting them live in his home and helping them find jobs, in exchange for them not being kept in the local jail (Fields, 2012). Augustus interviewed each individual and conducted his own unofficial risk assessment and background screening before agreeing to supervise each individual (Lindler, 2007). While he originally started working with adult males, he later opened up this opportunity to women and children as well.

This idea became popular in both the juvenile and adult justice systems with **probation** now being defined as the conditional release of a convicted adult or adjudicated youth under the community supervision of a court officer (i.e., the probation officer). However, unlike the original model formed by Augustus, you will not find a juvenile probation officer bringing a youth to his/her home, and the contact will be much less frequent.

Probation
the conditional release of a convicted adult or adjudicated youth under the community supervision of a court officer

Standard Conditions

youth placed on probation must adhere to some things such as attending school and not breaking any other laws

Special Conditions

conditions of probation that are not standard for everyone but are specific to that youth and his/her risks and needs

Today a youth placed on probation will then be required to adhere to some **standard conditions** of probation that apply to all clients (such as attending school and not breaking any other laws) and also may have **special conditions** placed upon him or her. Such special conditions are the cornerstone of designing a disposition that meets the best interests of the child and protects the public; these conditions are specific to the youth's situation. For example, perhaps the child needs outpatient drug and alcohol treatment or some other type of counseling to overcome a problem. Mandating that the youth attend such a treatment program would be an example of a special condition of probation.

ORGANIZATION AND ADMINISTRATION OF PROBATION

Although formal probation is perhaps the backbone of the juvenile justice system, there are many differences in how it is administered across states. One difference is whether probation is administered at the state, county or local level and whether or not it is considered a judicial or executive function of government. Much of this depends on the size of the state and on the legal traditions within a state. For example, in 24 states juvenile probation is administered totally, or at least in part, by local juvenile courts. However, in 12 states it is run by a state-level executive agency such as a Department of Juvenile Justice or a child protection agency (Griffith & King, 2006). Although these differences have been documented, there is no real empirical research that attempts to define if one system actually works better than another in regards to treatment outcomes for youths.

Continuous Probation

a model of probation in which one officer is responsible for the youth from intake through release from the system

Specialized Probation

a model of probation in which different officers have responsibilities for different stages of the system

Another difference is in the actual division of responsibility of probation officers. In some jurisdictions a youth will maintain the same juvenile probation officer from intake to discharge. This means that the officer who first became familiar with the case, the youth and the family maintains responsibility for that youth throughout the process. This is often referred to as a **continuous probation** model and is thought to have many benefits such as the officer having a greater understanding of, and connection with, the youth. A second model utilized in many jurisdictions is a **specialized probation** model in which different officers have responsibilities for different stages of the system. For example, an intake officer would be a specialized juvenile probation officer who only deals with the initial intake of the case, deciding if the youth should be placed in pre-adjudicatory detention and whether or not the case should be formally petitioned to court. In jurisdictions such as these, a youth assigned to post-adjudicatory probation would receive a new probation officer at this time who would be responsible for overseeing the case. Some benefits of this system are that the officers are able to specialize in certain aspects of the system, and it is thought that such specialization can lead to better job performance. Again, while one might speculate why one system may be better than the other, there is no formal research comparing the continuous or specialized probation officer models.

"SPECIALIZED PROBATION"

While the previous paragraph discussed specialized probation, in which certain officers have designated responsibilities on either the front end or back end of system processing, there is yet another type of probation that is called "specialized probation." In this latter case the probation officer takes on a special type of caseload such as a high-risk offender, or a drug and alcohol dependent offender with the need to offer greater supervision and treatment services due to these special needs of the juvenile. One common such program is **intensive-supervision probation**. This type of probation is often reserved for more high-risk offenders who might, but for the availability of this option, be put in a residential placement. Intensive supervision probation differs from normal probation in several ways. First, the officers usually have reduced caseloads to allow them to pay more close attention to each case. Second, there are more required face-to-face contacts, sometimes as many as three or four a week, between the officer and the youth. Third, the intensive supervision unit may work in "teams" where each probation officer has aides to assist in tracking and counseling the youth. This higher level of attention helps to protect the community from any possible misdoings of the youth as well as allowing the probation officer to provide the youth with more services.

Intensive-Supervision Probation

a special classification of probation supervision that requires more frequent monitoring of the youth

HOUSE ARREST

Another step up from intensive supervision probation is what you might have heard referred to as **house arrest** or home confinement. This is a special condition placed on a youth (usually in conjunction with other probation conditions) that requires the youth not be allowed to leave the home except for designated activities such as school or an approved job. Leaving the house at any other time would be considered a violation of probation conditions and could result in the probation being revoked and the individual being put into placement. There are several benefits to house arrest in that it allows the juvenile to remain in the home with his/her parents and avoid the stigma or trauma of going to a residential placement. From a system perspective it is also cost effective as the youth remains

House Arrest

home confinement, where the youth is not allowed to leave home except for designated activities in the home rather than becoming a ward of the state (the cost of residential placement will be discussed below). It can also be helpful if, as is often the case, part of the youth's problems come from exposure to delinquent peers or other negative factors in the community. Parents indeed often use "grounding" as a form of punishment to keep youths at home away from such influences or when they break the law. House arrest is similar and gives the parents extra support/legitimacy in keeping the youth in the home.

On the other hand, this option is not for everyone. The probation officer must first ensure the home itself is a healthy environment; otherwise the influence of the family may actually work to increase rather than decrease delinquency (Baumer, Maxfield & Mendelsohn, 1993; Ball, Huff & Lilly, 1988).

ELECTRONIC MONITORING

Electronic Monitoring

achieved by the probationer wearing an electronic ankle bracelet or other device that constantly monitors their location through a computer

Electronic monitoring is a new condition of probation that is made possible through technology. **Electronic monitoring** is achieved by the probationer wearing an electronic ankle bracelet or other device that constantly monitors their location through a computer. In early versions of the technology the system would work through the individual's home phone letting the probation officer know if the individual went outside a given allowable perimeter. Today, the technology is advancing quickly, however, to allow for an individual's location to be more consistently tracked.

Similar to house arrest this technology allows an individual, even a fairly risky individual, to remain in the home rather than be put into placement, thus letting the youth develop in a more natural environment. Also, similar to house arrests, it helps to reduce system costs. Also, the device allows a probation officer to monitor many youths at once through the technological device (Vaugh, 1989). Despite these benefits, however, some worry about the invasion of privacy increasing with the advances in technology (Houk, 1984). In addition, even though the technology might be able to allow the probation officer to know where clients are at all times, it does not tell the probation officer what their client is doing. That is, just because a youth does not leave a designated area does not mean that he or she is not engaging in illegal activities in that area such as using or selling drugs (Cohn, 2000).

DAY REPORTING CENTERS

According to the Office of Juvenile Justice and Delinquency Prevention, **day treatment centers** (also known as **day reporting centers**, community resource centers, or day incarceration centers) are "highly structured, community-based, post adjudication, nonresidential programs for serious juvenile offenders." The goal of day treatment is to provide highly intensive supervision while still maintaining the youth in the home and community environment. In general, when assigned to day reporting, youths are usually required to be at the program after school until a said curfew when the youth is returned home. Typical activities at these centers include mentoring, help with homework, perhaps group counseling sessions and even athletics. All these things are designed to keep the youth safe and off the streets from the period after school until bed time.

Day Reporting Centers

a highly structured, community-based, post adjudication, nonresidential program

Connections: In Chapter 3 you learned that most juvenile crime happens between the hours of 3 and 6 pm. This is thought to be because it is most likely at these times the youth are unsupervised as they are home from school but their parents may still be at work. In addition to just supervising these youth during these hours, day treatment centers ensure that the youth is not being exposed to negative influences by other peers or in the community and instead provides positive services the youth might need such as the tutoring with homework or counseling.

Originating in the United Kingdom in the 1970s, day reporting centers became popular in the United States in the 1990s during the "get tough" movement. They were seen as a way to keep the youth in the community while still providing more significant intervention than normal probation and keeping the community safe (Parent, 1995).

However, despite their increased use, empirical evaluations of the effectiveness of these centers are scarce. Winokur Early, Hand, Blankenship and Chapman (2010) is a recent exception. This study examined the impact of one center, the AMIkids Community-based Day Treatment Services, which offers services to at-risk and delinquent youth in Florida. Services provided at the center include mental health and substance use treatment, cognitive–behavioral therapy and skills therapy among other services. **Cognitive-Behavior Therapy** is a broad term for services that are designed to help youth replace criminogenic thinking with better decision-making that will then lead to behavioral changes. **Skills Therapy** (or skillstreaming) is designed to help youth learn better social skills and to deal with

Cognitive-Behavior Therapy

services that are designed to help youth replace criminogenic thinking with better decision-making that will lead to behavioral changes

Skills Therapy

designed to help youth learn better social skills and to deal with difficult social situations difficult social situations. In addition to these child-focused services, program staff also address issues in both the home and neighborhood, conducting home visits and working on family integration.

The evaluation found that youth who received services through AMIkids Community-based Day Treatment were significantly less likely to be rearrested, rearrested for a felony offense, adjudicated or convicted for an offense, convicted for a felony offense, and subsequently committed, placed on adult probation or sentenced to prison within 12 months of release compared with youth who completed residential programming (Winokur Early et al., 2010).

COSTS, FINES AND RESTITUTION

Court Costs

monies paid directly to the court for services rendered and can include such things as payment to a general fund to cover public attorneys or payment for probation supervision

There are three different types of monetary sanctions that can also serve alone as a dispositional outcome or be combined with other types of dispositions such as probation. These three are court costs, fines and restitution. **Court costs** are monies paid directly to the court for services rendered and can include such things as payment to a general fund to cover public attorneys or payment for probation supervision. It is probably a little known fact that many, if not most, individuals on probation pay a fee each week to help cover the cost of their supervision. This type of fee can be very taxing on families in poverty and, as you learned in Chapters 6, 7 and 8, poverty can be a key risk factor and correlate of delinquency.

Fine

the payment of money as a punishment, not directly related to the costs of the case

A **fine** is probably a concept with which you are more familiar. If you violate a law, you pay a fine to the state. The money goes into the state's general fund, or a specialized fund (such as emergency management or victim compensation). The most common fine most individuals face is a speeding ticket, but a fine can actually be attached to most other delinquent or criminal activities as well.

Restitution

the payment of money to repair harm done to a victim

Restitution is slightly different in that the juvenile is still required to pay money, but instead of to the state, the money goes to the victim. A restitution order is supposed to be based on the amount of harm done to the victim and is linked with the concept of restorative justice you learned about last chapter. It is meant to hold the offender accountable rather than just punish. For example, if you broke your neighbor's window playing baseball, your parent would probably make you pay for the window. That is the concept behind restitution. It is thought to be much more effective than costs or fines in which there is a financial burden placed on the youth that has little relevance to the victim, or the crime committed.

Although there have been few studies directed at the use of restitution in the juvenile justice system, one study that reported results from four juridictions—Boise, Idaho; Washington, D.C.; Clayton County, Georgia and Oklahoma County, Oklahoma—that randomly assigned youths to either conditions of restitution or traditional services found that in all four sites youths randomly assigned to restitution recidivated the same or less than youths assigned to more severe interventions (Schneider, 1986).

However, one problem with all of these financial penalties is that most youths do not have independent sources of income. Therefore, it is their parent, who may also have limited financial means, who has to struggle to pay these fees. Another disposition that may be used to hold a youth accountable in accordance with restorative justice standards but that may be less burdensome on the family is community service.

Community Service
doing any activity that repays the community

Community service is a broad term that refers to doing any activity that repays the community. It ranges from picking up trash along a highway or in a park to serving dinners at a homeless shelter or working at a Habitat for Humanity ReStore. The idea is that instead of being ostracized from society the youth is being more integrated into it by participating in activities that connect him/her with the other members of society.

Restorative Justice
a theory of justice the focuses on restoring the victim or community, to the extent possible, to the state before the crime happened rather than on punishing or treating the offender

Connections: Again, this idea is integrated with **restorative justice** and can be linked back to **reintegrative shaming theory** as proposed by Braithewaite. According to this philosophy the youth makes amends for the harm done to the victim or community without being removed from the community. Instead of being shunned, the youth remains integrated, or if not integrated, it is hoped that he/she develops ties to the community through the process.

Multisystemic Therapy
it assesses the youth and family and also addresses the social context of youth development, including the school, the youth's peers and the community

INTEGRATED CHILD, FAMILY AND COMMUNITY SERVICES

One last program that needs to be mentioned that can be used alone or in conjunction with many of the above-noted services is **multisystemic therapy (MST)**. Championed by Scott Henggeler at the Medical University of South Carolina, this approach is unique in that it not only assesses the youth and the family, but also addresses the social context of youth development, including the multiple systems of the school, the youth's peer group and the community. The approach recognizes that the family is usually the cornerstone of youth development and the focus of much of the attention of family relationships. A typical caseworker would have a caseload of only four to six families to allow for dedicated attention. In addition to this attention to the family the caseworker also assists that youth in addressing school problems, is able to address problems in the community and connect the youth and family to available community resources, and seeks to promote positive peer associations. Several evaluations of this approach suggest that it not only costs less than placing a youth in residential treatment, but at this reduced cost it reduces delinquency, future arrests and placements. For example, with a sample of violent and chronic juvenile offenders at imminent risk of incarceration, Henggeler and his colleagues (Henggeler, Melton & Smith, 1992; Henggeler, Melton, Smith, Schoenwald & Hanley, 1993) found that MST improved family functioning, reduced incarceration and reduced arrests. Similarly, with a sample of chronic juvenile offenders, Borduin et al. (1995) showed that MST improved individual and family functioning and reduced delinquency over a four-year follow-up period.

Evidence-Based Practice (EBP)
using programs that have some scientific evidence showing their effectiveness

Model Programs
the programs with the strongest scientific support

Promising Programs
show great promise but have not been proven effective yet

FOCUS ON POLICY: Evidence-Based Practice and Blueprints for Healthy Youth Development

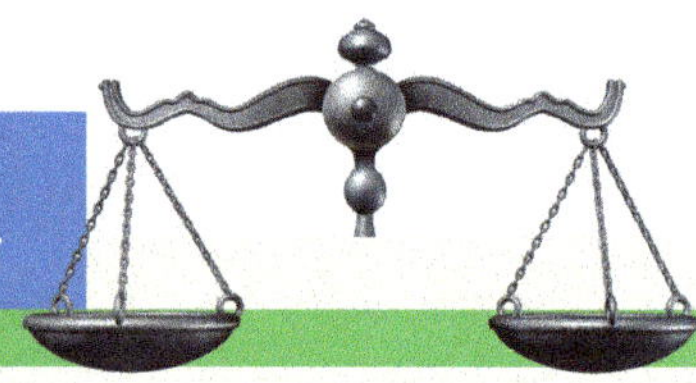

With the variety of treatment options available to the juvenile justice system, and often scarce financial resources to fund them, it is increasingly important for the system to understand which programs work and why, and not to just implement programs that "sound good." For example, Drug Abuse Resistance Education (DARE) is a program that sounds good as it brings police officers into the schools to teach about the dangers of drug abuse and to help students develop strategies to resist peer pressure to use drugs. However, evaluation after evaluation has shown that this program is not effective in reducing drug use and in some situations even increases drug use. What does work then? The focus on **evidence-based practice (EBP)** has led to lists being compiled of programs that have been proven effective by independent evaluations. The Blueprints for Healthy Youth Development (http:/www.blueprintprograms.com) is one such source. Each program provided on this list has been independently evaluated by experts and determined to improve youth outcomes. **Model programs** are ones with the strongest scientific support and **promising programs** are those that show great promise but have not been proven effective yet. The programs span a variety of possible problems and no two are quite the same. Yet, one thing that is clear in even reading the names of the programs are that these successful programs combine the youth, school, family and community in the treatment.

In addition to these individual programs promoted by the Office of Juvenile Justice and Delinquency Prevention, there has also been a quest to determine what makes these programs, or any one program, effective. Perhaps the most comprehensive information comes from a meta-analysis performed by Lipsey (2009), which found that the common denominators for successful programs were that the programs targeted high-risk offenders, were therapeutic rather than punitive in nature and had a high level of implementation fidelity. **Implementation fidelity** refers to the extent to which the program operates as intended. For example, with the multisystemic therapy noted above, the suggested caseload is four to six families. If a jurisdiction implemented this program but did not have enough caseworkers and each worker has 10 to 12 families, it may not be as successful, as this model does not allow the caseworker to devote enough time to each family. Similarly, if the program is to address mental health and substance abuse problems but only has services for mental health, this would be another example of poor implementation fidelity.

With this evolving focus on evidence-based practice many states have begun to implement best-practice centers or institutes to help coordinate and implement best practices. Examples include Pennsylvania's EPISCenter, located at Penn State University College Park, Connecticut's Tow Youth Justice Institute located at New Haven University and New York State's Youth Justice Institute located at the University at Albany, SUNY.

Implementation Fidelity

refers to ensuring that a program treats the clients for which it was supposed and delivers all the services required

Residential Placement

The term **residential placement** is a kind of catch-all term for when a youth is removed from the home and placed to "reside" in a facility. Notice the terminology here; instead of being incarcerated the juvenile is "placed," and instead of being in a jail or prison, he/she is in a "residence." Can you see the connections back to the original juvenile court when youth were in the "House of Refuge"? Although just as these houses sounded good on the surface, the terminology did not always match the reality. Hence the Illinois Supreme Court decision in the case of Daniel O'Connell; and the same holds true today, even with the best-intentioned placement facilities. Below you will learn about different levels of placement a judge could order at the disposition hearing. Remember, you already learned about one type of placement—juvenile detention—that a judge orders traditionally pre-adjudication if the juvenile poses a risk to him/herself or others. In some cases, a juvenile may return to a detention center after adjudication for further diagnosis or to await an open bed in the facility to which the judge has ordered treatment. However, these detention centers are not really equipped to handle this type of

Residential Placement

a catch-all term for when a youth is removed from the home and placed to "reside" in a facility population and provide treatment as are the other options specifically designed for post-adjudicatory placement discussed below.

The Cottage System

Cottage System Model

harkens back to the original "parens patriae" mission of the juvenile court which is to provide the child with a home-like environment in which he/she can develop into a productive young adult rather than a criminal

You started the chapter with a brief discussion of a cottage-style home for juveniles operated in Missouri. This model, sometimes called the Missouri model and other times simply referred to as the **cottage system model** truly harkens back to the original "parens patriae" mission of the juvenile court, which is to provide the child with a home-like environment in which he or she can develop into a productive young adult rather than a criminal.

In a cottage-style environment a small number of youths live in a house or cottage with house parents taking shifts living in the cottage with them. All treatment and education is given within this "homelike" environment. Benefits of this type of program include the youth feeling less stigmatized and less like a criminal and more like a normal teen. The house-like environment, rather than a cell, allows the child to move about more freely and experience a somewhat normal life, even though for whatever reason the judge determined that it was not safe for the youth to remain in their regular home. The downside is that, like all other programs discussed, the quality of the housing itself and the treatment provided within the cottage vary by area. That is, not all cottages will look as nice as the one depicted at the beginning of this chapter. In fact, the Missouri cottage system model is touted as the best in the country and has received the "Innovations in American Government Award" presented by the Ash Institute of Harvard University (McGarvey, 2005).

Private Placements

Another method used by some states to avoid placing kids in large prison-like facilities is to use private providers. Originally it was thought that these private placements could provide smaller, more therapeutic environments, while others feared that the for-profit nature of private companies might compromise the well-being of youth. As it turns out, both can be true. Below, I will give one example of what is considered a successful private model of juvenile rehabilitation, followed by an example of how corruption can overtake private detention centers.

VISION QUESTION

Vision Question is a private treatment program that currently operates in six states (Arizona, Delaware, Florida, Maryland, Pennsylvania and Texas). Originally designed as a "wagon train" experience, the program has grown into more of a system of small residential-based placement services that work with not only delinquent youth, but also dependent youth and in some states youth in, or transitioning from, foster care. Similar to the cottage-style homes above, these communities are usually small and the living arrangements resemble a home-like environment more than a jail. While the programs vary from site to site, Vision Quest has a tradition of having youth work with animals, grow and sell vegetables and participate in other outdoor and team-building activities and has more recently become dedicated to providing "evidence-based practices" which you learned about above. Such EBPs provided through Vision Quest include:

- Sanctuary Model® (thesanctuaryinstitute.org)
- Cognitive Behavioral Therapy (CBT) (nacbt.org)
- Aggression Replacement Training (ART) (aggressionreplacementtraining.com)
- The Seven Challenges (sevenchallenges.com)
- Street Smart (cdc.gov)
- Parenting with Love and Limits (PLL) (gopll.com)
- Functional Family Therapy (FFT) (fftinc.com)

Source: http://www.vq.com/

While a program such as this can seem to have many benefits, there is also a danger when a for-profit private company operates a detention center, placement center or an adult jail or prison. That is, the main goal can be to make a profit. In the following example, a worst-case scenario is provided for comparison.

KIDS FOR CASH: THE PENNSYLVANIA EXPERIENCE

Perhaps the worst example of such a practice gone wrong is the "Kids for Cash" scandal that surfaced in 2008 in Luzerne County, Pennsylvania. In this particular instance a private for-profit company was providing juvenile detention services to the county. The judge for the county, Mark Ciavarella, was quickly adjudicating juveniles for minor offenses such as mocking the principal, or minor shoplifting and removing them from the home and placing them in the private detention facility. It was later found out that over 50 percent of the children coming before the judge in the time period in question (2003 to 2008) lacked legal representation and about 60 were removed from their homes. The Pennsylvania Juvenile Law Center was at the heart of the investigation as this practice goes against the philosophy of rehabilitation, and of the child and family centered services that are the cornerstone of the juvenile system. It turned out the Judge was receiving kickbacks from the facility provider for each youth sent to the facility; thus he was literally receiving "cash" for each "kid" sent to the facility, padding both his pockets and those of the facility owner. Two judges, President Judge Mark Ciavarella and Senior Judge Michael Conahan, were later convicted of accepting money from Robert Mericle, the builder of two private, for-profit youth centers for the detention of juveniles, in return for contracting with the facilities and imposing harsh adjudications on juveniles brought before their courts to increase the number of residents in the centers. Both are now behind bars themselves on charges of corruption and fraud among other counts. Believed to be the largest judicial corruption scandal in modern history, the scandal was featured on *20/20* (an ABC show) in 2009 as well as in the film *Capitalism: A Love Story* by Michael Moore, a full-length documentary of the scandal entitled *Kids for Cash*, and on an episode of the crime documentary series *American Greed* in April 2014.

Connections: These examples provide two extremes and offer some distinctions. First, many private placements are with not-for-profit providers, which might make a difference in their intentions and philosophies compared to the for-profit facilities. Second, the first program described operates small units offering rehabilitation services, where the second was more of a jail-like placement facility designed to hold, not rehabilitate, youth. These two distinctions perhaps exemplify the fact that while noble in intent, the philosophy of the juvenile justice system is not always operationalized into practice and that youth need legal protections (like the right to counsel provided by the Supreme Court in the case of *In re Gault*), to avoid such grave miscarriages of justice as the one noted above.

BOOT CAMPS

Correctional Boot Camp

a type of placement that mimics a military boot camp focusing on physical activity and derogation of the juvenile to instill discipline

A **correctional boot camp** is a type of program that can be run either by the state or by a private entity as noted above. The idea behind a boot camp, if you cannot guess, is taken directly from the military. Youths are brought to the facility, their heads are shaved and they are given military-style uniforms. They rise early and answer to a drill sergeant who takes them on long runs, and forces them to endure other physically demanding challenges. Saying "Yes sir," "No sir" (or ma'am) and doing push-ups for non-compliance are all part of the routine. Most boot camps, however, also offer educational and counseling programs throughout the day. While this type of program on the surface seems to satisfy both those who want to get tough on kids—forces them to follow a strict schedule and partake in physically punishing regimens—and those who want to be lenient—provides for a short period of stay in a facility rather than lengthy sentences—the research on the effectiveness of such programs is dismal. Perhaps it is because the programs are short in nature—usually six to nine months—or perhaps it is because the environment inside the program is so different than that of the youth's daily life, but whatever the reason, multiple evaluations have found that these military-style boot camps have little to no effect on recidivism (Bottcher & Ezell, 2005; Cronin, 2004; MacKenzie, 1994; Parent, 2003).

STATE INSTITUTIONS

State institutions are typically reserved for the most serious and chronic offenders who have either committed crimes so serious they are seen as a threat to the community if not held in secure lock-up, or who have failed to be reformed when extended other, less intrusive services in the juvenile justice system. These facilities often look like small prisons. The facilities are considered "closed" or "secure" facilities, which means the youths spend most of their time behind bars in a facility with locks and even barbed wire fences. Perhaps the most extreme example is the California Youth Authority of which you saw a picture at the beginning of the chapter.

While I stated that these facilities are for the most serious offenders, some statistics suggest that less than half of the youths spending time in such facilities actually committed serious crimes. Recent statistics suggest what while just over a third of youths in such institutions actually committed a crime against a person (typically referred to as a violent crime), almost a quarter of the youths in such facilities are there for technical violations of court orders or conditions of probation (Sickmnund et al., 2011). This of course varies by state and the state emphasis of the juvenile justice system. However, what can be generalized across states is that these large institutions, whether they are "called" reform schools, training schools or merely youth facilities, harken more to an adult jail or prison than to the envisioned home-like care and rehabilitation promised by the underlying philosophy of the juvenile justice system.

Over recent decades many of these larger facilities have come into question not only for their lack of rehabilitation of youths, but for abuse of youths within their walls, as well as homicides and suicides. However, this crisis is not a new event. In 1967 a Massachusetts state senate report described that state's youth training schools as "a continuing nightmare," and found that "the majority of children" confined in the state's facilities did not belong there. In response, by 1973 Massachusetts had become the first state to literally close all of its state juvenile institutions and turn to the sole use of community corrections for delinquent and dependent youths.

While many initially questioned this decision, a decade later, a study by the National Council on Crime and Delinquency (NCCD) found that Massachusetts had the lowest juvenile recidivism rate of any state studied at only 25% (Krisberg & Austin, 1993). Moreover, the study found that the Massachusetts model saved state taxpayers over $11 million per year (Howell, 1996).

FOCUS ON RESEARCH: Disproportionate Minority Confinement

In Chapter 9 you learned about police encounters with minority juveniles and continuous concern over possible bias in system response to minority youths. In Chapter 10 you then learned more about the Juvenile Justice and Delinquency Prevention Act and its core requirements, one of which is to address disproportionate minority contact with the juvenile justice system. This requirement was first introduced in the 1992 version of the Act and was, at that time, a mandate to address disproportionate minority confinement. However, upon study of the problem, it was revealed that the disproportion of minorities in our nation's juvenile and adult institutions is not simply the result of sentencing and disposition decisions, but is part of a longer process that starts with the first system contact, usually a police officer, and follows through all points of contact from formal arrest decisions, diversion or formal processing decisions, pre-adjudicatory detention or jail decisions and ultimately the final disposition or sentencing outcome. Thus, the 2002 revision of the Act changed the mandate to states to address the broader concept of Disproportionate Minority Contact. The purpose of the mandate, however, remains the same: "The purpose of the core requirement remains the same: to ensure equal and fair treatment for every youth in the juvenile justice system, regardless of race and ethnicity" (Slowikowski, 2009).

Disproportionate minority contact (DMC) simply means that minorities have more contact with the juvenile/criminal justice systems than you would expect based on their proportion in the population. That is, if minorities make up 10% of the population, they should be expected to make up 10% of police contacts, arrests and placements. However, that is not the case, as shown by the following statistics:

	Population	Referrals	Detained	Petition	Adjudicated	Placed	Waived
White	78%	67%	60%	64%	68%	63%	62%
Black	16%	29%	36%	32%	29%	33%	35%
Other	6%	4%	4%	4%	3%	4%	3%

Stahl, A., Finnegan, T., & Kang, W. (2005). http://ojjdp.ncjrs.org/ojstatbb/ezajcs

OJJDP requires each state to provide a three-year plan to address DMC in order to be eligible for certain types of federal formula grant funding for their juvenile justice system. The plan requirements by OJJDP have five phases:

1. **Identification.** In this phase, the state must assess if disproportionality exists at nine specific contact points in the juvenile justice system (i.e., arrest; referral to court; diversion; case petitioned; secure detention; delinquency finding; probation; confinement in secure correctional facility; and cases transferred, certified, and waived to adult criminal court). To assess this, the state is to use the relative rate index (RRI) that computes the rate of activity involving minority youth divided by the rate of activity involving majority youth. Any number more than 1 indicates disproportionality except at the diversion and probation contact points in which case a number greater than 1 would mean minorities were benefiting from the system.
2. **Assessment/Diagnosis.** If the state determines disproportionality exists, the next stage is to determine what might be leading to it. This involves collecting data, analyzing data and assessing various possible explanations at each stage.
3. **Intervention.** After a state is able to determine what might be leading to disproportionality, the next step is to design efforts to address it and improve the system. System improvement activities may include many activities such as advocating for legislative reforms, expanding the availability of diversion options, implementing evidence-based programming and providing greater structure and oversight at the various decision-making points in the juvenile justice system.
4. **Evaluation.** An important aspect of any juvenile justice initiative is its evaluation. As you have learned by now, many programs that sound good on the surface (houses of refuge, DARE, boot camps), may actually do harm in the end. Thus, the OJJDP plan requires states to conduct systematic, objective and unbiased evaluation of all programs implemented to reduce DMC.
5. **Monitoring.** The final phase then ensures progress is maintained and assessing any fluctuation in the states' trends that may require additional attention to sustain DMC-reduction efforts.

Overall, while great strides have been made, there is still a long way to go. According to the latest information available from OJJDP, only 29 states have addressed all nine contact points of the system (phase 1), and only 18 states have completed the assessment and diagnostic phase. However, many states seem to be moving on to program implementation/intervention, perhaps without proper guidance or assessment, as 34 states report having implemented strategies to reduce DMC (Hanes, 2012).

End of the Line: Juveniles in Adult Jails and Prisons

One step worse, however, than these juvenile facilities, is perhaps the fate of many youths who find themselves in adult jails and lock-ups. These "adult-juveniles" (Barrett, 2013) as they have been coined, still bear all the resemblance to adolescents, based on their cognitive development, decision-making and general mental capacity. Yet, because of the offense committed, or a combination of past offenses and current state policies, they find themselves being redefined as an "adult" at least, and probably only for, criminal justice processing purposes.

There are, as you learned previously, a variety of ways in which juveniles can be transferred to adult courts for processing, including judicial waiver, legislative or statutory exclusion and direct file provisions. Also, several states have historically set the age of criminal responsibility below the traditional age of 18, although most of these states have recently, or are in the process of, changing these distinctions. For example, North Carolina, Connecticut and New York have historically simply defined all 16 and 17 year olds as adults. However, in 2010 Connecticut redefined 16 year olds as juveniles and in 2012 redefined 17 year olds as juveniles as well. In April 2017, New York raised the age of criminal responsibility to 18, making all 16 and 17 year olds "juveniles" again.

Despite this trend in raising the age, there are still many youths who find themselves transferred to adult court based on the severity of the offense, their prior records or a combination of the two. The distinction in purpose and practice between juvenile and adult court justice systems has led many scholars to question whether such transfer is indeed wise—even for the most severe and chronic youth. Early studies of transfer seemed to suggest that juveniles punished in adult courts did indeed fare worse in terms of likelihood of future criminality (Bishop & Frazier, 1991; Bishop et al., 1996; Goodstein & Sontheimer, 1987; Fagan, 1991, 1996; McNulty, 1996; Winner et al., 1997).

However, it is easy to argue that this may simply be because it is a group of worse youths (i.e., more serious and chronic offenders) who are generally transferred to adult court for processing. Several studies have tried to overcome this problem by using alternative sampling techniques. For example, Fagan (1991) capitalized on cross-jurisdictional differences between New Jersey and New York to identify a sample of violent youthful offenders ages 15–16 who would be originally adjudicated in juvenile court in New Jersey and in adult court in New York. This research found the New Jersey policy of retaining these youth in juvenile court led to lower recidivism rates. Additionally, for those youths processed in the juvenile court who *did* experience a new arrest, the average time to rearrest was longer than for youths processed in the adult court. Regarding the finding that youths treated in adult court had higher crime rates, Fagan (1991) suggests, "the criminalization of delinquency may actually have criminogenic effects with respect to recidivism." A later study by Fagan (1996) also found that those youths who actually experienced *incarceration* in the adult system had even greater likelihood of later recidivism and violence.

Researchers exploring Florida's transfer/waiver policy took a different approach, using statistical matching techniques to try to identify a sample of youths transferred to adult court by judges or prosecutors and compare them to youth retained in juvenile courts. Overall, these studies similarly suggest that youths retained in juvenile court have lower recidivism rates and when re-arrested were likely to have longer times to re-arrest and to be arrested for less-violent offenses (Bishop, Frazier, Lanza-Kaduce & Winner, 1996; Winner, Lanza-Kaduce, Bishop & Frazier, 1997; Lanza-Kaduce, Frazier, Lane & Bishop, 2002).

Several more recent studies using econometric methods of analyses, however, have found null effects, or even lower rates of recidivism, for youths processed in adult courts, bringing back into question whether these prior studies have adequately controlled for issues of selection bias. For example, Loughran et al. (2010) found overall null effects when comparing reoffending of a matched group of serious juvenile offenders in Pennsylvania and Arizona adjudicated in either juvenile court or adult court via transfer and Loeffler and Grunwald (2015), employing a regression discontinuity design, found processing juveniles as adults resulted in a three to five percent reduction in likelihood of recidivism when they compared felony drug offenders processed in juvenile and adult courts in Chicago over the course of four years.

What is one then to make of such mixed findings? Zane, Welsh and Mears (2016) attempt to answer this question by conducting a meta-analysis of the most methodologically sound studies of juvenile transfer. Using meta-analytic techniques to combine the effect sizes across studies, these researchers conclude that transfer to adult court has a small but statistically insignificant impact on recidivism. Perhaps more importantly, however, the authors conclude that this null effect appears to be tied to heterogeneous effects across studies with outcomes highly dependent upon the exact transfer policy of the jurisdiction involved. In plain English, that means, transfer exerted "different effects, whether because of the type of transfer, offender, offenses, or sanctions that youth receive" (p. 916).

Aftercare

Aftercare
designed to help youths re-adjust to being home and in community after residential placement

One last topic to address is what happens to youth after they are released from a placement. Most return home on some type of formal probation or parole supervision. However, some agencies have implemented more formal **aftercare** programs that are designed to help these youths re-adjust to being home and in their home community. These are, after all, the conditions under which the original delinquency developed. So while it is fine and dandy that a youth does well in placement, what really matters is how he/she does when returned to society where he/she is now expected to be a productive and law-abiding citizen.

For this reason, in the 1980s, the U.S. Justice Department's Office of Juvenile Justice and Delinquency Prevention (OJJDP) began funding research on efforts to help young offenders re-enter the community. In 1994, a series of studies by Altschuler and Armstrong (1994a, 1994b, 1994c) led to the development of a **national intensive aftercare program (IAP) model**. According to Altschuler and Armstrong, that IAP is explicitly designed to address two problems: 1) institutional confinement does not adequately prepare youth for return to the community where at least part of the problem has its origins and continues to reside, and 2) lessons and skills learned in confinement are not systematically monitored, much less reinforced, on the "outside." The model has three primary phases which include working with the youth prior to release to ensure he/she is ready to re-enter the home community, working with the family and home community to establishe links with available private and public sector services that might be beneficial to the youth and, finally, ensuring that the youth and the youth's family actually receive services upon release.

This model was tested in four states (Colorado, Nevada, New Jersey and Virginia); however, each site seemed to implement the program a bit differently, emphasizing different services or targeting different types of youths for services. The result was a mixed bag of evaluation findings, with some components of the program found successful in some areas, and others not so much. The take away message proposed by the evaluators was that although "The results of this evaluation do not allow for a simple characterization of the effectiveness of IAP . . . The model warrants additional efforts at implementation and testing" (Weibush et al., 2010).

Despite the immediate findings of this one particular aftercare program analysis, the fact remains that youth develop, learn and grow within a broader social context, and whether or not original services are provided in this setting, or the youth is removed from the setting for some period of time while in residential placement, the youth will ultimately continue to develop in this setting—thus, community services, such as aftercare, need to remain a key focus of the juvenile justice system.

Key Words

Aftercare
Cognitive-Behavior Therapy
Community Service
Continuous Probation
Correctional Boot Camp
Cottage System Model
Court Costs
Day Reporting Centers
Disposition
Electronic Monitoring
Evidence-Based Practice (EBP)
Fine
House Arrest
Implementation Fidelity
Intensive-Supervision Probation
Model Programs
Multisystemic Therapy
Probation
Probation Supervision
Promising Programs
Residential Placement
Restitution
Restorative Justice
Skills Therapy
Special Conditions
Specialized Probation
Standard Conditions

Chapter Summary

In this chapter you learned of a variety of options the juvenile court judge has at the point of "disposition." That is, after it has been determined that the youth did indeed commit the act in question. If it is determined that the youth does not require services, there can indeed be a disposition that involves no further action. However, the most popular dispositions utilized by the juvenile court are those that work with the youth in the home and community setting.

Probation supervision as you saw is the most popular outcome of a case. This allows the youth to remain in the home, school and community while abiding by some standard and specialized conditions of probation that include such things as going to school, obeying their parents, and usually some counseling or other guidance type activity to help the youth "get back on track."

Options that the juvenile court judge can use alone or in combination with probation include the paying of costs, fines and restitution; completion of community service hours; house arrest or electronic monitoring and even day reporting centers.

If none of these community-based options are deemed appropriate, based on either the risk the youth poses to the community or the safety of the youth in the home environment, then a residential placement may be ordered. Such a placement can be secure or non-secure, and can be in a public, state-run facility or a private for-profit or non-for-profit facility. While each has its strengths and weaknesses, the cottage system model, specifically the Missouri model, is one that has been recognized nationally for providing youth with the most "home-like" environment and for effective service delivery. This contrasts starkly with the prison-like environments of many state-run public juvenile facilities, such as the California Youth Authority depicted at the beginning of the chapter.

Worse yet, however, are adult jails and prisons, which are the fate of numerous youth across the nation, who, despite their young age and lack of maturity, find themselves before adult court judges because of the seriousness of the offense committed and the state's specific jurisdictional and transfer policies. Much empirical research has been directed at these youths and overall, while the findings are mixed they suggest 1) that youth tend to fair worse when prosecuted and punished as adults and 2) each state's specific policies leads to different outcomes. This suggests that greater information is needed on which youth fare the best and/or worst when subject to transfer so that states can begin to implement informed policies rather than policies that "sound good" to politicians and the media.

Finally, for those youth removed from the home, unless the crime was so severe it led to a sentencing of life in prison (which is severely limited for juveniles), society must realize these youths will be returning home. What then? How do we ensure that these youth continue any positive transformation gained during placement? Aftercare is one suggested pathway that provides continued services to the youth once he/she returns home. Although evaluations of one specific aftercare model proved mixed, there is much room for implementation, experimentation and evaluation of such services in the future of juvenile justice.

Discussion Questions

1. How is a disposition in juvenile court the same as adult sentencing? How is it different? In what ways are these differences important?
2. Since a focus of the juvenile system is to keep the youth in the home whenever possible there are usually several community-based options available to the juvenile court judge. What ones did you learn about in this chapter? Which do you think might be the most effective? When do you think it is not appropriate to use community-based sanctions?
3. When a youth is placed outside the home, there are also several options. What is the difference between a state training school and a cottage system? What is the key difference between a public or private placement? What are some key benefits of each?
4. At the end of the line, there is a significant number of juveniles who find themselves in adult jails and prisons. Do you think this is appropriate? If so, why? If not, why not? What does the research suggest is the impact of adult court processing on later criminality? Returning to the theories of delinquency you have learned, can you argue why this might be?

5. In this chapter you learned about several promising programs or model programs for evidence-based practice. Visit the websites for two of these programs and compare and contrast them.

REFERENCES

Altschuler, D. M., & Armstrong, T. L. (1994). *Intensive aftercare for high risk juveniles: A community care model.* Summary. Washington, DC: U.S. Department of Justice, Office of Justice Programs, Office of Juvenile Justice and Delinquency Prevention.

Ball, R., Huff, R., & Lilly, R. (1988). *House arrest and correctional policy: Doing time at home.* Newbury Park, CA: Sage.

Barrett, C. (2013). *Courting kids: Inside an experimental youth court.* New York: NYU Press.

Baumer, T. L., Maxfield, M. G., & Mendelsohn, R. (1993). A comparative analysis of three electronically monitored home detention programs. *Justice Quarterly, 10,* 121–142.

Bishop, D. M., & Frazier, C. E. (1991). Transfer of juveniles to criminal court: a case study and analysis of prosecutorial waiver. *Notre Dame Journal of Law, Ethics and Public Policy,* 5, 281–302.

Bishop, D. M., Frazier, C. E., & Henretta, J. (1989). Prosecutorial waiver: Case study of a questionable reform. *Crime and Delinquency, 35,* 179–201.

Borduin, C. M., Mann, B. J., Cone, L. T., Henggeler, S. W., Fucci, B. R., Blaske, D. M., & Williams, R. A. (1995). Multisystemic treatment of serious juvenile offenders: Long-term prevention of criminality and violence. *Journal of Consulting and Clinical Psychology, 63*(4), 569–578.

Bottcher, J., & Ezell, M. E. (2005). Examining the effectiveness of boot camps: A randomized experiment with a long-term follow-up. *Journal of Research in Crime and Delinquency, 42,* 309–332.

Cohn, A. W. (2000). Electronic monitoring and graduated sanctions. *Journal of Offender Monitoring,* 13, 19–20.

Cronin, R. C. (1994). *Boot camps for adult and juvenile offenders: Overview and update.* Washington, DC: National Institute of Justice.

Fagan, J. (1991). *The comparative impacts of juvenile and criminal court sanctions on adolescent offenders.* Washington, DC: U.S. Department of Justice, Office of Justice Programs, Office of Juvenile Justice and Delinquency Prevention.

Fagan, J. (1996). The comparative advantage of juvenile versus criminal court sanctions on recidivism among adolescent felony offenders. *Law and Policy, 18*(1–2), 77–114.

Fields, C. (2012). Augustus, J. In S. M. Barton-Bellessa (Ed.), *Encyclopedia of Community Corrections* (pp. 17–18). Newbury Park, CA: Sage.

Goodstein, L., & Sontheimer, H. (1987). *A study of the impact of ten Pennsylvania residential placements on juvenile recidivism: Prepared for the Pennsylvania juvenile court judges' commission.* Center for Juvenile Training and Research, Shippensburg University.

Griffith, P., & King, M. (2006). *National overviews state juvenile justice profiles.* Pittsburgh PA: National Center for Juvenile Justice.

Hanes, M. (2012). *In focus: Disproportionate minority contact.* Washington DC: U.S. Department of Justice, Office of Justice Programs, Office of Juvenile Justice and Delinquency Prevention.

Henggeler, S. W., Melton, G. B., & Smith, L. A. (1992). Family preservation using multisystemic therapy: An effective alternative to incarcerating serious juvenile offenders. *Journal of Consulting and Clinical Psychology, 60*(6), 953–961.

Henggeler, S. W., Melton, G. B., Smith, L. A., Schoenwald, S. K., & Hanley, J. H. (1993). Family preservation using multisystemic treatment: Long-term follow-up to a clinical trial with serious juvenile offenders. *Journal of Child and Family Studies, 2*(4), 283–293.

Houk, J. M. (1984). Electronic monitoring of probationers: A step toward Big Brother? *Golden Gate University Law Review, 14,* 431–466.

Howell, J. C. (1996). *Guide for implementing the comprehensive strategy for serious, violent, and chronic juvenile offenders.* Washington, DC: U.S. Department of Justice, Office of Juvenile Justice and Delinquency Programs.

Krisberg, B., & Austin, J. F. (1993). *Reinventing juvenile justice.* Newbury Park, CA: Sage Publications.

Lindler, C. (2007). Thacher, Augustus, and Hill: The path to statutory probation in the United States and England. *Federal Probation Journal, 71,* 36–41.

Lipsey, M. W. (2009). The primary factors that characterize effective interventions with juvenile offenders: A meta-analytic overview. *Victims and offenders, 4*(2), 124–147.

Lipsey, M. W., & Cullen, F. T. (2007). The effectiveness of correctional rehabilitation: A review of systematic reviews. *Annual Review of Law and Social Science, 3,* 297–320.

Loughran, E. J. (1997). The Massachusetts experience: A historical review of reform in the Department of Youth Services. *Social Justice, 24*(4), 170–186.

Lowenkamp, C. T., & Latessa, E. (2005). *Evaluation of Ohio's reclaim funded programs, community corrections facilities, and DYS facilities.* Cincinnati, OH: University of Cincinnati.

MacKenzie, D. L. (1994). Results of a multisite study of boot camp prisons. *Federal Probation, 58*(2), 60–66.

McGarvey, J. (2005). A culture of caring. *The American Prospect,* (September), A12–A14.

McNulty, E. W. (1996). The transfer of juvenile offenders to adult court: Panacea or problem? *Law and Policy, 18,* 61–76.

Office of Juvenile Justice and Delinquency Prevention. Day Treatment Centers. Washington, DC: U.S. Department of Justice. Retrieved from https://www.ojjdp.gov/mpg/litreviews/Day_Treatment.pdf

Parent, D. G. (2003). *Correctional boot camps: Lessons from a decade of research.* Washington, DC: National Institute of Justice.

Parent, D., Byrne, J., Tsarfaty, V., Valdae, L., & Esselman, J. (1995). *Day reporting centers (Vols. 1–2).* Washington, DC: U.S. Department of Justice, Office of Justice Programs, National Institute of Justice.

Payne, B. K., & Gainey, R. R. (2000). Electronic monitoring. *Journal of Offender Rehabilitation, 31,* 3–4, 93–111.

Puzzanchera, C., Adams, B., & Hockenberry, S. (2012). *Juvenile court statistics 2009.* Pittsburgh, PA: National Center for Juvenile Justice.

Schneider, A. L. (1986). Restitution and recidivism rates of juvenile offenders: Results from four experimental studies. *Criminology, 24*(3), 533–552.

Slowikowski, J. (2009). *Focus: Disproportionate minority contact.* Washington DC: U.S. Department of Justice, Office of Justice Programs, Office of Juvenile Justice and Delinquency Prevention.

Stahl, A., Finnegan, T., & Kang, W. (2005). Retrieved from http://ojjdp.ncjrs.org/ojstatbb/ezajcs

Vaughn, J. B. (1989). A survey of juvenile electronic monitoring and home confinement programs. *Juvenile and Family Court Journal,* 40, 1–36.

Wiebush, R. G., McNulty, E., & Le, T. (2000). *Implementation of the intensive community-based aftercare program.* Bulletin. Washington, DC: U.S. Department of Justice, Office of Justice Programs, Office of Juvenile Justice and Delinquency Prevention.

Winner, L., Lanza-Kaduce, L., Bishop, D. M., & Frazier, C. E. (1997). The transfer of juveniles to criminal court: Reexamining recidivism over the long term. *Crime and Delinquency, 43*(4), 548–563.

Winokur Early, K., Hand, G. A., Blankenship, J. L., & Chapman, S. F. (2010). Experimental community-based interventions for delinquent youth: An evaluation of recidivism and cost effectiveness. Unpublished manuscript. Tallahassee, FL: Justice Research Center.

Zane, S. N., Welsh, B. C., & Mears, D. P. (2016). Juvenile transfer and the specific deterrence hypothesis. *Criminology & Public Policy*, *15*(3), 901–925.

Section 4

Challenges and Directions for the Future

Challenges Facing the Juvenile Justice Sytem: Vulnerable Populations

12

© Robert Nickelsberg/Contributor/Getty

In the next few chapters you are going to explore some of the biggest challenges facing the juvenile justice system. As you have learned from Chapter 1, the intentions of those addressing juvenile delinquency are usually good, but the outcomes do not always match the intentions. This is because delinquency, and crime in general, are not phenomena that happen within the realm of the criminal or juvenile justice system. Their roots, as you have learned, grow deep in society, and thus, so do their answers.

The first challenge that we will explore is the fact that many juvenile delinquents are themselves the victims of crimes, be it family abuse or neglect, bullying in the school or exposure to violence in the community. The fact is, youth are highly vulnerable to victimization, particularly in the home. Moreover, there is a definite link between experiences of victimization and later delinquency—thus the youth in juvenile court today for a charge of delinquency may also be the youth in child protective services yesterday, today or tomorrow.

Second, in this chapter you will explore what I deem as the "forgotten" delinquent, or the female delinquent. It is a fact that males account for much more delinquency than females (Chapter 3), but it is also a fact that girls account for more delinquency today than in the past, even violent and gang-related delinquency. However, most of the theories of delinquency you learned about (Section 2) which are used to inform juvenile justice practice (Section 3) ignore the female delinquent. Thus, we will learn here about the few theories that do address female delinquency and the few gender-specific program initiatives that have developed to serve this population.

CHAPTER GOALS

At the end of this chapter you should be able to:

1. Define and understand the "victim/offender" overlap.
2. Name specific challenges to the juvenile justice system presented by this overlap.
3. Understand a "unified court system" and argue whether or not it is a good approach to the victim/offender overlap problem.
4. Discuss and contrast the differences between theories that address gender (extensions of early theories) and theories that center on gender (feminist theories).
5. Argue whether or not you believe traditional theories of delinquency apply to females as well as males, or whether different theories, and thus, different programs, are needed for female delinquents.

Challenge 1: The Victim/Offender Overlap

VICTIMIZATION OF CHILDREN

When it comes to crime victimization, children and teenagers are some of the most vulnerable members of our society (Finkelhor et al., 2001). For young children, this victimization usually occurs in the home, with parents or caregivers often being the perpetrators of the crime (Sickmund & Puzzanchera, 2014). According to the most recent data available almost half (40%) of all victims of child abuse and maltreatment are under the age of four and almost three-quarters (73%) are under the age of 10 (Annie. E. Casey Foundation, 2014). In addition, 61 percent of youth under the age of 18 report being either exposed to, or victimized by, violence in the past year (Finkelhor et al., 2009).

In addition to these overall alarming numbers, the patterns vary by gender, race and familial socio-economic status as well. For example, girls are sexually abused at a rate of about 3.8 per 1,000, compared to a rate of only 1.0 per 1,000 for boys. However, boys are more likely to be the victims of physical assaults. Trends also vary by race with Black, non-Hispanic youth being the most vulnerable to victimization with a rate that is almost double that of white youths (see Table 12.1).

TABLE 12.1 Rate of Juvenile Victimization, by Race

Victim race/ethnicity	1,000 in race/ethnicity group
Black	14.6
Multiple Races	12.7
American Indian	11.0
Pacific Islander	10.9
Hispanic	8.8
White	7.8
Asian	1.9

(Sickmund and Puzzanchera, 2014, p. 30)

Other parental and family factors also impact the rate of victimization. For example, children with an unemployed parent and those with no parent in the labor force have a much higher risk of experiencing abuse. Children with no parent in the labor force had the highest rate of abuse (15.2 per 1,000), two or more times higher than the rates for children of working parents (5.8 per 1,000) or with an unemployed parent (7.5 per 1,000) (Sickmund & Puzzanchera, 2014). Parental neglect of a child is also significantly higher for children of parents who do not have steady work. Children of working parents have a rate of neglect of only 12.8 per 1,000 compared to 46.4 per 1,000 for children with no parent in the labor force.

In addition to simply not having work, having a low income is also related to factors of abuse and neglect. Children living in these more impoverished environments were more than five times as likely to be maltreated, three times as likely to be physically abused and seven times as likely to be neglected than youths from more affluent households (Sickmund and Puzzanchera, 2014). Definitions of living in an **impoverished environment** include having a family income under $15,000 per year, having parents who did not graduate from high school, and living in a household that receives public benefits such as food stamps, free school lunches or public housing (Sickmund and Puzzanchera, 2014). As neglect can include such things as failure to provide proper food and shelter it is easy to see how the inability to support one's family can lead to charges of neglect. Also, not being able to provide for one's family can lead to stress and strain, which may then turn to abuse.

Impoverished Environments include having a family income under $15,000 a year, having parents who did not graduate from high school, and living in a household that receives public benefits such as food stamps, free school lunches or public housing

Trends in Victimization

While the point of this section is to address the victim/offender overlap, I would be remiss if I did not indicate that the most recent statistics show that youth victimization has been decreasing steadily since the 1990s, as has crime overall. This is important to point out and will be a bigger focus in the next and concluding chapter of the text when we discuss the future of juvenile justice and how public perceptions (and often faulty public perceptions), rather than true empirical evidence, drive trends in juvenile justice. For example, Table 12.2 following shows the reported victimization rate of youth from 1994 through 2010. The first year, 1994, was the height of the get tough movement and you can clearly see why at this time youth crime and violence were such a great concern. However, compare the 63.3 per 1,000 victimization rate of 12 to 14 year olds in 1994 to the most recent rate reported of 12 per 1,000. Clearly, despite the challenges to the juvenile justice system and society in general, we are doing at least something "right."

DATA SOURCES

How do we know this? In Chapter 3 you learned about various sources of information on juvenile delinquency and delinquents, for example, the Uniform Crime Report and the Juvenile Court Archive. The numbers reported above come from the National Crime Victimization Survey (which you also learned about in Chapter 3) as well as several other data sources directed at covering the "victims" rather than the offenders of crime. In specific, in the Child Abuse Prevention and Treatment Act Congress mandated two specific data collection efforts to help collect and understand information on child abuse: the National

TABLE 12.2 Serious violent victimizations per 1,000 in age group, 1994 to 2010

Year	12 to 14	15 to 17
1994	63.3	60.6
1995	47.6	56.7
1996	36.1	52.9
1997	40.8	47.6
1998	39.4	38.6
1999	30.7	39.9
2000	27.3	29.9
2001	23.4	20.1
2002	17.7	20.8
2003	14.3	25.8
2004	12.5	24.3
2005	11.7	17.0
2006	14.2	17.4
2007	13.0	21.2
2008	12.4	20.0
2009	15.1	16.0
2010	12.0	15.9

Sickmund and Puzzanchera, 2014, p. 39

Child Abuse and Neglect Data System (NCANDS) and the National Incidence Study of Child Abuse and Neglect (NIS). The first, the NCANDS, provides data on all cases referred to child protective services (CPS) in a given year. The second, the NIS, uses a sampling methodology to represent the incidence of child abuse and neglect in the United States as recognized by mandated reporters (e.g., teachers and doctors) to show how many of these maltreated children actually receive a CPS investigation.

What exactly is a child protective service (CPS) agency? **Child protective services (CPS)** agencies are governmental agencies authorized to act on behalf of a child when parents are unable or unwilling to do so. Now this might sound familiar to you as it goes hand in hand with the parens patriae logic of the juvenile justice system that allows the state to act as a parent when the parent is not fulfilling that duty.

Child Protective Services (CPS) governmental agencies authorized to act on behalf of a child when parents are unable or unwilling to do so

Indeed, there are many similarities with the ways in which child protective services handles a referral and the way the juvenile justice system handles a referral—this is not a coincidence.

Connections: Remember the juvenile justice system was born out of the Progressive Era and championed by social workers. Indeed the history of the juvenile justice system and the child welfare system can be closely traced. For further reading on this topic see *The Juvenile Court and the Progressives* by Victoria Getis.

---

1. When a report is made to CPS regarding suspected abuse or neglect a screening is done to determine if further investigation is warranted. This screening seeks to determine if the report is legitimate and how serious the situation is to determine the urgency of a response.
2. CPS agencies assess child and family needs before developing a case plan.
3. When possible, the child is kept in the home and preventive and interventive services are given to help the parent with childrearing responsibilities.
4. When the situation is so severe that keeping the child in the home presents a risk to the child or others, the child can be placed in protective services such as a group home or foster care.

Also, much like the juvenile justice system, some cases end up in court. In these cases the judge must decide if it is in the best interests of the child to leave him/her in the home or not. Although the placements vary, the intent is the same—to provide the youth with the best possible setting for development, acknowledging that in some cases, that setting may not be the home.

In addition to these similarities between systems, it is important to note that many juvenile delinquents are indeed victims of abuse/neglect or other crimes. Data show that 6 in 10 youths referred to the juvenile justice system for the first time had a history of child welfare involvement. Moreover, 9 in 10 youths previously referred for an offense (i.e., repeat offenders) had child welfare system involvement. Youth with multi-system involvement begin their delinquent activity earlier and are detained more frequently (and for longer periods of time) than youth without such involvement (Halemba & Siegel, 2011). Finally, those youths reporting involvement in both systems—dual system involvement—were more likely to recidivate than other youths.

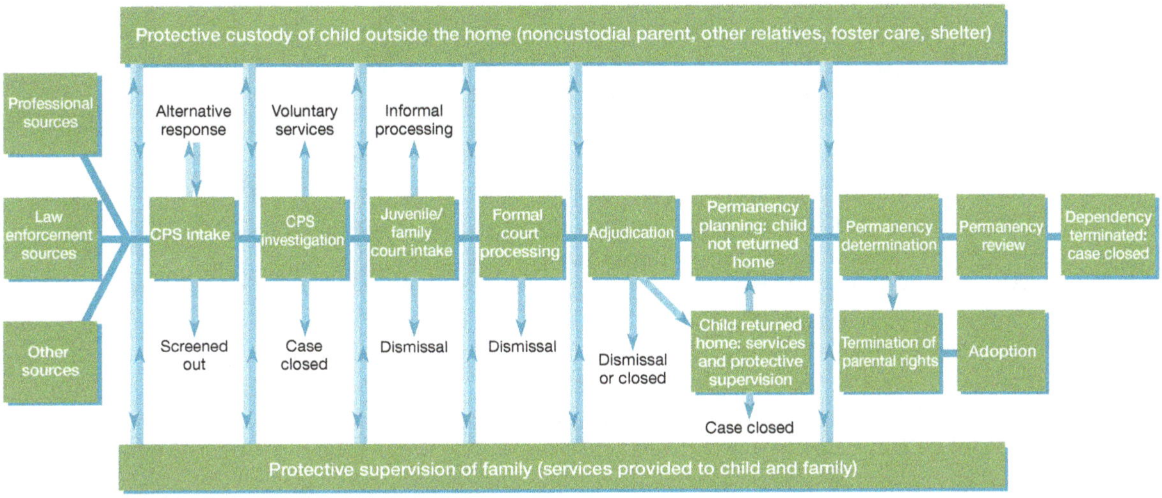

Note: This chart gives a simplified view of caseflow through these systems. Procedures may vary among jurisdictions.

TABLE 12.3 What are the stages of child maltreatment case processing in the child protective services and juvenile/family court systems?

Source: National Center for Juvenile Justice, December 2014. Juvenile Offenders and Victims: 2014 National Report, page 24.

This cross-system involvement is important to note because it indicates that there are youths that have multiple problems that extend beyond them and impact the family as well. In recognition of this phenomenon a specific terminology has evolved to describe and define these youths. Some popular terms are as follows:

- **Dual-status youth**: Youths who come into contact with both the child welfare and juvenile justice systems and occupy various statuses in terms of their relationship to the two systems defined below.
- **Dually identified youth**: Youth who are currently involved with the juvenile justice system and have a history in the child welfare system but no current involvement.
- **Dually involved youth**: Youth who have concurrent involvement (diversionary, formal or both) with both the child welfare and juvenile justice systems.

FOCUS ON POLICY: The Unified Court: Project ONE

Because so many youths cross systems there is a call for a cross-system solution. The National Council of Juvenile and Family Court Judges (NCJFCJ) with support from the MacArthur Foundation's "Models for Change" initiative has been promoting and evaluating an effort to unify efforts between the child welfare and juvenile justice systems because of the dual nature of so many youth. In 2010, with funding from the Office of Juvenile Justice and Delinquency Prevention to support critical cross-departmental and cross-system work, the NCJFCJ began work on the Multi-Court Collaboration (MCC) Initiative (now known as Project ONE) to signify a holistic approach to families. The word ONE is used as an acronym in which "O" stands for "one family/one judge," meaning that the same judge will hear and decide all matters pertaining to a family; the "N" stands for "no wrong door," meaning that it does not matter how the youth and family enter the system, the approach should be the same and finally, the "E" stands for "equal and coordinated access to justice."

Central to Project ONE is a holistic view of individuals and families and the life-course perspective on human development that you learned about in Chapter 9. Among the key principals of this Project are respect for the cultural diversity of youth, families and victims coming before the system, the right and ability of all to actively engage in the court and treatment process, and the responsibility of the judges to make timely and fair determinations in all cases that take into account the needs of the youth, the family, the victim and communities.

At the time of the writing of this text, the Courts and Lead Judges were:

- Jefferson County Family Court, Louisville, Kentucky; Honorable Gina Calvert, Co-Lead Judge and Honorable Tara Hagerty, Co-Lead Judge
- Milwaukee County Circuit Court, Milwaukee, Wisconsin; Honorable Lindsey Grady, Lead Judge
- North Okaloosa County Unified Family Court, Crestview, Florida; Honorable Terrance Ketchel, Lead Judge
- Orleans Parish Juvenile Court, New Orleans, Louisiana; Honorable Judge Tammy Stewart, Lead Judge
- Sixth Judicial Circuit Court (Pasco County), Dade City, Florida; Honorable Lynn Tepper, Lead Judge
- Second Judicial District Court, Family Division (Washoe County), Reno, Nevada; Honorable Egan Walker, Lead Judge

In 2009, NCJFCJ's Cross-Over Committee developed a Unified Model Court Concept Paper which discusses the need for collaboration among courts in order to achieve best outcomes for dually involved children, youth and families. For further reading this paper can be accessed at: http://www.ncjfcj.org/sites/default/files/Cross-Over%20Concept%20Paper%20RESOLUTION_07-22_1.pdf

FOCUS ON RESEARCH: Human Trafficking

Human trafficking has become the fastest growing and the third-largest international crime industry (behind illegal drugs and arms trafficking). According to the International Labor Organization, in 2004 human trafficking was a $30 billion industry but by 2014 it had grown to over $150 billion. The Guardian Group, one U.S.-based organization dedicated to fighting sex trafficking, estimates that up to 200,000 children are forced into the sex industry every year in the United States (The Guardian Group, 2017).

Human trafficking involves selling an individual into prostitution/the pornography industry, slavery or involuntary servitude. Estimates are that upwards of 80% of all trafficking is for sexual exploitation as compared to all other purposes, with the majority of victims being women and young girls (National Coalition Against Domestic Violence, 2016). In fact, the average age of entering into sex work in the United States is ages 12 to 14, with many of these being young runaways (Clawson et al., 2014).

Indeed, the National Council of Juvenile and Family Court Judges reports that one out of every six runaways reported to the National Center for Missing and Exploited Children is likely to be a victim of sex trafficking (National Council of Juvenile and Family Court Judges, 2015). This report goes on to detail that in the United States between 100,000 and 300,000 youth are "at risk" for commercial sexual exploitation annually. At particular risk are youth who run away from home—about 1.6 million children annually (National Runaway Safeline, 2012). These youth are at such a high risk because they are mentally, physically and financially vulnerable. Moreover, studies have found that many of these youth have prior child welfare system contact and that 70 to 90% were previously sexually abused, most likely in the home (Shared Hope International, 2009).

Thus, while there is much attention currently on international human trafficking, it is important to realize that many of our own youth here in America are victimized by this same crime. Indeed, as noted above, the average age of entry into the sex trade in the United States is between 12 and 14—which is considerably below the age of majority. Many of these young victims then go on to be criminalized as prostitutes and sex workers and further victimized by the system (Shared Hope International, 2009).

What can and is being done to address this problem? On September 29, 2014, President Obama signed the Preventing Sex Trafficking and Strengthening Families Act into law. Section 104 of this law specifically adds two new requirements for state child welfare agencies to report missing youth to law enforcement and to the National Center for Missing and Exploited Children within 24 hours. Now you might think that a parent would of course report a child missing fairly quickly; however, many runaways happen not just from home, but from foster homes and other child welfare and non-secure juvenile facilities. These already troubled youth may be even more vulnerable, and they may not have been officially reported missing until their next officially required court visit or until a formal hearing was held. Under this new law, which went into effect in October of 2016, the child must now be reported missing within 24 hours.

This is important because time is literally of the essence when locating missing children. However, beyond simply locating a child when he or she goes missing, if we realize that many of these youth are at risk because of negative home environments that lead to system placement and/or running away this calls on us as a society to address the factors that lead to the originating circumstance, and not just respond retroactively after a child is missing.

However, law enforcement attention must be focused on the perpetrators of human trafficking rather than merely the victims. In 2000, Congress passed the Trafficking Victims Protection Act (TVPA) that created the first comprehensive federal law to address trafficking. The law provides "a three-pronged approach: *prevention* through public awareness programs overseas and a State Department-led monitoring and sanctions program; *protection* through a new T Visa and services for foreign national victims; and *prosecution* through new federal crimes and severe penalties" (Trafficking Victims Protection Act, Pub. L. No. 106-386 (2000), codified at 22 U.S.C. § 7101, et seq).

As a result of the passing of the TVPA, the Office to Monitor and Combat Trafficking in Persons was established in October 2001. U.S. Immigration and Customs Enforcement (ICE) is one of the lead federal agencies charged with enforcing the TVPA as would-be terrorists and criminals often can access the same routes and use the same methods as human traffickers. The FBI is also a lead agency in enforcing the TVPA within the U.S. borders, as much trafficking occurs within and across state lines.

Human Trafficking

involves selling an individual into prostitution/the pornography industry, slavery or involuntary servitude

Sex

the biological differences between males and females

Gender

the socialized identity and behaviors associated with a given sex

Challenge 2: The Forgotten Female

Almost every theory of delinquency you have learned about was developed and tested solely on male youths. This is because males historically commit more delinquency and more serious delinquency. Indeed, in the earliest theories, such as Lombroso's theory of the Atavist, he merely posited that females were weaker and less intelligent than men, and therefore were not capable of serious and violent crimes. Rather, their criminality would mainly relate to crimes of a sexual nature (e.g., prostitution). Indeed, many other early attempts to explain female delinquency focused on biological differences between the sexes. To be clear for this conversation **sex** will refer to biological differences between males and females and **gender** will refer to socialized identity and behaviors associated with a given sex.

Some of these approaches focused clearly on genetics. For example, males produce more testosterone than females. Testosterone is a hormone that has been connected to aggression. Thus, one purely biological explanation for the difference between male and female offending would be the difference across the sexes in the production of testosterone (Walsh, 2002).

Other theories combined aspects of biological sex with their impact on the psyche. For example, Otto Pollak, in his book *The Criminality of Women*, hypothesized that females have a biological nature that leads them to engage in sexual delinquency and to use deceitful and manipulative techniques to get their way. Pollak, however, was the first to suggest that females were perhaps more delinquent than we know but that their delinquency is often overlooked by society because men are "protective" of women (Pollak, 1950). This **chivalry hypothesis** is the notion that the system will respond in a protective manner to female delinquents rather than arresting and prosecuting them.

Chivalry Hypothesis
the notion that the system will respond in a protective manner to female delinquents rather than arresting and prosecuting them

However, while females do offend less than males, the truth is they can and do commit serious crimes and the difference between male and female offending has become less in recent decades. Sociological theories of delinquency, most of which were not tested on females, make a different assumption. They assume that all of the same factors that impact male delinquency will impact female delinquency and that they will do so in the same way. For example, strains in the home such as exposure to negative stimuli (i.e., General Strain Theory) and attachment to parents (Social Bond Theory) should matter the same to boys and girls.

While this might sound logical at first, one must then question why females have such a lower rate of delinquency. Are male and female siblings in the same home, school and community not exposed to similar factors? If so, offending rates should be similar across crime types. As Table 12.4 clearly shows, rates are not the same; however, trends over time seem to be very similar for many crimes.

As Table 12.4 shows, females commit far less violent crime (as suggested by Lombroso) but rates are more similar for some minor crimes and females are more likely to be arrested for prostitution.

This suggests that either different factors impact female delinquency or females respond differently to factors than do males. There have been two approaches to addressing this question: 1) Extensions of existing theories to address differential treatment of girls in society and 2) the development of feminist or gender-specific theories that incorporate socialized gender roles and biological truths into the theory.

TABLE 12.4 Ten-Year Arrest Trends by Sex, 2006–2015

[9,581 agencies; 2015 estimated population 199,921,204; 2006 estimated population 186,371,331]

	Male						Female					
	Total			Under 18			Total			Under 18		
Offense charged	2006	2015	Percent change	2006	2015	Percent change	2006	2015	Percent change	2006	2015	Percent change
TOTAL[1]	**6,605,457**	**4,913,199**	**-25.6**	**922,499**	**405,325**	**-56.1**	**2,070,999**	**1,826,164**	**-11.8**	**357,696**	**173,213**	**-51.6**
Murder and nonnegligent manslaughter	6,292	5,463	-13.2	612	394	-35.6	812	738	-9.1	30	27	-10.0
Rape[2]	13,932	13,536	-	2,071	2,154	-	188	409	-	40	85	-
Robbery	60,460	46,060	-23.8	16,413	8,658	-47.2	7,977	7,943	-0.4	1,788	1,095	-38.8
Aggravated assault	216,482	179,138	-17.3	27,741	13,273	-52.2	55,258	52,690	-4.6	8,243	4,444	-46.1
Burglary	159,767	110,416	-30.9	45,896	19,254	-58.0	28,355	26,049	-8.1	6,057	2,802	-53.7
Larceny-theft	418,187	424,952	+1.6	106,506	60,365	-43.3	261,103	328,713	+25.9	74,117	41,533	-44.0
Motor vehicle theft	59,234	36,177	-38.9	14,361	6,029	-58.0	13,416	10,286	-23.3	3,290	1,518	-53.9
Arson	8,738	4,633	-47.0	4,538	1,536	-66.2	1,707	1,104	-35.3	685	275	-59.9
Violent crime[3]	297,166	244,197	-17.8	46,837	24,479	-47.7	64,235	61,780	-3.8	10,101	5,651	-44.1
Property crime[3]	645,926	576,178	-10.8	171,301	87,184	-49.1	304,581	366,152	+20.2	84,149	46,128	-45.2
Other assaults	592,204	486,355	-17.9	101,366	52,882	-47.8	199,974	192,182	-3.9	51,030	30,807	-39.6
Forgery and counterfeiting	41,028	22,493	-45.2	1,513	470	-68.9	27,291	12,418	-54.5	775	162	-79.1
Fraud	99,184	52,967	-46.6	3,297	1,811	-45.1	82,679	33,517	-59.5	1,793	965	-46.2
Embezzlement	6,101	4,850	-20.5	517	220	-57.4	6,907	5,073	-26.6	432	171	-60.4
Stolen property; buying, receiving, possessing	63,904	45,331	-29.1	11,930	5,514	-53.8	15,173	12,587	-17.0	2,102	1,086	-48.3
Vandalism	158,590	97,844	-38.3	66,281	23,174	-65.0	31,277	26,214	-16.2	9,921	4,619	-53.4
Weapons; carrying, possessing, etc.	105,054	78,496	-25.3	25,051	10,331	-58.8	9,050	7,947	-12.2	2,656	1,283	-51.7
Prostitution and commercialized vice	11,754	7,103	-39.6	182	85	-53.3	21,648	10,560	-51.2	551	184	-66.6

Offense charged	Male						Female					
	Total			Under 18			Total			Under 18		
	2006	2015	Percent change	2006	2015	Percent change	2006	2015	Percent change	2006	2015	Percent change
Sex offenses (except rape and prostitution)	47,168	29,862	-36.7	9,029	4,914	-45.6	3,488	2,494	-28.5	919	729	-20.7
Drug abuse violations	865,257	715,904	-17.3	93,508	49,170	-47.4	212,899	212,218	-0.3	19,624	13,865	-29.3
Gambling	2,366	1,272	-46.2	279	121	-56.6	441	385	-12.7	13	12	-7.7
Offenses against the family and children	60,217	41,552	-31.0	2,070	1,379	-33.4	19,351	16,825	-13.1	1,278	829	-35.1
Driving under the influence	738,512	508,633	-31.1	9,943	3,251	-67.3	187,306	167,327	-10.7	3,004	1,043	-65.3
Liquor laws	294,825	123,435	-58.1	60,064	17,707	-70.5	113,686	50,795	-55.3	34,665	11,823	-65.9
Drunkenness	310,500	202,628	-34.7	8,281	2,503	-69.8	57,771	48,796	-15.5	2,812	1,025	-63.5
Disorderly conduct	308,923	171,960	-44.3	87,098	29,356	-66.3	113,264	68,763	-39.3	42,850	16,303	-62.0
Vagrancy	13,876	11,847	-14.6	2,390	457	-80.9	4,230	3,170	-25.1	1,085	141	-87.0
All other offenses (except traffic)	1,902,249	1,477,329	-22.3	180,909	77,354	-57.2	575,732	520,470	-9.6	67,920	29,896	-56.0
Suspicion	869	384	-55.8	157	95	-39.5	256	96	-62.5	46	32	-30.4
Curfew and loitering law violations	40,653	12,963	-68.1	40,653	12,963	-68.1	20,016	6,491	-67.6	20,016	6,491	-67.6

[1] Does not include suspicion.

[2] The 2006 rape figures are based on the legacy definition, and the 2015 rape figures are aggregate totals based on both the legacy and revised Uniform Crime Reporting definitions. For this reason, a percent change is not provided.

[3] Violent crimes are offenses of murder and nonnegligent manslaughter, rape, robbery, and aggravated assault. Property crimes are offenses of burglary, larceny-theft, motor vehicle theft, and arson.

From Crime in the United States 2015 https://ucr.fbi.gov/crime-in-the-u.s/2015/crime-in-the-u.s.-2015/tables/table-33

EXTENDING EXISTING THEORIES OF DELINQUENCY

This approach involves taking the traditional theories of delinquency that you have already learned, and incorporating into them the fact that boys and girls are socialized differently. For example, boys are taught not to cry while girls are taught that it is ok to express emotion. Boys are taught to be aggressive while girls are taught to be nurturing. Think about what toys you might buy for a 5 year old for Christmas? How might these differ if it was a boy or a girl? Did you think about fire trucks and toy guns for the boys? Perhaps a Barbie doll for the girl? These images depict how we raise boys and girls differently in society and can lead to the same elements influencing boys and girls differently.

Now move on to middle school. What is important for male acceptance? Usually, again, aggression, sports involvement. For girls acceptance is often based on appearance. Also, it is argued that boys are controlled less by parents—given more freedoms—thus they are more subject to influences from peers and the social environment than girls are who are more likely to be kept in the home and monitored.

Incorporating these notions of differential gender roles, socialization and social control of girls into existing theories of delinquency, then, may offer some insight into different rates and types of offending across the sexes. If girls are kept in the home more, then they would be more likely to be influenced by familial risk factors and less influenced by peers and community factors. For example, there is evidence that girls experience a greater number of negative life events during adolescence and that they may be particularly sensitive to such events when they originate in the home (Ge et al., 1994). If, as suggested by our earlier discussion of female victimization in the home, girls might be more likely to run away from home and to end up in lives of prostitution when such events occur we would expect females to have higher rates of running away and prostitution. Indeed these are two "crimes" for which females have higher rates of delinquency than males.

Also, if females are kept in the home more they should be less influenced by peers and community risk factors. Again, this is a finding supported by research (Farrell & Bruce, 1997; Bottcher, 2001).

If female acceptance is based on appearance, then many girls who cannot afford make-up or fancy clothes might be expected to shoplift such items, while boys would partake in fighting and other means of asserting "masculinity" to gain acceptance. Indeed, again, the data generally support such patterns in male versus female offending (Chilton & Datesman, 1987; Federal Bureau of Investigation, 2015).

Labeling and conflict theories have been two of the theories extended to explain female delinquency. Concerning Labeling Theory (Chapter 7), it is thought that young girls who are labeled as "promiscuous" early on, perhaps due to appearance or other factors, may indeed adapt this identity (Shur, 1984). Conflict theories, which we did not explore in depth in this text as they usually address broader economic conditions and adult delinquency, have also been applied to explain the offending of young girls. Conflict theories focus on the oppression of one group, or groups, in society by others. **Conflict theories** thus suggest that those who are more oppressed will either act out through crime or turn to crime to obtain things they desire (e.g., actual items such as clothes, or status such as the respect of others). Young girls then who are from more economically challenged homes would be expected to be more likely to shoplift and engage in other property crimes (Chesney-Lind & Shelden, 2004).

Conflict Theory

a theory of crime that focuses on conflict between groups, with specific focus on conflict between majority and minority groups in a society and their economic means

One particularly well-known theory of conflict and delinquency is **Hagan's Power-Control Theory**. In this theory, Hagan connects family structure and economic activity to delinquency and risk taking. He notes that in traditional patriarchal families the father works outside of the home while the female stays home to rear the children. In these homes the sons are thus prepared by their parents to enter the workforce and the daughters are prepared to become homemakers themselves. This leads to large differences in gender role identities, risk taking and delinquency. On the other hand in more egalitarian families, both the mother and father work outside the home and thus prepare offspring of either gender for the workforce and are less controlling of their daughters. Therefore, the minor delinquency of youth from these families tends to be less gendered. The empirical support for this theory is, however, mixed with some early studies finding support (Singer & Levine, 1988) and later studies with larger samples finding less support (Jensen & Thompson, 1990). The theory has also been criticized for conceptualizing parenting style with mere parental supervision and ignoring other facets of social structure as well (Curran & Renzetti, 1994; Ackers 1994).

Power-Control Theory

connects family structure and economic activity to delinquency and risk taking

From conflict theories, a substrain of what are known as more radical theories have evolved that particularly focus on gender and crime, although they traditionally address adult female rather than juvenile female offending.

FEMINIST THEORIES OF DELINQUENCY

Feminist Theory

incorporate gender, not just as a new variable in a traditional sociological theory, but rather use gender as the key theoretical construct upon which to build the theory

Feminist theories of delinquency incorporate gender, not just as a new variable in a traditional sociological theory, but rather use gender as the key theoretical construct upon which to build the theory. More simply put, gender is center stage rather than a supporting actor.

These theories differ from other theories in that:

1. They focus on gender not as a reality but as a socially and culturally constructed idea that changes over time.
2. They recognize that these notions of gender then order social life and social institutions.
3. This proposes that gender roles, as historically constructed, have led to a patriarchal society in which men economically, politically and socially dominate over women.
4. They propose that knowledge itself is gendered and is influenced by the thinking of the dominant group (in this case males).
5. Females are at the center of, rather than the periphery of, theory construction.

(Daly & Chesney-Lind, 1984; Regoli, Hewitt & DeLisi, 2011)

As an example of how these concepts work, Chesney-Lind and Faith (2000) argue that, unlike most other correlates of crime, gender has historically and remains one of the most significant predictors. Thus, they contend that sex and gender roles must be a central focus of more modern theorizing on delinquency and crime. While a full discussion of feminist criminology that focuses mainly on patriarchal structures of society and the role of child bearing may be beyond the reach of this introductory text, suffice it to say that these theories impress upon us all the importance of recognizing the role of women in society, the experiences of women as victims and the system's responses to female delinquents/criminals as central to understanding not only why females offend less, but why they offend when they do and why the system may need to have a differential response to those girls who do make it into the system.

IMPLICATIONS FOR JUVENILE JUSTICE PROCESSING OF FEMALES

These are two obvious implications, and perhaps one not-so-obvious implication, for the juvenile justice system from the above discussion. First, because most of the theories of delinquency were designed based on the study of male delinquency, most programs in the juvenile justice system based off such theories are naturally designed to "treat" male and not female delinquents.

Second, although there is a recognition that the juvenile system lacks programming for females, there is an argument over whether existing programs need only to be modified to adjust for female gender roles (extending upon traditional sociological theories) or whether entirely new programs need to be developed if indeed the causes of female delinquency are different than those of male delinquency (radical theories).

The Office of Juvenile Justice and Delinquency Prevention has recognized this need through the creation of a special funding stream for "**Gender-Specific Services**" that encourages local entities to research and develop programs specifically designed to meet the needs of young girls. A report by the Girls Gender Gap study group acknowledges the possibility of biological and psychological differences between the genders that may lead to differences in the way males and females experience stressors (Hawkins et al., 2010). This study, however, also acknowledges the gendered nature of society and the differential exposure of females and males to delinquency (Hawkins et al., 2010). For example, while both boys and girls who have experienced abuse in the home are more likely to be delinquent, girls experience sexual violence more often than males (Snyder, 2000; Hennessey et al., 2004) and these experiences are linked to greater levels of violent delinquency among females (Poe-Yamagata & Butts, 1996; Smith, Leve & Chamberlain, 2006). Moreover, Herrera and McCloskey (2001) found that girls who experienced severe child abuse were more than seven times as likely as non-abused girls to commit a violent act that was referred to the juvenile justice system.

Gender-Specific Services

encourages local entities to research and develop programs specifically designed to meet the needs of young girls

Somewhat related, or perhaps primarily related to this, many girls in the juvenile justice system are found to suffer from depression and **Post Traumatic Stress Disorder (PTSD)**. **PTSD** is a condition that is triggered by a traumatizing life event—i.e., either experiencing or witnessing violence. The symptoms vary but may include such things as anxiety, depression, sudden flashbacks and nightmares (Mayo Clinic, 2017).

Post Traumatic Stress Disorder

a condition triggered by a traumatizing life event where the symptoms may include anxiety, depression, sudden flashbacks and nightmares

While mental health disorders impact both male and female delinquency, the types of disorders differ across the sexes. For example, boys outnumber girls by a ratio of 3:1 in the diagnoses of attention-deficit/hyperactivity disorder (ADHD) and conduct disorder, which are known risk factors for problem behavior and delinquency (Chapter 5) (Barbaresi et al., 2002; Lahey et al., 1999). On the other hand mental health problems linked to life stressors and experiences of victimization, such as depression, anxiety and posttraumatic stress disorder, are much more common in girls in the juvenile justice system (Teplin et al., 2002).

Female delinquency is also linked to early onset of puberty, which impacts the way girls are treated by others. One particular pathway between early-onset puberty and delinquency in girls is association with older romantic partners (Castillo Mezzich et al., 1997). Early maturing girls are more likely to date at younger ages and to affiliate with older males who may be inclined toward delinquent activity and involve the girls in their antisocial behavior (Haynie, 2003). Moreover, Haynie et al. (2005) found that romantic partners' delinquency did influence the likelihood of delinquency and that the dynamic had stronger relevance for girls' delinquency than for boys'. Giordano, Cernkovich and Rossol (2002) further found that girls may adopt drug and alcohol use to cope with partner abuse, to win their partner's approval, or to fit in with peers.

Other studies of family and school risk factors, however, find that for the most part they seem to operate in a similar way for boys and girls (Hawkins et al., 2010) with a notable exception that school attachment seems to matter more for girls than boys (Crosnoe, Erickson & Dornbusch, 2002). What does this mean for the juvenile justice system? According to this report, while overall the literature suggests that risk and protective factors for female delinquency are similar to those for male delinquency, there are some key differences that should be considered, including:

- Attention to the physical and sexual maltreatment of females that often leads them into the juvenile justice system.
- Responses to mental health problems such as depression, anxiety and posttraumatic stress disorder should be integral components of programming for girls.
- Interdisciplinary models that place behaviors in social, psychological and biological context for girls are critical in understanding and responding to early puberty as a risk factor.

The need for such interdisciplinary models that address family, peers, schools and communities leads us naturally to the second chapter on key challenges to the juvenile justice system where we will further explore these dynamic influences.

Key Words

Child Protective Services (CPS)
Chivalry Hypothesis
Conflict Theory
Dual-Status Youth
Dually Identified Youth
Dually Involved Youth
Feminist Theory
Gender
Gender-Specific Services
Human Trafficking
Impoverished Environments
Post Traumatic Stress Disorder
Power-Control Theory
Sex
Unified Court

Chapter Summary

In this chapter you learned about two special challenges to the juvenile justice system. The victim/offender overlap and the delinquency of females. These topics are further overlapped as noted above in that females are particularly vulnerable to victimization, especially physical and sexual abuse in the home, and that such victimization leads these youth to often run away from home and/or find themselves in the juvenile justice system.

The victim/offender overlap is important to understand as it means many of the youth coming before the system have multiple problems and are not just guilty of committing a delinquent act, but have deeper rooted problems that most likely lead them to commit these acts. Since the system is designed to treat and rehabilitate and not simply punish youths this scenario takes on much more importance than it would for the punishment-focused adult system of justice.

There are two important points to take away from your lesson on the victim/offender overlap. First, this overlap is not equal across genders, races/ethnicities and socio-economic status. Thus, while you learned in Chapter 3 that delinquents are much more likely to be male, come from poor socio-economic backgrounds and to be minorities, in this chapter you learned that females are much more likely to be victims of crime and that this too is linked with other social factors. Second, you also learned that female victimization tends to manifest itself differently than in males with females being more likely to run away from the home and end up in the system for different reasons. Their double vulnerability leaves them subject to further victimization on the streets through prostitution and human trafficking.

This then leads naturally to the second topic of the chapter, which is the treatment of females in the juvenile justice system. Because most of the theories of delinquency were developed studying males, it is unclear if they apply to females and what the proper system response to females should be. For example, do we just add "being female" as a variable to Social Control Theory and assume females are less likely to be delinquent because they are more controlled by their parents? Or, do we use sex and gender roles as a key consideration in understanding the lives of these young girls and design special gender-specific programs that incorporate these differences? While there is still debate in the field, I would suggest that the answer is leaning toward the second option and that theories that incorporate both biological sex differences and gender social role identities may help us to better understand how and why young girls become delinquent and, thus, how to better address their needs once they are in the system.

The discussion questions in this chapter are specifically designed to help you think deeper about some of these issues and challenge contemporary ideas. At this point in the text you should realize the issues before the juvenile justice system are not "black and white" and that there is much room for debate and improvement. In the next chapter you will learn more about some other challenges unique to juvenile versus adult justice and again be challenged to think critically about solutions to such issues and the future of juvenile justice.

Discussion Questions

1. Crime victimization has real physical and emotional tolls on those impacted. In your daily life what do you do to avoid being victimized by crime? How might this be different for young children? What measures might we take as a society to protect children from crime as they are unable to protect themselves?
2. One approach to addressing the victim/offender overlap is the Unified Court system that would address both issues of abuse and neglect (social welfare issues) and issues of delinquency (juvenile justice issues). Do you think this is a good idea? Or do you think the issues are separate and should remain separate? Is being abused ever an excuse for delinquency? If so when and why? If not, why not?
3. In this chapter you also learned about human trafficking. We often think of slavery as a thing of the past and not as a current-day problem, but the truth is slavery exists. How does this type of slavery compare to your images of slavery in the past? What efforts should be taken to combat modern-day slavery?
4. Take a position on whether you believe there is a need for gender-specific theory and services in the juvenile justice system. Defend your position using what you have learned about offending behavior, exposure to and responses to victimization and system programming.

REFERENCES

Ackers, R. (1994). *Criminological theories*. Los Angeles: CA: Roxbury.

Annie. E. Casey Foundation, Kids Count Data. Retrieved from http://datacenter.kidscount.org/data/tables/6225-children-who-are-confirmed-by-child-protective-services-as-victims-of-maltreatment-by-age-group?loc=1&loct=1#detailed/1/any/false/869,36,868,867,133/62,2594,2595,113,36/12945,12944

Bagley, C., & Young, L. (1987). Juvenile prostitution and child sexual abuse: A controlled study. *Canadian Journal of Community Mental Health,* 6(1), 5–26.

Barbaresi, W. J., Katusic, S. K., Colligan, R. C., Pankratz, V. S., Weaver, A. L., Weber, K. J., . . . Jacobsen, S. J. (2002). How common is attention-deficit/hyperactivity disorder?: Incidence in a population-based birth cohort in Rochester, Minnesota. *Archives of Pediatrics and Adolescent Medicine, 156,* 217–224.

Bottcher, J. (2001). Social practices of gender: How gender relates to delinquency in the everyday lives of high-risk youths. *Criminology, 39*(4), 893–932.

Castillo Mezzich, A., Tarter, R. E., Giancola, P. R., Lu, S., Kirisci, L., & Parks, S. (1997). Substance use and risky sexual behavior in female adolescents. *Drug and Alcohol Dependence,* 44(2–3), 157–166.

Chesney-Lind, M., & Faith, K. (2000). What about feminism? In R. Paternoster & R. Bachman (Eds.), *Explaining Criminals and Crime, pp. 28–302.* Los Angeles: Roxbury.

Chesney-Lind, M., & Sheldon, R. W. (2004). *Girls, delinquency and juvenile justice* (3rd ed.). Belmont CA: Brooks/Cole.

Chilton, R., & Datesman, S. K. (1987). Gender, race and crime: An analysis of urban trends. *Gender and Society, 1,* 157–171.

Clawson, H. J., Dutch, N., Solomon, A., & Goldblatt Grace, L. *Human trafficking into and within the United States: A review of the literature.* Study of HHS Programs Serving Human Trafficking Victims. Retrieved from http://aspe.hhs.gov/hsp/07/humantrafficking/LitRev/

CNN. "The CNN Freedom Project." Retrieved from

Council for Prostitution Alternatives. (1991). *Annual report.* Portland, Oregon.

Crosnoe, R., Erickson, K. G., & Dornbusch, S. M. (2002). Protective functions of family relationships and school factors on the deviant behavior of adolescent boys and girls. *Youth and Society, 33*(4), 515–544.

Curran, D., & Renzetti, C. (1994). *Theories of crime*. Boston: Allyn and Bacon.

Daly, K., & Chesney-Lind, M. (1984). Feminism and criminology. *Justice Quarterly, 5,* 497–538.

Estes, R., & Weiner, N. (2001). *Commercial sexual exploitation of children in the U.S., Canada, and Mexico*. Philadelphia: University of Pennsylvania.

Farrell, A. D., & Bruce, S. E. (1997). Impact of exposure to community violence on violent behavior and emotional distress among urban adolescents. *Journal of Clinical Child Psychology,* 26(1), 2–14.

Federal Bureau of Investigation. (2015). *Crime in the United States*. Washington DC U.S. Department of Justice.

Finkelhor, D., Turner, H., Ormrod, R., & Hamby, S. L. (2009). Violence, abuse, and crime exposure in a national sample of children and youth. *Pediatrics, 124*(5), 1411–1423.

Ge, X., Conger, R. D., & Elder, G. H. (1996). Coming of age too early: Pubertal influences on girls' vulnerability to psychological distress. *Child Development, 67,* 3386–3400.

Ge, X., Conger, R. D., Lorenz, F. O., & Simons, R. L. (1994). Parents' stressful life events and adolescent depressed mood. *Journal of Health and Social Behavior,* 35, 28–44.

The Guardian Group. (2017). Retrieved from https://theguardiangroup.org/?gclid=CMqQsKLD4N-MCFZi1wAodsxUNxw

Halemba, G., & Siegel, G. (2011). *Multi-system involvement of delinquent youth in King County (Seattle, WA)*. Pittsburgh, PA: The National Center for Juvenile Justice.

Haynie, D. L. (2003). Contexts of risk? Explaining the link between girls' pubertal development and their delinquency involvement. *Social Forces, 82,* 355–397.

Haynie, D. L., Giordano, P. C., Manning, W., & Longmore, M. A. (2005). Adolescent romantic relationships and delinquency involvement. *Criminology, 43*(1), 177–210.

Hennessey, M., Ford, J. D., Mahoney, K., Ko, S. J., & Siegfried, C. B. (2004). *Trauma among girls in the juvenile justice system.* Los Angeles, CA: National Child Traumatic Stress Network.

Jenson, G., & Thompson, K. (1990). What's class got to do with it? *American Journal of Sociology, 95,* 1009–1023.

Lahey, B. B., Goodman, S. H., Waldman, I. D., Bird, H., Canino, G., Jensen, P., . . . Applegate, B. (1999). Relation of age of onset to the type and severity of child and adolescent conduct problems. *Journal of Abnormal Child Psychology, 27,* 247–260.

Mayo Clinic. *Post traumatic stress disorder.* Retrieved from https://www.mayoclinic.org/diseases-conditions/post-traumatic-stress-disorder/symptoms-causes/syc-20355967

Murphy, P. (1993). *Making connections: Women, work, and abuse*. Florida: Paul M. Deutsch Press.

National Coalition Against Domestic Violence. Human trafficking facts. Retrieved from

National Runaway Safeline. (2012). Retrieved from http://www.1800runaway.org/faq/#

Poe-Yamagata, E., & Butts, J. A. (1996). *Female offenders in the juvenile justice system: Statistics summary.* Washington, DC: U.S. Department of Justice, Office of Justice Programs, Office of Juvenile Justice and Delinquency Prevention.

Regoli, R. M., Hewitt, J. D., & DeLisi, M. (2011). *Delinquency in society, the essentials.* Sudbury, MA: Jones and Bartlett.

Shared Hope International. (2009). *National report on domestic minor sex trafficking: America's prostituted children.* Washington, DC.

Sickmund, M., & Puzzanchera, C. (Eds.). (2014). *Juvenile offenders and victims: 2014 national report*. Pittsburgh, PA: National Center for Juvenile Justice.

Singer, S., & Levine, M. (1988). Power-control theory, gender and delinquency. *Criminology, 26*, 627–647.

Smith, D. K., Leve, L. D., & Chamberlain, P. (2006). Adolescent girls' offending and health-risking sexual behavior: The predictive role of trauma. *Child Maltreatment,* 11, 346–353.

Snyder, H. (2000). *Sexual assault of young children as reported to law enforcement: Victim, incident, and offender characteristics report.* Washington, DC: U.S. Department of Justice, Office of Justice Programs, Bureau of Justice Statistics.

Teplin, L. A., Abram, K. M., McClelland, G. M., Dulcan, M. K., & Mericle, A. A. (2002). Psychiatric disorders in youth in juvenile detention. *Archives of General Psychiatry, 59*, 1133–1143.

Walker-Rodriguez, A., & Hill, R. (2011). *Human sex trafficking*. FBI Law Enforcement Bulletin. The Federal Bureau of Investigation. Washington, DC: U.S. Department of Justice.

Wiig, J. K., Tuell, J. A., & Heldman, J. K. (2013). *Guidebook for juvenile justice & child welfare system coordination and integration* (3rd ed.). Washington, DC: Models for Change, Justice Policy Institute.

Challenges Facing the Juvenile Justice System: Schools, Peer Groups and Gangs

13

© Kevin Moloney/Contributor/Getty

Pictured above are Dylan Klebold and Eric Harris whom you probably better know as the assailants in the Columbine massacre, in which they killed 13 people (including themselves), and injured 20 others. This massacre was one of the largest school crimes in our nation's history and changed the discourse about youth and school crime. While many blamed the youth for being part of the "new breed of juvenile offender" noted before and saw them as having no remorse or empathy, others blamed the parents for not noticing anything was wrong or better raising their children. Still others point the finger at the school environment itself where these two youths were subject to ridicule and bullying by other students. And, finally some even looked to the broader social norms of the community that seemed to promote military-style violence and the "trench coat" mafia gang of which the boys were later said to be members.

In the movie *Bowling for Columbine*, produced by Michael Moore, Moore interviews musician Marilyn Manson, who was one of the boys' favorite artists and who too was "blamed" for the attack, with some saying that the lyrics of his music promoted violence. In an iconic moment in this film Moore asks Manson what would he have said if he had been able to talk to Eric Harris and Dylan Klebold. Manson answers that he would not say anything; he would just listen. This simple statement indicates that he too, perhaps, felt the boys were victims as well as perpetrators and that if someone had listened to their pain, their story, earlier, this massacre could have been avoided.

In this chapter you will learn about two additional challenges to the juvenile justice system. The first, the school environment, is truly unique to juveniles. Due to compulsory education laws, youths spend much of their time in the school environment. While our schools are designed to be positive environments, our school are to promote healthy development and to prepare youths for work as adults, much like the Houses of Refuge were, there are inherent problems with our schools and educational system today that lead to fights in schools, student failures and in some instances delinquency.

You will also learn about how friends and playgroups can turn into violent environments, how gangs form and how youths come in and out of gang membership. This is inherently related to the neighborhoods and communities in which youths live, but can also spill over into the schools, linking these two social environments. Gangs are probably one of the longest standing problems facing juvenile justice and one of the most feared aspects of juvenile crime. Gang members are often seen as a different breed of youth without feelings or empathy for their victims. In fact, there was a period of time in which it was reported that police departments in several major cities would refer to gang members as "NH" or non-humans. But nothing could be further from the truth. Gang members are not only humans, but simply youths who have grown up in, and been exposed to, violent environments. As you will learn, one of the major reasons youth say they join a gang is for "protection." Thus, understanding these youths and how our society contributes to their gang joining and then gang-related criminal activity is important for the safety of us all—including the gang-involved youths.

CHAPTER GOALS

By the end of this chapter you should be able to:

1. List the types of crime and delinquency that most often occur in school.
2. Use theory to explain why delinquency occurs in schools.
3. Use these theories to critique the various delinquency prevention programs implemented by schools and argue for which strategy you believe is best.
4. Understand the gang problem in the United States, particularly as it relates to juveniles.
5. Explain the reasons why youths join gangs, leave gangs and what being in a gang means for youths.
6. Use theories of delinquency to critique gang prevention and intervention efforts.

Challenge 3: Schools and Delinquency

THE AMERICAN PUBLIC SCHOOL

In America public education is considered a right, not a privilege. Therefore, our public school system was designed to provide each child with an equal opportunity for an education and later life success. Or, at least, that is how the story goes. However, historically, minority populations, particularly African-Americans, were excluded from educational opportunities. In fact, as you might already know, it was not until May 1954 that the U.S. Supreme Court ruled in a unanimous decision that separate schools were not equal schools and that black and white children should attend the same schools (***Brown v. the Board of Education*** 347 U.S.482).

However, without going too far into politics and policy, it is important to note that our nation's public schools are mainly funded through local sources of income such as property taxes and not federal or state income taxes. Therefore the quality of an education one receives is inherently tied to where one lives and the financial resources of that community.

In addition, we have compulsory attendance laws in the United States that mandate youths attend school until a certain age (usually 16 but it varies by state). In fact you also learned that failure to go to school, called truancy, is considered a status offense for which a youth can be arrested and punished. Thus, school is not just a right, it is a legally mandated responsibility for youths to go to school every day of the school year.

Parents send their children off every day of the school year to this environment so that they can learn and prepare to be productive adults. Yet, for many children, the school environment can be a negative experience, and these negative experiences can culminate either in crime and violence within the school or the youth dropping out of school, which in turn, can contribute to delinquency.

Delinquency in the School

To understand the problem fully, it is first important to understand the nature and extent of delinquency in schools. The news media, as is the case with all crime, tends to cover only the most unusual and horrific events. Thus, your perception of school crime is probably related to school shootings such as the Columbine tragedy. Luckily, these are relatively rare instances , although they appear to be on the rise recently. School crime, however, is not a rare event overall compared to other types of youth crime.

While data from the National Center for Educational Statistics shows that there were 53 school-associated violent deaths from July 1, 2012, through June 30, 2013, in 2014 there were also about 850,100 nonfatal victimizations at schools that included 363,700 theft victimizations and 486,400 violent victimizations, such as simple assault and serious violent victimizations (Zhang, Musu-Gillette & Oudekerk, 2015). In addition, during the 2013–14 school year, this report indicates that there were 1.3 million reported discipline incidents in U.S. schools for alcohol, drugs, violence or weapons possession.

To understand these numbers better it helps to place them in a broader trend to let you know if school crime is increasing or decreasing. Overall, it has been decreasing for over the past twenty years. For example, from 1992 to 2014, the total victimization rate at school declined from 181 victimizations per 1,000 students in 1992 to 33 victimizations per 1,000 students in 2014, which represents an 82% decrease. This trend is also similar to the total victimization rate of youths away from school which declined 86 percent over a similar time period.

But, just as crime in general is not divided equally among society, so it does not occur equally at all schools. One fact that might be surprising is that violent incidents are actually more likely at rural schools (53 incidents per 1,000 students) than at suburban (28 incidents per 1,000 students) or urban (32 incidents per 1,000 students) schools (Zhang, Musu-Gillette & Oudekerk, 2015).

Other differences include that minority students are more likely to report access to illegal drugs at schools and gang-related activities at their schools than are white students, and middle school students are the most likely to report experiencing bullying and cyberbullying.

These nuances to the problem of school delinquency (e.g., is it violent or nonviolent; is it gang related; what age, race and ethnic groups are most vulnerable) are very important for school officials to understand in order to design proper strategies to prevent and respond to school crime. In the next section we therefore turn to understanding school delinquency.

Causes of School Problems

SCHOOL BONDS

In Chapter 7 you learned about Hirschi's Social Bond Theory that discussed the importance of bonds to society. These bonds include attachment, commitment, involvement and beliefs. The first three of these concepts have been heavily applied in understanding student behaviors at school. Constructs such as being attached to one's teacher, being committed to getting good grades and pursuing higher education and involvement in pro-social clubs and school activities have all been found to reduce the likelihood that a youth will engage in delinquency both in and out of school (Hirschi, 1969). Tests of this theory over time, while finding school attachment, commitment and involvement to matter, have found these bonds to be reliant upon parental/family relations (Liska & Reed, 1985) and also peer relationships (Lawrence, 1985). Thus once again empirical studies reinforce the mingling of family, schools and peers as simultaneous influences on a juvenile's life.

Tracking

accepted practices in schools where students' standardized test scores and other measures of intelligence used to group students. This can set some students up for school failure, impacting their attachment to school and lead to delinquency

LABELING

It has historically been an accepted practice in schools to track students according to their perceived academic ability as evidenced on standardized tests or other measures of intelligence. These **tracking** mechanisms are blamed for setting some students up for school failure, which in turn can impact their attachment/commitment to school and their delinquency. Studies have also found that teachers do indeed respond to students differently based on such labels. For example, Schafer and Polk (1976) found correlations between teachers' perceptions of educational deficiencies and problem behavior in students. In line with the labeling perspective, this study found that when teachers labeled some students as "stupid" or "bad" and the students became aware of these labels, it resulted in the students feeling alienated from school and was correlated with increased truancy from school and other forms of delinquency.

In fact, much of the link between IQ and delinquency noted in Chapter 5 has been attributed not to direct correlations, but rather indirect correlations whereby those youths labeled as less intelligent receive differential negative treatment in the schools. In addition, many studies find that the behavior of the youths labeled as learning disabled do not really differ from the behavior of other youths, but merely, that these behaviors are more likely to be classified as delinquent for the labeled youths (Keilitz et al., 1979; Border et al., 1981).

It has also been found that this relationship can work in the opposite direction. For example, one fairly famous study by Rosenthal and Jacobson entitled "Pygmalion in the Classroom" (1968) examined how labeling could actually impact a student's educational performance. In this classic study, teachers were informed that some of the students in their classroom were identified as "growth spurters" by a test called the Havard Test of Inflected Acquisition. The trick was there was no such test and the students were randomly assigned as "growth spurters." The outcome was that these students received special attention and treatment by the teachers and by the end of the year had actually made large gains in academic achievement. This study is just one of many to show that teachers' perceptions of students and their abilities directly impact educational outcomes.

STRAIN

Just as being labeled or tracked in school can have very real consequences for a youth, so can the feeling of strain or frustration one might feel from such tracking. Explanations of school structure and delinquency highlight how tracking such as that noted above can lead students to feel blocked from opportunity. Moreover, school failure in general, that is the inability to meet parents' and teachers' or even one's own expectations for performance, can lead to negative feelings such as anger, frustration and depression. According to the General Strain Theory, these negative emotions, if experienced consistently enough, can become negative affective states and impact how an individual perceives and interacts with the world around them.

Also Merton's Theory of Anomie pointed out that while all are taught to seek the American Dream, only some are given the legitimate opportunities to achieve it. Think about how being "tracked" into a non-academic or non-college-bound curriculum might limit one's ability to achieve this dream.

> **Connections:** Other theories you have learned that combined these influences were Elliot et al.'s Integrated Theory, Sampson and Laub's Age-Graded Theory and Thornberry's Interactional Theory (Chapter 8). Think about what connections you can draw here?

School Context and Delinquency

In addition to direct links between the academic setting of school and delinquency, it is important to view the school as a social environment as well in which youths develop and grow. As such, this social environment provides both opportunities for positive growth through acceptance by peers and the learning of social norms, and opportunities for negative behaviors. In this section we explore two unique aspects of the school social environment as it relates to juvenile delinquency and victimization.

OPPORTUNITY FOR DEVIANCE

On the most basic level, school, being the place where children and adolescents spend a majority of their waking hours, provides the social context in which delinquency can happen. From a routine activities perspective, unlocked lockers and cell phones left unattended become easy "targets" for theft, and unsupervised hallways, bus stops and cafeterias provide unguarded places in which crime of various forms can happen. The school is also what might be referred to as a forced environment in which youths from diverse backgrounds and with diverse interests must interact on a daily basis. That is, unlike peer groups (explored in the following section of the chapter), in which youths select the people with whom they want to interact, schools force youths, many of whom do not like each other, to interact and even compete on a daily basis.

In some ways, this forced interaction can be a good thing because it forces individuals to be exposed to different lifestyles and, it is hoped, gain some level of tolerance and respect for each other. However, this forced interaction can also backfire in the form of insults, fights and in many cases bullying.

BULLYING

Bullying

using one's strength or social status to intimidate, humiliate, or injure another person usually of lesser strength or status. Can be physical, verbal or emotional

Bullying is generally defined as one using one's strength or social status to intimidate, humiliate, or injure another person usually of lesser strength or status. Bullying can take various forms, including:

- Physical bullying that involves actual physical harm through hitting, kicking or other forms of violence (e.g., the classic example of shoving a kid in his/her locker),
- Verbal bullying which includes name calling, taunting and teasing and, finally,
- Emotional bullying which encompasses manipulative behavior such as spreading false rumors about another.

Some scholars/texts also include sexual abuse as a form of bullying. Depending on the nature of the activity it could actually fall into a separate category or into many of the above categories as well such as physical violence, verbal teasing and emotional distress. In general what differentiates bullying from other types of aggressive behaviors are the power imbalance between the bully and bullied and the repetitive and directed nature of the "attacks."

Regarding the bully him/herself it is estimated that nearly 2 million children admit to bullying another child (National Institute of Child Health and Human Development). Bullying is most likely to occur during the middle school years, and while both boys and girls bully they do so differently, with boys being more likely to report physical and sexual bullying and girls more likely to report verbal and emotional bullying.

Regarding the victims of bullies, about 1 in 3 children ages 12 to 18 admit to being bullied (Tanner, 2001) and more recent work suggests that almost one-quarter of students admit to being the victim of cyberbullying (Dehue et al., 2008).

IMPACT OF BULLYING

There are two important components to the bullying problem from a delinquency perspective. First, the bully him/herself is engaging in antisocial behavior that can rise to the level of delinquency and which is often consistent with other forms of delinquency exhibited by the bully. Second, the victim of the bullying can him/herself be traumatized and this trauma can lead to delinquent behaviors, violence and even suicide. Indeed, the Columbine shooting depicted at the beginning of this chapter was carried out by youths who felt bullied and ostracized by the school environment. And it was perhaps this incident that brought the topic of school bullying into the national spotlight and led schools to begin to take measures to address the problem.

Overall, it has been found that bullies themselves are more likely to go on to become delinquent than other youths. While I would not suggest that bullying causes delinquency, the research suggests that bullying is one manifestation of underlying problems that can also lead to delinquency and, therefore, intervention with the bully may be warranted before the behavior progresses to more serious anti-social and criminal behaviors.

Being the victim of bullying also has detrimental effects. Students who are bullied may develop physical symptoms such as stomach pains or sleeping problems, may be afraid to even go to school or to certain places in the school such as the cafeteria or playground where bullying may be more likely due to less direct supervision. Bullied students often lose confidence in themselves and may either have negative behaviors that turn inward such as depression and "cutting" or even suicide, or negative behaviors that turn outward such as that evidenced in the Columbine massacre (Olweus, 2016).

Olweus Anti-Bullying Prevention Program
a whole-school-based program that utilizes the school, the classroom and individuals (school administrators, teachers, staff and students) to simultaneously address bullying while also including parents and community member

Connections: Here we see another clear example of the victim/offender link in which the victim of bullying can become the deviant him/herself in response. Another point to note is that it is thought that many "bullies" themselves come from home environments where they are abused or are exposed to violence. Thus, their bullying behavior in school can be viewed as an expression of their victimization in other settings.

FOCUS ON POLICY: The Olweus Anti-Bullying Program

With this problem being so prevalent, what can schools do to combat it? One effective approach is known as the Olweus Bullying Prevention Program. The **Olweus Bullying Prevention Program** (OBPP) is probably the most researched and best-known bullying prevention program.

OBPP is a whole-school-based program that utilizes the school, the classroom and individuals (school administrators, teachers, staff and students) to simultaneously address bullying. The method also includes parents and community members, which may be particularly important given the rise in cyberbullying that may have its roots in school but continues into the evening hours and the home.

While a discussion of the entire program is beyond the scope of this text, in a nutshell it includes specific goals and tasks for the various levels of involvement. For example, at the school level an anti-bullying committee is formed and this committee should include community members from outside the school to raise awareness of the problem. Committee trainings are held to help staff recognize and know how to address bullying. A school-wide questionnaire is also given to students to assess the prevalence and specific nature of bullying in the school. At the student/parent level individual meetings are held with students who are bullied or who bully and their parents and intervention plans developed. Overall, the goal is to develop a culture in which bullying is looked down upon, and in which students and teachers know how to prevent and intervene when bullying does occur.

The OBPP is probably also the most thoroughly evaluated bullying prevention/reduction program with six large-scale evaluations conducted worldwide involving more than 40,000 students. Overall these studies found that the program resulted in an average reduction of up to 50 percent in student reports of either bullying or being bullied. In addition to direct effects on bullying the program was also found to have the added benefit of reducing student reports of general antisocial behavior, such as vandalism, fighting, theft, and truancy, and improving classroom social climate as reflected in students' reports of positive social relationships and positive attitudes toward school. However, the results were not as strong in some American replications of the program and overall the program seems to be more effective for white than for African-American youth, suggesting that there may be some different causal factors in bullying across race/ethnic groups that call for differential responses.

For more information on the OBPP see:

Amundsen, E. J., and E. Ravndal. 2010. Does successful school-based prevention of bullying influence substance use among 13- to 16-year-olds? *Drugs: Education, Prevention and Policy, 17*(1): 42–54.

Bauer, N. S., P. Lozano, and F. P. Rivara. 2007. The effectiveness of the Olweus Bullying Prevention Program in public middle schools: A controlled trial. *Journal of Adolescent Health, 40*(3): 266–274.

Bowllan, N. M. 2011. Implementation and evaluation of a comprehensive, school-wide bullying prevention program in an urban/suburban middle school. *Journal of School Health, 81*(4):167–173.

Prevention. Washington, DC: Office of Juvenile Justice and Delinquency Prevention.

Olweus, D. 1993. *Bullying at school: What we know and what we can do.* Oxford, England: Blackwell.

Olweus, D. 2005. New positive results with the Olweus Bullying Prevention Program in 37 Oslo schools. The HEMIL-Center, University of Bergen.

Pepler, D. J., W. M. Craig, S. Ziegler, and A. Charach. 1994. An evaluation of an anti-bullying intervention in Toronto schools. *Canadian Journal of Community, 13*: 95–110.

Smith, P. K. 1997. Bullying in schools: The UK experience and the Sheffield anti-bullying project. *The Irish Journal of Psychology, 18*: 191–201.

Yaakub, N. F., F. Haron, and G. C. Leong. 2010. Examining the efficacy of the Olweus prevention programme in reducing bullying: The Malaysian experience. *Procedia Social and Behavioral Sciences 5*: 595–598.

Delinquency and Dropout

In addition to providing an environment in which deviance and victimization can occur, schools are also part of what has been deemed the "**school to prison pipeline**" in which school failure can lead to negative feelings about one's self (e.g., Labeling Theory noted above) and harsh school discipline such as **suspensions** and **expulsions** (which reduce bonds to school) and ultimately can lead to school dropout. Dropping out of school can be a major negative turning point in a student's life. Now instead of spending the day in a structured environment being prepped to enter the labor force as a competitive worker, the youth is often spending most of his/her time in unstructured socializing situations, which, as you have previously learned, can be criminogenic (Christle, Jolivette & Nelson, 2005).

School to Prison Pipeline
the process through which school failure leads to delinquency and, ultimately, prison. It is suggested this pipeline is almost inescapable for many minority youth from poor neighborhoods who are much more likely to spend time in prison than to finish school

Suspensions
student is temporarily removed from their school setting

Expulsions
student is permanently removed from their school setting

You have already learned about the impact of tracking and labeling of students, another key factor in student failure can be the reliance of schools on suspension and expulsion as disciplinary actions. When youths face such disciplinary actions they are often left home alone unsupervised while their parent is at work. Not only does the student fall further behind academically because he or she is missing school days, but he or she is also often unsupervised and hanging out with other peers who are suspended, expelled or who have dropped out of school.

Statistics also show that most students who experience suspension and expulsion live in impoverished communities (Lugalia, 2003) and that between 70 and 87% of youths in the juvenile justice system have a learning disability or emotional problems that impact their ability to perform in the American school environment, thus furthering the link between school failure and delinquency (Coalition for Juvenile Justice, 2001).

However, there is some disagreement among scholars about the delinquency and drop-out link with some studies showing that delinquency is the highest right before drop out and that delinquency may actually decrease after drop out as the youth experiences less feelings of frustration and stress after dropping out (Elliot & Voss, 1974). Other studies have found the opposite, however, showing that even though youth may be involved in delinquency before dropping out of school, dropout significantly increases their delinquent activity as well as prospects of unemployment (Farrington et al., 1986; Thornberry, Moore, & Christenson, 1985).

Responses to Delinquency in Schools

In addition to the Olweus bullying prevention program described in the Focus on Policy section, you also learned about the use of school resource officers as an approach to reduce delinquency in schools. Other measures being adopted include:

- Suspensions/expulsions of students for disruptive behaviors
- Zero tolerance policies that mandate the suspension or expulsion of students for certain behaviors
- Search and seizures policies that allow teachers, school resource officers or even outside police to search individual students, their lockers and belongings such as backpacks
- The installation of metal detectors that students must pass through on their way into school.

While these policies are met with mixed responses, one of the least popular and most criticized are the **zero-tolerance policies** that can be interpreted as "zero-thought" policies. These policies typically vaguely detail a type of behavior that will not be allowed and dictate that any student violating the rule will be suspended or expelled. The administrators then put zero thought into the actual behavior or the intent behind it, leading to such policies that denounce "any weapon" or "any sexual misconduct," leading to ridiculous outcomes. As a personal example, my six-year-old niece was once suspended from school because her mother packed a packet of plastic utensils in her lunch box that included a "knife." On a national level other examples include:

Zero Tolerance Policies
vaguely detail a type of behavior that will not be allowed and dictate that any student violating the rule will be suspended or expelled

The 14-year-old "terrorist" who was arrested for bringing in a homemade clock which the school determined to be an "explosive" device;

A seven-year-old who was suspended from his Maryland elementary school for chewing his Pop-Tart into a gun and pointing it at fellow students; and

A six-year-old Colorado student who was expelled and charged with sexual harassment for kissing his classmate's hand.

Such policies are thought to contribute to the school to prison pipeline mentioned above as students who experience suspensions and expulsions have reduced odds of ever finishing school.

What does work, then? As you might expect from everything you have learned so far, while there is no one clear-cut answer, what seems to work are efforts that are individualized to the youth and the particular circumstance and programs that involve not just the youth, but the peers, the school, the family and the community. As we recognize the greater embeddedness of the youths in these broad social contexts and their combined influence on development, these lead us naturally to the last challenge to be discussed in this text: the role of peer groups in delinquency and the development of youth gangs from such naturally occurring youth peer groups.

Gangs
first defined as a phenomenon of human ecology as groups of youth band together. Sociological and Law enforcement definitions differ and are provided later in the chapter

Challenge 4: From Playgroup to Gang: Peers and Delinquency

As first proposed by W. I. Thomas (1968), **gangs** are a "phenomenon of human ecology" arising in the disordered interstitial spaces on the edges of the encroaching business district (p. 23). It is these interstitial spaces that lie "between" two things that allow chaos to ensue. In this case it is between the business district and the area of working men's homes as proposed by Shaw and McKay in Social Disorganization Theory that such disorder arises and gives rise to formation of youth gangs.

In this area, what most of us would call the ghetto or the slums of a city, he witnessed what he called "swarms" of children hovering in parking lots and streets with little to do. In this overcrowded and unsupervised area the playgroups of children became the "embryos" of gangs (pg. 26). Just as schools provide a forced structural social environment for youths, so do their communities. These youths "hang out" there not by choice, but because it is where their parents live. Often these hangouts are in poor and overpopulated communities with little to no structured social activities for the youths.

Connections: Remember from Chapter 6, Social Disorganization Theory focused on the breakdown of social institutions such as families, schools and churches. In these impoverished communities the youths have little structure and, as proposed by Miller in his Focal Concerns Theory, they turn to the streets and each other for a sense of family and to determine what it means to "be a man."

While these youths may have little, what they do have, as proposed by Focal Concerns Theory, Code of the Streets and other subcultural theories you have learned about, is the need for a sense of belonging and respect. In control of perhaps little else in their lives, these youths turn to the gang for a sense of protection, status and control. Just as Durkheim proposed deviance can play an important function in society and having a common enemy is often a unifying force, the gang serves a purpose for these youths and provides a common enemy—typically rival gangs often of different racial and ethnic compositions.

Thus, these interstitial spaces as proposed by Thomas are not just between the business district and the suburbs, they are the areas between racial groups, ethnicities and immigrants that compete with each other for the scarce resources available in these impoverished communities. It is in these areas that escape the organization and social control of broader society that the gang forms as the new means of social order for these youths.

The Gang Problem

While the basic reasons and processes for gang formation may not differ much today than they did when Thomas was writing the classic work referenced above, the gang problem in general, the types and extent of criminality perpetrated by gangs and our understanding of gangs have vastly changed.

According to the FBI, 33,000 violent street gangs, motorcycle gangs and prison gangs with about 1.4 million members are criminally active in the United States and Puerto Rico today. However, all of these members are of course not juveniles. Some gangs are exclusively juveniles, others more exclusively adults (e.g., most motorcycle gangs) and others have mixed membership ranging from early adolescence through adulthood.

When one thinks of juvenile gangs they typically think of neighborhood gangs, also known as street gangs, where youths from a given community band together. But how do criminal justice officials define a gang? Formal definitions of gangs typically include the notion of illegal activity, but can vary greatly from jurisdiction to jurisdiction. While there is no one accepted definition, here I provide two examples of definitions, one from the sociological tradition and one from law enforcement:

SOCIOLOGICAL DEFINITION:

A gang is a group of recurrently associating individuals with identifiable leadership and internal organization, identifying with or claiming control over territory in a community, and engaging either individually or collectively in violent or other forms of illegal behavior (Miller, 1975).

FEDERAL LAW ENFORCEMENT DEFINITION:

The federal definition of gang as used by the Department of Justice and the Department of Homeland Security's Immigration and Customs Enforcement (ICE), is [1]:

A. An association of three or more individuals;
B. Whose members collectively identify themselves by adopting a group identity, which they use to create an atmosphere of fear or intimidation, frequently by employing one or more of the following: a common name, slogan, identifying

sign, symbol, tattoo or other physical marking, style or color of clothing, hairstyle, hand sign or graffiti;

C. Whose purpose in part is to engage in criminal activity and which uses violence or intimidation to further its criminal objectives;

D. Whose members engage in criminal activity or acts of juvenile delinquency that if committed by an adult would be crimes with the intent to enhance or preserve the association's power, reputation or economic resources.

E. The association may also possess some of the following characteristics:
   1. The members may employ rules for joining and operating within the association.
   2. The members may meet on a recurring basis.
   3. The association may provide physical protection of its members from others.
   4. The association may seek to exercise control over a particular geographic location or region, or it may simply defend its perceived interests against rivals.
   5. The association may have an identifiable structure.

(National Institute of Justice, 2011)

You might be particularly familiar with some of these more recognizable notions of a gang, including the use of colors, signs and symbols to signify gang membership. For example, the graffiti pictured depicts symbols for the Crypts and the hand signal is a sign for the Bloods:

© Boston Globe/Contributor/Getty

© Steven D Starr/Contributor/Getty

In addition to these well-known national gangs that have "chapters" in various cities across the nation, many cities also have their own local gangs that develop based on the social structure and make-up of that individual city. Regardless of whether that gang is a chapter of a larger structure, or a local identity, street gangs have been historically and remain a problem for our nation's cities, both large and small. Recent data shows that about 42% of all gangs are in what are considered the nation's largest cities, such as Los Angeles, New York, Chicago and Philadelphia, while another 27% are in suburbs of these cities and 25% in smaller cities. Only a small portion of gangs are in rural areas and these are typically not "street" gangs but rather motorcycle gangs and/or extremist gangs.

It is hard, as you can imagine, to get an exact tally on numbers and make up of gang members, but it is estimated that fewer gang members are juveniles today than in the past. According to the National Gang Center, in 1996 about half of all gang members were juveniles under the age of 18 and that has reduced to only about 35% today (Table 13.1):

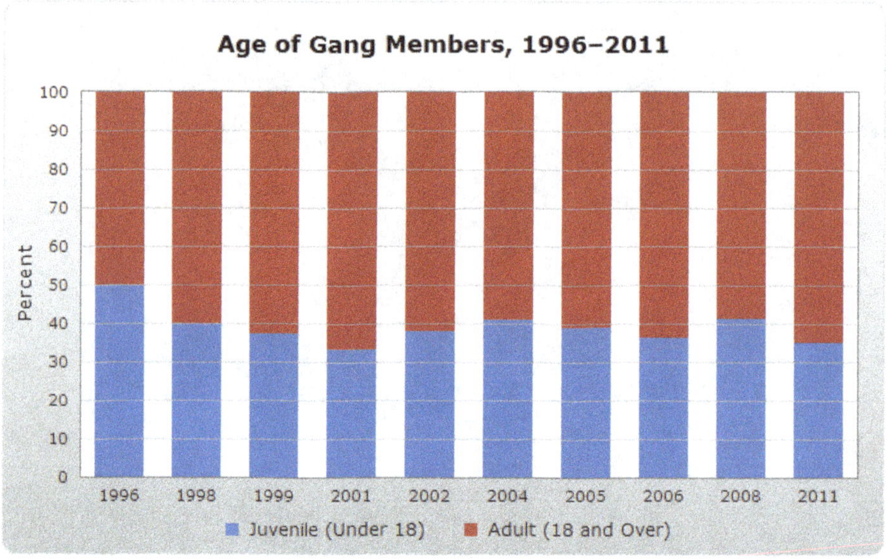

TABLE 13.1 Age of Gang Members
(https://www.nationalgangcenter.gov/Survey-Analysis/Demographics#anchorage)

Estimates of the race/ethnicity of gang members also show that gang members are also more likely to be Hispanic or African-American than all other races/ethnicities (Table 13.2):

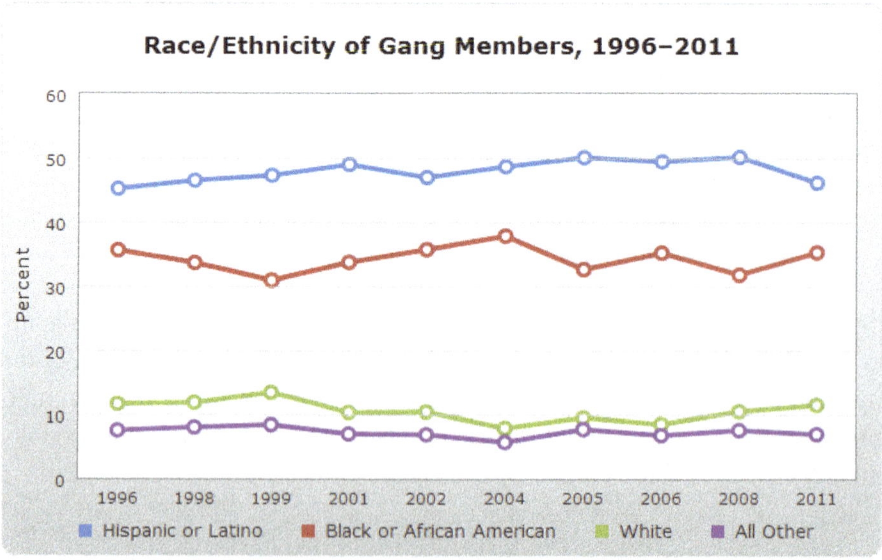

TABLE 13.2 Race/Ethnicity of Gang Members.
National Gang Center. *National Youth Gang Survey Analysis*.
from http://www.nationalgangcenter.gov/Survey-Analysis

It is easier to capture the types of crime for which gang members are arrested as this becomes formal administrative data. While gangs are most often associated with drug dealing and various forms of violence that go along with drug dealing, as the following chart shows, gang criminality is highly varied in nature (Table 13.3):

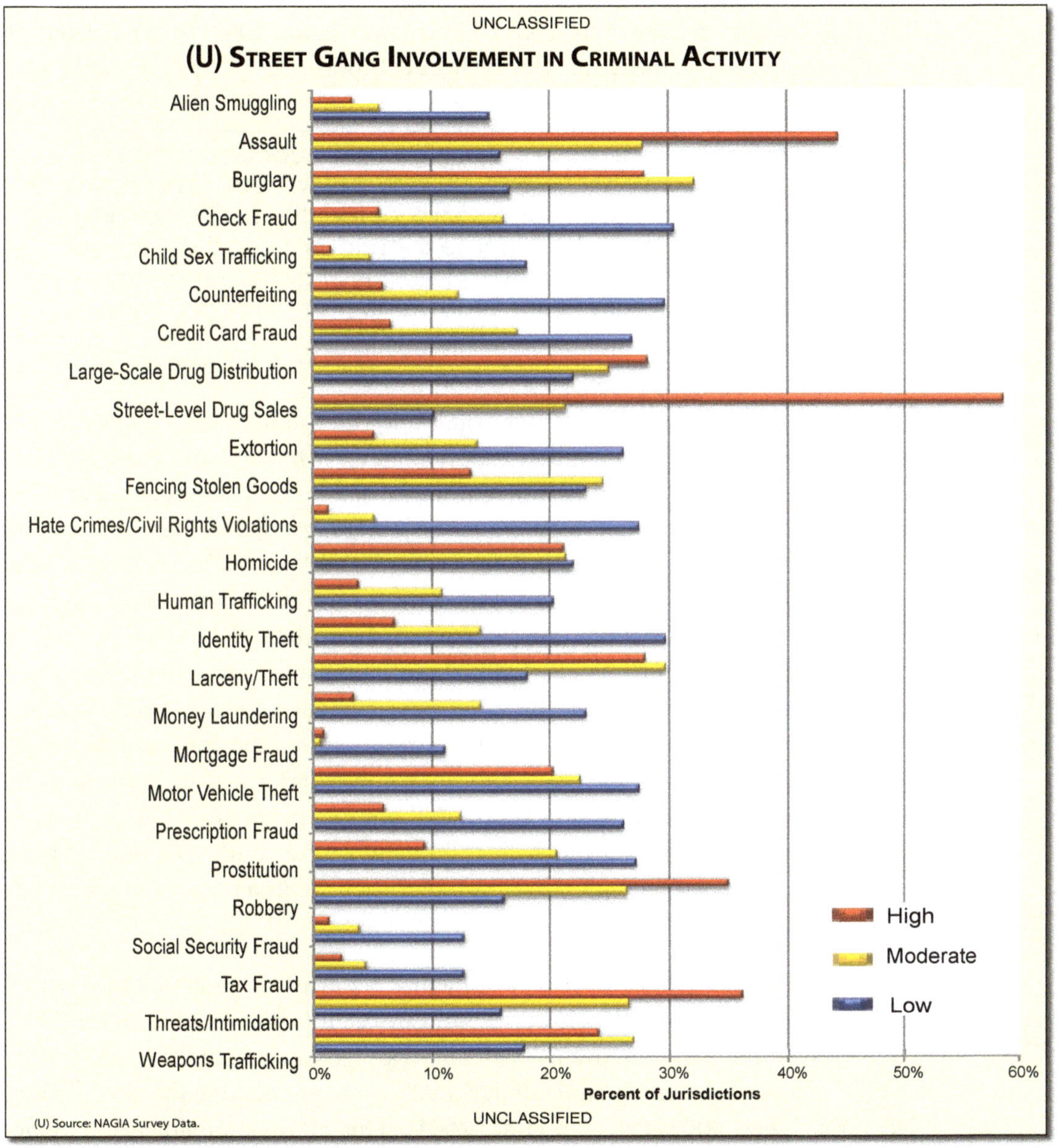

(U) The survey question asked respondents to indicate the level of street gang involvement in various criminal activities. The choices were High, Moderate, Low, Unknown, and None. The graphic depicts the percent of jurisdictions reporting High, Moderate, and Low gang involvement for each criminal activity.

TABLE 13.3 Criminal Activity of Gangs
(FBI National Gang Report, 2015, p. 14.)

Research on Gangs

A lot of research has focused on understanding why youths choose to join gangs in the first place, and how the time spent in a gang impacts their life trajectory. Most of the research suggests that youth join the gang either for reasons of protection (Peterson, Taylor, & Esbensen, 2004; Thornberry et al., 2003) or for reasons of respect and identity (Anderson, 1999; Short & Stodtbeck, 1965; Zastrow, 1992).

> **Connections:** As previously learned under subcultural theories, many youth from poor neighborhoods and without stable home lives look to the streets for a sense of identity and belonging. Joining a gang to help promote such identity and a sense of masculinity is in line with various theories of delinquency including Anderson's Code of the Streets and Miller's Focal Concerns Theory.

Selection Model

youths already disposed to delinquency seek out like others and thus join the gang

Facilitation Model

otherwise non-delinquent youth become involved in delinquency because they join a gang and are influenced by delinquent peers.

Enhancement Model

delinquent-prone youth seek out the gang and the gang in turn increases and promotes their delinquency to higher levels

The next question is what happens to youth once they join a gang? While it might seem like an obvious statement that youths in gangs commit crime, there is a classic chicken or the egg dilemma inherent in discussions of gang delinquency. Do youths who are more prone to delinquency join gangs or does joining the gang make a youth delinquent? The answer is "yes" and "yes." That is, youths who join gangs seem to be already committing some levels of delinquency, but after joining the gang their delinquency increases substantially (Keenan et al., 1995; Decker, 1996; Thornberry et al., 2003). Thornberry and colleagues define these processes as a combination of the **selection model** in which youths already disposed to delinquency seek out like others and thus join the gang and the **facilitation model** in which the group processes and dynamics of the gang actually promote and cause delinquency. Together, these two processes work to produce the **enhancement model** in which delinquent-prone youth seek out the gang and the gang in turn increases and promotes their delinquency to higher levels (Thornberry et al., 1993).

Contrary to the popular myth that gang members stay in the gang for life, research shows that gang membership is mostly transitory and short-lived in nature. Perhaps most ironic, while many individuals report joining a gang for protection, research shows that their victimization actually increases once in the gang (Curry, Decker & Egley, 2002; Peterson et al., 2004). This increase in violence and victimization is key to gang-leaving, with most gang members eventually exiting the group within one year (Thornberry et al., 2003). Of those leaving, many report leaving due to violence (Decker & Lauritsen, 2002; Decker & Van Winkle, 1996). For example, 14 of the 24 former gang members interviewed by Decker and Van Winkle said they had left the gang because a friend had been killed while in the gang, while four others left the gang because they were personally shot or stabbed (1996, p. 269).

Girls in Gangs

While gangs, just like delinquency in general, are predominantly a male phenomenon, that does not mean that some girls do not join gangs. Data from the National Gang Center estimates that females comprise about 7% of all gang members, with this percent holding relatively stable over the past two decades at least.

Although, just like male gangs, it is difficult to collect exact data on this phenomenon we do know several things about female gang membership. First, there are two predominant ways in which females join gangs: 1) as auxiliary members of a male gang or 2) in all-female gangs. In either case females report some of the same reasons for joining gangs as males, including protection, in this case, however, often from an abusive home environment (Moore & Hagedorn, 2001) rather than from other street violence. In this way that gang provides a refuge from the abuse and perhaps also a sense of power for the young female. Some girls also join gangs because their boyfriend or brother is already a member while others might do so out of a sense of rebelliousness or even financial necessity.

Second, we know that once in gangs, females can be just as violent and criminal as their male counterparts (Esbensen et al., 2003; Miller, 2001). For example, while early ideas were that girls in gangs were most likely just there as sex options, in interviews with girls in gangs in St. Louis, Missouri and Columbus, Ohio, Miller found that girl gang members were just as likely to steal cars, commit larceny, intimidate others and commit vandalism. While this study did not find that girls sought out violence perhaps as readily as their male counterparts, they would use it to establish credibility within the gang culture.

Preventing and Responding to Gang Delinquency

Primary Prevention
refers to prevention efforts that target all youth, regardless of their individual risk of gang joining

Secondary Prevention
targets only those youth who are somehow identified as being at personal risk for gang joining

Tertiary Prevention
refers to efforts directed at youths who have already joined a gang

Efforts to prevent gang delinquency have been divided into three categories of prevention as defined by the CDC: Primary prevention, secondary prevention and tertiary prevention. **Primary prevention** refers to prevention efforts that target all youth, regardless of their individual risk of gang joining. **Secondary prevention** on the other hand targets only those youth who are somehow identified as being at personal risk for gang joining. Finally, **tertiary prevention** refers to efforts directed at youths who have already joined a gang. Some would therefore also call this third level an intervention. Primary prevention programs could be educational programs directed at all youths in a community, or it could involve efforts to actually make changes to the community that would reduce exposure to violence and other factors known to promote gang involvement generally. Secondary prevention is different in that it uses some criteria to define who is at risk of joining a gang, and then delivers specific services to those youths and families seen as being at risk. The Broader Urban Involvement and Leadership (BUILD) program could be seen as a combination of these two strategies. This program involves a 12-week educational component on gang violence, substance abuse, gang recruitment strategies and the negative consequences of gang membership that is delivered to all students in lower or lower-middle-class neighborhoods in Chicago. Then, youths in these schools who are seen as being particularly at risk of gang joining are provided with additional afterschool programs, job training, and recreational activities (Thompson & Jason, 1988).

Tertiary prevention is perhaps more difficult because it involves trying to change the behavior and attitudes of youth who are already involved in gangs. This means the workers must identify gang members and convince them to participate in programs that help them "quit" the gang. One such program is Homeboy Industries operating in Los Angeles, California. The program targets youth and young adults ages 14 to 30 at risk of joining or already active in gang activity. The program provides a host of services to these youth from mental health services and job training, to legal help and tattoo removal. Program officials report that most youth come to the program with a variety of needs and start with one service and then stay for more. The job training and placement component is one of the key functions of the program that works to show these youths that there are other, and better, options to life on the streets (Franke & Leap, 2011).

FOCUS ON RESEARCH: G.R.E.A.T.

Gang Resistance Education and Training (G.R.E.A.T.) is a program first developed by the Phoenix Police Department in 1991. It is a school-based intervention program that is designed to provide students with real tools for resisting the pressures and lures of gang joining. The program as originally designed was taught as a nine-week curriculum that focused on the negative aspects of gang life as well as conflict resolution skills and cultural sensitivity. In 1992 the U.S. Bureau of Alcohol, Tobacco and Firearms began financial funding of the program and by 1996 it had spread to schools in 47 states (Esbensen & Osgood, 1999).

A national evaluation of the program was funded by the National Institute of Justice. This first evaluation covered students in 42 schools from 11 cities in 11 states. The sample of 2,635 youths who reported completing the program were found to be significantly less likely to report gang affiliation, drug use and delinquent activities a year later than were the sample of 3,207 youths who did not complete the program (Esbensen & Osgood, 1999).

However, a follow-up study that looked at longitudinal outcomes of a smaller sample of G.R.E.A.T. participants over time found that while there were differences in some attitudinal measures, there were fewer differences in behavior. G.R.E.A.T. kids had lower levels of victimization and risk-seeking, had more prosocial peer relationships and had more positive views of police and more negative views about gangs; however, these differences were all attitudinal and did not result in the G.R.E.A.T. participants reporting less gang involvement (Esbensen et al., 2001). In response to these more negative findings, the G.R.E.A.T. curriculum was reviewed and revised. The new curriculum is longer (13 weeks instead of 9) and includes family and community components (see G.R.E.A.T. families website at https://www.great-online.org/Home/Training/GFT for more information on the family component).

A 2011 evaluation of this curriculum examined 3,427 students in 31 schools located in 5 different cities who either did (treatment group) or did not (control group) complete the program. Similar to the previous study, this study also found that G.R.E.A.T. students were more likely to have positive attitudes about police and more negative attitudes towards gangs. In addition, however, this study did find the program to be effective in reducing gang membership, with G.R.E.A.T. participants reporting lower rates of gang membership (Esbensen et al., 2011).

In addition to these prevention strategies, the police also use suppression and abatement tactics to try to protect communities from the potential crimes and violence committed by gang members.

Suppression

refers to efforts to remove gangs and indiviaul gang members from the streets

Abatement

a practice by which known gang members are prevented from hanging out in certain areas or participating in otherwise law abiding activities

Displacement

refers to when a crime-control policy fails to reduce the actual activity but just changes it location from one place to another

Suppression refers to efforts to remove gangs and individual gang members from the streets. These strategies may involve sentencing enhancements for individuals affiliated with gangs and special prosecution units designed to expedite the processing of cases involving suspected gang members. These efforts, however, are most often only applicable to youths transferred to the adult system. The Chicago Police Department's Flying Squad and the Los Angeles Police Department's Community Resources Against Street Hoodlums (CRASH) are examples of suppression programs.

Abatement, also referred to as an injunction, is a process by which gang members are defined as a "public nuisance" and prohibited from engaging in certain activities or hanging out in certain areas, such as near schools. Nationally it is estimated that about 12 percent of law enforcement agencies use such practices. Evaluations of these efforts show that while the most gang-ridden communities reported a reduction in gang presence, gang activity actually increased in less gang-ridden neighborhoods, suggesting the policy may only have **displaced** rather than reduced gang activity (Maxon, Henningan & Sloan, 2005). **Displacement** refers to when a crime-control policy fails to reduce the actual activity but just changes its location from one place to another.

Key Words

Abatement
Bullying
Displacement
Enhancement Model
Expulsions
Facilitation Model
Gangs
Olweus Anti-Bullying Prevention Program
Primary Prevention
School to Prison Pipelin
Secondary Prevention
Selection Model
Suppression
Suspensions
Tertiary Prevention
Tracking
Zero Tolerance Policies

Chapter Summary

This chapter brings together many of the key theories you already learned and applies them to two additional challenges faced by Juvenile Justice: the social environments and schools and peers/gangs and their influence on delinquency.

Schools are a unique setting in which youths from many different backgrounds are forced to interact and to compete for grades, at sports and for social popularity. Thus, it is not surprising that these environments would lead to delinquency. While Social Bond Theory predicts that students who are most committed and involved in school activities will be less delinquent, labeling and strain theories can be applied to show why specific characteristics of our nation's schools, such as tracking, can lead to delinquency.

Although school shootings are the type of school crime that most often makes it onto television, such events are rare, while more minor physical fights and thefts are common on school property. The school provides both easy opportunities for such crimes to occur, especially in less supervised areas of the school such as the hallways or the buses, and also provides a social context in which conflict can occur.

In this chapter you also learned about the impact of bullying on students and how such bullying can lead the one-time victim to overlap into offender. Indeed many of the most severe instances of school crime have been perpetrated by students who felt they were the victims of extreme bullying such as Eric Harris and Dylan Klebold.

Schools respond to such delinquency in many ways, from hiring school resource officers and installing metal detectors to suspending and expelling troubled students. However, policies that suspend or expel already troubled students can lead to even lower bonds with the school and further academic problems, which increase the risk of drop out and fuel the school to prison pipeline. Thus, recommended policies are those that keep children in school, increase supervision and reduce opportunities for delinquency in the school and promote healthy and tolerant school environments in which students are less likely to feel threatened or bullied.

The second challenge explored in this chapter is that of youth gangs, which typically form and operate in the community at a neighborhood or block level. Gangs have been a long-standing problem in the nation's urban areas and have spread to smaller cities and suburbs as well. Gangs are a concern because they are responsible for much crime in the city, including drug dealing and violent crimes such as robbery and homicides. While it is argued that youth are drawn to the gang because they are delinquent, research suggests that many youths actually join gangs because they feel the gang will protect them from the violence in the community—only to then be further put at risk of violence. Research also shows that while gang membership is a short-lived experience for many youth, their delinquency increases during the time they are in the gang, and although it reduces somewhat after leaving the gang, it does not necessarily return to the level before gang joining. Thus, this short time spent in a gang can have life-long consequences.

Most programs designed to address gangs either work to try to prevent youths from joining gangs (primary and secondary prevention) or to convince young gang members that there are better options and that they should leave the gang (tertiary prevention). You also learned about some law-enforcement efforts that are aimed at suppression of gang activity by removing gang members from the streets and by specifically forbidding known gang members from participating in certain activities (this latter approach is called abatement). Unfortunately, while some of the prevention programs show some success in reducing gang membership, youth gangs remain a significant problem in our nation's inner cities.

Discussion Questions

1. Most of you have just recently graduated from high school. Think back to your experience. What kinds of delinquency do you remember happening in your school? Drug use? Fights? Theft? Where in the school did these incidents happen? What do you think your school administrators could have done differently to reduce these incidents?
2. Several of the theories you have previously learned were applied to explain delinquency in schools. Which of these theories do you think makes the most sense? Or are they all important?
3. In this chapter you learned about the connection between bullying and school crime and violence. You also learned about the Olweus Bullying Prevention Program. Go online and search bullying prevention. What other programs can you find? How are they similar to or different from the Olweus model?

4. In Thrasher's famous book, *The Gang*, he described the evolution of youth playgroups into gangs. Were there gangs in the community where you grew up? If not, use what you have learned in this chapter and previous chapters to explain why you think your community was gang free. If so, use the knowledge you have gained to explain why you think these gangs were able to form and what purpose they served.
5. Based on what you have learned in this chapter, develop a gang prevention or intervention strategy. What would your strategy focus on? Would it focus on just the youths? Community institutions? Schools? Whom would it target? All youth? At-risk youth? Youth already in the gang? Defend your program as a "good" strategy.

REFERENCES

Broder, P. K., Dunivant, N., Smith, E. C., & Sutton, L. P. (1981). Further observations on the link between learning disabilities and juvenile delinquency. *Journal of Educational Psychology, 73* (December), 838–850.

Christle, C. A., Jolivette, K., & Nelson, C. M. (2005). Breaking the school to prison pipeline: Identifying school risk and protective factors for youth delinquency. *Exceptionality, 13*(2), 69–88.

Coalition for Juvenile Justice. (2001). Annual report overview, abandoned in the back row: New lessons in education and delinquency prevention. Retrieved from www. juvjustice.org/publications/overview2001.pdf

Curry, G. D., Decker, S. H., & Egley Jr., A. (2002). Gang involvement and delinquency in a middle school population. *Justice Quarterly*, *19*(2), 275–292. doi:10.1080/07418820200095241

Decker, S. (1996). Collective and normative features of gang violence. *Justice Quarterly, 13,* 243–264.

Decker, S. H., & Lauritsen, J. (2002). Leaving the gang. In C. R. Huff (Ed.), *Gangs in America III* (pp. 51–67). Thousand Oaks, CA: Sage Publications.

Decker, S. H., & Van Winkle, B. (1996). *Life in the gang: Family, friends, and fiolence.* New York, NY: Cambridge University Press.

Esbensen, F.-A., Deschenes, E. P., & Winfree Jr., L. T. (2003). Differences between gang girls and gang boys. In Rebecca D. Peterson (Ed.), *Understanding Contemporary Gangs in America.* Upper Saddle River, NJ: Prentice Hall.

Esbensen, F.-A., & Osgood, D. W. (1999). National evaluation of the gang resistance education and training program (G.R.E.A.T.). *Journal of Research in Crime and Delinquency,* 2, 194–225.

Esbensen, F.-A., Osgood, D. W., Taylor, T. J., Peterson, D., & Freng, A. (2001). How great is G.R.E.A.T.?: Results from a quasi-experimental design. *Criminology & Public Policy, 1*, 87–118.

Esbensen, F.-A., Peterson, D., Taylor, T. J., Freng, A., Osgood, D. W., Carson, D. C., & Matsuda, K. (2011). Evaluation and evolution of the gang resistant education and training (G.R.E.A.T.) program. *Journal of School Violence,* 10, 53–70.

Farrington, D., Gallagher, B., Morley, L., St. Ledger, R. J., & West, D. J. (1986). Unemployment, school leaving and crime. *British Journal of Criminology,* 26, 335–356.

Franke, T., & Leap, J. (2011). Homeboy Industries: Los Angeles county gang intervention and re-entry program second quarter report. Retrieved from http://zevyaroslavsky.org/wp-content/uploads/Homeboy-Industries-2nd-Quarter-Report-2011.pdf

Hirschi, T. (1969). *Causes of delinquency*. Berkeley: University of California Press.

Keenan, K. (1995). The influence of deviant peers on the development of boys' disruptive and delinquency behavior: A temporal analysis. *Development and Psychopathology, 9,* 715–726.

Keilitz, I., Zaremba, B. A., & Broder, P. K. (1979). The link between learning disabilities and juvenile delinquency: Some issues and answers. *Learning Disability Quarterly,* 2, 2–11.

Kelly, D. H., & Pink, W. T. (1982). School crime and individual responsibility: The perpetuation of a myth? *Urban Review, 14*(1),47–63.

Lawrence, R. (1985). School performance, containment theory and delinquent behavior. *Youth and Society,* 17, 69–5.

Liska, A. E., & Reed, M. D. (1985). Ties to conventional institutions and delinquency: Estimating reciprocal effects. *American Sociological Review,* 50, 547–560.

Lugalia, T. A. (2003). *A child's day: 2000. Selected indicators of child well-being.* Washington, DC: U.S. Census Bureau.

Maxon, C., Hennigan, K., & Sloane, D. (2005). It's getting crazy out there: Can a civil gang injunction change a community? *Criminology and Public Policy, 4,* 577–606.

Miller, J. (2001). *One of the guys: Girls, gangs and gender.* New York: Oxford University Press.

Moore, J., & Hagedorn, J. *Female gangs: A focus on research.* Washington DC: U.S. Department of Justice, Office of Justice Programs, Office of Juvenile Justice and Delinquency Prevention.

Oliver Brown et al. v. Board of Education of Topeka, 347 U.S. 483.

Peterson, D., Taylor, T. J., & Esbensen, F.-A. (2004). Gang membership and violent victimization. *Justice Quarterly, 21*(4), 793–815. doi:10.1080/07418820400095991

Rosenthal, R., & Jacobson, L. (1968). Pygmalion in the classroom. *The Urban Review, 3*(1), 16–20.

Shafer, W. E., & Polk, K. (1976). Delinquency and the schools. In *Task Force Report: Juvenile Delinquency and Youth Crime,* 228–234. The President's Commission on Law Enforcement and the Administration of Justice. Washington DC: U.S. Government Printing Office.

Short, J. F., & Strodtbeck, F. L. (1965). *Group process and gang delinquency.* Chicago: University of Chicago Press.

Thomas, W. I., & Znaniecki, F. (1918). *The Polish peasant in Europe and America: Monograph of an immigrant group* (Vol. 2). Chicago: University of Chicago Press.

Thompson, D. W., & Jason, L. A. (1988). Street gangs and prevention interventions. *Criminal Justice and Behavior, 15,* 323–333.

Thornberry, T. P., Krohn, M. D., Lizotte, A. J., & Tobin, K. (2003). *Gangs and delinquency in developmental perspective.* New York: Cambridge University Press.

Thornberry, T., Marvin, P., Krohn, D., Lizotte, A. J., & Chard-Wierschem, D. (1993). The role of juvenile gangs in facilitating delinquency behavior. *Journal of Research in Crime and Delinquency, 30,* 55–87.

Thornberry, T., Moore, M., & Christenson, R. L. (1985). Dropping out of high school and subsequent criminal behavior. *Criminology,* 23, 3–18.

Thrasher, F. M. (1927). *The gang: A study of 1,313 gangs in Chicago.* Chicago: Chicago University Press.

Zastrow, C. (1992). *Social problems: Issues and solutions* (3rd ed.). Chicago: Nelson-Hall.

Zhang, A., Musu-Gillette, L. & Oudekerk, B. A. (2016). Indicators of school crime and safety: 2015. NCES 2016-079. NCJ 249758. National Center for Education Statistics.

The Future of Juvenile Justice

14

© Rawpixel.com/Shutterstock.com

Throughout this text you have learned about the beginnings of the juvenile justice system from the definition of the "delinquent act" and the "delinquent youth" as something different from adult crime to the formation of this separate and unique system of justice designed to treat and rehabilitate rather than punish these youths. From its beginnings in social work and the Houses of Refuge, through the evolution of state training schools, detention centers and even the transfer of juveniles back to adult courts, you have reviewed a variety of approaches to youth justice, some of which embody the original mission of the child savers and many which do not.

You have also now learned about the many theories of delinquency that have developed over time, some of which focus on specific biological and psychological characteristics and others that focus on elements of the social structure or social processes. These theories all seem to come to fruition in the development of holistic theories such as developmental and integrated theories that address the youth as a whole person and incorporate the multiple environments in which each youth develops.

Finally, you have seen that, for as far as the juvenile justice system has come, it has much farther to go to truly combat the problem of youth crime. Perhaps this is because the juvenile justice system does not cause crime in the first place. It can intervene in the lives of youths in a way that either perpetuates (e.g., Differential Association Theory and Labeling Theory) or reduces (e.g., Deterrence Theory) crime. However, while each of these theories offers us new insight into the problem of delinquency and while each program offered by the system has the potential to increase or reduce delinquency, one important takeaway message I would like you to keep with you as you finish this text is that the juvenile justice system, on its own, is not the root cause of delinquency and therefore it can never be the sole solution to the problem.

As you learned in Chapters 9, 10 and 11, some of the most effective programs utilized by the juvenile justice system are those designed to encompass the physical and social environments of the juvenile, as suggested by the developmental and integrated theories, instead of programs that just treat the youth as if something is wrong with him or her. Approaches such as multi-systemic therapy and family functional therapy appear to hold much promise for the system. Similarly, there has been a movement—slow and incomplete perhaps—but a movement nonetheless toward a unified court system that will be designed to treat all issues involving a family within one court and by one judge for unity purposes. A system such as this would further return to the social welfare roots of juvenile justice, recognizing the victim/offender overlap and the comorbidity of family and social problems.

Continued movement toward treatment is apparent at the time of the writing of this text; however, it is also underscored by some voices again calling for the system to get tougher on youth as, for the first time in two decades, crime is on the rise. For example, when I began writing this text, North Carolina and New York were the only two states to still process 16 and 17 year olds as adults. As I close the writing, New York has passed legislation that will take effect in 2018 to "raise the age" of adult court responsibility to 18, leaving North Carolina as the stand-alone state treating all 16 and 17 year olds as adults. Similarly, Connecticut, a state that had previously raised the age to 18 has a governor who is mandating the shutdown of all state training schools, just as was done in Massachusetts in the 1970s. This same governor of Connecticut is also asking the state legislature, in light of the emerging research on brain development and adolescent decision-making, to consider further raising the age of adult responsibility into the early 20's when science indicates the brain is more complete and individuals are more capable of making rational decisions—hence a time at which deterrence theories and rational choice theories might be more relevant to criminal justice philosophy.

However, as promising as some of these changes might seem to those who carry a deep-seated belief in a different juvenile justice system and treatment for youth, I have tempered optimism for the future. In the *Cycle of Juvenile Justice* (Bernard & Kurlychek, 2010), my mentor Thomas Bernard, building off the work of Ferdinand (1989), proposed that a cycle existed in which society at all times thought they were in the midst of a juvenile crime wave, whether indeed they were or were not. Hence society would blame whatever policies were in place at the time (lenient policies or punitive policies) for the crime wave and swing the pendulum back in the other direction. The recent two years show the first upswing in juvenile crime in almost two decades and thus I seem to be hearing again among certain circles a call to start cracking down on juvenile crime—that is, placing blame for this upswing on the juvenile justice system and its policies rather than delinquency's root causes. Thus, we may see states begin to return to harsh punishments if this trend or perception of a trend continues.

However, unlike the conclusions made by myself and Dr. Bernard in that earlier book, I am more optimistic today that instead of repeating history we are indeed moving toward an era of learning from it. As proof of this I would turn to the *Roper v. Simmons* decision that relied at least partially on social science and medical science evidence to determine that it was cruel and unusual punishment to subject an individual who was under the age of 18 at the time of his/her crime to the death penalty. Previous decisions on the death penalty relied more on an emerging morality, or a sentiment of what is right and wrong, and the states' ability to administer the death penalty in an unprejudiced manner. *The Roper* decision was in this sense unique and its logic was later extended to the use of mandatory life without parole for minors as well. If we continue to follow this science, then it may be possible that society realizes many other adult outcomes and punishments are just not appropriate or even useful in dealing with youth crime.

If adult punishments are not appropriate, then what does science suggest is appropriate? Here, I am also encouraged by the national movement toward evidence-based practice. Evidence-based practice means more than going to a list of proven programs, however; it involves encouraging local innovation in the treatment of youth and setting the stage for these new programs to be evaluated. As noted in Chapter 11, youth justice institutes and best practice centers are popping up in states across the country to support fidelity in program implementation through technical assistance and the formal and independent evaluation of programs to determine effectiveness. As our knowledge of "what works" and "what works for which kids" grows, it will help states and localities to better direct often-scarce resources. I think both of these developments—legislative and judicial reliance on science to inform policy, and practitioner reliance on and investment in evidence-based practice—represent some of the more positive trajectories in the juvenile justice system that I hope continue into the future.

That is not to say that the system does not still face many challenges, as outlined in the previous chapters: there is a dearth of programming available for female offenders, mainly based on a lack of understanding of gender/sex issues in delinquency. While the victim/offender overlap is important to consider and there is a call for "trauma-informed" practice, there is little coordination between the juvenile justice system and other social welfare agencies that would help prevent such trauma, abuse and victimization from occurring in the first place. And, there is even further disconnect between the juvenile justice system and education, economic and housing programs—all of which we know can be connected to the origin of delinquency.

While recognition that children are different than adults is a good starting point and basing treatment of juveniles upon such differences is important (as it has been since the Progressive Era), this still is only treating the problem after it has occurred and in some ways blaming the youth for problems that have originated far beyond his/her control. Thus, while I would not go so far as to say "it is" the future of juvenile justice, I would call for it to be the future of juvenile justice that the child is not seen just as embedded within the family, school and even community, but within a larger social structure that dictates both opportunities and experiences and is fraught with institutionalized bias. Thus, the solutions to juvenile crime must include the solutions to broader social issues of injustice in our society. I would therefore like to end this text with a quote from the mission statement of the National Center for Juvenile Justice that I believe reminds us all of the importance of the juvenile justice system and its role in shaping the future of society:

"The way in which a society treats its children, its young people, says something about the future of that society, its beliefs, and the viability of those beliefs. The way in which a society treats those of its children who break its laws says something about its humanity, its morality, its resilience, and its capacity for self-correction."

(National Center for Juvenile Justice, 1999).

REFERENCES

Bernard, T. J., & Kurlychek, M. C. (2010). *The cycle of juvenile justice.* New York: Oxford.

Ferdinand, T. N. (1989). Juvenile delinquency or juvenile justice: Which came first? *Criminology*, *27*(1), 76–106.

National Center for Juvenile Justice. (1999). Annual Report. Retrieved from http://www.ncjj.org/pdf/Annual%20Reports/NCJJ_1999_AnnRep.pdf

Glossary

Abatement a practice by which known gang members are prevented from hanging out in certain areas or participating in otherwise law abiding activities

Absconding running away and/or failure to appear for a scheduled hearing

ADHD symptoms include an inability to pay attention and to sit still for developmentally appropriate periods of time

Adjudication a finding of "guilt." Meaning the judge has enough evidence to determine the youth committed the act in question and is in need of treatment and care

Administrative Data often referred to as "official data" because they are reported through official juvenile and criminal justice agencies such as the police, courts, state departments of corrections, and even federal agencies such as the FBI

Adolescence the period of life between puberty and adulthood

Aftercare designed to help youths re-adjust to being home and in community after residential placement

Age-crime curve a pattern in which offending begins to increase in early adolescence, peaks around age 17 or 18, and thereafter declines

Amenability to Treatment means able to be changed through treatment

Atavist a human that is not genetically evolved and thus more animal like

Attachment the emotional connection that you have with others in their lives

Autonomy not succumbing to authority, particularly authority by of police, teachers or even parents

Balanced and Restorative Justice a philosophy of juvenile justice that attempts to balance the needs of the youth with the need to protect the community and repair harm done to a victim

Belief beliefs about right and wrong

Blending Sentencing a policy that "blends" sentences from the juvenile and adult court allowing the judge to use options from either or both systems

Broken-Windows Policing focuses on making the streets of the community unattractive for crime and making the citizens feel safe again

Bullying using one's strength or social status to intimidate, humiliate, or injure another person usually of lesser strength or status. Can be physical, verbal or emotional

Certainty the likelihood that one will actually experience the consequence given he/she commits the offense

Cesare Beccaria, Marchese d. Beccaria linked to the Classical School of Criminology. His classic essay "On Crimes and Punishments" brought together the thinking of some key philosophers of the time and provided a new approach to criminal justice.

Child Protective Services (CPS) governmental agencies authorized to act on behalf of a child when parents are unable or unwilling to do so

Childhood the period of life between infancy and adolescence—most commonly between the ages of 2 and 12

Chivalry Hypothesis the notion that the system will respond in a protective manner to female delinquents rather than arresting and prosecuting them

Chronic Offender typically defined as an offender who has had 5 or more contacts with the juvenile and/or criminal justice system

Classical Conditioning a person learning to associate an outcome with a stimulus

Classical School of Criminology the primary theory behind the development of our nation's adult criminal justice system that rests on assumptions of rationality, free will and hedonism

Cognitive-Behavior Therapy services that are designed to help youth replace criminogenic thinking with better decision-making that will lead to behavioral changes

Cohort Study follows a group of people over time that share some common characteristic

Collective Efficacy ability of members of a community to come together to achieve a common goal

Commitment how committed you are to traditional beliefs and behaviors

Community Review Boards volunteer community members who hear the cases of youth being diverted from formal court processing

Community Service doing any activity that repays the community

Community-Oriented Policing relies on a mutual sense of trust between community members and the police

Concentrated Poverty when all of your neighbors are as poor as you or have even less. It causes decreases in quality schooling, access to positive role models for youth and access to jobs and even marriage partners

Conduct Disorder symptoms of Oppositional Defiant Disorder along with aggression and bullying, destruction of property, deceitfulness and more serious violations of the rules

Conflict Pathway begins with simple stubborn behavior which leads to defiance of authority and eventually avoidance of any authority

Conflict Subculture youths rebel against everything middle class and form their own definitions of success that often center on violence and defending their territory

Conflict Theory a theory of crime that focuses on conflict between groups, with specific focus on conflict between majority and minority groups in a society and their economic means

Conformist conforms to both society's goals and their means for achieving them

Contaminants strictly defined as a pollutant or poisonous substance. In this case referring to pollutants or poisonous substances in one's environment that delay or impair development

Continuous Probation a model of probation in which one officer is responsible for the youth from intake through release from the system

Conventional Level internalize conventional standards of right and wrong with a high regard for authority and maintaining social order

Correctional Boot Camp a type of placement that mimics a military boot camp focusing on physical activity and derogation of the juvenile to instill discipline

Cottage System Model harkens back to the original "parens patriae" mission of the juvenile court which is to provide the child with a home-like environment in which he/she can develop into a productive young adult rather than a criminal

Court Costs monies paid directly to the court for services rendered and can include such things as payment to a general fund to cover public attorneys or payment for probation supervision

Covert Pathway begins with simple lying but may escalate into shoplifting, fraud and other types of theft and property crimes

Criminal Subculture A culture that values criminal means to achieving goals rather than the traditional legal means in a society

Cross Sectional Survey looks at a cross-section of the population at a given time

Culpability how responsible one is for an act/action

Cultural Transmission the process through which a culture of delinquency is handed down from older youth to younger youth creating a subculture of crime

Daniel O'Connell the youth at the center of the second case to challenge the placement of a youth in a House of Refuge. In this case, the court sided with the youth/parent

DARE a curriculum taught by police officers to middle and high school children to help them understand the dangers of illegal drugs and learn tactics to resist peer pressure to engage in illegal drug use

Dark Figure of Crime crimes that go unreported to the police

Data Mining a technique in which researchers are able to literally "mine" a data set created for other purposes to find valuable information related to their research purpose

Day Reporting Centers a highly structured, community-based, post adjudication, nonresidential program

Defendant person accused in a court of law

Delinquent a delinquent is a youth who commits an act that would be a crime if he was an adult

Delinquent Act an act that would be considered a crime if committed by an adult

Delinquent Offense an act that would be a crime if committed by an adult

Demeanor a person's attitude toward and response toward the police officer

Dependent Child a child in need of care by the state because such care is not being provided in the home

Detention Review Hearing a hearing, usually held within 24 to 72 hours of pre-adjudicatory detention placement in which the judge decides if the placement is warranted. Similar to a bail hearing in adult court, however, most states do not set bail for youth

Developmental Theory focus on an aspect or multiple aspects of development over time

Differential Associations our associations with other people that give us various messages about the appropriateness of rules and laws

Differential Social Organization communities that are organized around a different set of norms and values

Direct File a situation in which the decision to file charges in either juvenile court or adult court is left in the hands of the prosecutor instead of the judge

Discretion police have the freedom to decide what the best course of action is in a situation

Discrimination when an individual receives a different and more severe outcome than another individual based on uncontrollable factors such as race, age or gender

Disintegrative Shaming not only punish a youth for their action, but applying the unmistakable and inescapable label of delinquent upon the youth

Displacement refers to when a crime-control policy fails to reduce the actual activity but just changes it location from one place to another

Disposition Hearing the hearing at which the judge hands down the final outcome of the case such as a term of probation or placement in a residential facility

Disposition the final outcome of a juvenile court proceeding after a youth is adjudicated delinquent

Disposition the phase of the juvenile justice system that would be similar to "sentencing" in adult court. It is the final outcome after an adjudication of delinquency has been made

Disproportionate Minority Contact minority youth are more likely to be arrested and referred on to juvenile court than white youths

Disproportionate Minority Contact occurs when minorities are represented in the criminal justice system at a rate greater than their representation in the general population

Domination when the new species overtakes the area

Dramatization of Evil instead of seeing the act as evil or bad, the person committing the act is seen as bad or evil

Dual-Status Youth youths who come into contact with both the child welfare and juvenile justice systems

Dually Identified Youth youth who are currently involved with the juvenile justice system and have a history in the child welfare system but no current involvement

Dually Involved Youth youth who have concurrent involvement (diversionary, formal or both) with both the child welfare and juvenile justice systems

Duration how long a person is exposed to a message

Early Intervention intervening at a young age is crucial to help youth avoid problems

Electronic Monitoring achieved by the probationer wearing an electronic ankle bracelet or other device that constantly monitors their location through a computer

Enhancement Model delinquent-prone youth seek out the gang and the gang in turn increases and promotes their delinquency to higher levels

Evidence-Based Practice (EBP) using programs that have some scientific evidence showing their effectiveness

Excitement risky activities that break up the monotony of everyday life

Exclusionary Rule excludes any evidence from court that is not collected according to constitutional search and seizure rules

Expulsions student is permanently removed from their school setting

Extra-Legal Factors factors such as race, age or gender not related to the crime

Extroversion outgoing and social

Facilitation Model otherwise non-delinquent youth become involved in delinquency because they join a gang and are influenced by delinquent peers

Fate a belief that life and its circumstances are largely beyond our control

Feminist Theory incorporate gender, not just as a new variable in a traditional sociological theory, but rather use gender as the key theoretical construct upon which to build the theory

Fine the payment of money as a punishment, not directly related to the costs of the case

Free Will the belief that man makes his/her own choices and is not controlled by outside forces such as demons

Frequency how often a person is exposed to a message

Gangs first defined as a phenomenon of human ecology as groups of youth band together. Sociological and Law enforcement definitions differ and are provided later in the chapter.

Gender the socialized identity and behaviors associated with a given sex

Gender-Specific Services encourages local entities to research and develop programs specifically designed to meet the needs of young girls

General Deterrence the idea that you will not commit an offense based on general knowledge of possible negative consequences and/or seeing these negative consequences applied to others you know

Habeas Corpus presenting the body

Hate Crimes any crime motivated by biases based on race, gender, gender identity, religion, disability, sexual orientation and/or ethnicity

Hedonistic work to serve their own self interests unless otherwise directed

Hierarchy Rule when an offender is charged with multiple crimes at arrest, but only the most serious crime per arrest is recorded

Hormones regulatory substances in the human body that influence mood and behavior. Certain hormones have been attached to specific behavioral patterns such as testosterone with aggression.

Hot-Spots Policing focuses police presence in areas known to have high crime rates

House Arrest home confinement, where the youth is not allowed to leave home except for designated activities

House of Refuge a house designed to hold youth up until their 21st birthday when the state determined that the youth needed to be removed from his parent's care for proper development

Human Trafficking involves selling an individual into prostitution/the pornography industry, slavery or involuntary servitude

Identity Reformation the process through which labeling theory suggests the label applied by others can become a self-fulfilling prophecy

Imitation mimic behaviors of those around us

Immigrants those flocking to America in search of a better life often with little resources or the ability to read or speak English

Implementation Fidelity refers to ensuring that a program treats the clients for which it was supposed and delivers all the services required

Impoverished Environments include having a family income under $15,000 a year, having parents who did not graduate from high school, and living in a household that receives public benefits such as food stamps, free school lunches or public housing

In re Gault in 1967 the first official challenge to the court's practice for procedural safeguards

In re Winship The Supreme Court decision in which the burden of proof in the juvenile court was changed from preponderance of the evidence to beyond a reasonable doubt

Individual Justice recognizes that because people are different and come from different circumstances, the response to crime must be individualistic

Informal Adjustments the handling of a juvenile's case outside of the formal court system, usually reserved for first-time offenders or less serious offenders

Informal Probation a period of probation supervision agreed upon by the youth, the youth's family and the probation officer but not formally ordered by a judge

Informal Social Control controls exerted by families, schools and community members rather than the formal justice system

Inner Containment more than just one's conscience, also involves the notion of one's self-concept or self-esteem

Innovator has the goals instilled but not the legitimate means to achieve them so they must make, or innovte, up their own means

Intake Units units in which officers are assigned to ONLY conduct intake assessments and are responsible for all front-end decision making regarding a case

Integrated Theory takes ideas or components from other theories and ties them together into one broader theory

Intelligence Quotient based on a scale such that a score of 100 indicates an individual is at the appropriate mental capacities for his/her age

Intensity how much a person cares about the person giving him/her the message

Intensive-Supervision Probation a special classification of probation supervision that requires more frequent monitoring of the youth

Introduction of Negative Stimuli strain happens when a negative new factor is introduced

Invasion process by which a new "species" comes into an area

Involvement the more time spent in conventional settings, the less time there is to be deviant

Judicial Waiver a decision by the juvenile court judge to "waive" a youth to adult court. This indicates the judge believes the youth is not treatable as a juvenile and requires punishment

Juvenile Justice System a separate system of justice designed just for processing youth

Kent v. United States The Supreme Court case in which the court gave additional rights to youth facing waiver or transfer to adult court

Legal-Factors factors specifically related to the crime, including seriousness of the crime and the presence of a victim or witness

Legitimate Means approved avenues for achieving success such as education and employment

Mandatory Waiver Hearings a hearing at which it is mandatory for the juvenile court judge to waive a youth to adult court if the facts are confirmed such as the youth's age, prior record and severity of offense

Mary Ann Crouse The youth at the center of the first court case challenging the state's right to place children in such a house if they had not committed a crime. The court sided with the state

McKeiver v. Pennsylvania The Supreme Court case in which the Court decided that a youth did not have the right to a trial by a jury of his peers in the juvenile court

Mens Rae a guilty mind

Middle-Class Measuring Rod the middle class standard to which all students are typically held in American schools

Miranda Warning a formal statement of the accused's constitutional rights including the right to remain silent and the right to an attorney that police must read to all individual's upon arrest

Mitigating Circumstances circumstances beyond the individual's control that may impact his/her ability to make a rational decision

Model Programs the programs with the strongest scientific support

Multisystemic Therapy it assesses the youth and family and also addresses the social context of youth development, including the school, the youth's peers and the community

Narcissism egocentric and less critical of themselves also likely to report feelings of not being appreciated or recognized by others

National Crime Victimization Survey (NCVS) a representative sample of about 90,000 households each year, which consist of nearly 160,000 persons

National Juvenile Court Data Archive contains over 15 million automated case records with nearly all records containing demographic information on age, gender, race, county of residence, offense(s) charged, use of pretrial detention, adjudication, and disposition

National Longitudinal Study of Youth (NLSY) a nationally representative sample of approximately 9,000 youths who were 12 to 16 years old as of December 31, 1996.

Nature genetics/biology

Needs areas of a youth's life in which his or her needs are not being met, regardless of whether they directly contributed to the behavior at hand

Neo-Classical School introduces mitigating circumstances and individual justice to the original Classical School

NIBRS National Incident-Based Reporting System which reports and connects all data by criminal incident

Nurture social environment

Office of Juvenile Justice and Delinquency Prevention (OJJDP) the federal office in charge of setting rules and regulations for state juvenile justice policy and providing funding for juvenile justice services

Olweus Anti-Bullying Prevention Program a whole-school-based program that utilizes the school, the classroom and individuals (school administrators, teachers, staff and students) to simultaneously address bullying while also including parents and community member

Operant Conditioning learning is based on rewards and punishments

Oppositional Defiant Disorder a pattern of behavior that defines how a person interacts with others

Outer Containment reaches beyond the family and more to the general social environment of the individual

Overt Pathway begins with problem behavior such as bullying in school which escalates into violence such as assault and robbery

Parens patriae state as the parent

Pauper a poor person who does not work

Personality Theory assumes individuals are born with inherent behavioral traits that influence the way they respond to their environment

Petition a formal legal document that alleges that a youth is delinquent and asks the juvenile court to take jurisdiction over the case

Post Traumatic Stress Disorder a condition triggered by a traumatizing life event where the symptoms may include anxiety, depression, sudden flashbacks and nightmares

Post-Conventional Level realizes laws represent agreed-upon standards and are there for a reason, also realizing there could be a good reason to violate the law. Also the level when people respect differing opinions. Not all people reach that part of the level.

Poverty defined as living with an income below that needed to survive in a society. Today that figure is $30,750 in America for a family of four

Power-Control Theory connects family structure and economic activity to delinquency and risk taking

Pre-Adjudicatory Detention holding a youth in a detention facility while awaiting a formal hearing. Traditionally used to prevent the youth from absconding or to protect the community or the youth

Pre-Conventional Level avoids punishment and does what is necessary to satisfy needs

Pre-Disposition Report a report that outlines the youth's situation including risks, needs and strengths and makes a recommendation to the judge for a disposition

Preliminary Hearing the first hearing before a judge in which he/she determines if the case has merit. Similar to arraignment in adult court

Presumption Waiver Hearing a hearing at which the law presumes the youth should be treated as an adult, but the judge retains some discretion to retain the youth in juvenile court if he finds the youth amenable to treatment

Primary Deviance a deviant act one commits, whether serious or minor, as a normal part of growing up

Primary Prevention refers to prevention efforts that target all youth, regardless of their individual risk of gang joining

Priority how early in life a person receives a message

Probable Cause the set of facts known to the police officer at that time that would lead a reasonable person to conclude that a crime has occurred and that the person being arrested had committed it

Probation Supervision a period of formal court ordered supervision of a youth during which the juvenile probation officer, much like an adult probation officer, ensures that the youth adheres to all conditions placed upon him/her by the judge

Probation the conditional release of a convicted adult or adjudicated youth under the community supervision of a court officer

Problem-Solving Policing a tactic in which police work proactively to reduce the factors in a community that lead to crime rather than reacting to the crime after it happens

Progressive Era maintained a positive focus on the evolution of man and of society to an ever better state, with confidence in the role of medicine and technology to get us there

Promising Programs show great promise but have not been proven effective yet

Property Crime Index includes Burglary/Breaking or Entering, Larceny/Theft, Motor Vehicle Theft and Arson

Proportionality Severity the punishment should be proportional to the amount of damage the crime inflicted upon the victim and/or society

Protective Factor the absence of risk and characteristics that interact with risk factors to decrease delinquent behavior

Psychodynamic Theory from Freud's early work who proposed that healthy human development occurs through a process of psychosexual development from birth to adulthood

Psychopath an individual who did not suffer from hallucinations or delusions and was in control of their behavior, but exhibited extreme rage and immoral behavior

Racial Heterogeneity refers to how many different races/ethnicities and types of people live in an area. The more people are alike the more they share common values. The more they are different, the greater the potential for their values to conflict

Rational Choice Theory the emphasis is on understanding why in certain circumstances an individual chooses to commit a crime

Rationality a human's ability to weigh the cost and benefit of an action before choosing a course

Reaction Formation alternative behaviors that emerge to deal with the inability to achieve traditional measures of success

Rebellion can be criminal or related to progress of a society as some goals and things should be changed

Recidivism is the commission of a new crime after an initial crime is committed. This is usually measured by a new arrest, but could be measured by self-report data, conviction data or placement data as well

Reintegrative Shaming doing something but ensuring that the consequence keeps the youth connected to society and recognizing his/her own potential to be a good person in the end

Removal of Positively Valued Stimuli a strain occurs when something that is valued is taken away

Residential Mobility refers to people moving in and out of an area quickly. The longer someone stays the more ties and commitments are made to the neighborhood

Residential Placement a catch-all term for when a youth is removed from the home and placed to "reside" in a facility

Restitution the payment of money to repair harm done to a victim

Restorative Justice a theory of justice the focuses on restoring the victim or community, to the extent possible, to the state before the crime happened rather than on punishing or treating the offender

Retreatist separated from society no longer holding goals of success. They may suffer mental illness or turn to drugs or alcohol to ease their strain

Retreatist Subculture a type of subculture that develops when both legitimate and illegitimate means are blocked. This subculture revolves around escaping society, perhaps through drugs and alcohol, rather than trying to achieve within it

Risk Factor things such as poverty that increase the probability of delinquency

Risks problems the youth is facing that make him or her more likely to continue in delinquency and anti-social behaviors

Routine Activities Theory assumes everyone could be a motivated offender given the right circumstance assumes three things must be present for an offense to happen: a motivated offender, a suitable target and the lack of a capable guardian

RYDS Rochester Youth Development Study where 1,000 inner-city youth were studied beginning in 1987 and continues today (2018) looking at the influence of the inner-city on their development over the life course

School Resource Officers police officers stationed in schools to increase safety

School to Prison Pipeline the process through which school failure leads to delinquency and, ultimately, prison. It is suggested this pipeline is almost inescapable for many minority youth from poor neighborhoods who are much more likely to spend time in prison than to finish school

Secondary Deviance an act of deviance that occurs after someone internalizes the label of delinquent

Secondary Prevention targets only those youth who are somehow identified as being at personal risk for gang joining

Selection Model youths already disposed to delinquency seek out like others and thus join the gang

Self-control to control impulses and act in socially appropriate ways

Self-Report Surveys studies that ask individuals to self-report their delinquent behaviors."

Sex the biological differences between males and females

Shelter or Respite Care another type of pre-adjudicatory holding of a youth that is used when it is unsafe for the juvenile to return home. This type of facility is traditionally less secure than a formal detention center

Situational Crime Prevention changing the immediate environment to make it more difficult for someone to commit the crime

Skills Therapy designed to help youth learn better social skills and to deal with difficult social situations

Social Networks a person's network of relationships. That is, the other people with whom one interacts on a regular basis

Sociopath an individual who, due to some great or prolonged trauma such as severe child abuse, has extreme rage and immoral behavior

Special Conditions conditions of probation that are not standard for everyone but are specific to that youth and his/her risks and needs

Specialized Probation a model of probation in which different officers have responsibilities for different stages of the system

Specific Deterrence the idea that once you as an individual experience a punishment for your offense you will know that the negative consequence outweighs any possible gain and therefore will not commit offenses in the future

Stakes in Conformity what you have to lose by committing a delinquent act

Standard Conditions youth placed on probation must adhere to some things such as attending school and not breaking any other laws

Station Adjustment when a police officer makes the decision to take the juvenile to the station, but then decides not to proceed with a formal arrest

Statistical Metropolitan Area an area consisting of a central city and its surrounding suburbs

Status Frustration the feelings of frustration that occur when one is not able to meet these middle class definitions of success

Status Offense a behavior that is only illegal because of one's status as a juvenile

Statutory Exclusion when the legislature passes a statute that requires certain youth to be tried as adults based on combinations of age, offense history and current offense

Strain Theories focus on society or the individual as they are situated in society. It is deeply rooted in the concept of American capitalism with some at a disadvantage

Strengths things a youth is particularly good at and which can be used to help him or her succeed in life

Succession when the area stabilizes with a new balance

Suppression refers to efforts to remove gangs and indiviaul gang members from the streets

Suspensions student is temporarily removed from their school setting

Swiftness how quickly a punishment is applied to an offender after he/she is caught

Symbiosis a relationship between two organisms living in close proximity to each other (be it plants or people) that provides mutual benefits

Systemic Theory viewed neighborhoods as an interrelated group of social networks

Target Hardening practices such as adding lighting and locks to make it harder for an individual to commit a "successful" crime

Teen Courts a program through which the case is heard by a jury of the teens peers rather than being sent to the formal juvenile justice system

Tertiary Prevention refers to efforts directed at youths who have already joined a gang

Totality of Circumstance states a youth can only waive the right to an attorney if it can be determined that the youth fully understood his or her rights before waiving them

Toughness ability to physically dominate other males

Tracking accepted practices in schools where students' standardized test scores and other measures of intelligence used to group students. This can set some students up for school failure, impacting their attachment to school and lead to delinquency

Trajectory the path a person is following

Transition a time in life when things are changing

Trouble being able to cause trouble without getting caught, or into trouble

Turning Point when a transition leads to a change or turn in a developmental trajectory--either for better or worse

Unified Court a court system that puts one judge in charge of all matters involving one family to provide a unified response to all of a families needs and problems

Uniform Crime Report reported annually by the FBI, this data set compiles data from over 97% of police departments in the United States

Violent Crime Index includes Criminal Homicide, Rape, Robbery and Aggravated Assault

Zero Tolerance Policies vaguely detail a type of behavior that will not be allowed and dictate that any student violating the rule will be suspended or expelled

Zone of Transition Zone II which separates business from more residential housing

Index

A

B

C

D

E

F

G

H

I

J

N

Q

R

S

T

U

V

W

Y

Z

CPSIA information can be obtained
at www.ICGtesting.com
Printed in the USA
LVHW01s2201270718
585079LV00001B/1/P